INDEX
1947-1976

NATIONAL
GEOGRAPHIC

INDEX

1947-1976

INCLUSIVE

NATIONAL GEOGRAPHIC SOCIETY

WASHINGTON, D. C.

Contents

A publication of the National Geographic Society.

STAFF FOR THIS BOOK:

Editor: JOHN SCOFIELD

Project Editor: HOWARD E. PAINE

Text: ALLEN A. BORAIKO

Expeditions and Researches: PAUL H. OEHSER

Index: JOLENE M. BLOZIS, *Chief, Indexing Division;* MARTHA K. HIGHTOWER, GEORGE I. BURNESTON III, PHILIP G. GUTEKUNST, BARBARA L. KLEIN, ANNE K. McCAIN, BRIT A. PETERSON, JESSICA C. TAYLOR, VIRGINIA C. THOMPSON, LINDA C. CORBIN, ELLA L. SMITH

Research: ANN K. WENDT, *Chief;* FRANCES H. PARKER, *Associate Chief;* CAROLYN H. ANDERSON, LESLEY B. ROGERS, MICHAELINE A. SWEENEY

Design and Production: N. TAYLOR GREGG, ROBERT E. PULLMAN, CHARLES C. UHL

Engraving and Printing: JOHN R. METCALFE

OVERLEAF: CLOAKED IN SPRAY, A SOUTHERN RIGHT WHALE BREACHES OFF PATAGONIA'S DESERT COAST. PHOTOGRAPH BY DES AND JEN BARTLETT.

Foreword

"I AM NOT A SCIENTIFIC MAN, nor can I lay claim to any special knowledge that would entitle me to be called a 'Geographer.'" Modest words like these often appear in the letters fellow National Geographic Society members write to me. It would surprise many of them to find that they are echoing the soft denial made in 1888 by Gardiner Greene Hubbard, a founder and first President of the Society.

Geographer or not, any member of the Society can come to know the world in astonishing and intimate detail. The key to this remarkable familiarity lies in this book and its companion volume, *National Geographic Index, 1888-1946*. With these comprehensive reference tools, past issues of NATIONAL GEOGRAPHIC yield a trove of authoritative information and rich images.

ROBERT S. OAKES

This volume, *National Geographic Index, 1947-1976,* contains more than 14,000 entries spanning thirty years and more than 2,000 lucid and fascinating articles. It guides you to the summit of Mount Everest and the face of the moon, directs you to intriguing facts about subjects as varied as Polynesia and plankton, and charts your course through time from ancient China to scientific breakthroughs as new as tomorrow.

Also in this volume, a special "Picture History of National Geographic, 1947-1976" recalls the phenomenal growth and change in your Society and its official journal during the past three decades. In 1947 the Society already numbered more than a million and a half members, a tremendous tribute to the late Gilbert H. Grosvenor, master builder of GEOGRAPHIC and Editor from 1899 to 1954. Working closely with him was the late John Oliver La Gorce, Editor from 1954 to 1957. Another close colleague, Thomas W. McKnew, former Secretary and now Advisory Chairman of the Board, helped encourage the Society's expansion to a worldwide membership of nearly 9 1/2 million at the end of 1976.

Outstanding editorial direction continued at NATIONAL GEOGRAPHIC under Melville Bell Grosvenor, who became Editor in 1957 and whose infectious enthusiasm inspired many Society projects: the first National Geographic globe and World Atlas, the modern Book Service and Special Publications, and an award-winning series of television specials. Now Editor Emeritus, he was succeeded in 1967 by Frederick G. Vosburgh, who ensured that accuracy, grace, and style continued to be the hallmark of GEOGRAPHIC writing.

In the introduction that follows, Gilbert M. Grosvenor, Editor since 1970, outlines the reasons for NATIONAL GEOGRAPHIC's success, among them an adherence to high editorial standards and a willingness to pioneer new processes and directions to achieve what has always been the Society's, and the magazine's, primary purpose, "the increase and diffusion of geographic knowledge."

Many of the letters I receive close with the gratifying postscript that, better than anything else, NATIONAL GEOGRAPHIC offers its readers the pleasure and excitement of having the world at their fingertips. You'll discover that the way to that pleasure and excitement is also at your fingertips—in this new *National Geographic Index, 1947-1976.*

Robert E. Doyle

PRESIDENT

Bringing the World Into Your Home

AN INTRODUCTION BY GILBERT M. GROSVENOR

Editor, National Geographic Magazine

David Lewis and Ice Bird *enter Antarctica's Penola Strait.*

OVEMBER 29, 1972: *The situation is not encouraging. My 32-foot steel sloop* Ice Bird *lies dismasted, wallowing uncontrollably in the wild seas of the sixtieth southern parallel, swept by zero-temperature winds and snow showers. . . . the life raft is gone.*

Aboard the battered *Ice Bird,* seaman and adventurer David Lewis ponders "what seems like a certain rendezvous with death." Six weeks and 3,600 nautical miles out from Sydney, Australia, the first singlehanded attempt to circumnavigate Antarctica's frozen perimeter nears a premature conclusion in the hurricane-force winds of the "screaming sixties", breeding ground of one-hundred-foot-high waves. Incredibly, *Ice Bird* rides out the storm to limp 2,500 miles eastward to Palmer Station, a U. S. Antarctic research base. Months of refitting make her seaworthy again, but a second dismasting cuts short

Ice Bird's odyssey for good, and on March 20, 1974, she motors into the harbor of Cape Town, South Africa, final port in an 11,000-mile voyage around two-thirds of the southernmost continent.

Published in the December 1973 and August 1975 NATIONAL GEOGRAPHICS, David Lewis's vivid and sometimes heart-stopping narrative of his Antarctic enterprise is a classic adventure story, one that illustrates what GEOGRAPHIC does best: It interprets the world to its readers through the lens of personal experience, be it the reader's own, that of the author, or that of the author's subject. Reporting from a personal perspective is an editorial tradition at NATIONAL GEOGRAPHIC. One of the keys to the magazine's outstanding success, it broadens isolated and solitary adventures like that of *Ice Bird* and her master into accounts that call up common intuition to illuminate uncommon experience. Few of us will ever suffer the unique rigors or taste the secret satisfaction of a lone voyage around the greater part of Antarctica, but in reading his story, we can grasp David Lewis's will to survive, his pride in achievement, and his hope in the face of failure. Universally familiar feelings thus sensitize us to the magnitude of another's rare accomplishment.

T HERE IS MORE in the pages of NATIONAL GEOGRAPHIC than adventure and exploration, of course. Traditionally, GEOGRAPHIC has chronicled the fundamental changes that overtake and transform great civilizations and tiny tribes. This, too, it does with the human interest and sympathetic understanding of people that are hallmarks of GEOGRAPHIC reporting.

Take, for example, the pageant of "The Lost Empire of the Incas," a December 1973 article. Titling themselves "Sons of the Sun," in 1438 Inca lords embarked on a whirlwind series of conquests. By 1525 they had expanded their formerly minor agricultural state into the "Four Quarters of the World"—an imperial domain stretching 2,500 miles southward from the Equator through Ecuador and Peru to central Chile. Backbone of this realm was the Andes, a sawtooth mountain chain that provided what is for me the real highlight of this report on one of aboriginal America's greatest empires: the stunning photograph (right) of an Inca child who froze to death some five hundred years before my birth.

Seemingly asleep, a young boy about 8 or 9 years of age huddles beneath a llama-wool tunic. Perhaps drugged with some of the narcotic coca leaves found in the feathered pouch beside him, he died of exposure when entombed on Chile's 17,815-foot El Plomo peak near the southern edge of the once flourishing Inca Empire. Most probably he was left in that desolate spot as a sacrifice to the sun—a high honor in Inca eyes. Miniature idols and keepsakes surround him: the costumed silver image of an Inca goddess, llama figurines of gold and shell, and leather pouches holding his baby teeth and fingernail parings, left with the boy so that in the afterlife he would not have to search for missing parts of his body. NATIONAL GEOGRAPHIC's emphasis on human interest allows

Time rests lightly on the face of an Inca boy who froze to death in the Andes five centuries ago.

LOREN MCINTYRE

this image of a long-ago child to leap five centuries and achieve its full effect on our imagination, reminding us that back of any larger-than-life civilization there lies a more intimate and immediate human dimension, one that lingers long after its mother culture has vanished.

IN ALL ITS REPORTING, NATIONAL GEOGRAPHIC demonstrates a sure instinct for the exciting and revealing, the products of which are superlative imagery and fascinating text. This is especially true of the magazine's coverage of science and natural history, traditional areas of interest for a journal whose parent society numbered no fewer than 16 scientists and naturalists among its 33 founding members.

The combination of educational value and pictorial beauty that distinguishes GEOGRAPHIC articles on science and nature is one of the most important elements in the magazine's enormous and long-standing popular appeal. These qualities of instruction and graphic attractiveness lend individual issues of NATIONAL GEOGRAPHIC enduring value as reference works on topics as varied as the how and why of our planet's climate and geology, the subtle mysteries of our universe and its physics, and the rainbow-hued creatures of the Red Sea, such as the hawkfish (right).

Technology now alters our environment more rapidly and with greater effect than ever before in history. As it does so, NATIONAL GEOGRAPHIC's science and nature coverage becomes increasingly important for readers who seek reliable information in order to form their own opinions on issues that are sometimes debated without benefit of solid fact or reasoned argument. Here is where GEOGRAPHIC, with its straightforward, lucid, and comprehensive reporting, has a special contribution to make.

One of the most recent entries in this index is "The Pipeline: Alaska's Troubled Colossus." Published in November 1976,

In undersea plaid, a hawkfish patrols a Red Sea coral reef.

DAVID DOUBILET

it proved to be one of the year's most popular articles. It deals with a controversial subject and reveals much about the character of NATIONAL GEOGRAPHIC.

Almost to the moment of publication, the pipeline story was reviewed, revised, and rewritten to keep pace with continuing construction of the mammoth Alaskan project. Such up-to-the-minute coverage is more than a hasty installment in a simple monthly accounting of change: it draws upon the basic continuity of GEOGRAPHIC reporting. When our staff began work on this piece, they were taking up a subject—our fuel resources and how to manage them—that is hardly new to NATIONAL GEOGRAPHIC: In 1904 we surveyed the "Natural-Gas, Oil, and Coal Supply of the United States"; in 1918 we discussed oil shales; and in 1920 we presented "Where the World Gets Its Oil: But Where Will Our Children Get It . . . ?" In 1972 we published "The Search for Tomorrow's Power" and followed it two years later with "Oil: The Dwindling Treasure." Since then articles on wind power and solar energy have appeared, and others on geothermal energy, nuclear power, and energy conservation are in preparation. The consistent ability of NATIONAL GEOGRAPHIC to combine continuity and topicality results, as in the pipeline story, in timely coverages backed by solid, factual reporting, which may stretch back over many decades.

A S NATIONAL GEOGRAPHIC documents the changes sweeping our world, it is constantly challenged to present the compellingly human side of a story or issue and to report at the same time without speculation or exaggeration. This difficult demand is best met by letting the facts speak for themselves, as we did in "Brazil's Kreen-Akarores: Requiem for a Tribe?", a February 1975 look at a beleaguered Indian tribe deep in the jungled Amazon Basin.

Beset by highway builders, stricken with foreign disease, and awed by a non-Indian material culture far in advance of their own, the Kreen-Akarores are nearing both tribal and personal extinction. In reporting the irreversible changes that "progress" is working on these Stone Age people, we chose to do no more than portray the fundamental humanity of their plight, believing that strong enough in itself to make the case for the survival and protection of the Kreen-Akarores. This approach yielded sad and powerful vignettes: a chief with skin so weather-hardened that at first it resisted and broke penicillin needles that could save him from the white man's influenza, and a young boy presented with a gift of fishing line that he cannot yet use because he has never seen such a thing before.

Occasionally, the task of reporting without polemicizing is best accomplished through photographs: An affecting image can go far to make a point without disturbing the factual balance of an article. This is true of the haunting portrait of famine (right) that illustrated a July 1975 survey of our world's growing population and strained food supply. Equally eloquent images have appeared in GEOGRAPHIC articles on pollution, mercury poisoning, and endangered whales, where they serve the same purpose—to educate without editorializing.

N OT LONG AGO I came across a yellowed brochure written in 1915 and intended for advertisers in the pages of NATIONAL GEOGRAPHIC. Its author was John Oliver La Gorce, Editor of the magazine from 1954 to 1957.

Sketching the character of NATIONAL GEOGRAPHIC for his readers, the future Editor summed up the matter in a single sentence: "The Geographic seems to anticipate where the world's attention is to be focused and turns its searchlight there— it presents to its readers what they want, when they want it, in a comprehensive and illuminating way. . . ." As Editor, I like to think that NATIONAL GEOGRAPHIC readers would find that simple description as fitting today as it was in 1915—only more so.

Sad-eyed and stoic, a Bengali girl endures famine in Bangladesh.
STEVE RAYMER

A Picture History of National Geographic 1947-1976

THREE GENERATIONS of readers have grown up with the unique institution known as NATIONAL GEOGRAPHIC. Often they have inherited shelves of back issues of the magazine from parents or grandparents. Just as often, they add to these carefully stored collections of the yellow-bordered journal, intending to pass them on to their own children and grandchildren.

Longtime readers of GEOGRAPHIC regard it with the loyalty they would show a member of the family. They seldom discard an issue or allow it to go unread, nor do they have the magazine bound just to place it high on some inaccessible bookshelf. And unlike some things handed down through the family and maintained only for display or out of sentiment, GEOGRAPHIC remains in constant use: by schoolchildren seeking essay topics, by parents who value it as a teaching aid or reference work, and by the entire family as a source of intriguing information not always available elsewhere and rarely in so fascinating a format.

Finally, GEOGRAPHIC fascinates as much by what it says about itself as by the endless variety and color of its contents. The following picture history forms an absorbing almanac of the magazine's evolution during three decades and demonstrates why NATIONAL GEOGRAPHIC has attracted millions of readers who call it "their" magazine.

1947

• *Aided by a Society grant, an oceanographic expedition surveys topography, geology, and marine life of the Mid-Atlantic Ridge.*

• *A joint Geographic — U. S. Army Air Forces expedition studies a solar eclipse in Brazil.*

• *A Society — Smithsonian Institution expedition finds evidence of a previously unknown preceramic culture in southern Mexico.*

1948

• *National Geographic joins with the Smithsonian Institution in Arnhem Land to survey Australia's Aboriginal culture, and in Panama to discover the first urn burials ever found between the southeastern United States and Ecuador.*

• *The Society announces discovery in Alaska of the nesting place of the bristle-thighed curlew, a mystery for 163 years.*

The face of a long-dead Olmec lives on in a colossal stone head (**below**). Discovered by a Society — Smithsonian Institution expedition, the pre-Maya sculpture appeared in a 1947 article on Mexico's ancient past.

Bottom-dwelling spider at lower right and the brittle star just above it appeared in a 1948 article on oceanographic probes along the Mid-Atlantic Ridge. Touching bottom at 5,850 feet, a camera equipped with an electronic flash raised the silt swirl at left.

During the U. S. Navy Antarctic expedition of 1946-47, officer-in-charge Rear Adm. Richard E. Byrd, Jr., (**above**) takes his bearings with a sun compass on a flight near the south magnetic pole. Byrd also used the device, more reliable in polar regions than the magnetic compass, on his 1926 flight over the North Pole. The late Albert H. Bumstead, chief cartographer of the Society, invented the sun compass for Byrd's historic polar ventures.

Winged miniature, a ruby-throated hummingbird visits a feeder of honey water in a 1947 GEOGRAPHIC photograph by Dr. Harold E. Edgerton, father of the electronic flash. Dainty wings "scull" the air in a figure-eight motion as the bird hovers above the quarter-size floor of its nest.

15

PAINTING BY ROBERT WILLIAM BUSS

1949

- *Society-backed expeditions gather data on the scarlet ibis in Venezuela and capture a specimen of Nepal's rare spiny babbler, the first such bird taken by a scientist in more than a century.*

- *The National Geographic – Palomar Observatory Sky Survey begins to map the heavens to a depth of one billion light-years for a monumental sky atlas.*

1950

- *Beginning a three-year Society-funded study, University of Miami scientists identify previously unrecognized larval fishes among plankton in the Florida Current.*

- *Jean and Franc Shor take the highroad in Afghanistan in the November 1950 issue, commencing their career as NATIONAL GEOGRAPHIC's husband-and-wife writer-photographer team.*

Daydreaming amid his characters, Charles Dickens figured in a 1949 GEOGRAPHIC devoted entirely to "The British Way."

Nepali child bride, arrayed in silk, jewels, and gold, appeared in the January 1950 issue.

First Grosvenor Medal goes to namesake Dr. Gilbert H. Grosvenor (**below**, at left) on May 19, 1949. Dr. Charles Franklin Kettering, a Trustee of the Society, presents the honor to Dr. Grosvenor on the latter's Golden Jubilee as Editor.

VOLKMAR WENTZEL

THE WASHINGTON POST

Victorious in his war chariot, King Thut-mosĕ III of Egypt draws his bow against Syrians at the Biblical Armageddon. The colorful painting by H. M. Herget was one of a series illustrating the Society's popular 1951 book, *Everyday Life in Ancient Times.*

Horned brow marks a placid cowfish (**lower left**) from a 1952 article on Bahamian sea life.

"I Sailed With Portugal's Captains Courageous" in 1952 highlighted this slickered Grand Banks doryman.

1951

● *The Society supports an aerial and ground survey of giant gravel pictographs of Indian origin in southeast California.*

● *The magazine receives U. S. Camera's Achievement Award for its use of editorial color photography.*

1952

● *Britain's Royal Geographical Society and Cambridge University join National Geographic to sponsor geological studies on Norway's West Spitsbergen Island.*

● *A Society research grant aids astronomer Dr. George A. Van Biesbroeck of Yerkes Observatory in making star-field measurements at Khartoum, Sudan, during the February 25, 1952, total solar eclipse. His findings substantially confirm Albert Einstein's theory of relativity.*

PAUL A. ZAHL

ALAN VILLIERS

17

JEAN SHOR

Perilous span of worn cables and cracked branches set a stride apart carries Franc Shor of the Foreign Editorial Staff over Central Asia's Hunza River 500 feet below, an adventure described in the October 1953 GEOGRAPHIC.

Circled cross marks an ice floe directly above the North Pole at 11:29 a.m. EST on May 20, 1953. Circling the Pole in an airplane GEOGRAPHIC Editor Gilbert H. Grosvenor became the first to locate the spot by photographing it from all sides. Plotting the lines of focus on 15 photographs, he pinpointed the Pole's position. U. S. Coast and Geodetic Survey calculations and grid lines, shown on this photograph, confirmed Dr. Grosvenor's computations.

WILLARD R. CULVER

ALFRED GREGORY (C) R. G. S. AND ALPINE CLUB

- *NATIONAL GEOGRAPHIC publishes the first aerials of the North Pole, the first pictures of birds of paradise displaying in the wild, and the first color pictures of living deep-sea fishes . . .*

- *. . . and joins forces with Eastman Kodak and others to produce the first color photographs and depth map of New Mexico's Carlsbad Caverns.*

- *The La Belle Award of the Photographic Society of America is presented to NATIONAL GEOGRAPHIC for outstanding contributions to the development of color photography for magazine use.*

- *With Society backing, ornithologist E. Thomas Gilliard renews studies of New Guinea bird life and Stone Age natives.*

Edmund Hillary leads as he and his Sherpa companion Tenzing Norgay labor up the southeast ridge of Mount Everest en route to the first conquest of the world's tallest peak on May 29, 1953. As a member of an unsuccessful Swiss-led assault on the 29,028-foot Himalayan giant, Norgay had passed this way the previous spring. Hillary recounted "The Conquest of the Summit" for GEOGRAPHIC readers in the July 1954 issue.

Society Trustees join Gen. George C. Marshall, standing, in honoring Dr. Gilbert H. Grosvenor, far right, at his retirement on May 5, 1954. Editor of NATIONAL GEOGRAPHIC for 55 years and President of the Society since 1920, Dr. Grosvenor was succeeded in those posts by longtime Associate Editor and Vice President Dr. John Oliver La Gorce (at far end of table).

Diver *extraordinaire*, Capt. Jacques-Yves Cousteau recounted his discovery of the remains of a 2,200-year-old Greek merchant ship in the January 1954 GEOGRAPHIC. The Society sponsored the early work of this French aquanaut, here holding a bronze spike from the ship, which went down off Marseille.

HAROLD E. EDGERTON

- *President Dwight D. Eisenhower presents the Society's gold Hubbard Medal to the British Everest expedition. Leader Sir John Hunt and climbers Sir Edmund Hillary and Tenzing Norgay receive bronze replicas as personal awards.*

- *The Society supports an archeological expedition to probe the origin of Canada's Dorset Eskimo culture.*

- *Honor Award for Distinguished Service in Journalism is given to NATIONAL GEOGRAPHIC by the University of Missouri School of Journalism.*

- *Work begins on a two-year, Society-supported study of Mars.*

ARTHUR JOHNSON

PAINTING BY W. LANGDON KIHN

Solemn-faced Shawnee, Chief Tecumseh (**above**) appeared in the Society's 1955 book, *Indians of the Americas*.

Land diver prepares to leap 78 feet from a tower of branches and vines (**left**) in a January 1955 article on New Hebrides Islanders.

"Stars and Stripes nailed to the Pole." On April 6, 1909, Robert E. Peary carried a taffeta flag made by his wife (**lower left**) to the North Pole. Caching pieces of it en route and depositing a strip at the Pole, Peary reduced the banner to a patchwork. In 1955 his widow presented the much-worn memento to the Society.

1955

● *Mrs. Robert E. Peary is awarded the Society's Special Gold Medal for contributions to her husband's Arctic explorations.*

● *Renewed Society funding enables specialists from the University of California and the Smithsonian Institution to clear the main ceremonial court of La Venta in southern Mexico. Archeological fieldwork at the ancient urban-ceremonial site establishes La Venta as a capital of Olmec civilization as long as 2,500 years ago.*

● *President and Editor Dr. John Oliver La Gorce celebrates his Golden Jubilee at NATIONAL GEOGRAPHIC and is awarded the Society's Grosvenor Medal.*

BROOKS HONEYCUTT

LUIS MARDEN

PHILIP DRUCKER

More of man's past in the Americas appeared in the pages of GEOGRAPHIC during 1956. Russell Cave in Alabama (above) yielded traces of man dating back 8,000 years. Pre-Columbian Olmec figurines of jade and serpentine (upper right), perhaps representing priests at sacrifice, came to light at La Venta, Mexico.

1956

• *Photography is completed for the National Geographic Society— Palomar Observatory Sky Atlas, which expands known space twenty-five times.*

• *As part of the International Geophysical Year, and with the Society's support, a shipboard geophysical observatory studies earth's magnetic field and measures cosmic-ray intensities.*

• *National Geographic Society— Smithsonian Institution excavations at Russell Cave in Alabama unearth bones, tools, and weapons indicating human occupancy of the cave from 6200 B.C. to A.D. 1650. The Society purchases the cave site for later presentation to the Federal Government as a national archeological monument.*

Fatally attractive, a bristling lionfish scouts a sponge-mantled coral shelf in the Red Sea. The venom-spined creature appeared in a 1956 GEOGRAPHIC article on marine photography.

21

1957

- *Grants from the Society and the Smithsonian Institution make possible field studies of Ecuador's primitive Indian tribes.*

- *The Society's modern Book Service is formally organized;* The World in Your Garden *inaugurates its new series.*

- *With Tulane University, the Society cosponsors excavation and restoration of Dzibilchaltun, an ancient Maya urban center in Yucatán, Mexico.*

Suns glow green in a filtered multi-exposure taken at the U. S. South Pole station by GEOGRAPHIC staff man Thomas J. Abercrombie in November 1957. First civilian photographer to reach the station, Abercrombie spent three weeks there.

In the wake of history, *Mayflower II* spans the Atlantic during a British reenactment of the original 1620 Pilgrim crossing (**left**). Longtime seaman and NATIONAL GEOGRAPHIC author Alan Villiers skippered the ship and described her voyage in the November 1957 issue.

Beached and burned on January 23, 1790, the mutiny ship *Bounty* lay undetected off Pitcairn Island in the South Pacific for 167 years until NATIONAL GEOGRAPHIC's Luis Marden (**right**) discovered her remains in Bounty Bay in January of 1957. Here Marden retrieves ship's fittings he chiseled out of limy growths that marked the line of the vessel's keel.

Newly elected President and Editor Melville Bell Grosvenor (**below,** center) with his executive staff on January 8, 1957. Seated are Dr. Thomas W. McKnew, Vice President and Secretary (left), and Robert V. Fleming, Treasurer. Standing: Melvin M. Payne, Senior Assistant Secretary (left), and Frederick G. Vosburgh, Associate Editor.

THOMAS CHRISTIAN

VOLKMAR WENTZEL

ANGELO CARUSO, JR.

"**Aviation will conquer** the Arctic—and the Antarctic, too." First to fly over the North Pole in 1926 and the South Pole in 1929, Trustee Adm. Richard E. Byrd died March 11, 1957.

23

1958

- *National Press Photographers Association (NPPA) honors Thomas J. Abercrombie of the Foreign Editorial Staff as Magazine Photographer of the Year.*

- *The Society's Hubbard Medal is presented to Dr. Paul A. Siple, scientific leader of the first group to winter at the South Pole.*

- *Society and American Museum of Natural History funding enables ornithologists to make the first color record of courting ritual among greater birds of paradise.*

- *Thomas W. McKnew is elected Executive Vice President and Secretary; Robert E. Doyle, Associate Secretary.*

- *March GEOGRAPHIC publishes the deepest undersea photographs made to this date, from 25,000 feet down in the mid-Atlantic's Romanche trench.*

Brooding cliffs in the Judaean wilderness and the sectarians they once sheltered were featured in a 1958 article. About 100 B.C. the Essenes, a Jewish religious group, retired to the cliffs at Wadi Qumran near the northwest shore of the Dead Sea. There they prepared and stored copies of the Old Testament, creating cave libraries and the famous Dead Sea scrolls. To date, copies of all Old Testament books except Esther have been found at Qumran.

Lightning erupts above lava-flanked Ilha Nova (New Island) in the Azores in a 20-minute time exposure (**below**). Rising in September 1957, the volcano sank back into the sea in October, only to reappear in November; by March 1958 it squatted as a steaming quarter-mile-wide islet at the western end of Fayal Island. The up-and-down evolution of Ilha Nova appeared in the June 1958 GEOGRAPHIC.

Atomic kaleidoscope at the tip of a platinum needle (**below**) appeared in the September 1958 article "You and the Obedient Atom." Magnified 750,000 times and supercooled, individual atoms glow as blobs of light.

ROBERT F. SISSON

Best preserved of the Dead Sea manuscripts, this leather scroll contains the full 66 chapters of the messianic Book of Isaiah, a favorite Old Testament text of the Essene scribes who copied it.

Stubborn stump of bristlecone pine (**lower right**) resists time in California's White Mountains. A March 1958 article on these oldest known living things included this 4,000-year-old tree, its wood polished by wind-borne grit.

Polar crossings, over the ice and beneath it, were reported in the January 1959 NATIONAL GEOGRAPHIC. British Commonwealth Trans-Antarctic expedition tractors set out from Shackleton Base on the Weddell Sea in late 1957 and paused at Amundsen-Scott Station at the South Pole on January 19, 1958 *(above).*

1959

- *Hubbard Medal awarded to Sir Vivian Fuchs, leader of the British Trans-Antarctic expedition.*

- *GEOGRAPHIC's John E. Fletcher places first, J. Baylor Roberts second and third in color class in White House News Photographers Association contest.*

- *The September NATIONAL GEOGRAPHIC bears the first of a continuing series of color covers.*

- *Vice Chairman of the Board and retired Editor Dr. John Oliver La Gorce dies December 23.*

- *The Aviation/Space Writers Association's James J. Strebig Memorial Award goes to Assistant Editor Allan C. Fisher, Jr., for "Cape Canaveral's 6,000-mile Shooting Gallery" (October).*

The expedition covered 2,158 miles in all, arriving at McMurdo Sound on March 2, 1958. Painting (**facing page**) shows the atomic-powered submarine *Nautilus* passing beneath the frozen Chukchi Sea during the first Arctic transpolar voyage. *Nautilus* reached the North Pole on August 3, 1958.

Nearly complete skull of "East Africa Man" elates prehistorian Louis S. B. Leakey (**lower left**). Later supported by the Society, Dr. Leakey and his wife unearthed *Zinjanthropus boisei* in 1959 in Tanzania's Olduvai Gorge. First sign of the landmark discovery was a fossilized jaw dated at 1,750,000 years (**below**).

U. S. and Asian leaders — President Dwight D. Eisenhower and Indian Prime Minister Jawaharlal Nehru meet at the University of Delhi in December 1959 (**above**). Ike donned cap and gown at this midpoint of a 22,000-mile goodwill tour of Europe, Asia, and Africa, reported in the May 1960 GEOGRAPHIC.

Undersea butterfly, explorer Jacques-Yves Cousteau's diving saucer (**far left**) glides over a marine meadow in the Caribbean off Guadeloupe. Construction of the two-man submarine was made possible by grants from the National Geographic Society.

Pre-Columbian Peruvian grave doll (**left**) illustrated a June 1960 article on the Smithsonian Institution. The National Geographic Society and the Smithsonian have long shared a common purpose: the increase and diffusion of knowledge.

New presses, paper, and inks make up the September 1960 NATIONAL GEOGRAPHIC (**lower left**). By the beginning of 1960, rising Society membership required a monthly edition of 2 1/2 million copies of the magazine, prompting a successful eight-month printing transfer from Washington, D. C., to new presses in Chicago, Illinois.

1960

● *National Geographic scientist Barry C. Bishop joins Sir Edmund Hillary in winter high-altitude research in the Himalayas.*

● *The Society deeds Alabama's Russell Cave, occupied by man 8,000 years ago, to the National Park Service.*

● *Titles are added to the magazine's spine for easy reference, beginning with the January issue.*

● *First bound and indexed set of Geographic maps offered:* **Atlas of the Fifty United States.**

● **Wild Animals of North America** *issued by the Book Service.*

● *The Society assists in the first probe with free-diving gear of the Well of Sacrifice at Chichén Itzá, Yucatán. Thousands of artifacts are recovered.*

Abandoned to ruin and loose rock, cliff houses at Wetherill Mesa in Colorado's Mesa Verde National Park once sheltered the Anasazi—the Ancient Ones—the Pueblo culture that succumbed to a late 13th-century drought. Long House (**above**) stretches 295 feet along a canyon face; multistory apartments and storage rooms, 181 in all, conform in size and shape to the irregular rock of the mesa. The December 1961 President's Annual Message to Members pointed to archeological and restoration work at Wetherill Mesa as an example of research assisted by the Society.

1961

- *First political Geographic world globe offered to members.*

- *Robert E. Doyle elected Vice President of the Society.*

- *Staff photographer Dean Conger chosen NPPA Magazine Photographer of the Year.*

- *"Countdown for Space" in the May* NATIONAL GEOGRAPHIC *earns senior editorial staff member Kenneth F. Weaver the Aviation/Space Writers Association Writing Award of the Year.*

- *GEOGRAPHIC reports discovery by E. Thomas Gilliard of previously unknown New Britain birds.*

- *The Society begins its support of Jane Goodall and her studies of chimpanzee behavior at Gombe Stream National Park in western Tanzania.*

"Geography in the round": The Society's globe, with its unique plastic "thinking cap," was introduced in 1961.

Burnished by sunset, a gun battery (**left**) marks the line held by Stonewall Jackson at the first Battle of Bull Run in 1861. Stilled cannon appeared in the April 1961 Civil War Centennial issue.

29

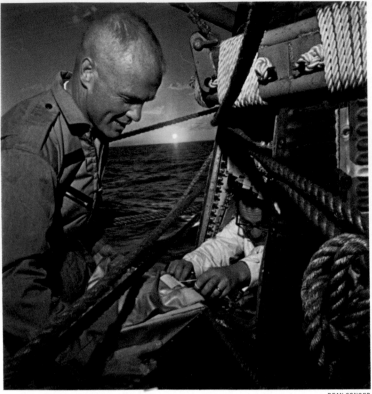

DEAN CONGER

Riding *Friendship 7* through three sunsets in space, Astronaut John Glenn (**above**, left) splashed down on February 20, 1962 in time for a fourth sunset in the At-

lantic. Shown aboard a recovery ship collecting gear from his capsule, the first American to orbit earth received the Society's Hubbard Medal on April 9, 1962.

New headquarters of the National Geographic Society take shape in the heart of Washington, D. C. By 1962 the Society's steadily expanding membership and

WINFIELD PARKS

Pleased President and Mrs. John F. Kennedy accept presentation copies of *The White House: An Historic Guide,* requested by Mrs. Kennedy and prepared by

GEORGE F. MOBLEY

the Society in 1962 as a public service. On the cover is an unusual view of the Executive Mansion taken from atop an extended firetruck ladder.

1962

- *Lt. Col. John H. Glenn, Jr., carries Geographic flag on first U. S. orbital spaceflight.*

- *East African fossil discoveries earn Dr. and Mrs. Louis S. B. Leakey the Society's Hubbard Medal.*

- *The* GEOGRAPHIC *publishes more editorial color this year than any other magazine.*

- *Thomas W. McKnew becomes Vice Chairman of the Board of Trustees; Melvin M. Payne, Secretary and Executive Vice President.*

- *The Society issues* **Men, Ships, and the Sea,** *a history of seafaring from raft to atom-powered ship.*

services required construction of new offices. Much praised for its architectural excellence, the ten-story glass and marble building was dedicated in 1964. It houses Magazine and Society staffs, photographic laboratories, and Explorers Hall, a museum of adventure, exploration, and science. Open to the public, the hall and its changing exhibits display the results of many Society-supported expeditions. The Society's old headquarters building, at far left, continues in use.

Through time and cultures, 1962 articles carried GEOGRAPHIC readers to New Guinea (**above**); to Outer Mongolia, where Supreme Court Justice William O.

Douglas watches staff photographer Dean Conger eat a mutton rib Mongol fashion (**above**); and to Turkey's seacoast for the salvage of Bronze Age relics (**right**).

KATHLEEN REVIS JUDGE

Marking 75 years of NATIONAL GEOGRAPHIC and 63 years of marriage, Gilbert H. Grosvenor and his wife, Elsie May Bell, observe the Society's Diamond Anniversary at Beinn Bhreagh, their summer home near Baddeck, Nova Scotia. Dr. Grosvenor was Editor of the Society's journal for fifty-five years; Mrs. Grosvenor created its familiar blue, brown, and green flag.

NATIONAL GEOGRAPHIC
ATLAS OF THE WORLD

Long famous for the quality of its map supplements, the National Geographic Society in 1963 issued the first edition of its *Atlas of the World*. Revised three times, the atlas continues to be one of the most accurate, detailed, and timely volumes of its kind ever produced. More than 650,000 copies have been distributed.

1963

• *The Society celebrates the 75th anniversary of its founding in 1888.*

• *A five-year joint National Park Service—National Geographic project to excavate and study Indian cliff dwellings at Wetherill Mesa in Colorado is completed.*

• *Evidence is found at L'Anse aux Meadows in Newfoundland by a Society-funded investigation that Norsemen reached North America five centuries before Columbus.*

• *The Geographic flag is raised atop the world's highest mountain by the Society-supported American Mount Everest expedition.*

• *A National Geographic grant makes possible a National Park Service study to preserve California's coast redwoods. The survey later aided establishment of Redwood National Park.*

• *The Society's Book Service publishes* **Great Adventures With National Geographic.**

Beneath a flag at half-staff, the caisson bearing the casket of John F. Kennedy draws up at the Capitol on Sunday, November 24, 1963. A restive black gelding, riderless and with black boots reversed in silver stirrups, suggests the fallen leader's spirit. The March 1964 NATIONAL GEOGRAPHIC carried a special tribute to the President who gave "The Last Full Measure."

White House ceremony honors the American Mount Everest expedition as President Kennedy awards the Hubbard Medal to team leader Norman Dyhrenfurth on July 8, 1963 (**lower left**). Soci- ety President Melville Bell Grosvenor and Executive Vice President Melvin M. Payne applaud at left. GEOGRAPHIC's Barry Bishop was one of six climbers to reach the summit (**below**).

"**Invite exploration . . . .**" So urges President Lyndon B. Johnson at the dedication of new Society headquarters on January 18, 1964 (**above**). Guests in Explorers Hall included Justices of the Supreme Court, Cabinet members, and Society officers.

Street boys in Sana, capital of Yemen, flick disks into the corner pockets of a carom board in a popular Yemenite game similar to

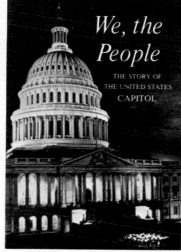

Floodlit classic, the U. S. Capitol crowns the cover of *We, the People,* second of the Society's public-service books. In 1964 the history and guide won the George Washington Honor Medal of the Freedoms Foundation.

billiards (**facing page, lower**). The youngsters added a peaceful vignette to a March 1964 article on Yemen's civil war.

Mirrored in the eyes of mother and child (**below**), harsh life of Andean Indians was one of "The Five Worlds of Peru" in 1964.

World's tallest tree, the California coast redwood at center was reported in 1964 by GEOGRAPHIC naturalist Dr. Paul A. Zahl.

1964

- *The Society grants research funds for an ethnological study of the vanishing Ainu people of Hokkaido, Japan.*

- *Elsie May Bell Grosvenor, "first lady of National Geographic" and designer of the Society's flag, dies December 26.*

- *Reprints of 179 rare issues covering the magazine's first 20 years are offered by the Society.*

- *A new book,* **Song and Garden Birds of North America,** *is issued, accompanied by the Society's first recording.*

- **The Presidents of the United States,** *another Geographic public-service book, appears.*

Words of courage and resolution from Sir Winston Churchill inspired the free world. A record accompanying the August 1965 NATIONAL GEOGRAPHIC contained excerpts of Churchill's address to a joint session of Congress on December 26, 1941 (left), and the pageantry and sorrow of his funeral in London on January 30, 1965 (below). Flag-draped and topped by the Order of the Garter insignia on a black velvet cushion, the casket of "the greatest Englishman" rides a gun carriage drawn in slow march by a Royal Navy crew.

WIDE WORLD

STUART HEYDINGER

WINFIELD PARKS

Television joined print and photographs at Geographic in 1965 with airing of the Society's first television special, "Americans on Everest." At left, President and Editor Melville Bell Grosvenor confers with executive producer Robert C. Doyle beside gear used in the 1963 American Everest ascent.

Uncommon beauty of a common egret (right) appeared in the Society's 1965 book *Water, Prey, and Game Birds of North America*. Records of bird songs were included with this and its companion volume, *Song and Garden Birds of North America*.

FREDERICK KENT TRUSLOW

JAMES A. MCDIVITT, NASA

● *Special Publications Division officially established.*

● *Joining with several other contributors, the National Geographic Society helps finance a project for the preparation and publication of a six-volume work on the wild flowers of the United States, under the aegis of the New York Botanical Garden.*

● *The Book Service publishes* **Wondrous World of Fishes.**

● *George Washington Honor Medal of the Freedoms Foundation is awarded the Society for its public-service books.*

Up a tree for science, chimpanzee-watcher Jane Goodall seeks a vantage point in Tanzania's Gombe Stream National Park. The photograph of the Society-supported zoologist appeared in the December 1965 magazine.

A golden tether secures slow-motion spacewalker Maj. Edward H. White II (**above**) as he floats 100 miles above earth on June 3, 1965. The first American to walk in space, White used the guidance gun in his right hand to maneuver alongside Gemini 4, reflected in his helmet visor. Exhausting the gun's compressed oxygen, White later pulled on the gold-plated tether to change his position. The cord carried oxygen and voice contact with White's partner, Maj. James A. McDivitt. In September 1965 GEOGRAPHIC published dramatic photographs of the 21-minute, 6,000-mile stroll through space.

BARON HUGO VAN LAWICK

Staff photographers collected 29 magazine awards in the 1966 "Pictures of the Year" competition. Winners included Thomas R. Smith, seated far left, who placed first in Picture Editing for the Winston Churchill articles in the August 1965 GEOGRAPHIC, which itself won an award for the year's best use of photographs in a magazine. Other winners in 1966 were, seated with Smith, Winfield Parks and William Albert Allard; standing, left to right, Albert Moldvay, David S. Boyer, W. E. Garrett, Bruce Dale, and James P. Blair.

B. ANTHONY STEWART

Ravaging the Renaissance heart of Florence on November 4, 1966, the flooding Arno River turns the Ponte Vecchio (Old Bridge), downstream at left, into a half-submerged weir. Palazzo Vecchio and city cathedral are at center and right. The July 1967 issue told of the disaster and the city's recovery effort.

Cavalry carrying the field, Norman knights crack Anglo-Saxon ranks at the Battle of Hastings in a panel from the Bayeux Tapestry (center). The medieval epic in cloth celebrates the Norman Conquest of England on October 14, 1066. Reproduction of the entire tapestry appeared 900 years later in the August 1966 GEOGRAPHIC.

GIANNI TORTOLI

1966

MILTON A. FORD AND VICTOR R. BOSWELL, JR.

Face-lift for a pharoah: Sandstone visage of Ramesses II swings free from a statue at Abu Simbel on the Nile (right). A 40-million-dollar international rescue effort was mounted under United Nations, Egyptian, and United States auspices to save the desert shrine, threatened by rising river waters impounded by Egypt's Aswan High Dam. The 3,200-year-old temples were sawed into blocks, marked, and then meticulously reassembled atop a plateau overlooking the new lake. The epic salvage job was reported in the May 1966 and May 1969 GEOGRAPHICS.

GEORG GERSTER

39

Portrait of planet earth, first in color from space, emerged in 1967 from the Johns Hopkins Applied Physics Laboratory. Society technicians, using the guide at top, helped correct the color.

On top of the bottom of the world, the 1966-67 American Antarctic Mountaineering expedition scaled that continent's loftiest peaks, an exploit honored by the Society's first John Oliver La Gorce Medal.

Educational filmstrips for secondary schoolchildren were the Society's new venture for 1968. Offerings ranged from "Ancient Times" and "Washington, D. C." (**above**) to "Southeast Asia."

Glowing lake mirrors twilight at the Membership Center Building, opened in 1968. The Gaithersburg, Maryland, structure, containing 400,000 square feet of space, replaced a bulging 43-year-

old records facility in downtown Washington, D. C. The Membership Center houses the Cartographic Division, which produces the Society's outstanding maps, globes, and atlases. Also at the

1967

- **My Friends the Wild Chimpanzees,** *an account of zoologist Jane Goodall's pioneering field studies of free-roaming chimpanzees in Tanzania, is issued by the Society's Special Publications Division.*

- *Air-route pioneer and National Geographic Society Trustee Juan T. Trippe is awarded the Hubbard Medal for his lifetime of service to the art and science of aviation.*

- *Geographic's Bruce Dale is named NPPA Magazine Photographer of the Year.*

- *NATIONAL GEOGRAPHIC Director of Photography Robert E. Gilka receives the Joseph A. Sprague Memorial Award, the NPPA's highest recognition to an individual for contributions to photography.*

JAMES E. RUSSELL

Change of command at the Society and its magazine occurred again in 1967: longtime President and Editor Melville Bell Grosvenor became Chairman of the Board and Editor-in-Chief. In front of him are new Editor Frederick G. Vosburgh at his right and new President Melvin M. Payne to his left. Flanking the three are new Associate Editor Gilbert M. Grosvenor at far left and newly elected Society Secretary Robert E. Doyle.

JAMES L. STANFIELD

building, more than a thousand employees and two computers handle records and correspondence of the National Geographic Society's more than nine million members.

1968

- *NATIONAL GEOGRAPHIC Assistant Editor W. E. Garrett is named NPPA Magazine Photographer of the Year.*

- *A Society grant makes possible a behavioral and ecological study of the little-understood and possibly endangered Florida manatee.*

- *The first volume in a series of Research Reports summarizes scientific findings of Society-sponsored research projects.*

- *The Society awards its John Oliver La Gorce Medal to Harold E. Edgerton, "father" of electronic flash equipment.*

- **Man's Conquest of Space,** *a Society Special Publication, wins first prize, book category, in Aviation/Space Writers Association competition.*

Sailor's self-portrait captures Robin Lee Graham during his lone round-the-world cruise aboard *Dove,* a feat followed in the October 1968, April 1969, and October 1970 GEOGRAPHICS.

Historic lunar reconnaissance: The 1968 Apollo 8 Christmas flight around the moon furnished amazing photographs for the May 1969 issue, including "earth rise" (**above**). Man first stepped on the lunar surface on July 20, 1969.

Visor of Apollo 11 Astronaut Edwin E. Aldrin (**below**) reflects fellow moon explorer Neil A. Armstrong and the lunar lander *Eagle*. Third crew member Michael Collins remained in moon orbit in the command module *Columbia*.

Applying shadows with an airbrush, a GEOGRAPHIC relief artist portrays the moon's far side (**above**). Photograph of the crater Tsiolkovsky guides him.

1969

- *Apollo 11 astronauts carry the Geographic flag to the moon.*

- *"The Music of Greece" issued as first of a series of stereo Sounds of the World recordings.*

- *The Society's Cartographic Division produces the first map to show the entire lunar surface on a single sheet.*

- **The Age of Chivalry** *issued.*

1970

- *Bringing to a close nearly 37 years of full-time service to the Society and to its journal, Vice President and Editor Frederick G. Vosburgh retires on October 1, retaining his position on the Board of Trustees. Gilbert M. Grosvenor is elected to succeed him.*

- *Hubbard Medal awarded to Apollo 11 Astronauts Neil A. Armstrong, Edwin E. Aldrin, Jr., and Michael Collins in recognition of their role in the historic moon landing of July 1969.*

Industrial river of sorrows, the Cuyahoga struggles through a Cleveland, Ohio, factory district. The sluggish, soiled waterway carries the pollution burden of steel mills, municipal sewers, chemical plants, and fertilizer runoff from upstream farms into oxygen-starved Lake Erie. The Cuyahoga's desperate condition emphasized the seriousness of "Our Ecological Crisis" in the December 1970 issue of NATIONAL GEOGRAPHIC.

Spiky pondside sentinels, cattails suggest a delicate defense against environmental abuse: heightened awareness of our world's fragile beauty. Like the grace of the mother robin stilling her nestling's hunger (**above,** right), much of earth's simple charm goes unremarked and seems beyond our perception — until we suddenly note its absence. Such thoughts led to the December 1970 portfolio: "The Fragile Beauty All About Us."

43

LILA M. BISHOP

W. E. GARRETT

MELVILLE BELL GROSVENOR

1971

• *The Society offers its first ethnic map,* **The Peoples of Mainland Southeast Asia,** *inaugurating a political and cultural map series.*

• *First photographs of snow leopards in the wild published in the November* GEOGRAPHIC.

• *National Geographic Physical Globe, one of the first to depict earth's major undersea surface features, is offered to Society members.*

• **Grcat Religions of the World** *issued by Society's Book Service.*

Lands and peoples of Asia appeared often in the pages of GEO-GRAPHIC during 1971. Barry C. Bishop (**top**, second from right) traveled to western Nepal for a November article on life in that changing kingdom. The Society's first ethnic map (**above, left**) supplemented the March issue, which portrayed mainland southeast Asian tribespeople such as the silver-trinketed Akha woman from northern Laos (**above**).

Hunting prehistory in East Africa, anthropologist Dr. Louis S. B. Leakey (**upper right**) and his wife Mary recovered a series of spectacular fossils during 13 years of Society-aided fieldwork. He died October 1, 1972.

1972

• *The Society announces support for a joint project with the Boston Museum of Science to map a ten-mile stretch of the Grand Canyon's South Rim, the area most visited by tourists.*

• *Two new ethnic supplement maps cover the Middle East (July) and North American Indians (December).*

• *A new Geographic book,* **The Marvels of Animal Behavior,** *is added to the Society's Natural Science Library.*

NATIONAL MUSEUMS OF KENYA

JAMES L. STANFIELD

Introducing beginning readers to nature, science, and geography, in 1972 the Society combined learning and entertainment in a new series of National Geographic children's books (**above**). Created especially for ages 4 through 8, Books for Young Explorers now include 20 titles, ranging from *How Animals Hide* to *Cowboys;* over six million have been distributed.

Mapping America anew for a people eager to see their country, a new Geographic regional map series began to appear in 1973: "Close-up: U.S.A.—The Northwest" (**top center**) is designed for vacation-bound Americans.

1973

● *Mars map supplement accompanies the February issue of* NATIONAL GEOGRAPHIC.

● *A Society grant aids publication of maps of the ruins of Chan Chan, Peru, perhaps the largest prehistoric city in the Americas.*

● *The Society's Book Service focuses on America's wild regions in* **Wilderness U.S.A.**

● *Society support begins for University of Texas radio sky-mapping project.*

Many-sided man, Dr. Leonard Carmichael, shown above with an infant orangutan, died September 16, 1973. After a lifetime of achievement as author, scholar, teacher, university president, and museum director, Dr. Carmichael served the last nine years of his full life as the National Geographic Society's gracious and vigorous Vice President for Research and Exploration.

In the family tradition, Richard E. Leakey proposed in a June 1973 NATIONAL GEOGRAPHIC article that fossil skull 1470 (**bottom center**) may be evidence of the existence of early man as long ago as 2.8 million years.

Solar spectacle millions of miles wide, the sun's outer atmosphere, the corona, unfurls in a view color-coded to distinguish levels of brightness. A coronagraph aboard NASA's orbiting Skylab observatory masks the solar disk, indicating the vast extent of the hot gases enveloping the sun. NATIONAL GEOGRAPHIC's three-part Skylab coverage appeared in the October 1974 issue.

Diaphanous drifter on wings of latticed muscle fiber, the oceanic snail *Corolla spectabilis* seines Gulf Stream currents for food. Classed as plankton—plant and animal organisms that ride the currents—the ghostly snail is an important element in the marine food web. Gossamer geometry of *Corolla* and other free-floating life was portrayed in a 1974 article on blue-water plankton.

SKYLAB 2, NASA

● *Continuing a long tradition of support for scientific and geographic research, the Society approves its 1,000th project, which makes possible a study of canals and reservoirs at the ancient Maya urban-ceremonial center of Etzna in Campeche, Mexico.*

● *"Rare Look at North Korea" by H. Edward Kim in the August NATIONAL GEOGRAPHIC wins the Overseas Press Club of America Award for best reporting on Asia.*

● *Melville Bell Grosvenor, Editor-in-Chief and Chairman of the Board of Trustees, receives the Grosvenor Medal in recognition of his fifty years of outstanding service to the increase and diffusion of knowledge through NATIONAL GEOGRAPHIC.*

PAINTING BY JEAN-LEON HUENS

Exploring hometown earth from the suburbs of space, the 100-ton Skylab laboratory drifts above the cloud-flecked Amazon River Delta 270 miles below. For 5 1/2 months in 1973 and 1974, Skylab astronauts trained sensors on the planet to monitor croplands and weather and to detect hints of new fishing grounds and ore deposits. The October 1974 issue carried this lofty view.

Centuries of belief decreed earth the navel of the universe, until in 1543 astronomer Nicolaus Copernicus enthroned the sun at the center of our planetary system. Overturning tradition established by Ptolemy, a 2d-century A.D. Greek, Copernicus laid the foundations of the modern astronomy covered in the May 1974 NATIONAL GEOGRAPHIC.

PAINTING BY JEAN-LEON HUENS

Rash sea dog even on land, Francis Drake (**left**, with pistols) waits to ambush a Spanish mule train in Panama's bush in 1573. A favorite of Queen Elizabeth I, he was profiled in February 1975 by Alan Villiers, a seagoing favorite of GEOGRAPHIC readers.

Unraveling the riddle of the ancient Maya, tracing Columbus' voyages, and locating the wreck of the Civil War ironclad *Monitor* were among the GEOGRAPHIC's 1975 highlights.

Serpents and glyphs weave across the Madrid Codex (**top right**), a folding 22-foot almanac consulted by Maya priests to foretell the future.

Map (**center right**) was drafted after 1500 by Juan de la Cosa, shipmate of Columbus on his second New World voyage in 1493-96. Green coast of a new land fills the left border of the chart, first to show mainland America.

Armor-plated wreck of the *Monitor* lies bottom up off Cape Hatteras, North Carolina, where she foundered in 1862 (**lower right**). Displaced gun turret protrudes at upper right.

A new magazine for youngsters, *World* replaced the familiar *School Bulletin* in 1975. Enthusiastic reception boosted circulation to more than 1,300,000 by mid-1976. *We Americans,* published by the Book Service for the country's Bicentennial, records 200 colorful years of U.S. history.

NATIONAL GEOGRAPHIC
world

SEPTEMBER 1975
Backpacking
Volcano!
Pygmy Chimps
Cobras

We Americans

1975

● *"The Arab World, Inc." by John J. Putman in the October* GEOGRAPHIC *is judged "Best Magazine Reporting from Abroad in 1975 by Overseas Press Club.*

● *Trustee Alexander Wetmore is awarded the Hubbard Medal in honor of his lifetime of contribution to ornithology.*

OTIS IMBODEN AND VICTOR R. BOSWELL, JR.; MUSEO DE AMÉRICA, MADRID

MUSEO NAVAL, MADRID

PHOTOGRAPHS BY GLEN TILLMAN, ALCOA MARINE CORPORATION; PHOTOMOSAIC BY U. S. NAVY

Touching up the continental United States, Tony Rossi of the General Electric Photographic Engineering Laboratory refines a billboard-size mosaic of 569 color prints made from images scanned by Landsat satellites. From this first coast-to-coast photomosaic of the 48 contiguous states came *Portrait U.S.A.,* a July 1976 map supplement.

Zeroing in on Antarctica, the Nimbus 5 satellite equipped with microwave radiation detectors produced this color-coded view of the South Polar ice cap, published in a November 1976 article on the world's changing climate. Ice sheet glows green and dark blue at center, revealing the relatively slow snow buildup of Antarctica's high summer.

Building life, geological violence and atmospheric fury fuse simple molecules into organic compounds about four billion years ago (**below**). Primitive protein chains link up with nucleic acids, and eons later a self-replicating cell appears. "Exploring the New Biology," in the September 1976 GEOGRAPHIC, presented this theory of life's beginnings on earth.

Forty-ton madonna, a mother humpback whale lazes with her calf off Maui, Hawaii. They were among "The Imperiled Giants" in the December 1976 GEOGRAPHIC.

Still-fresh wounds are reopened on the tundra as the Alaska pipeline is checked for defective welds. GEOGRAPHIC covered the oil line in November 1976.

1976

● *Robert E. Doyle elected Society President; Owen R. Anderson, Vice President and Secretary; Melvin M. Payne, Chairman of Board of Trustees.*

● *NPPA cites GEOGRAPHIC for "Best Use of Photography by a Magazine," presents its Magazine Picture Editor's Award to GEOGRAPHIC's David L. Arnold, and names staff photographer Steve Raymer Magazine Photographer of the Year.*

● *National Geographic Society membership, averaged over the year, reaches 9,350,000, an increase of 7,880,000 in the 30-year period covered by this index.*

Expeditions and Scientific Researches of the National Geographic Society

By MELVIN M. PAYNE

*Chairman, Board of Trustees,
and Chairman, Committee for Research and Exploration*

"UNBELIEVABLE! What a glorious, incredible sight!" In January 1976 Canadian zoologist Fred A. Urquhart stood on the flanks of central Mexico's Sierra Madre and watched countless millions of monarch butterflies stain the volcanic slopes a vibrant, quivering orange. After decades of search, and aided by the National Geographic Society through six grants from its Committee for Research and Exploration, he had located the overwintering site of the eastern population of the North American monarch. Only a simple and half-whispered "glorious, incredible sight!" caught the wonderment of the moment.

Making such moments possible for "the increase and diffusion of geographic knowledge" has always been a major aim of the National Geographic Society. Within two years of its founding in 1888, the Society endorsed geographic and geological studies in Alaska's St. Elias Mountains. While on that expedition, scientists (including two of the Society's first members) discovered Mount Logan, North America's second highest peak.

In the nearly nine decades since that 1890 expedition, the Society has aided or sponsored more than 1,300 individual researches and explorations. Some, like the 1915-1920 Mount Katmai expeditions to Alaska's Valley of Ten Thousand Smokes, have resulted in the addition of spectacular scenery to our

system of national parks. Many others have fostered signal contributions to every conceivable field of geographic and scientific interest.

A sampling of projects encouraged by the Society quickly becomes a catalog of human achievement and a vivid record of the expansion of knowledge: At the ends of the earth, the Society assisted Robert E. Peary's epic 1909 "dash to the Pole" and supported two of Richard E. Byrd's historic stays at Little America in Antarctica.

Uncovering man's past in the Americas, in 1912 explorer Hiram Bingham led Society–Yale University excavations at the ruins of Machu Picchu, the lost mountaintop citadel of Peru's once great Incas. In 1938, with Society backing, Dr. Matthew W. Stirling began to uncover Mexico's pre-Columbian Olmec civilization and a stela bearing one of America's oldest written dates, equivalent to 31 B.C.

Nearly thirty years and more than 32,000 feet separate William Beebe's record-breaking 1934 bathysphere descent off Bermuda and the American Mount Everest expedition's conquest of the world's loftiest mountain in 1963. Both undertakings had Society support.

In East Africa, first the late Louis S. B. Leakey and his wife, Mary, and now their son Richard unlock the prehistoric mysteries

Fossil jaw in hand, the late Dr. Louis S. B. Leakey, at left, describes his early-man discoveries to the author.

of Tanzania's Olduvai Gorge and Laetolil and Kenya's Lake Rudolf (now Lake Turkana), pushing man's history back more than three million years. Also in Tanzania, Jane Goodall observes her free-roaming friends the wild chimpanzees. In England archeologists sift the possible site of King Arthur's "Camelot." And in the United States a University of Texas radio sky survey maps the "chatter" of distant galaxies, extending our vision of the universe. All these projects receive Society aid.

Through its Committee for Research and Exploration, the Society annually approves more than one and a half million dollars in new and continuing grants to excavations, expeditions, and researches of all kinds. The following section of this index contains a list-ing of the Society's research grants and expeditions through 1976. Concise résumés summarize the aims and results of major projects and point both interested layman and questing scholar to detailed technical monographs collected in the Society's *Research Reports,* a series now complete through 1968.* Many of these projects have also appeared in the pages of NATIONAL GEOGRAPHIC.

Describing his butterfly find to the Committee for Research and Exploration, Fred Urquhart called it "a tremendous discovery." It was indeed, and others await you in the pages that follow.

*Copies of the first nine volumes of *Research Reports* may be obtained for $5 each, postpaid, by writing to Dept. 100, National Geographic Society, Washington, D. C. 20036. Request later billing if desired.

Aeronautics and Atmospheric Science

Air-quality measurement device: development. John S. Hall. 1974

Da Vinci–Trans-America Manned Scientific Balloon Flight. Rudolf J. Engelmann. 1973

Explorer I (balloon). William E. Kepner, Albert W. Stevens, and Orvil A. Anderson. 1934

Explorer II (balloon): altitude record. Albert W. Stevens and Orvil A. Anderson. 1935. *Lifting a ton of scientific instruments and two aerial photographers,* Explorer II *reached an altitude of 13.71 miles, a record that stood unchallenged for 21 years.*

Stratosphere sampling. Bismarck, North Dakota. National Bureau of Standards. 1940-41

Anthropology

ARCHEOLOGY
North America

Agate Basin ancient Indian camp. Wyoming. Frank H. H. Roberts and William M. Bass. 1959, 1961

Arizona, central: prehistoric human adaptation in an environmental transition zone. George J. Gumerman. 1973

Baffin Island, Northwest Territories, Canada. Lorna M. McKenzie-Pollock. 1968-69

Balankanche Cave, Chichén Itzá, Mexico. E. Wyllys Andrews IV. 1959

Basket Maker occupation, Upper Grand Gulch, Utah. William D. Lipe. 1968-69

Bering Strait, Alaska. Henry B. Collins. 1936

Bison-kill site, Jones-Miller Paleo-Indian. Colorado. Dennis J. Stanford. 1973-76. *Ten thousand years old, this kill and butchering* *area provides a firsthand look at the daily economy of prehistoric North American Indians.*

Carter's Grove, Virginia. Ivor Nöel-Hume. 1976. *Seventeenth-century settlement sites near Williamsburg add to our knowledge of the colonial South and America's early material beginnings.*

Caves and rock-shelters. Dominican Republic. Marcio Veloz Maggiolo. 1976

Chaco Canyon, New Mexico: remote-sensing analysis of prehistoric human occupations. Thomas R. Lyons. 1973

Chalcatzingo, Morelos, Mexico. David C. Grove. 1971-72

Colima, Mexico. Isabel T. Kelly. 1968, 1970

Coxcatlán, Puebla, Mexico. Richard S. MacNeish. 1971-73

Cuicuilco ruins, Mexico. Byron Cummings. 1924-25. *A vast ceremonial mound, sealed and preserved for many centuries by lava flows, bears impressive witness to the early beginnings of urban life among ancient Americans.*

Culture ecology, early. Mexican Gulf Coast. S. Jeffrey K. Wilkerson. 1973-75

Dorset Eskimo sites. Southampton Island, Hudson Bay. Henry B. Collins. 1954

Dry Creek, central Alaska. William R. Powers. 1976

Dzibilchaltun, Yucatán, Mexico. E. Wyllys Andrews IV. 1957-66. *Perhaps the largest and longest-inhabited site in prehistoric America, this ruined metropolis speaks eloquently of the vanished glories of Maya civilization.*

Engelbert site: Indian burials. Nichols, New York. William D. Lipe. 1968

Environmental archeology and cultural systems. Hamilton Inlet, Labrador. William W. Fitzhugh. 1971-72

Etzna: prehistoric house mounds and canals. Campeche, Mexico. Ray T. Matheny. 1974

"Exploration of Early Man Sites in Alaska" project. 1976. *The Society has joined the National Park Service in a three-year project to locate and date traces of early man in his dispersal through North America.*

Finger Lakes region, New York. Marian E. White. 1975

Gatecliff Shelter, Nevada. David H. Thomas. 1975-76

Grand Canyon, Arizona: North Rim. Douglas W. Schwartz. 1968-71

Grasshopper Pueblo habitat. Arizona. William A. Longacre. 1974

Hell Gap site. Wyoming. Cynthia and Henry T. Irwin and George A. Agogino. 1962-66

Hirundo site. Maine. David Sanger. 1972-73, 1975

Katmai National Monument, Alaska: ancient Aleut and Eskimo site. Donald E. Dummond. 1967-68

King site. Floyd County, Georgia. David J. Hally. 1973

Lahonton Lake, Nevada. Phil C. Orr. 1957

Larsen archeological site. South Dakota. William M. Bass. 1970

Lehner Paleo-Indian site. San Pedro Valley, Arizona. C. Vance Haynes and Emil W. Haury. 1973, 1975

Maya sites. Becan, Campeche, Mexico. Prentice M. Thomas, Jr. 1972-73

————Yucatán Peninsula, Mexico. E. Wyllys Andrews IV. 1968, 1970. *Dramatic artistic and scientific discoveries in the Yucatán Peninsula reflect the greatness of Maya culture at its zenith.*

Meadowcroft Rockshelter and Cross Creek Drainage. Pennsylvania. James M. Adovasio. 1976

Mississippi, southwestern. Stephen Williams. 1970, 1972

Mississippi Valley protohistoric and early 18th-century Indian-French contact period. Jeffrey P. Brain. 1974

Mummy Cave, Wyoming. Harold McCracken. 1965

Olmec sites. La Venta, Tres Zapotes, and San Lorenzo, Mexico. Philip Drucker, 1955; Robert F. Heizer, 1955, 1965-69; Matthew W. Stirling, 1938-46. *Eight successive dry-season expeditions produced a series of superlative finds illuminating Olmec culture: one of America's oldest dated works—a stela bearing a date equivalent to 31 B.C., colossal stone heads, greenstone "tiger" masks, and two ruined cities.*

Paleo-Indian quarry and living sites. Shenandoah Valley, Virginia. William M. Gardner. 1970

Port Royal, Jamaica. Edwin A. Link. 1959

Post-Hopewellian subsistence change: testing a model for. Stuart Struever. 1973

Pueblo Bonito, New Mexico. Andrew Ellicott Douglass, 1923-29; Neil M. Judd, 1920-27, 1929. *Communal dwellings in northwestern New Mexico yielded clues to the prehistory of the Southwest; tree rings in housing beams have dated their construction at A.D. 919 to 1130.*

Puerco River Valley, New Mexico: resettlement of Puebloan populations after the abandonment of Chaco Canyon. Cynthia Irwin-Williams. 1970-73

Quintana Roo: Cobá mapping project. Mexico. George E. Stuart. 1974-75

——Tancah and Tulum: murals and architecture. Mexico. Arthur G. Miller. 1972-75

Río Bec region: ecological change and cultural history. Yucatán Peninsula, Mexico. Richard E. W. Adams. 1972

Russell Cave, Jackson County, Alabama. Carl F. Miller, 1956-58. *Artifacts recovered here reveal continuous human occupancy from about 6200 B.C. to A.D. 1650. The Society bought and deeded the site to the Federal Government for preservation as a national archeological monument.*

Salts Cave, Mammoth Cave National Park, Kentucky. Patty Jo Watson. 1968-69

San Juan County, Utah. Neil M. Judd. 1923

Sandia Cave, New Mexico. George A. Agogino. 1961

Santa Rosa Island, California. Phil C. Orr. 1957

"Spanish Diggings" aboriginal flint quarries. Southeastern Wyoming. John M. Saul. 1964

Stone spheres. Jalisco, Mexico. Matthew W. Stirling. 1967-68

Tellico Reservoir, Tennessee. Jefferson Chapman. 1976

Thule culture. Northwest Hudson Bay. Charles F. Merbs. 1968-70

Towers of Hovenweep National Monu-ment. Mesa Verde, Colorado. Ray A. Williamson. 1976

Turner Farm site. North Haven, Maine. Bruce J. Bourque. 1974-75

Upper Delaware Valley Early Man Project. Charles W. McNett, Jr. 1974-76

Viking site. L'Anse aux Meadows, Newfoundland. Helge Ingstad. 1963-65. *This site has produced evidence that Norse settlers touched the North American Continent some five centuries before Columbus.*

Voyageur fur-trade materials. Minnesota-Ontario border. Robert C. Wheeler. 1963-66

Voyageurs: Fort Charlotte Underwater Project. Grand Portage National Monument, Minnesota. Robert C. Wheeler. 1975

Well of Sacrifice probe. Chichén Itzá, Mexico. William J. Folan. 1960-61. *The first exploration with modern free-diving equipment and air lift at this old Maya city's cenote brought to light jade, metal, and ceramic ornaments and figurines.*

Wetherill Mesa, Colorado. Douglas Osborne. 1958-63. *Painstaking excavation efforts co-sponsored by the Society and the National Park Service resurrected the cliffside dwellings of Indians who vanished 700 years ago.*

Xitle (volcano) and Cuicuilco (pyramid), Mexico. Robert F. Heizer. 1957

Yucatán Peninsula, Mexico: settlement patterns, pre-Columbian. Edward B. Kurjack. 1975

Central and South America

Abaj Takalik, Guatemala. John A. Graham. 1975-76. *Exploratory studies at this extensive and little-investigated group of ruins revealed chronological overlap between two ancient Middle American cultures—the Olmec and the Maya.*

Agronomy potential. Bajo de Santa Fe, El Petén, Guatemala. Bruce H. Dahlin. 1975

Architectural stones and sculpture. Peru and Bolivia. Robert F. Heizer. 1963

Ariari River Basin, Colombia: archeological chronology. John P. Marwitt. 1973-74

Chan Chan-Moche Valley Project, Peru. Carol J. Mackey and Michael E. Moseley. 1969-74. *An urban settlement on Peru's north* coast, Chan Chan was built between the 13th and 15th centuries A.D. and served as the capital city of the Chimu people before being conquered around 1470 by highland Incas.

Chicama-Moche Canal Project, Peru. James S. Kus. 1968-69

Culebra, Bay of, Costa Rica. Frederick W. Lange. 1976

Cupisnique culture: Caballo Muerto complex. Peru. Thomas G. Pozorski. 1973

Ecuador Indian tribes and pre-Columbian sites. Matthew W. Stirling. 1957

Gold artifacts, pre-Columbian: catalog. Panama. Reina Torres de Arauz. 1971

Honduras cultural change (pre-Columbian Mesoamerican frontier). Paul F. Healy. 1975-76

Incas. Machu Picchu, Peru. Hiram Bingham. 1912, 1914-15. *Discovered in 1911 by explorer Hiram Bingham, Machu Picchu had been concealed from the outside world by jungle for nearly four centuries. Bingham later headed a Society–Yale University expedition to clear this lost mountaintop citadel of the Incas.*

Maya highlands, Guatemala. Robert J. Sharer. 1972-73

Maya vessels: search for evidence of seaborne contact with highland cultures of Mesoamerica. Nancy M. Farriss. 1974-75

Middle American Research Institute archeological publication. New Orleans, Louisiana. E. Wyllys Andrews IV. 1975

Monte Alto, Guatemala. Lee A. Parsons, 1968-70

———— Edwin Martin Shook. 1972

Nazca lines. Peru. Gerald S. Hawkins. 1967

———— Maria Reiche. 1974

Panama. Matthew W. Stirling. 1948-49, 1951, 1953

Prehistoric maize spread, ceramic evidence of. Peru. Mary Eubanks Dunn. 1975

Quichean civilization, central Guatemala. Kenneth L. Brown. 1976

Quiriguá, Guatemala. William R. Coe, 1974-75; Robert J. Sharer, 1976. *Long-range investigations at this site in the Maya lowlands are*

filling important gaps in our knowledge of the ancient Maya culture.

Williamsburg and Palmar Sur, Costa Rica. Matthew W. Stirling. 1964

Pacific

Huahine, Society Islands. Yosihiko H. Sinoto. 1974-75

Lau Island, Fiji. Roger C. Green. 1976

Asia

Abu Salabikh, Iraq (Sumerian city). John N. Postgate. 1976

Antiochus I: tomb. Nemrud Dagh, Turkey. Theresa Goell. 1963-64

Aphrodisias, Turkey. Kenan T. Erim. 1966-76. *As a result of this ambitious archeological project, an acropolis, a theater, a stadium, and magnificent statuary have emerged as sublime witnesses to the grandeur of the ancient Greco-Roman world.*

Bronze Age settlement. Cyprus. James R. Carpenter. 1974

Cyprus. James M. Adovasio. 1973

Jerusalem. Kathleen M. Kenyon. 1962-67

Palawan caves. Palawan Island, Philippines. Robert B. Fox. 1965-66

Radiometric dating of Paleolithic sites. Israel and Hungary. Henry P. Schwarcz. 1975

Routes through the Bakhtiari Mountains, Iran. Allen Zagarell. 1976

Samosata Mound, Turkey. Theresa Goell. 1967, 1969

Sarepta (Zarephath), Lebanon: Phoenician and Biblical city. James B. Pritchard. 1968-72. *Once a great port city that could boast of a visit by the prophet Elijah, Sarepta is now farmland harboring important Phoenician and Biblical remains.*

Shahr-i Qumis. Lost capital of Parthian Iran. John F. Hansman. 1970, 1975

Syria. Trevor F. Watkins. 1975

Tal-i Malyan, Fars, Iran. Robert H. Dyson, Jr. 1976

Tell Jemmeh, Israel. Gus W. Van Beek. 1975-76. *This site dating from the 13th century B.C. offers evidence of ancient trade and cul-*

tural contacts between the areas of present-day Israel and the Arabian Peninsula.

Tell Keisan, Israel. Roland DeVaux. 1971

Europe

Amber artifacts: spectroscopic provenance analysis. Curt W. Beck. 1973

Anglo-Saxon royal burial ground. Sutton Hoo, Suffolk, England. Rupert L. S. Bruce-Mitford. 1968, 1970

Apollo sanctuary. Halieis, Greece. Michael H. Jameson. 1973-74

Architecture and village layout in ancient Greece. William A. McDonald. 1971

Argolid Peninsula, Greece: postglacial environmental history. Donald R. Whitehead. 1972-73

"Camelot." South Cadbury, Somerset, England. Leslie Alcock. 1970. *Excavations of this and other sites lend credence to medieval legends of King Arthur's royal city.*

Caves of Quaternary and Holocene origin. Spain. William H. Waldren. 1971, 1973

Greece: society, culture, economy in the later Roman period. Timothy E. Gregory. 1974

Helice, Greece. Harold E. Edgerton and Peter Throckmorton. 1970-71

Ice Age Franco-Cantabrian caves: photography and analysis. Alexander Marshack. 1973

Monastery, seventh-century. Jarrow, England. Rosemary J. Cramp. 1973

Neolithic fortress site and rock paintings. Sierra de Taibilla, Spain. Michael J. Walker. 1968-70

Porto Longo Harbor, Sapienza Island, Greece. Harold E. Edgerton and Peter Throckmorton. 1970

Stonehenge, England; Callanish, Scotland. Gerald S. Hawkins. 1965

Tower of the Winds. Athens. Derek J. de Solla Price. 1964

Trade in prehistoric amber. A. Colin Renfrew and Curt W. Beck. 1975

Africa

Aten, temple of: computerized study. Kar-nak, Egypt. Ray W. Smith. 1968-69

Bamenda-Koumbo area, West Cameroon. Donald D. Hartle. 1967

Cave research. Mali. Johan Huizinga. 1970

Chad and Libya: archeological reconnaissance. Carleton S. Coon. 1966-67

Colossi of Memnon, Egypt. Robert F. Heizer. 1971

Engaruka, Tanzania, cultural site of early man. Hamo Sassoon. 1967

Gebel Adda, Egypt. Nicholas B. Millet. 1963-65

Iron Age settlement survey. Upper Zambezi Valley, Zambia. Joseph O. Vogel. 1976

Karamoja District, Uganda. Hamo Sassoon. 1972

Libyan Desert, Egypt: geological-anthropological survey. C. Vance Haynes. 1974-76

Megaliths of central Africa. Nicholas C. David. 1974

Mosaics of Tunisia. Margaret A. Alexander. 1973, 1976

Ngamiland, Botswana. John E. Yellen. 1973

Pyramids, cosmic-ray research in. Egypt. Luis W. Alvarez. 1968

Underwater

American Revolutionary gunboat. Lake Champlain. Philip K. Lundeberg. 1968

Battle of Lepanto shipwrecks: Greece. Spyridon Marinatos. 1971

Bermuda waters. Mendel L. Peterson. 1965-67

Byzantine shipwrecks. Turkey. George F. Bass. 1961-69, 1976. *New underwater excavation techniques allow the recovery of ship remains that shed new light on nautical architecture of the 7th through 12th centuries.*

Greek cargo ship, seventh-century. Sicilian waters. Edwin A. Link. 1962

Iron Age shipwreck. Turkey. George F. Bass. 1974-75. *An unlooted shipwreck from the seventh century B.C. promises new insight into the shipping and daily life of archaic Greece, a period little known from dry-land remains.*

Kyrenia, Cyprus. Michael L. Katzev. 1967-72. *This underwater project located and excavated a fourth-century B.C. Greek merchantman, the finest preserved ship of Greece's classical period ever found.*

Kyrenia Ship Project film documentary. Susan W. Katzev. 1975

Mediterranean Sea search. Peter Throckmorton. 1975

———— survey. George F. Bass. 1973

Monitor **search.** Cape Hatteras area, North Carolina. John J. Newton and Harold E. Edgerton. 1973-74. *The wreck of the celebrated Civil War ironclad was discovered in August 1973 by this expedition. Side-scan sonar equipment confirmed the wreck's location in 220 feet of water off Cape Hatteras.*

Porto Longo, Greece: sonar search. Peter Throckmorton. 1968-69

Portuguese frigate search. Mombasa Harbor, Kenya. Hamo Sassoon. 1975

Punic ship, third-century B.C. Sicily. Honor E. Frost. 1973

Sonar gear supplied. Eastern Mediterranean. Harold E. Edgerton. 1968

Spanish Plate Fleet research. Florida. Kip L. Wagner. 1965

ETHNOLOGY

Chewing sticks. West Africa, Egypt, and Pakistan. Memory P. Elvin-Lewis and Walter H. Lewis. 1975

North America

Aleutian survivors of the Bering land bridge. William S. Laughlin. 1972

Aleuts: Russian influence on ecology, culture, and physical anthropology. Christy G. Turner, 2d. 1972-73

Eskimo linguistics and religion. Canada. Svend Frederiksen. 1965

Hinds Cave, Val Verde County, Texas. Vaughn M. Bryant, Jr. 1975

Indian ethnobotany. California. Lowell J. Bean. 1975

Otomi Indians: resource cognition. Mexico. Kirsten J. Haring. 1973

Preceramic culture. Chiapas, Mexico. Philip Drucker. 1947

Pre-Columbian cultural change. Cozumel, Mexico. Jeremy A. Sabloff. 1971-73

Rock art, prehistoric. Nevada caves. Robert F. Heizer. 1975

Tarahumara people. Mexico. Robert A. Bye, Jr. 1972

Tlapanec Indians. Tlacoapa, Mexico. Marion Oettinger, Jr. 1971

Washo Indians: art. Nevada. Norval C. Kern, Jr. 1970

Central and South America

Afkodre **magic and religion:** Creoles. Surinam. Benjamin E. Pierce. 1971

Black Caribs. Central America. William V. Davidson. 1973-74

Chickens, black-boned: distribution and use. Middle America. Carl L. Johannessen. 1976

Copablanca Festival: ethnographic and ethnomusicological survey. Bolivia. Edwin E. Erickson. 1973

Maya salt trade. Anthony P. Andrews. 1975

Mesoamerican pottery techniques. Lewis A. Krevolin. 1972

Peasant livelihood behavior. Trinidad. Bonham C. Richardson. 1971

Prehistoric cultural development. Peruvian highlands. Clifford Evans and Betty Meggers. 1968-69

Waurá Indians. Mato Grosso, Brazil. Harald Schultz. 1961-64

Welsh colony. Patagonia. Glyn Williams. 1968-69

Pacific

Caroline Islanders: ethnohistory. Saul H. Riesenberg. 1973

Child behavior. New Hebrides. E. Richard Sorenson. 1971. *A comparative study of child-rearing behavior and its relationship to cultural organization, this project employed motion-picture filming of natives relatively untouched by European influences.*

Dani people, material culture. Netherlands New Guinea. Robert G. Gardner. 1962

Diseases and cures, native. Torres Strait Islands. George J. Simeon. 1974

Fore and Bahinemo peoples: facial expression of emotions. New Guinea. E. Richard Sorenson. 1968-69

Maori. New Zealand. William N. Fenton. 1974

New Guinea natives: religious symbolism. Wilson G. Wheatcroft. 1968-70

Polynesian dances. Cook Island. E. Richard Sorenson. 1975

Tanna Island, New Hebrides. Kalman A. Muller. 1974

Trade, migration, and marriage. New Guinea. Deborah Gewertz. 1974

Australia

Aborigines. Arnhem Land, northern Australia. Charles P. Mountford. 1948. *A comprehensive eight-month survey brought together cultural and natural history data on an aboriginal reserve the size of Maine.*

Art sanctuary. Koonalda Cave, South Australia. Christine Elvera Sharpe. 1975

Tiwi culture. Melville Island, Australia. Charles P. Mountford. 1954

Asia

Ainu of Hokkaido, Japan. M. Inez Hilger. 1965-66

Arab potters. Israel. Owen S. Rye. 1976

Bakhtiyārī tribe: role in history. Iran. Gene R. Garthwaite. 1971

Burial ritual. North Borneo. Peter A. Metcalf. 1975

Karnali Zone: cultural-ecological analysis. Western Nepal. Barry C. Bishop. 1968-69, 1971

Kenyah Dayaks: religion and social organization. Sarawak, Malaysia. Herbert L. Whittier. 1973

Kinship and marriage: hierarchy and amity. South Asia. Anthony T. Carter. 1973

Kurds. Khorasan, Iran. Robert E. Peck. 1967

Lua tribe. Northern Thailand. Peter Kunstadter. 1963-64

Man, protohistoric and early historic: interaction with environment. Isthmian Thailand. Janice Mary Stargardt. 1973

Mesolithic occupations. Cyprus. James M. Adovasio. 1972-73

Pashtoon pastoral nomadism. Afghanistan. Asen Balikci. 1972

Pastoralism in southern Sinai. Ofer Bar-Yosef. 1976

Religious centers of the Himalayas. Barbara N. Aziz. 1975

Shabakites. Northern Iraq. Sami Sáid Ahmed. 1973

Sherpa culture. Nepal and Sikkim. Luther G. Jerstad. 1965

Yazidies religious group. Middle East. Sami Sáid Ahmed. 1967

Europe

Depopulation and cultural change. Islands of western Ireland. Kevin C. Kearns. 1975

Symbol systems, Paleolithic. East Europe and the Soviet Union. Alexander Marshack. 1975-76

Africa

Afar nomadism. Ethiopia. Robert G. Gardner. 1965

Bani-Niger people: African migrants. Johan Huizinga. 1974

Fulani people: social system with their cattle. Northern Nigeria. Dale F. Lott. 1973

Kwanyama linguistic group: ethnobotany. Ovamboland, South-West Africa. Robert J. Rodin. 1972

Mandinko people: history, social structure, and ethnobotany. Pakao, southern Senegal. David M. Schaffer. 1973, 1975

Migration and communication of people of the Kisii district, Kenya. Ronald D. Garst. 1975

Ngamiland peoples: demography. Okavango River and delta, Africa. Thomas J. Larson. 1971

Rural migration: relationship to expansion of

commercial agriculture. Tanzania. Marilyn Silberfein. 1973

West African settlement geography along a linguistic and environmental transect. Reed F. Stewart. 1976

Women's role in the Pokot of Kenya. Elizabeth L. Meyerhoff. 1976

Yoruba geophagy. Nigeria. Donald E. Vermeer. 1975

PHYSICAL ANTHROPOLOGY
and
PALEOANTHROPOLOGY

African sites: Fort Ternan, Kenya; Lake Rudolf, Kenya; Olduvai Gorge, Tanzania; Omo Valley, Ethiopia. Louis S. B. Leakey, Mary Leakey, and Richard E. Leakey. 1960-68. *The Leakeys have filled major gaps in the record of early man. One of their most exciting finds was the discovery, in 1959, of* Australopithecus (Zinjanthropus) boisei, *shown by later tests to have lived 1,750,000 years ago.*

Arikara burial sites. South Dakota. T. Dale Stewart. 1971

———— Indian skeletons. North Dakota. William M. Bass. 1968-69

Calico Mountains, Mojave Desert, California. Louis S. B. Leakey, Thomas Clements, Gerald A. Smith, and Ruth D. Simpson. 1964-67

Centre for Prehistory and Palaeontology, Nairobi, Kenya. Louis S. B. Leakey. 1971

Disease, pre-Columbian American. Marvin J. Allison. 1971, 1973-74, 1976. *Analysis of diseases of mummies from graves dating as far back as A.D. 825 shows, among other things, black lung (miner's) disease and tuberculosis.*

East Africa. Louis S. B. Leakey. 1971-72.

Ecuador, coastal: demography. Douglas H. Ubelaker. 1974

Ethiopia's Upper Pliocene localities. Francis H. Brown and F. Clark Howell. 1974

Extinct fauna and early man. Mojave Desert, California. Emma Lou Davis. 1970-71

Hadar, central Afar, Ethiopia. Donald Johanson. 1975-76. *The dramatic discovery, in one small area, of skeletal remains of five to seven individual hominid specimens indicates the possibility that a prehistoric social group — perhaps a family — was caught in a mass disaster.*

Kathmandu Valley and Siwalik deposits, Nepal. Elwyn L. Simons. 1974

Laetolil beds, Tanzania. Raymonde Bonnefille. 1976

———— Mary D. Leakey. 1975-76. *Mammalian fossils found in the upper part of the Laetolil sequence have been dated as 3.35 to 3.75 million years old. Hominid remains from the same sequence bear striking similarities to material found in Ethiopia.*

Olduvai Gorge, Tanzania. Raymonde Bonnefille. 1976

———— Mary D. Leakey. 1970-75. *Continuing fieldwork at this premier archeological and paleontological site permits an ever firmer dating of fossil remains.*

Rudolf, Lake, Kenya. Richard E. Leakey. 1965-76. *Discovery at this site of skull 1470, nearly three million years old, compelled a rethinking of mankind's pedigree. It has been tentatively classified as a direct ancestor of present-day* Homo sapiens.

———— discoveries: report. F. Clark Howell. 1974

Sherpas: high-altitude adaptation and genetics. Georgio P. Morpurgo. 1976

Skeletal biology. Corinth, Greece. Henry S. Robinson. 1975

Astronomy and Astrophysics

Asteroids: Geographos and others. A. M. J. Gehrels. 1971

Astronomical alignment of Canadian Indian cairns and medicine wheels. John A. Eddy. 1975

Auroras. Carl W. Gartlein. 1938-56. *Eighteen*

Astronomy and Astrophysics

years of observations by professional and amateur astronomers produced valuable data on the brightness, color, variety, and sequence of auroras.

Beta Scorpii and companion: occultation by Jupiter. David S. Evans. 1971

Cosmic-ray monitoring. Martin A. Pomerantz. 1946-53, 1956-58, 1964

"Einstein Shift" verification. Khartoum, Sudan. George A. Van Biesbroeck. 1952. *Starfield measurements made during and after the February 25, 1952, solar eclipse substantially confirmed Einstein's theory of relativity.*

Galaxy clusters: size. Hale Observatories. Thomas W. Noonan. 1974

Geographos (asteroid 1620). Betty F. Mintz. 1968-69

────── orbit study. Samuel Herrick. 1968-69

Gravitational light-deflection effect: improved measurement. Bryce S. DeWitt. 1973

Interstellar deuterium. Jay M. Pasachoff. 1974

Kohoutek, comet, and the annular solar eclipse. Donald H. Menzel. 1973

Mars. Bloemfontein observatory, South Africa. E. C. Slipher. 1954-56. *Greenish patches and mysterious "canals" lacing the Martian surface were among the subjects of this two-year study of the red planet.*

Mars and Jupiter: spectroscopic studies. Mauna Loa, Hawaii. C. C. Kiess and C. H. Corliss. 1956-57

"Martian Pavilion," Georgetown College Observatory, presented by the Society. 1956

Planetary systems search. Arizona. A. M. J. Gehrels and Krzysztof Serkowski. 1974-76. *If successful, the search for solar-type stars with large orbiting planets can improve our estimate of the probability of life elsewhere in the universe.*

Planets, brighter. Photographic atlas prepared. E. C. Slipher and John S. Hall. 1962-63

Sky mapping, radio. James N. Douglas. 1973-75. *Radio telescopes monitor the infrared emissions of distant stars that lie beyond the range of optical telescopes.*

Sky survey, infrared photographic. Eric R. Craine. 1976

Sky survey, Palomar Observatory–National Geographic Society: photomapping. 1949-58. *A monumental sky atlas, extending to a depth of one billion light-years, resulted from this photographic survey of the heavens, which expanded the known sky 25 times.*

────── Palomar Observatory–National Geographic Society: transparent overlay map preparation. John D. Kraus. 1976

Solar corona: photography of the spectrum, polarization, and form. Donald H. Menzel. 1972

Solar corona at eclipse: spectrographic study. Donald H. Menzel. 1969

Solar eclipse. Africa. Donald H. Menzel. 1972

────── Australia. Donald H. Menzel. 1976

────── Bocaiúva, Brazil. Lyman J. Briggs. 1947. *Observations made during this Society–U. S. Army Air Forces expedition included photographs of the May 20, 1947, solar eclipse taken from 30,000 feet.*

────── Burma to the Aleutian Islands. Lyman J. Briggs. 1948

────── Canton Island, Pacific. Samuel A. Mitchell. 1937

────── Maine-New Hampshire. Albert W. Stevens and Paul A. McNally. 1932

────── Norfolk, Virginia. Simon Newcomb and Alexander Graham Bell. 1900

────── Northern Canada. Wolfgang B. Klemperer. 1963

────── Patos, Brazil. Irvine C. Gardner. 1940

────── Trans-African baseline. Jay M. Pasachoff. 1973

────── U.S.S.R. Irvine C. Gardner. 1936

────── U.S.S.R. Paul A. McNally and W. Robert Moore. 1936

Solar radiation. Mount Brukkaros, South-West Africa. Charles G. Abbot. 1925-29

Stars, peculiar early-type. Deane M. Peterson. 1974

Uranus occultation (1977). William B. Hubbard, Jr. 1976

Zodiacal light. Colorado-Nebraska border. George A. Van Biesbroeck. 1954

Biology

Animal hard parts: biological destruction of, in marine environment. Peter M. Kranz. 1973

Aquatic animals: behavior in relation to polarized light. Talbot H. Waterman. 1970-71

Biological and archeological expedition. Southeast Oceania. John E. Randall. 1969

Biological colonization of a recently formed volcanic island. Motmot, Papua New Guinea. Eldon E. Ball. 1972, 1974, 1976

Biological investigation; disease study. Bolivia. Richard G. Van Gelder. 1964

Biological studies of the northern Cordillera Vilcabamba. Peru. John W. Terborgh. 1966-68. *Much new information on biological relationships has emerged from this study of the effect of altitude upon the diversity of plant and animal species.*

Cerro Tacarcuna, Panama-Colombia border: biological exploration. Alwyn H. Gentry. 1974

Deep reefs: ecology. Western Caribbean. Walter A. Starck II. 1970

Deep-sea fauna: biology and distribution. Tropical Atlantic Ocean. Gilbert L. Voss. 1963-73. *This project included research on population dynamics, life histories and biology of species, and the physical and chemical character of ocean environments.*

Gombe National Park: establishment. Tanzania. 1968

——— support. D. N. Bryceson. 1973

Hudson Bay and Labrador: biological expedition. W. E. Clyde Todd. 1912, 1914, 1917

Natural history collection. Inner Mongolia, China. Frederick R. Wulsin. 1923-24

Netherlands Indies: collection of rare species for zoos. Sumatra. William M. Mann. 1937

Organisms from simple environments. Nicholas C. Collins. 1976

Río Camuy Cave, northwestern Puerto Rico. Russell H. Gurnee, Brother G. Nicholas, and John V. Thrailkill. 1963

Urubamba Valley, biological expedition. Peru. Frank M. Chapman. 1916

BOTANY

Algae. Australia. Ralph A. Lewin. 1976

Alpine cushion plants. George G. Spomer. 1974

Araucarian cones. Southern Argentina. Thomas N. Taylor. 1973

Asteraceae: biosystematic studies. South America. Robert Merrill King. 1973

Bahama, Turks, and Caicos Islands. William Thomas Gillis, Jr. 1973

Bali and Celebes Islands. Willem Meijer. 1976

Bamboos and bambusoid grasses: Brazil. Thomas R. Soderstrom. 1971, 1975

Bracken-fern gametophytes: comparative normal and abnormal development. Carl R. Partanen. 1971

Bromeliads. Brazilian mountains. Margaret U. Mee. 1966

Bryophytes. Southern Chile. John J. Engel. 1975

Capsicum pubescens complex: biosystematics and evolution. W. Hardy Eshbaugh. 1970-71

Chondrus crispus alga. Esther L. McCandless. 1970

Cycad *(Zamia)*. Knut Norstog. 1975

Death Valley, California. Frederick V. Coville. 1931

Desert plants; *Welwitschia*. South-West Africa. Chris H. Bornman. 1968

Flax *(Linum)*. Mediterranean region. Claude M. Rogers. 1971

Forest reserves in the "Green Plan." Austria. Else A. Schmidt. 1968-69

Forest types. North Cascade Range, Washington. Richard N. Mack. 1973

Forests: establishment. Celebes. Willem Meijer. 1975

Grasses: biosystematic investigation. Oaxaca and Chiapas, Mexico. Frank W. Gould. 1973

Hanging gardens. Colorado Plateau. Stanley L. Welsh. 1972

Kakabekia, microorganism with Precambrian affinities: paleobiology. Iceland. Sanford M. Siegel. 1971. *Straddling the thin line between inorganic material and living substance, the microorganism* Kakabekia *is a living fossil plant virtually identical with the earth's earliest organisms. Research on it hints at what life was like at its very beginning.*

Kokechik Bay area, Alaska. Charles M. Kirkpatrick. 1972

Kwangsi, China. G. Weidman Groff. 1937

Lepidoptera: host plants. Aldabra Atoll, Indian Ocean. Jay C. Shaffer. 1967

Lichen growths on Maya ruins. Mason E. Hale. 1975

Lichens *(Stereocaulon paschale)* as caribou fodder. K. A. Kershaw. 1976

———— (Thelotremataceae): systematics and evolution. Lesser Antilles. Mason E. Hale. 1971

———— and bryophytes. Galapagos Islands. William A. Weber. 1975

Lodgepole pine forests: biotic succession following fire. Yellowstone National Park. Dale L. Taylor. 1971

Log-fern hybrids *(Dryopteris).* Great Dismal Swamp, Virginia. Lytton J. Musselman. 1976

Madagascar. Peter Goldblatt. 1973

Mangroves: evolutionary mechanisms. Philip B. Tomlinson. 1976. *This project and the following research entry are designed to win a deeper knowledge of the breeding mechanisms of mangroves in order to draw up management policies that will halt their wholesale destruction.*

———— Old World (Indo-Pacific). Philip B. Tomlinson. 1973

———— Oriental. A. Malcolm Gill. 1968-69

Marquesas Islands. Marie-Helene Sachet. 1974

Maya Mountains, British Honduras. John D. Dwyer. 1972

Microflora: composition, variation, and ecology. Arctic Sea ice. Spencer Apollonio. 1971

Mistletoes: biogeographical affinities and chromosomal relationships. Africa. Delbert Wiens. 1971

Orchids, terrestrial: pollination. Australia. Warren P. Stoutamire. 1972-73

Phytogeographic studies. Burica Peninsula, Panama and Costa Rica. Thomas B. Croat. 1972

Plankton, blue-water. William M. Hamner. 1970

Plant collecting. Sierra de San Lazaro, Baja California. Amy Jean Gilmartin. 1968-69

Plant communities: effects of pollinating bats. Costa Rica and Arizona. Donna J. Howell. 1974

Plant succession on Soufrière of St. Vincent, Leeward Islands. John Stanley Beard. 1971

Plants and landforms. Tristan da Cunha and St. Helena Islands. Nigel M. Wace. 1975

Psilotum: classical culture, mutants, and wild occurrences. Japan. Albert S. Rouffa. 1972

Pteridophytic plants: phytogeography. Chocó, Colombia. David B. Lellinger. 1968-69

Rattan–palm collection. Asian rain forests. Jack B. Fisher. 1976

Redwoods: preservation. California. Chester C. Brown. 1963. *A National Geographic grant made possible this National Park Service survey of coast redwoods. The study eventually prompted the establishment of a new national park to preserve the giant trees.*

Sage *(Salvia).* James L. Reveal. 1974

Spore research. West Indies and northern South and Central America. Fred C. Meier. 1935

Stromatolites and algal carbonate structures of the Recent Epoch: ecology. Shark Bay, Australia. Stjcpko Golubic. 1973

Subarctic plant systems and water conservation. Wayne R. Rouse. 1971

Sunflower family (Compositae): as source of fish poisons. Tod F. Stuessy. 1976

Tierra del Fuego, Argentina-Chile: study, collection, and illustration of flora. Rae Natalie P. Goodall. 1970-72. *The first fully gener-*

alized botanical collecting done in little-known Tierra del Fuego since 1764, this project aimed at the collection and description of plants native to the area before they were further disturbed by agriculture.

Wheats, cultivated: origin and ancestry. B. Lennart Johnson. 1972

Wild flowers of the United States. New York Botanical Garden. 1965. *Preparation and publication of a six-volume work on U. S. wildflowers was aided by this Society research grant.*

ECOLOGY

Camera equipment for marine biology research. Harold E. Edgerton. 1974

Dead Sea system: limnology and ecology. Joel R. Gat. 1976

Dugongs and sea turtles: exploitation. Torres Strait. Bernard Nietschmann. 1976. *The marine resource system of the strait between New Guinea and Australia contains some of the tropics' last dugongs, sea turtles, sea-grass pastures, and the human marine hunters dependent upon them.*

Ecological surveying in East Lake Rudolf, Kenya. Michael Norton-Griffiths. 1976

Everglades ecology. Everglades National Park, Florida. Frank C. Craighead, Sr. 1966, 1970

Falkland Islands: natural history and ecology. Olin S. Pettingill, Jr. 1970

Forests, semideciduous: ecology of the canopy. Panama. Pedro Galindo. 1973

Little Dunk's Bay, Great Lakes system: ecosystem. Joseph B. MacInnis and Alan R. Emery. 1970

Moose and wolf relationships. Isle Royale, Michigan. Durward L. Allen and Peter A. Jordan. 1964-65. *A complex ecological drama— the survival of an island population of moose in the face of intensive predation by timber wolves—was the substance of this project.*

New Guinea mountains. J. Linsley Gressitt. 1968-69

Papyrus swamps: effect on ecology. Lake Naivasha, Kenya. John J. Gaudet. 1971, 1973, 1975

Pollution: 70-year evaluation. Dry Tortugas, Florida. Richard H. Chesher. 1972

Protozoan communities: ecology. Lake Waiau, Hawaii. Raymond D. Dillon. 1970

Submarine limnological study. Great Lakes. Joseph B. MacInnis. 1968-69

Tidal marsh: ecosystem. Trenton, New Jersey. Dennis F. Whigham. 1974

Titicaca, Lake. Peru-Bolivia. Carl Widmer. 1972

Wildlife-habitat classification by satellite imagery. John J. Craighead. 1975

ZOOLOGY

Cave fauna. Yucatán Peninsula. Robert W. Mitchell. 1974-75

Marine organisms, complex: sensory information processing and visual behavior. Talbot H. Waterman. 1968-69, 1973-76. *Wholly new data concerning the migratory navigation of fishes are emerging from these studies of the perception of polarized light by marine vertebrates.*

Reptiles, amphibians, and insects. Ethiopia. Thomas P. Monath. 1964

Vertebrate genetic systems: comparative population cytogenetics and evolutionary roles. William P. Hall, 3d. 1971

Vertebrates: locomotion. East Africa. Charles R. Taylor. 1976

———— Neotropical: seasonal patterns. Sinaloa, Mexico. Terry A. Vaughan. 1970

———— populations in strip-mine areas. Frederick J. Brenner. 1971, 1973-74

Wildlife survey and collection of specimens. Nepal. S. Dillon Ripley. 1948-49

Vertebrate Zoology

HERPETOLOGY

Alligator, American: thermoregulation and ecology. Frederick R. Gehlbach. 1971

———— thermoregulation. Clifford Ray Johnson. 1974

Amphibians. Seychelles Islands, Indian Ocean. Ronald A. Nussbaum. 1976

Amphibians and reptiles. Andes. William E. Duellman. 1974

———— Colombia. Victor H. Hutchison. 1965

Frogs: relation of activity periods to phototactic behavior. Robert G. Jaeger. 1972

———— telmatobiid; physiological ecology. Lake Titicaca, Peru-Bolivia. Victor H. Hutchison. 1973

———— and reptiles: collecting specimens. New Guinea. Richard G. Zweifel. 1968

Iguanas, land *(Conolophus pallidus* and *C. subcristatus).* Dagmar I. Werner. 1975-76. *Introduced predators threaten the survival of land iguanas native to the Galapagos Islands. This study of their life history may suggest ways to preserve these reptiles against outside environmental pressures.*

Lizards. Kalahari Desert, Africa. Raymond B. Huey. 1975

———— *(Anolis).* Bahamas and West Indies. Thomas W. Schoener. 1968-70

———— *(Anolis):* island ecology. Caribbean. George C. Gorman. 1971

———— *(Anolis limifrons):* functions and social displays. Thomas A. Jenssen. 1971

———— iguanid *(Sceloporus grammicus):* biogeography of karyotype variation. William P. Hall, 3d. 1970

Salamanders, tropical: behavioral defense mechanisms. Edmund D. Brodie, Jr. 1973, 1975

Snakes and amphibians. French Guiana. Thomas P. Monath. 1963

Toads, Yosemite *(Bufo canorus):* energetics and natural history. Martin L. Morton. 1973

Tortoises, Galapagos. James L. Patton. 1976

———— William G. Reeder. 1968-69. *Giant tortoises are in danger of extinction and exist today only on the Galapagos Islands and on Aldabra Island in the Indian Ocean. This study of the population ecology of the Galapagos colony was undertaken to provide basic facts for use in conservation efforts.*

Turtles. Africa: Roger C. Wood. 1967

———— fresh-water chelid: taxonomy, distribution, and ecology. Australia. John M. Legler. 1972, 1974, 1976

Turtles, giant leatherback: taxonomic study. Surinam. Wayne F. Frair. 1968-69

———— green. Ascension Island. Archie F. Carr. 1976

———— Pacific green. Galapagos. Craig G. MacFarland. 1975-76

———— Pacific ridley: nesting biology. David A. Hughes. 1971

———— pleurodiran: systematics, evolution, and ecology. South America. Roger C. Wood. 1970

———— sea, hawksbill: exploitation and ecology. Bernard Nietschmann. 1972

———— slider *(Pseudemys scripta).* Panama. John M. Legler. 1966

ICHTHYOLOGY

Characid, splashing *(Copeina arnoldi):* reproductive and parental behavior. Guyana. Charles O. Krekorian. 1973

Coelacanth *(Latimeria chalumnae).* Indian Ocean. Keith Stewart Thomson. 1972

Eels, garden. Red Sea. Eugenie Clark. 1971. *Scientist, diver, and underwater photographer, Eugenie Clark made use of all her talents in this ecological and behavioral study of compact colonies of Red Sea garden eels.*

Fishes. Lord Howe Island. New South Wales, Australia. Frank H. Talbot. 1972

———— collection. Río Nichare, Venezuela. James E. Böhlke. 1976

———— coral-reef. Bahamas. Raymond D. Clarke. 1974

———— coral-reef. Moluccas, Indonesia. Victor G. Springer. 1973

———— coral-reef. Solomon Islands. John E. Randall. 1973

———— electric. Walter F. Heiligenberg. 1976

———— electric, mormyriform. Peter Moller. 1975

———— electric, mormyriform. Gabon. Carl D. Hopkins. 1976

———— genetics. Atlantic and Pacific Oceans. Dennis A. Powers. 1975

———— labrid. David R. Robertson. 1975

Fishes, marine invertebrates, and algae. Southeast Oceania. John E. Randall. 1969. *Society support enabled this scientist not only to collect, photograph, and study marine specimens from the waters off Easter Island but also to conduct an onshore archeological reconnaissance.*

────── osteoglossid. South America. Joan Dorothy Fuller. 1972

────── pelagic. F. G. Walton Smith and Hilary B. Moore. 1953-60. *This project embraced a search for unknown larval stages of sport and food fishes in order to complete their life histories.*

────── pelagic. North Atlantic. Frank J. Mather 3d. 1962

────── *(Poecilia):* ethology. Mexico. Joseph S. Balsano and Ellen M. Rasch. 1976

────── survey. Congo River's lower rapids. Tyson R. Roberts. 1972

────── toxic-repellent effect of certain species on sharks. Red Sea. Eugenie Clark. 1972. *Toxic even when diluted, a marine poison secreted by the Red Sea sole offers clues in the search for an effective synthetic shark repellent.*

────── tropical reef. Caribbean. Robert R. Warner. 1976

Killifish, annual: systematics, ecology, and distribution. Northern South America. Jamie E. Thomerson. 1971

Lungfish *(Clarias)* and *Tilapia.* East Africa. Geoffrey Moriaso Ole Maloiy. 1974-75

River fishes. Australia. Tim M. Berra. 1968-69

Sharks, bull: speciation. Lake Nicaragua. Jack D. Burke. 1970

────── gray reef: social behavior and aggression. Donald R. Nelson. 1971-72

────── reef. Rangiroa, French Polynesia. Donald R. Nelson. 1973

────── sleeping. Mexican caves. Eugenie Clark. 1973-74.

────── teleost symbionts. Japan. Eugenie Clark. 1975

Shore fishes. Easter Island. John E. Randall. 1968-69

Stingrays: freshwater adaptation. Thomas B. Thorson. 1974, 1976. *Most stingrays live in a marine environment, but some tolerate brackish and fresh water. How they do so was the object of this study.*

Tuna: body-temperature study. Francis G. Carey. 1967-69

MAMMALOGY

Animal tracking by satellite. Frank C. Craighead, Jr. 1970. *A dramatic advance in research technique, satellite radio tracking and biotelemetry of large mammals literally moves biology into the Space Age.*

Antelopes. East Africa. Richard Despard Estes. 1974

────── bongo: search for. Kenya. Theodore H. Reed. 1968

────── sable. Angola and Kenya. Richard Despard Estes. 1968-70, 1975

────── topi. Mara Game Preserve, Tanzania. Geoffrey Moriaso Ole Maloiy. 1972

Baboons, olive: ecology and behavior. Gilgil, Kenya. Robert S. O. Harding. 1974

Bats, false vampire: social, foraging, and roosting behavior. Terry A. Vaughan. 1972

Bears, black: satellite monitoring during winter sleep. John J. Craighead. 1971

────── brown. Alaska Peninsula. Allen W. Stokes. 1972-73

────── grizzly: habitat survey by Landsat. John J. Craighead. 1976

────── grizzly. Yellowstone National Park, Wyoming. Frank C. Craighead, Jr., and John J. Craighead. 1959-67

────── polar: behavior and ecology. North Twin Island, Northwest Territories, Canada. Brian M. Knudsen. 1970-71

────── polar: survey of dens. Svalbard, Arctic Ocean. Thor Larsen. 1971

Biotelemetry systems for wildlife research. Frank C. Craighead, Jr., and John J. Craighead. 1968-69

Bison, American: social and sexual behavior. Montana. Dale F. Lott. 1967-71

Burros, wild: social organization and communication behavior. Patricia D. Moehlman. 1970, 1972

Bushbaby, thick-tailed: ecology and behavior. South Africa. Gerald A. Doyle. 1968, 1970

Caribou telemetry tracking. Idaho. Donald R. Johnson. 1974

Cat, Iriomote *(Mayailurus iriomotensis):* ecology and conservation. Japan. Paul Leyhausen. 1973

Cetacea, cervico-spinal rete mirabile of. Merrill P. Spencer. 1974

Cheetahs. Botswana. Mark J. Owens and Delia Owens. 1974

Chimpanzees. Gombe Stream, Tanzania. Jane Goodall. 1961-71, 1976. *Spectacular new facts on chimpanzee behavior and a unique scientific record resulted from this project.*

———— communicative capacity. R. Allen Gardner and Beatrice T. Gardner. 1968-69

Deer, Key. Florida. Willard D. Klimstra. 1968-71

Dolphins, dusky. Argentina. Roger S. Payne. 1974

———— dusky and southern common. Argentina. Charles Walcott. 1975-76

———— Franciscana: life history, behavior, and acoustics. Uruguay. Robert L. Brownell, Jr. 1972-73

Dugongs. Cape York Peninsula, Australia. Paul K. Anderson. 1975

Ferrets, black-footed, and prairie dogs. Wyoming. Timothy W. Clark. 1973

Gazelles, desert. Charles R. Taylor. 1971

Gorillas, lowland: ecology. West Africa. Julie C. Webb. 1974-75

———— lowland: interrelationships with chimpanzees. Río Muni, West Africa. Arthur J. Riopelle. 1966-69

———— lowland, juvenile. Francine G. Patterson. 1976

———— mountain. Virunga Mountains, Rwanda. Dian Fossey. 1967-76. *Feeding and grooming habits, play, sexual behavior, nest building and social systems, as well as range and habitat were included in this field study highlighted by overt acceptance of the researcher by the fast-disappearing mountain gorillas.*

Gorillas, white ("Snowflake"): adolescent development. Barcelona, Spain. Arthur J. Riopelle. 1970

Guanaco. South America. William L. Franklin. 1976

Hutia, Haitian. Charles A. Woods. 1974-75

Jackals. Serengeti Plain, Tanzania. Patricia D. Moehlman. 1975-76

Jaguars. Mato Grosso, Brazil. George B. Schaller. 1976

Kobs: conventionality of territorial leks. Uganda. Helmut K. Buechner. 1971

Lemurs *(Varecia variegatus).* Madagascar and Comoro Archipelago, Indian Ocean. Ian Tattersall. 1974, 1976

Lions: ecology. Kitengela Conservation Area, Kenya. Judith Ann Rudnai. 1974

Macaques, Ceylonese. Wolfgang P. J. Dittus. 1975

———— wild bonnet. South India. Paul E. Simonds. 1975

Mammals. Chaco Boreal, Paraguay. Ralph M. Wetzel. 1973-75

———— Uintah Mountains, Utah. Gordon L. Kirkland, Jr. 1976

Mammals, large, high-altitude. Pakistan and Nepal. George B. Schaller. 1971-73. *Documenting animal life in one of the most mountainous and remote regions of southern Asia, this study resulted in a photographic "first"— published pictures of the rare, beautiful, and endangered snow leopard.*

———— Neotropical. Ralph M. Wetzel. 1968-69

———— nocturnal. Botswana. Reay H. N. Smithers. 1969

———— small: ecology on open-pit mine waste dumps. Gordon L. Kirkland, Jr. 1973

———— small: microdistribution at the coniferous-deciduous interface. Gordon L. Kirkland, Jr. 1972

———— small: speciation. Apostle Islands, Lake Superior. Richard R. Meierotto. 1970-71, 1973

———— and birds: collecting. Central Africa. Carnes Weeks and Gertrude S. Weeks. 1952

Manatees, Florida: behavior and ecology. Daniel S. Hartman. 1968. *Little understood and possibly endangered, the gentle Florida manatee and its movements, feeding, reproduction, and response to man formed the basis of this investigation.*

Marine mammals. Guadalupe and Cedros Islands, Baja California. G. Dallas Hanna and A. W. Anthony. 1922

Marsupials: evolution. South America. Larry G. Marshall. 1974

––––––– reproductive biology. South America. C. H. Tyndale-Biscoe. 1971

Martens: ecology. Grand Teton National Park, Wyoming. Timothy W. Clark. 1975

Mongoose, dwarf *(Helogale parvula)* and banded *(Mungos mungo):* ecology and social organization. Uganda. Jonathan P. Rood. 1973

Monkeys: red colobus and agile mangabey. Kenya. Colin P. Groves. 1972

––––––– rhesus: ecology and behavior. Nepal. Charles H. Southwick. 1973, 1975

––––––– talapoin: mating behavior. Reserved Forest of Maolmayo, Cameroon. Thelma E. Rowell. 1973

––––––– and lesser primates. Tigoni Primate Research Centre, Limuru, Kenya. Cynthia P. Booth. 1963

––––––– and loris. Ceylon. John F. Eisenberg. 1968

Nyala, mountain. Ethiopia. Leslie H. Brown. 1965

Opossum, brush-tailed *(Trichosurus vulpecula).* Ian D. Hume. 1975

Orangutans. Mount Looser Reserve, Sumatra, and Tanjung Puting Reserve, Borneo. Biruté Galdikas-Brindamour. 1971, 1973-76. *Lasting contributions to our knowledge of the orangutan have emerged from this study of their ecology and social development.*

Otters, giant Brazilian. Surinam. Nicole Duplaix-Hall. 1976

Peccaries. Peru. John W. Terborgh. 1976

Pigs, domestic and wild: cultural and ecological aspects. New Guinea. James A. Baldwin. 1973, 1976

Pika: ecological study. Western United States. Richard D. Bates. 1970-71

Primates: Neotropical. Manu National Park, Peru. John W. Terborgh. 1974-75

––––––– nonhuman. East Borneo. Peter S. Rodman. 1974

Raccoons, tropical: ecology and relationships. James D. Lazell, Jr. 1972

Sea lions: sonar. Thomas C. Poulter. 1970

––––––– Steller's. H. Dean Fisher. 1972

Seals, harbor and gray: feeding habits and population dynamics. Maine. David T. Richardson. 1972

––––––– Hawaiian monk *(Monachus schauinslandi).* Hawaii. G. Causey Whittow. 1976

Sheep, bighorn. Nez Perce Creek, Wyoming. E. Earl Willard. 1974-75

––––––– desert bighorn: environmental and physiological biology. Jack Chardon Turner. 1972

––––––– urial, and markhor goats. Pakistan. George B. Schaller. 1970

Shrew, golden-rumped elephant-shrew. Kenya. Galen B. Rathbun. 1971, 1974, 1976

Squirrels, Kaibab. Joseph G. Hall. 1970-71

Tenrecs. Madagascar. Edwin Gould. 1963

Whales, bowhead: population. Arctic. John R. Bockstoce. 1976

––––––– California gray: tracking. John E. Schultz. 1968-69

––––––– gray. Scammon Lagoon, Baja California. Merrill P. Spencer. 1966

––––––– heartbeat. Scammon Lagoon, Baja California. Paul Dudley White. 1956

––––––– humpback. Roger S. Payne. 1976

––––––– right. Charles Walcott. 1976

––––––– right: vocalizations and behavior. Roger S. Payne. 1971-73. *Large numbers of right whales congregate close to shore in remote bay areas on the Argentine coast. This investigation of their vocalizations and behavior seeks to shed new light on the communal urge of this endangered species.*

––––––– sperm: bioacoustic research. Kenneth S. Norris. 1970

Wildebeests. Ngorongoro Crater, Tanzania. Richard Despard Estes. 1963-66, 1972. *Close daily observation of wildebeest herds on the grassland and forest floor of this giant crater in East Africa has provided material for the definitive scientific work on these hoofed mammals.*

Wolverines: ecology. Northwestern Montana. Maurice G. Hornocker. 1973-75

Wolves, red, and coyotes: comparative study of vocalization. Howard McCarley. 1973

Yaks. Richard P. Palmieri. 1971, 1973

ORNITHOLOGY

Accipiters. North America. Noel F. R. Snyder. 1970-71

Albatrosses, Laysan: survival, longevity, and turnover in breeding populations. Harvey I. Fisher. 1971

Bee-eaters, African: cooperative breeding. Stephen T. Emlen. 1973-74

——— European. Fred N. White. 1975

Bird-fossil comparative study. Trindade Island, South Atlantic Ocean. Storrs L. Olson. 1974

Birds: adaptations for tropical survival. North America. Eugene S. Morton. 1973

——— ant-following. Brazil. Edwin O. Willis. 1974

——— community structure. Lowland forest. David L. Pearson. 1974, 1976

——— ecological studies. Amazon forest. Thomas E. Lovejoy III. 1971

——— Ethiopian: library study. Emil K. Urban. 1966, 1968

——— field studies and collecting specimens. New Guinea. Jared M. Diamond. 1965-68. *This series of ornithological expeditions furthered the classification and analysis of New Guinea's exotic bird life.*

——— high-Andean. François Vuilleumier. 1975

——— North American. Hudson Bay, Gulf of St. Lawrence, southern United States, Mexico, Georgia, Florida, North Dakota, New York. Arthur A. Allen. 1944-49. *Six successive seasons of bird observations from Alaska to Mexi-co were highlighted by the discovery in the Alaskan tundra of the nest and eggs of the bristle-thighed curlew on June 12, 1948. This shorebird, first described in 1785, was the only North American bird whose nesting place had not yet been located.*

Birds, piscivorous: effects of human disturbance on breeding success. Eagle Lake, California. James R. Koplin. 1971

——— post-fire competition among hole nesters. Dale L. Taylor. 1973

——— recolonization of exploded volcanic islands. New Guinea. Jared M. Diamond. 1972

——— Rift Valley lakes, Ethiopia. Emil K. Urban. 1970

——— Rio Grande do Sul, Brazil. William Belton. 1976

——— Simen Mountains, Ethiopia. Michel Desfayes. 1970

——— small mammals, and bat distribution. Peru. Asa C. Thoresen. 1964-65

——— social systems. Africa. J. David Ligon. 1975

——— songs. John R. Krebs and Malcolm L. Hunter, Jr. 1976

——— New Guinea. E. Thomas Gilliard. 1953-54

——— stranded on land-bridge islands. Jared M. Diamond. 1974

——— survey. Brazil and Venezuela. Ernest G. Holt. 1929-30

——— systematics. South America. Ned K. Johnson. 1974

——— tropical-forest communities. James Richard Karr. 1975-76

——— tropical Pacific islands. Jared M. Diamond. 1976

——— UHF radiolocation system. Frank C. Craighead, Jr. 1973

——— collection. New Britain. E. Thomas Gilliard. 1958-59. *Pioneering penetration of New Britain's rugged interior resulted in the discovery of bird species previously unknown to science.*

Birds-of-paradise study. Little Tobago, West Indies. E. Thomas Gilliard. 1958

Birds of prey: survey. South Africa. C. W. R. Knight. 1937

Bowerbirds, golden-fronted *(Amblyornis flavifrons):* search for. New Guinea. E. Thomas Gilliard. 1963. *Known only from a few specimens, capture of the golden-fronted bowerbird was the object of this expedition. Although this species was not found, important additions of other birds were made to ornithological collections.*

Brazil and Venezuela jungles: specimen collection. Orinoco headwaters. Ernest G. Holt. 1929-31

Cock-of-the-rock: dancing courtship. British Guiana. E. Thomas Gilliard. 1961

Condors: number and range; preservation. California. National Audubon Society. 1961-64

Duck, torrent: reproduction dynamics and behavior. South America. Marvin C. Cecil. 1968-70

Eagles, bald: post-fledgling activities. Thomas C. Dunstan. 1971.

―――― golden. Montana. John J. Craighead. 1973. *Banding and newly developed telemetry techniques were employed in this behavioral study of a diminishing and majestic species.*

―――― golden: nesting behavior. Texas. W. Grainger Hunt. 1975

Falcons, Eleanora's: territory and aggression. Morocco. Hartmut Walter. 1968-69

―――― peregrine: migration. Greenland to U. S.; South America. William W. Cochran. 1975

Finches: courtship behavior. Africa. Robert B. Payne. 1971

―――― Galapagos: genetic analysis of evolution patterns. Galapagos Islands. Robert I. Bowman. 1973

Flamingos: ecology and reproductive biology. Florida. M. Philip Kahl. 1972

―――― global study. M. Philip Kahl. 1974. *A worldwide survey of the population dynamics of flamingos, this is the most significant study of its kind ever attempted.*

―――― limnological studies of diets and distributions. Chile and Bolivia. Stuart H. Hurlbert. 1973, 1975

Flamingos, New World: population ecology. M. Philip Kahl. 1971

―――― photographic study. Andros Island, Bahama Islands. John Oliver La Gorce and Louis Agassiz Fuertes. 1920

Fowl, long-tailed. Japan. Frank X. Ogasawara. 1969

Geese, cackling: breeding ecology. Yukon and Kuskokwim River Deltas, Alaska. Peter G. Mickelson. 1971-72

―――― Canada: breeding biology. Yukon and Kuskokwim River Deltas, Alaska. Peter G. Mickelson. 1970

Grebes, hooded. Patagonia. Robert W. Storer. 1975

―――― pied-billed. Lake Atitlán, Guatemala. Anne LaBastille. 1967-68

―――― western. Gary L. Nuechterlein. 1975-76

Grouse, spruce *(Canachites canadensis).* Montana. Stanley S. Frissell. 1975

Hemipode *(Turnix sylvatica):* ecological relations, reproduction, and distribution. Andalusia, Spain. Gerald Collier. 1973

Hoatzin. British Guiana. J. Lear Grimmer. 1959-60

Hoopoes, green wood. Kenya. J. David Ligon. 1976

Hornbills, African. Fred N. White. 1976

Hummingbirds. South America. Augusto Ruschi. 1962

―――― ecology. Mexico, Central America, South America. Augusto Ruschi. 1974

―――― heat exchanges in nesting. Rocky Mountains. William Alexander Calder, Jr. 1972

―――― rufous: utilization of time and microhabitat. William Alexander Calder, Jr. 1973, 1975

Ibises, scarlet: search for rookery. Venezuela. Paul A. Zahl. 1949

Jay, green: ecology. Colombia. Humberto Alvarez. 1974

―――― Yucatán: social and reproductive biology. John William Hardy. 1973

Kiwi: olfactory sense. Bernice M. Wenzel. 1967

Oilbirds. Masakazu Konishi. 1975-76. *Undertaken in Colombia, this study concentrated on oilbird ecology, behavior, physiology, and anatomy.*

—— Venezuela. Bernice Tannenbaum. 1976

Ospreys: ecology. Connecticut River. Roger Tory Peterson and Peter Ames. 1962

—— pesticide influence on reproductive function. Flathead Lake, Montana, and northwestern California. James R. Koplin. 1968-70, 1972

Penguins, jackass. South Africa. Walter R. Siegfried. 1973, 1976

Petrels, Leach's and ashy: nocturnal orientation. Robert I. Bowman. 1971

Pheasants, mikado and Swinhoe's. Taiwan. Sheldon R. Severinghaus. 1971

Pigeons, homing: navigation analysis. Charles Walcott. 1968-69. *Aircraft tracking of homing pigeons has provided data suggesting that these birds may rely on the sun's position to orient themselves for flight.*

—— pink. Mauritius. Anthony S. Cheke. 1973

Plover, Egyptian. Thomas R. Howell. 1976

Prairie chickens and sharp-tailed grouse. North Dakota. Donald W. Sparling, Jr. 1976

Quails *(Coturnix):* calling behavior patterns. Wolfgang M. Schleidt. 1974

Raptors: tracking by satellite. Frank C. Craighead, Jr. 1976

Ruffs, male *(Philomachus pugnaz).* Julia Marian Wentworth-Shepard. 1974-75

Sea birds: ecology and reproductive behavior. Thomas R. Howell. 1969

—— ecology and tick distribution. Indian Ocean. Christopher J. Feare. 1976

—— ecology, numbers, and distribution. Aegean Sea. George E. Watson. 1966

Shorebirds, desert *(Peltohyas* and *Stiltia).* Australia. Gordon Lindsay Maclean. 1973

Storks: worldwide study of the 17 species. Asia and Africa. M. Philip Kahl. 1966-69.

This ambitious study is unprecedented in its broad and thorough treatment of the behavior, ecology, and movement of stork populations.

Swallows, Texas cave. Charles F. Martin. 1974

Swans, mute. Chesapeake Bay. Jan G. Reese. 1976

—— whistling: migrations. Alaska breeding grounds. William J. L. Sladen. 1972-74. *Conservation of the large and beautiful whistling swan has been greatly enhanced by data gathered during years of observation of this bird as it moves from its wintering grounds in the eastern U. S. to its Alaskan summer habitat, 3,500 miles away.*

Weaverbirds, sociable: ecological role of the nest. George A. Bartholomew. 1972-73

Woodpeckers: behavior, ecology, and taxonomy. Asia. Lester L. Short. 1971

—— ivory-billed, search for. Louisiana, East Texas. John V. Dennis. 1967

Invertebrate Zoology
ENTOMOLOGY

Ants, giant Amazon. Brazil. Paul A. Zahl. 1957

Army-ant mites and leafhoppers. Paraguay. Richard J. Elzinga. 1975

Bagworms: distribution and host-tree orientation of the eggs and parasites. Herbert M. Kulman. 1970

Butterflies, Alaskan: survey. Victoria Island, Canada. Kenelm W. Philip. 1974-75

—— ecology and specimen collection. Aldabra Atoll, Indian Ocean. Jay C. Shaffer. 1967

—— equatorial alpine. Colombia. Arthur M. Shapiro. 1976

—— (Hesperiidae): systematic and distributional study. Mexico. Hugh A. Freeman. 1973-75

—— monarch: migration. Texas, Florida, California, Australia, Mexico. Fred A. Urquhart. 1968-71, 1975-76. *A dogged, decades-long search culminated in the discovery in Mexico of the overwintering site of the eastern North American monarch butterfly.*

—— Neotropical. Trinidad. William Beebe and Jocelyn Crane. 1957

Butterflies, pierid: population ecology. Ward B. Watt. 1972

Fireflies *(Pteroptyx).* Asia. Ivan Polunin. 1971

———— luminescence. Far East. John B. Buck. 1965-68

Flies (Tabanidae). Thailand. John J. S. Burton. 1968-69

———— snail-killing: Pacific Northwest. Benjamin A. Foote. 1971

Hymenoptera, stinging: phenology, mimics, and insectivorous birds. Gilbert P. Waldbauer. 1972

———— Neotropical Ichneumonidae. Charles C. Porter. 1974-75

———— systematics and zoogeography. Charles C. Porter. 1973-75

Insects (Neuroptera). South America. Lionel A. Stange. 1974-76

———— aquatic. Ecuador. Paul J. Spangler. 1975

———— aquatic: zoogeographical connections. New Caledonia. William L. Peters. 1972

———— collection. Africa. Edward S. Ross. 1957-58

———— collection. Southern Asia; Australia. Edward S. Ross. 1961-62

———— dispersal of. Ethiopia. Jørgen Birket-Smith. 1966

Insects, orthopteroid. Madeira. S. K. Gangwere. 1975

———— water balance. Namib Desert, South-West Africa. Eric B. Edney. 1973

Spiders, funnel-web builders: niche analysis. Carrizozo Malpais, New Mexico. Susan E. Riechert. 1972, 1974

Treehopper, membracid *(Umbonia crassicornis).* Florida. Thomas K. Wood. 1974

Triatominae. Central and South America. Pedro W. Wygodzinsky. 1963

Worms, railroad *(Phrixothrix):* life history. Brazil. Darwin L. Tiemann. 1968-69

MALACOLOGY

Marine invertebrates: biogeography and history. Moluccas. Joseph Rosewater and Barry R. Wilson. 1969

Marine mollusks: ecology and distribution. South Pacific. Harald A. Rehder. 1965, 1967, 1973, 1976. *Thousands of marine mollusk specimens were collected on successive expeditions to the Samoa and Fiji Islands, Cook Islands, and others in a survey of the ecology and distribution of Pacific species.*

———— shallow-water. Yucatán Peninsula, Mexico. Walter E. Vokes. 1974

Snails: heat, desiccation, and starvation. Near East. Knut Schmidt-Nielsen. 1968-69

———— high-intertidal: crab predation and shell architecture. Geerat J. Vermeij. 1974

———— land: Hispaniolan urocoptid. Fred G. Thompson. 1975

OTHER INVERTEBRATES

Brachiopod fauna, recent: marine environment. Joyce R. Richardson. 1976

Cephalopods, deep-sea: photographic record. Noel Peter Dilly. 1971, 1973

Coral reefs. Florida. Gilbert L. Voss. 1961-63. *Society grants aided this research into coral growth rates, how much fish life coral areas can sustain, and the food-chain relationship between marine plants and animals.*

———— Jamaica. Judith C. Lang. 1975

———— community structure. Lizard Island, Australia. Michel Pichon. 1976

Corals and coral-reef destruction. American Samoa. Austin E. Lamberts. 1974. *A ten-acre area of coral-reef destruction caused by herbicides was the focus of this study.*

Crabs, brachyuran. Gulf of Guinea. Raymond B. Manning. 1972

———— fiddler. Europe. Jocelyn Crane. 1959

———— hermit: ethology. Alex Henderson and Syd Radinovsky. 1971

———— tropical land. Charles L. Hogue and Donald B. Bright. 1970

Foraminifera, large calcareous: ecology. Queensland Shelf and Great Barrier Reef, Australia. Charles A. Ross. 1970

Invertebrate predation and crustacean zooplankton. English Lake District. W. Gary Sprules. 1976

Lobster, spiny: mass migrations. William F. Herrnkind. 1973

Plankton: Florida Current. University of Miami Institute of Marine Sciences. 1950-52

Shrimp. Florida. Clarence P. Idyll and David A. Hughes. 1964-69

—— *Macrobrachium:* migration mechanisms. David A. Hughes. 1970

Sponges: morphological and ecological studies. Pacific reef caves. Willard D. Hartman. 1971

Squid fisheries. North Atlantic. Gilbert L. Voss. 1965

Starfish, coral-reef. Guam. Masashi Yamaguchi. 1974

—— crown-of-thorns *(Acenthaster planci):* biology and epidemiology. Walter A. Starck II. 1971. *Significant improvements in our understanding of coral-reef survival resulted from this survey of the sometimes devastating effect of crown-of-thorns starfish on corals.*

Geography

Aerial survey. Washington to Buenos Aires. Albert W. Stevens, Frederick Simpich, and Jacob Gayer. 1930

Africa: a history of exploration by Americans. James A. Casada. 1976

Agricultural development potential in a semiarid drainage basin. Central Tanzania. John W. Pawling. 1973

Alaska Peninsula and Aleutian Islands. Bernard R. Hubbard. 1934

Ancient environments and age of nonglaciated terrain. Southeastern Alaska. Ian A. Worley. 1971

Antarctic: air exploration. Lincoln Ellsworth. 1934

—— first Byrd expedition. Richard E. Byrd, Jr. 1928-30; second Byrd expedition, 1933-35. *Society grants helped Comdr. Richard E. Byrd, expedition leader, to achieve man's first flight over the South Pole. This expedition was followed by a second that explored and mapped 450,000 square miles of the southernmost continent.*

Arctic: Franz Josef Land islands (North Polar expeditions). Walter Wellman. 1898, 1906

—— MacMillan expedition. Donald B. MacMillan and Richard E. Byrd. 1925

—— survey, area north of Alaska. Robert A. Bartlett. 1924

Baseline study. Delaware Bay. William S. Gaither. 1970

Cape Horn region, South America. Amos Burg. 1934

Carlsbad Caverns, New Mexico. Willis T. Lee. 1924. *Exploration, mapping, and photographing led to Carlsbad Caverns' becoming a national park in 1930.*

China-Tibet frontier. Joseph F. Rock. 1923-30

Citröen-Haardt Trans-Asiatic Expedition. Beirut, Syria, to Peking, China. Georges-Marie Haardt. 1931. *This 7,370-mile overland exploration from the Mediterranean to the Yellow Sea was the first since the days of Marco Polo.*

Darwin Range, Santa Inés, Tierra del Fuego. E. Jack Miller and Paul H. Dix. 1964

Everest, Mount. Norman G. Dyhrenfurth and Barry C. Bishop. 1962-63. *This expedition brought not only the first American conquest of the mountain monarch but also important contributions to high-altitude research.*

Geographic education assistance. Association of American Geographers. 1962

Himalayan Mountains. Sir Edmund Hillary and Barry C. Bishop. 1960, 1962

Himalayan region, Bhutan. Pradyumna P. Karan. 1964-65

Ice caves. Canadian Cordillera. Derek C. Ford. 1973

Katmai, Mount, region, Alaska. Robert F. Griggs. 1915-20, 1930. *The Valley of Ten*

Thousand Smokes on the Alaska Peninsula was discovered, named, and explored by the Society's Katmai expeditions. The spectacular region was declared a national monument in 1918.

Land-use intensity and labor migration. St. Kitts and Nevis, Leeward Islands. Bonham C. Richardson. 1975

Landscape change. Green River area, Utah-Colorado. William L. Graf. 1976

McKinley, Mount, aerial photo survey. Bradford Washburn. 1936

Mountains and gorges, Yünnan-Szechwan, China. Joseph R. Rock. 1923, 1927, 1929

Mountains of eastern New Guinea. J. Linsley Gressitt. 1968-69

North Pole: attempt to reach. Walter Wellman. 1898

———— attempt to reach. William Ziegler, Anthony Fiala, William J. Peters. 1903

———— attempt to reach, by dirigible balloon. Walter Wellman and Henry E. Hersey. 1906-07

———— first successful effort to reach. Robert E. Peary. 1908-09

———— attempt to reach, on skis. Bjørn O. Staib. 1964

Rock, Joseph F.: biography. Stephanne B. Sutton. 1971

Reventazon and General Valleys: Quaternary river terraces. Costa Rica. Richard H. Kesel. 1974

Saharan expansion. Southern Tunisia. Ian A. Campbell. 1970

St. Elias, Mount, Alaska. Israel C. Russell. 1890-91. *First of the Society's expeditions, this undertaking included discovery of Mount Logan, Canada's highest summit, and the mapping of a 600-square-mile area.*

St. Elias Range, Alaska-Canada: Mount St.

Elias-Mount Logan: aerial photography. Bradford Washburn. 1938

St. Elias Range-Yukon Territory, Canada. Bradford Washburn. 1935

Theodore Roosevelt National Memorial Park, North Dakota: feasibility study for expansion. Paul B. Kannowski. 1972

Vilcabamba Range. Plateau between the Apurímac and Urubamba Rivers, Peru. G. Brooks Baekeland and Peter R. Gimbel. 1963

Vinson Massif ascent. Sentinel Range, Ellsworth Mountains, Antarctica. Nicholas B. Clinch. 1966

West African Grain Coast: ports. William R. Stanley. 1974

CARTOGRAPHY

American Revolution: military map sources. Douglas W. Marshall. 1976

Antarctic: mapping. Lincoln Ellsworth. 1934

Chan Chan-Moche Valley site: maps published. Peru. Carol J. Mackey and Michael E. Moseley. 1973

Grand Canyon of the Colorado: mapping. Bradford Washburn. 1971-72, 1974. *No large-scale map of the canyon's South Rim, the section most visited by tourists, has ever been compiled. When completed, this extensive mapping project will remedy this surprising cartographic oversight.*

Historical map testing. Roland E. Chardon. 1976

Kennedy, Mount, and Mount Hubbard: mapping. Canada. Bradford Washburn. 1965

———— mapping. Canada. Paul Ulmer. 1966

Roads Through History: map catalog publication. Peabody Institute Library. 1965

Sikkim: physical-cultural map. Pradyumna P. Karan. 1968

Geology

'Ai (Et-Tell), Israel: soils, construction, and geologic materials. George R. Glenn. 1970

Alpine chain: geological exploration. Southern Italy. Walter Alvarez. 1975

Carboniferous deposits: statistical analysis. Fife, Scotland. Edward S. Belt. 1972

Chubb Crater, Quebec. V. Ben Meen. 1951. *Chubb Crater was proved by this study to be one of the largest known earth scars created by meteor impact.*

Glacial and floral changes, climatic history, last 140 centuries. Argentina. John H. Mercer. 1974

Hydrographic evolution, Late Glacial to Recent. Western Mediterranean. Daniel J. Stanley. 1970

Kenya, Mount: Quaternary history. East Africa. William C. Mahaney. 1976

Labrador Crater, Canada. V. Ben Meen. 1953-54

Marble Canyon Quadrangle: geology. Death Valley, California. Edward A. Johnson. 1973

Messina earthquake study. Sicily. Charles Will Wright. 1909

Recent Nile Cone history based on sediment-core analysis. Daniel J. Stanley. 1974

Salmon River, Idaho: Idaho batholith. Philip J. Shenon and John C. Reed. 1935

Saltpeter conversion and cave nitrate origins. Carol A. Hill. 1974

Sedimentation patterns, submarine. Wilmington Canyon, off Delaware. Daniel J. Stanley. 1966

Sedimentological study. Volta Delta, West Africa. John K. Adams. 1972

Sediments, internal: interrelationships with submarine lithification. Robert L. Eutsler. 1973

Skaergaard region, Greenland. Alexander R. McBirney. 1974

Submerged beach-rock pavements. Bimini, Bahamas. Mahlon M. Ball. 1971

Trondhjemites: development and the earth's early sialic crust. Fred Barker. 1972

Turbidity maximum. Westerschelde Estuary, Netherlands. Richard W. Faas. 1973

Ultramafic inclusions: origin and relationship to basalt genesis. A. William Laughlin. 1972

West Spitsbergen Island, Norway: geology and glaciology. George H. Sutton and P. C. Parks. 1952

GLACIOLOGY

Alaska: glaciers. Ralph S. Tarr and Lawrence Martin. 1909-11

——— glacier studies. Maynard M. Miller. 1961-67. *This long-term program surveyed changes in glaciers along the southern Alaska coast, with special attention to the effects of the 1964 spring earthquake.*

Alaska-British Columbia Coast Mountains: glacier differentiation. Maynard M. Miller. 1968-69

Atlin Park glaciers, British Columbia. Maynard M. Miller. 1974

Austrian Alps: glaciation chronology. Henry W. Posamentier. 1975

Baffin Island, Canada: glacial erosion. David E. Sugden. 1975

Glacier Bay, Alaska: Late Wisconsin and neoglacial history. George M. Haselton. 1975

Glaciers: presurge dynamics. Sam G. Collins. 1971

St. Elias Mountains, Alaska: glaciers. Richard L. Cameron. 1968

——— region, Alaska-Yukon Territory: glaciers. Walter A. Wood. 1964-67

MINERALOGY

Clay sediments: mineralogy and distribution. Turnagain Arm region, Alaska. Neal R. O'Brien. 1973

Fire: man's use of, to shape earths and metals. Theodore A. Wertime. 1968, 1970, 1972

Gem study. Asia. V. Ben Meen. 1964-65

Meteorite and tektite collection. Australia. Brian H. Mason and E. P. Henderson. 1963-67

Meteorite craters. Mauritania. Robert F. Fudali. 1969-70

Mineralogical research. Prince of Wales Island, Alaska. George S. Switzer. 1967

Pegmatite mineral studies. Black Hills, South Dakota. George Rapp, Jr. 1964

Tektites. Bosumtwi Crater, Ivory Coast. John Saul. 1964

PALEONTOLOGY

Algae, calcareous. North Atlantic Ocean. Walter H. Adey. 1964-65

Amphibians and reptiles: Lower Pliocene. Kansas. J. Alan Holman. 1972-73

——— Upper Miocene. Nebraska. J. Alan Holman. 1975

Biostratigraphy, Tertiary molluscan. Tierra del Fuego and Patagonia. William J. Zinsmeister. 1975

Birds, terrestrial fossils (Upper Cretaceous). Baja California. William J. Morris. 1973

Bovidae from Tanzania and Kenya. Alan W. Gentry. 1964-65

Calvert Cliffs, Maryland. Robert E. Gernant and A. Lincoln Dryden. 1968. *This world-famous paleontological area has yielded fine fossil plant and animal collections.*

Catfish. Green River Formation, Wyoming. H. Paul Buchheim and Ronald C. Surdam. 1976

Cave with scavengers. Villafranca de los Barros, Spain. Emiliano Aguirre. 1971-72

Cetacean remains, Oligocene. South Carolina. Albert E. Sanders. 1972

Coral reefs, Cretaceous. Europe and Caribbean. Anthony G. Coates. 1975

Crabs, late Cretaceous. North America. Gale A. Bishop. 1976

Desmostylia (mammalian order). Roy H. Reinhart. 1973

Dinosaurian fauna, Jurassic. Colorado. James A. Jensen. 1975. *This project has yielded part of the world's largest dinosaur; it also harbors an accumulation of fossil bones of some 15 different species of reptiles.*

Dinosaurs. Gadoufaoua, Niger Republic. Philippe Taquet. 1973

——— Morrison Formation. Western United States. Peter Dodson. 1974-75

Dry Cave: Pleistocene paleoecology. New Mexico. Arthur H. Harris. 1971

Early man and extinct animals. China Lake, California. Emma Lou Davis. 1971

Flamingos, Eocene: nesting area. Wyoming. Paul O. McGrew. 1971, 1975

Footprint castings, Oligocene. Presidio County, Texas. John A. Wilson. 1975

Foraminifera: Jurassic and Cretaceous. Pacific Ocean. Robert G. Douglas. 1970, 1974

Fossil vertebrates. Australia. Thomas H. Rich. 1975

——— terrestrial. Canadian high Arctic. Mary R. Dawson and Robert M. West. 1976

Fossils: collecting. Kenya. Vincent J. Maglio. 1968-69, 1972

——— dating, using racemization of amino acids from Africa. Jeffrey L. Bada. 1973

——— dating, using racemization of amino acids from caves. John H. Ostrom. 1970

Geomagnetic chronology of late Cenozoic South American land-mammalian ages. Larry G. Marshall. 1974, 1976

Herbivores, wild: carcasses. Kenya. Diane P. Gifford. 1976

Malagasy lemur subfossils: crania and dentitions. Ian M. Tattersall. 1969

Mammal bones. Amboseli National Park, Kenya. Anna K. Behrensmeyer. 1975-76

Mammals. James S. Mellett. 1975

——— Cretaceous. Greenwood Canyon, Montague County, Texas. Bob H. Slaughter. 1973

——— early Cretaceous. North America. Farish A. Jenkins, Jr. and A. W. Crompton. 1974-75

——— small: biologic and geologic relationships. Austria. Robert W. Wilson. 1973

——— South Dakota. Robert W. Wilson. 1965, 1974

Mammoth-kill sites. Wyoming and New Mexico. George A. Agogino. 1959-65

——— Murray Springs, Arizona. C. Vance Haynes, Jr. 1966-72. *This long-term project explored occurrences of mammoth bones with potential human associations.*

Mammoth-kill sites, Selby and Dutton, Colorado. Dennis J. Stanford. 1976

Mammoth site, late Pleistocene. South Dakota. Larry D. Agenbroad. 1975

Mammoth skeleton; man-made stone tools. Wyoming. George A. Agogino. 1960-61. *This project located and saved from destruction the skeleton of a five-ton* Mammuthus columbi *of 11,000 years ago.*

Mesozoic and Tertiary fauna. Australia and New Zealand. Thomas H. Rich. 1973, 1975

Microvertebrates, Miocene and Pliocene. South Dakota. Morton Green. 1973

Old World monkey fossils *(Cercopithecoidea)*. Mediterranean region. Eric Delson. 1971

Paleontology and archeology. Lubbock Lake site. Texas. Craig C. Black. 1973-74

Permian conodont paleoecology. Wyoming. Fred H. Behnken. 1976

Pliocene fauna. Nebraska. Michael R. Voorhies. 1965

Pliocene fossil localities. Rift Valley, Kenya. Vincent J. Maglio. 1972

Plio-Pleistocene fossils. Iran. Douglas M. Lay. 1976

Pterosaurs, giant. Texas. Douglas A. Lawson. 1975

Rhinoceros and pig fossil bones. South Dakota. Joseph P. Connolly and James D. Bump. 1940

Rocks, minerals, and fossils: collecting for conservation. Badlands, South Dakota. Robert W. Wilson. 1965, 1968-69

Salamander and frog fossils: paleogeography. Richard Dean Estes. 1973

Stanton's Cave: Pleistocene paleoclimatology. Grand Canyon, Arizona. Robert C. Euler. 1969-70

Underwater paleontology. Florida. S. David Webb. 1968-69

Vertebrates. Baja California. Theodore Downs. 1974

—— Baja California. William J. Morris. 1965-71. *Field studies and collecting for this investigation were capped by the discovery of* the oldest Eohippus *(fossil horse) known to science.*

Vertebrates, Cenozoic. Australian Pilbara and Canning Basin areas. William D. Turnbull. 1976

—— Cenozoic. Eastern Canadian High Arctic. Mary R. Dawson and Robert M. West. 1973

—— Central America and Great American Interchange. S. David Webb. 1976

—— Jurassic and Cretaceous terrestrial. South America. José Fernando Bonaparte. 1975-76

—— late Arikarean. Nebraska. Margery C. Coombs. 1975

—— Lower Eocene. South-West Africa. John A. Van Couvering. 1975

—— Lower Triassic. Tasmania. John W. Cosgriff. 1970

—— mid-Tertiary. Charleston, South Carolina. Albert E. Sanders. 1971-72

—— Pleistocene. Lake Bonneville deposits, Utah. Wade E. Miller. 1973

—— terrestrial, present and fossil. Fernando de Noronha Island, South Atlantic. Storrs L. Olson. 1972

—— tropical South America. Bryan Patterson. 1974

STRATIGRAPHY
and PETROLOGY

Andean metamorphic rocks: petrology. Colombia and Ecuador. Tomas Feininger. 1971

Basalts: petrology and geochemistry. Snake River Plain, Idaho. William P. Leeman. 1969

Bentonite dating, Lower Paleozoic. Britain. Reuben J. Ross, Jr. 1976

Caledonides, Norwegian. William B. Size. 1976

Great Rift Valley: structural origin of the Ethiopian section. George H. Megrue and Paul A. Mohr. 1968-69

Laetolil Beds, Tanzania: stratigraphy. Richard L. Hay. 1976. *Resting ground of early-man fossils, the Laetolil Beds are 3.5 to 3.8 million* years old. *This study will improve understanding of the deposits themselves and also add to knowledge of the fossils they contain.*

Metamorphic rocks: petrographic mapping. New Caledonia. Philippa M. Black. 1970

Miocene rocks: stratigraphy and faunas. Northwestern Nebraska. Robert M. Hunt, Jr. 1972

Olduvai Gorge, Tanzania: geological studies. Richard L. Hay. 1962, 1968-70, 1972. *Spectacular fossil discoveries of early man by anthropologist Louis S. B. Leakey and his wife, Mary, have made Olduvai Gorge world famous. This investigation of the geology of the gorge provides an essential basis for the interpretation of the finds made by the Leakeys.*

Stuart, Mount, batholith: petrology and geochemistry. Cascade Range, Washington. Erik R. Erickson, Jr. 1971-72, 1974

Geophysics

Archeomagnetic chronology of the New World. Robert Lee DuBois. 1969-70

Joint and fracture patterns. Israel and Iceland. Amos A. Nur. 1974

OCEANOGRAPHY

Aquascope designed, built, and used in study of Chesapeake Bay. Gilbert C. Klingel. 1952-53

Bathysphere depth record set. Bermuda. William Beebe and Otis Barton. 1934. *Observations of deep-sea species never before seen by man were made during a record 3,028-foot descent.*

***Calypso* expeditions.** Jacques-Yves Cousteau. 1952-67. *In 1952 the Society began cosponsorship of the oceanographic expeditions of Captain Cousteau aboard his research vessel Calypso. The French diver's investigations included Mediterranean sea life, ancient shipwrecks, the Persian Gulf, and the Atlantic continental shelf off South America.*

Freshwater streams in the sea. Cephalonia, Ionian Sea. T. Nicholas Panay. 1953

"Knee-line" depths and positions: seismic study. Mediterranean Sea. Harold E. Edgerton. 1969

Man-in-Sea project. Mediterranean Sea, off Villefranche, France. Edwin A. Link and Robert Sténuit. 1963. *This test of an underwater habitat proved that divers, once acclimated to special atmospheric conditions in a* diving chamber, could live and operate at ocean depths of several hundred feet.

Marine photographic and echo-sounding research and equipment. Harold E. Edgerton. 1950, 1952-62, 1966, 1974. *Dr. Edgerton's innovations in cameras, ultrahigh-speed lighting equipment, and echo-sounding devices have played an important role in the success of many Society research projects, especially those involving marine photography.*

Marine sediments: bioturbation. Puerto Rico. Jack Morelock. 1973

Mid-Atlantic Ridge. Maurice Ewing. 1947-48. *Extensive summer surveys of this 10,000-mile-long submerged mountain range in the Atlantic Ocean produced data on the ridge's topography, geology, and sea life.*

Mid-Atlantic Ridge Rift Valley: sonar exploration. Harold E. Edgerton. 1969

Ocean floors: global physiographical study. Bruce C. Heezen. 1970. *Society maps of the Atlantic, Indian, and Pacific Ocean floors owe much to this study's successful conversion of massive amounts of ocean-sounding data into global sea-floor physiography.*

Photographic equipment developed for underwater use. Florida. Walter A. Starck II. 1964

VOLCANOLOGY

Arenal Volcano: eruption dynamics and petrology. Costa Rica. William G. Melson. 1969

Basement rock and Tertiary volcanic correlations. Gulf of California. R. Gordon Gastil. 1972

Katmai, Mount, Alaska: examination following eruption. George C. Martin. 1912

Mont Pelée, Martinique: eruption. Robert T. Hill, Israel C. Russell, Thomas A. Jaggar. 1902

Nunivak Island: volcanic ejecta. John Sloan Dickey, Jr. 1974

Pavlof Volcano, Alaska Peninsula. Thomas A. Jaggar. 1928

Santorini Volcano: eruption date (Bronze Age). Aegean Sea. Charles J. Vitaliano. 1974. *It has been theorized that the Minoan civilization of Crete was extinguished by volcanic eruption. An exact dating of the Bronze Age eruption of Santorini will aid in determining if it was indeed responsible for the decline of Minoan culture.*

Summit Crater area: geophysical and volcanological investigation. Mount Rainier, Washington. Barry W. Prather and Maynard M. Miller. 1970-71

Tonga Islands volcanoes: survey of recent activity. William G. Melson and W. B. Bryan. 1968

Volcanic flames and fume: spectroscopy. Hawaii. Dale P. Cruikshank. 1971

Volcanic gas and petrology. Galapagos Islands. Bert E. Nordlie. 1971

Volcanic rocks. Micronesia. Fred Barker. 1976

Volcanism. Austral Islands. Rockne H. Johnson. 1971

———— late Cenozoic. Zuni Centers, New Mexico. A. William Laughlin. 1973

Volcanoes, submarine. Near Samoa. Rockne H. Johnson. 1975

Social Sciences

HISTORY

Llanos, tropical plains frontier: historical research. Northern South America. Jane M. Loy. 1973

Manuscript collections: survey. Nepal, Sikkim, and Bhutan monasteries. John F. Staal and Lewis R. Lancaster. 1973. *As the modern world encroaches upon once remote monasteries, unique manuscript collections are threatened with destruction and dispersal. Preserving, microfilming, and indexing such treasures were the aims of this survey.*

Manuscripts. St. Mpatsis Monastery, Andros Island, Aegean Sea. Antonia Tripolitis. 1968-69

Metallurgic zones described by Homer and Strabo. Northern Turkey. Theodore A. Wertime. 1970

Naval documents: cataloging and indexing. Naval Historical Foundation. 1965

Persian Royal Road Survey. Anatolia, Turkey. S. Frederick Starr. 1961. *Intended to locate, map, and photograph parts of the ancient road that once connected Susa and Persepolis, the two capitals of the Persian Empire, this survey also located portions of old Roman, Byzantine, and Seljuk routes.*

SOCIOLOGY

City street life. New York City. William H. Whyte. 1972-73. *This project, directed toward finding novel ways of solving insistent urban problems, made use of specialized motion-picture techniques to study human behavior in a city setting.*

A brooding brown bear mother keeps close watch over her cubs in Alaska's wilderness.

ALLAN L. EGBERT

Medals and Awards of the Society

T O ENCOURAGE exploration, to promote scientific advance, and to recognize outstanding service to geography, the National Geographic Society presents medals, awards, and prizes for exceptional achievement. The dozens of distinguished men and women who have received these coveted honors are listed here:

MEDALS

Nine Presidents and three Vice Presidents of the United States have presented National Geographic Society medals, beginning with Theodore Roosevelt in 1906. The Hubbard Medal, named for Gardiner Greene Hubbard, first President of the Society, is awarded for distinction in exploration, discovery, and research; the Grosvenor Medal for outstanding service to geography; the Special Gold Medal for extraordinary geographic achievement; the John Oliver La Gorce Medal for accomplishment in geographic exploration, or in the sciences, or for public service to advance international understanding.

COMDR. ROBERT E. PEARY - 1906, Hubbard Medal: Arctic explorations. 1909, Special Medal of Honor: Discovery of North Pole.

CAPT. ROALD AMUNDSEN - 1907, Hubbard Medal: Traverse of Northwest Passage. 1913, Special Gold Medal: Discovery of South Pole.

CAPT. ROBERT A. BARTLETT - 1909, Hubbard Medal: Far-north explorations with Peary's 1909 expedition.

GROVE KARL GILBERT - 1909, Hubbard Medal: Thirty years of achievements in physical geography.

SIR ERNEST H. SHACKLETON - 1910, Hubbard Medal: Antarctic explorations and farthest south, 88° 23'.

COL. GEORGE W. GOETHALS - 1914, Special Gold Medal: Directing completion of Panama Canal.

VILHJALMUR STEFANSSON - 1919, Hubbard Medal: Discoveries in Canadian Arctic.

LT. COMDR., LATER REAR ADMIRAL, RICHARD E. BYRD, JR. - 1926, Hubbard Medal: First to reach North Pole by airplane. 1930, Special Medal of Honor: First to attain South Pole by air.

FLOYD BENNETT - 1926, Special Gold Medal: Flight to North Pole with Richard E. Byrd.

COL. CHARLES A. LINDBERGH - 1927, Hubbard Medal: New York-Paris solo flight.

HUGO ECKENER - 1930, Special Medal of Honor: First global navigation of an airship.

ROY CHAPMAN ANDREWS - 1931, Hubbard Medal: Geographic discoveries in Central Asia.

AMELIA EARHART - 1932, Special Gold Medal: First solo Atlantic flight by a woman.

ANNE MORROW LINDBERGH - 1934, Hubbard Medal: Notable flights, as copilot, on Charles Lindbergh's aerial surveys.

CAPTS. ALBERT W. STEVENS AND ORVIL A. ANDERSON - 1935, Hubbard Medals: World altitude record of 72,395 feet in balloon *Explorer II*.

LINCOLN ELLSWORTH - 1936, Hubbard Medal: Extraordinary achievements in polar exploration.

THOMAS C. POULTER - 1937, Special Gold Medal: Achievements, Byrd Antarctic Expedition.

GEN. H. H. ARNOLD - 1945, Hubbard Medal: Contributions to aviation.

GILBERT H. GROSVENOR - 1949, Grosvenor Medal: Outstanding service to geography as Editor of NATIONAL GEOGRAPHIC.

COMDR. DONALD B. MacMILLAN - 1953, Hubbard Medal: Arctic explorations, 1908-52.

BRITISH EVEREST EXPEDITION - 1954, Hubbard Medal: Ascent of Mount Everest.

MRS. ROBERT E. PEARY - 1955, Special Gold Medal: Contributions to husband's polar explorations.

JOHN OLIVER LA GORCE - 1955, Grosvenor Medal: Outstanding service to the increase and diffusion of geographic knowledge, 1905-55.

PRINCE PHILIP, DUKE OF EDINBURGH - 1957, Special Gold Medal: Promoting science and better understanding among the world's peoples.

PAUL A. SIPLE - 1958, Hubbard Medal: For 30 years of Antarctic explorations, including leadership of first group to winter at the South Pole.

U. S. NAVY ANTARCTIC EXPEDITIONS - 1959, Hubbard Medal: Antarctic research and exploration, 1955-59.

SIR VIVIAN FUCHS - 1959, Hubbard Medal: Leadership of British Trans-Antarctic expedition.

CAPT. JACQUES-YVES COUSTEAU - 1961, Special Gold Medal: Undersea exploration.

DR. AND MRS. LOUIS S. B. LEAKEY - 1962, Hubbard Medal: Anthropological discoveries in East Africa.

LT. COL. JOHN H. GLENN, JR. - 1962, Hubbard Medal: Space exploration.

AMERICAN MOUNT EVEREST EXPEDITION - 1963, Hubbard Medal: Contributions to geography and high-altitude research through conquest of earth's highest peak.

AMERICAN ANTARCTIC MOUNTAINEERING EXPEDITION - 1967, John Oliver La Gorce Medal: First ascent of Antarctica's highest mountain, 1966-67.

JUAN T. TRIPPE - 1967, Hubbard Medal: Contributions to aviation.

HAROLD E. EDGERTON - 1968, John Oliver La Gorce Medal: Contributions to photographic and geophysical technology.

PHILIP VAN HORN WEEMS - 1968, John Oliver La Gorce Medal: Contributions to marine, air, and space navigation.

APOLLO 8 ASTRONAUTS COL. FRANK BORMAN, USAF, CAPT. JAMES A. LOVELL, JR., USN, AND LT. COL. WILLIAM A. ANDERS, USAF - 1969, Hubbard Medal: Space exploration; first to orbit the moon.

APOLLO 11 ASTRONAUTS NEIL A. ARMSTRONG, COL. EDWIN E. ALDRIN, JR., USAF, AND LT. COL. MICHAEL COLLINS, USAF - 1970, Hubbard Medal: Space exploration; moon landing.

MELVILLE BELL GROSVENOR - 1974, Grosvenor Medal: Outstanding service to geography.

ALEXANDER WETMORE - 1975, Hubbard Medal: Contributions to ornithology.

AWARDS
JANE M. SMITH AWARD

Jane McGrew Smith of Pittsburgh, Pennsylvania, who died in 1911, made bequests to the National Geographic Society and 14 other educational and religious institutions. A life member of the Society deeply interested in its scientific work, Miss Smith directed that her gift be used to establish an award, including life membership in the Society, in recognition of notable contributions to geography.

ALFRED H. BROOKS	1917, Geologist
HIRAM BINGHAM	1917, Historian, explorer
HENRY PITTIER	1917, Agriculturist
GEORGE KENNAN	1917, Authority on Russia
FRANK G. CARPENTER	1919, Journalist
WILLIAM H. DALL	1919, Naturalist
WILLIAM H. HOLMES	1919, Art curator
STEPHEN T. MATHER	1919, Park Service Director
EDWARD W. NELSON	1919, Biologist
WALTER T. SWINGLE	1919, Plant explorer
ROBERT F. GRIGGS	1919, Botanist
O. F. COOK	1919, Plant explorer
JOSEPH STRAUSS	1919, Rear Admiral, USN
J. B. TYRRELL	1921, Canadian explorer
HERBERT E. GREGORY	1921, Geologist
FRANK M. CHAPMAN	1921, Ornithologist
R. G. McCONNELL	1921, Canadian explorer
DONALD B. MacMILLAN	1921, Explorer, Lieutenant, USNR
CHARLES SHELDON	1925, Alaska explorer
ROBERT A. BARTLETT	1925, Far-north explorer
NEIL M. JUDD	1925, Archeologist

JOSEPH F. ROCK   1925, Plant explorer

PHILIP SIDNEY SMITH   1925, Geologist

WILLIAM BROOKS CABOT
          1925, Author, engineer

KNUD RASMUSSEN
          1926, Greenland explorer

CHARLES A. LINDBERGH
          1927, Transatlantic flight pioneer

CURTIS D. WILBUR
          1929, Secretary of the Navy, retired

ANDREW E. DOUGLASS
          1929, Astronomer, dendrochronologist

HERBERT PUTNAM
          1929, Librarian of Congress

CORNELIUS A. PUGSLEY
          1929, Banker, conservationist

SIR WILFRED GRENFELL
          1930, Surgeon, missionary, author

ASHLEY C. McKINLEY
1931, Captain, USA, aerial photographer

DOUGLAS W. JOHNSON
          1931, Physiographer

ANDRÉ CITROËN 1931, French industrialist

ALBERT W. STEVENS 1931, Captain, USA,
          aerial photographer

LAURENCE M. GOULD   1931, Biologist

WILLIAM H. HOBBS   1933, Geologist

EUGENE EDWARD BUCK
          1934, President, American Society of
          Composers, Authors & Publishers

VERNON BAILEY   1934, Field naturalist

JAMES P. THOMSON
          1934, Royal Geographical Society
          of Australia

CHARLES F. MARVIN   1934, Meteorologist

W. COLEMAN NEVILS, S. J.
          1934, Classicist,
          President, Georgetown University

CLIFFORD K. BERRYMAN
          1934, Political cartoonist

LEONHARD STEJNEGER   1935, Biologist

JOSEPH P. CONNOLLY
          1935, Geologist, college president

WILLIAM R. POPE   1935, Colonel, USA

LAWRENCE J. BURPEE
          1936, Canadian commissioner

RANDOLPH P. WILLIAMS
          1936, Captain, U. S. Army Air Corps

ROGERS BIRNIE, JR.
          1936, Retired Army officer

SAMUEL S. GANNETT   1936, Geographer

HERBERT HOLLICK-KENYON
          1936, Pilot, Canadian Airways

HIS MAJESTY KING LEOPOLD
          1936, Brussels, Belgium

A. E. MURLIN
          1936, U. S. Geological Survey, retired

H. L. BALDWIN
          1936, U. S. Geological Survey, retired

ROBERT MULDROW
          1936, U. S. Geological Survey, retired

W. J. PETERS
          1936, U. S. Geological Survey, retired

PRINCE IYESATO TOKUGAWA
          1937, Tokyo, Japan

WEB HILL   1937, Merchant

STEPHEN R. CAPPS   1938, Geologist

FRANKLIN ADAMS
          1938, Authority on Latin America

GEORGE W. GODDARD
1940, Major, USAF, aerial photographer

J. FRED ESSARY   1941, Journalist

CHARLES H. DEETZ   1942, Cartographer,
          U. S. Coast & Geodetic Survey

SAMUEL WHITTEMORE BOGGS
          1943, Department of State geographer

ALEXANDER M. PATCH
          1943, Major General, USA

ELI HELMICK
          1943, Major General, USA, retired

HARRY WARNER FRANTZ   1943, Journalist

EDMUND W. STARLING
        1943, U. S. Secret Service

MRS. WILLIAM G. PADEN   1943, Author

CHRISTOVA LEITE DE CASTRO
        1944, Brazilian geographer

FRANK B. JEWETT   1945, President,
        National Academy of Sciences

FRANK M. MacFARLAND   1945, President,
        California Academy of Sciences

S. S. VISHER   1945, Geographer

SALVADOR MASSIP 1946, Cuban geographer

CHESTER W. NIMITZ   1946, Fleet Admiral,
        USN, Chief of Naval Operations

MALCOLM J. PROUDFOOT 1947, Geographer

GEOFFREY T. HELLMAN   1947, Essayist

MAURICE EWING   1947, Geologist

NICHOLAS H. DARTON   1948, Geologist

BENJAMIN R. HOFFMAN
1948, Geographical Society of Philadelphia

JOHN O'KEEFE
        1949, U. S. Army Map Service

GEORGE J. MILLER
        1949, Editor, *Journal of Geography*

EARL B. SHAW   1949, President,
        Council of Geography Teachers

MRS. ALBERT W. STEVENS
        1950, Smith life member widow

MRS. HENRY H. ARNOLD
        1950, Smith life member widow

ALBERT E. GIESECKE
        1951, Government adviser, Peru

HUGH L. DRYDEN
        1951, Director, National Advisory
        Committee for Aeronautics

HERBERT FRIEDMANN
        1951, Curator of Birds,
        U. S. National Museum

MRS. J. R. HILDEBRAND
        1951, Widow of Assistant Editor,
        NATIONAL GEOGRAPHIC

MRS. RUTH B. SHIPLEY
1951, Passport Office, Department of State

ANDREW GEORGE LATTA McNAUGHTON
        1952, General, Canadian Army, retired

MAYNARD OWEN WILLIAMS
        1953, Chief of Foreign Staff,
        NATIONAL GEOGRAPHIC

ROBERT B. ANDERSON
        1953, Secretary of the Navy

MRS. FRANKLIN L. FISHER
        1953, Widow of Illustrations Editor,
        NATIONAL GEOGRAPHIC

KENNETH H. GIBSON
        1953, Colonel, U. S. Air Force

IRA S. BOWEN   1955, Astronomer

ARDITO DESIO
        1955, Leader, K-2 Expedition

CHARLES P. MOUNTFORD
        1956, Anthropologist, Australia

SIR VIVIAN FUCHS
        1959, British geologist, explorer

ALBERT A. STANLEY
        1959, U. S. Coast & Geodetic Survey

P. V. H. WEEMS
        1959, Captain, USN, retired

EDWIN A. LINK
        1959, Inventor and undersea pioneer

SIR BRUCE INGRAM
        1959, Editor, *Illustrated London News*

ARLEIGH A. BURKE   1960, Admiral, USN,
        Chief of Naval Operations

LYNDON B. JOHNSON
1962, Vice President of the United States

DR. CALVIN H. PLIMPTON
        1964, President, Amherst College

FRANKLIN L. BURR AWARD

Mary C. Burr of Hartford, Connecticut, who died in 1930, bequeathed a fund to the National Geographic Society in memory of her father. Income from the fund is used to award cash prizes to leaders in the Society's expeditions and researches for especially meritorious work in the field of geographic science.

CAPT. ALBERT W. STEVENS
1933, 1936, Aeronaut

CAPT. ORVIL A. ANDERSON 1936, Aeronaut

CAPT. RANDOLPH P. WILLIAMS
1936, Aeronaut

DR. AND MRS. WILLIAM M. MANN
1938, Zoologists

BRADFORD WASHBURN
1939, 1965, Geographer

MATTHEW W. STIRLING
1939, 1941, 1957, Archeologist

MRS. MATTHEW W. STIRLING
1941, Archeologist

ALEXANDER WETMORE 1944, Ornithologist

THOMAS A. JAGGER   1945, Engineer

LYMAN J. BRIGGS
1945, 1954, 1962, Chairman, Committee for Research and Exploration, National Geographic Society

GEORGE VAN BIESBROECK
1947, 1948, 1953, Astronomer

EDWARD A. HALBACH, FRANCIS J. HEYDEN, S. J., CARL W. MILLER, CHARLES H. SMILEY
1948, Astronomers

ARTHUR A. ALLEN   1948, Ornithologist

CHARLES P. MOUNTFORD
1950, Anthropologist

FRANK M. SETZLER   1950, Anthropologist

HAROLD E. EDGERTON
1952, Electrical engineer

NEIL M. JUDD   1955, 1963, Archeologist

MRS. ROBERT E. PEARY
1955, Scientific collaborator

MRS. MARIE PEARY STAFFORD
1955, Scientific collaborator

ROBERT F. GRIGGS   1956, Geographer

CARL F. MILLER   1959, Archeologist

LOUIS S. B. LEAKEY AND MARY D. LEAKEY
1961, Anthropologists

JANE GOODALL   1962, 1964, Zoologist

REAR ADM. DONALD B. MacMILLAN
1963, Polar explorer

BARRY C. BISHOP
1963, Mountaineer and glaciologist

HELGE INGSTAD AND ANNE STINE INGSTAD
1964, Archeologists

RICHARD E. LEAKEY
1965, 1973, Anthropologist

NORMAN G. DYHRENFURTH
1965, Mountaineer

MAYNARD M. MILLER   1967, Glaciologist

DIAN J. FOSSEY   1973, Zoologist

KENAN T. ERIM
1973, Classical archeologist

OTHER SOCIETY AWARDS

HERBERT FRIEDMANN, WILLIAM J. MORRIS
Arnold Guyot Memorial Award, 1968, Paleontologists

ROBERT W. WILSON
Arnold Guyot Memorial Award, 1974, Paleontologist

HESLON MUKIRI GITHUA
Special National Geographic Society Award, 1968, Scientific collaborator

Meeting in Washington, D. C. – the 33 eminent

RESPONDING to an invitation to organize "a society for the increase and diffusion of geographical knowledge," the men gathered at the Cosmos Club on January 13, 1888. From this small beginning, the Society has extended its membership around the world.

Artist Stanley Meltzoff based his depiction of the meeting on individual photographs. Key at right identifies: **1** Charles J. Bell, banker; **2** Israel C. Russell, geologist; **3** Commodore George W. Melville, USN; **4** Frank Baker, anatomist; **5** W. B. Powell, educator; **6** Brig. Gen. A. W. Greely, USA, polar explorer; **7** Grove Karl Gilbert, geologist and a future President of the Society; **8** John Wesley

Powell, naturalist and explorer of the Colorado River; **9** Gardiner Greene Hubbard, Boston lawyer and first President of the Society, who helped finance the telephone experiments of Alexander Graham Bell; **10** Henry Gannett, geographer and a future Society Presi-

PAINTING BY STANLEY MELTZOFF

men who founded the National Geographic Society

dent; **11** William H. Dall, naturalist; **12** Edward E. Hayden, meteorologist; **13** Herbert G. Ogden, topographer; **14** Arthur P. Davis, civil engineer; **15** Gilbert Thompson, topographer; **16** Marcus Baker, cartographer; **17** George Kennan, author, lecturer, and explorer of Arctic Siberia; **18** James Howard Gore, educator; **19** O. H. Tittmann, geodesist and a future President of the Society; **20** Henry W. Henshaw, naturalist; **21** George Brown Goode, naturalist and author; **22** Cleveland Abbe, meteorologist; **23** Comdr. John R. Bartlett, USN; **24** Henry Mitchell, engineer; **25** Robert Muldrow II, geologist; **26** Comdr. Winfield S. Schley, USN; **27** Capt. C. E. Dutton, USA; **28** W. D. Johnson, topographer; **29** James C. Welling, journalist and educator; **30** C. Hart Merriam, Chief, U. S. Biological Survey; **31** Capt. Rogers Birnie, Jr., USA; **32** A. H. Thompson, geographer; **33** Samuel S. Gannett, geographer.

Presidents

THIRTEEN men—explorers, inventors, geographers, and men of letters—have served as President of the National Geographic Society. They are listed below with their terms of office.

GARDINER GREENE HUBBARD
January 27, 1888—died December 11, 1897

ALEXANDER GRAHAM BELL
January 7, 1898—resigned October 1903

W J MCGEE   March 5, 1904—April 1904

GROVE KARL GILBERT   Acting President, 1904

WILLIS L. MOORE
January 27, 1905—resigned December 1909

HENRY GANNETT
January 19, 1910—died November 5, 1914

O.H. TITTMANN
January 20, 1915—resigned April 1919

JOHN E. PILLSBURY
April 16, 1919—died December 30, 1919

GILBERT H. GROSVENOR
January 21, 1920—retired May 5, 1954, becoming Chairman of the Board of Trustees. (d. 1966)

JOHN OLIVER LA GORCE
May 5, 1954—retired January 8, 1957, becoming Vice Chairman of the Board of Trustees. (d. 1959)

MELVILLE BELL GROSVENOR
January 8, 1957—retired August 1, 1967, becoming Chairman of the Board and Editor-in-Chief. On June 1, 1976, he became Chairman Emeritus of the Board.

MELVIN M. PAYNE
August 1, 1967—retired June 1, 1976, becoming Chairman of the Board of Trustees.

ROBERT E. DOYLE   June 1, 1976—

Members of the Board of Trustees

CALLED the Board of Managers until 1920, the Society's Board of Trustees numbered 27 members at the end of 1976. Past and present members are listed below with year of election to the Board and year of their death or resignation.

CLEVELAND ABBE	1888(r. 1890)
ROBERT B. ANDERSON	1960(r. 1963)
H. H. ARNOLD	1938(d. 1950)
O. P. AUSTIN	1903(d. 1933)
CYRUS C. BABB	1893(r. 1895)
MARCUS BAKER	1888(d. 1903)
J. R. BARTLETT	1888(r. 1889)
R. N. BATCHELDER	1893(r. 1894)
ALEXANDER GRAHAM BELL	1898(d. 1922)
CHARLES J. BELL	1888(d. 1929)
ROGERS BIRNIE, JR.	1888(r. 1891)
HENRY F. BLOUNT	1892(d. 1917)
FRANK BORMAN	1975-
LYMAN J. BRIGGS	1933(d. 1963)
ALFRED H. BROOKS	1905(r. 1906)
J. CARTER BROWN	1976-
WARREN E. BURGER	1974-
GEORGE K. BURGESS	1930(d. 1932)
RICHARD E. BYRD, JR.	1953(d. 1957)
LEONARD CARMICHAEL	1957(d. 1973)
THOMAS H. CARROLL	1964(d. 1964)
T. C. CHAMBERLAIN	1905(r. 1911)
COLBY M. CHESTER	1904(d. 1932)
L. O. COLBERT	1938(d. 1968)
CALVIN COOLIDGE	1929(d. 1933)
FREDERICK V. COVILLE	1897(d. 1937)
C. W. DABNEY, JR.	1895(r. 1897)
WILLIAM H. DALL	1896(r. 1899)
GEORGE DAVIDSON	1901(r. 1911)
WILLIAM M. DAVIS	1901(r. 1904)
CHARLES G. DAWES	1924(d. 1951)
DAVID T. DAY	1896(r. 1903)
CHARLES DENBY	1907(r. 1907)
ROBERT E. DOYLE	1975-
HUGH L. DRYDEN	1951(d. 1965)
JOHN JOY EDSON	1901(d. 1935)
LLOYD H. ELLIOTT	1968-
DAVID FAIRCHILD	1905(d. 1954)
FRANKLIN L. FISHER	1945(d. 1953)
ROBERT V. FLEMING	1929(d. 1967)
JOHN FOOTE	1924(d. 1931)
HENRY GANNETT	1888(d. 1914)

WALTER S. GIFFORD 1933(r. 1951)
GROVE KARL GILBERT 1890(r. 1905)
DANIEL C. GILMAN 1901(d. 1908)
G. BROWN GOODE 1888(d. 1896)
J. HOWARD GORE 1906(d. 1939)
A. W. GREELY 1888(d. 1935)
CRAWFORD H.
GREENEWALT 1959-
EDWIN P. GROSVENOR 1929(d. 1930)
GILBERT H. GROSVENOR 1905(d. 1966)
   Chairman 1954-
GILBERT M. GROSVENOR 1966-
MELVILLE BELL
GROSVENOR 1945-
   Chairman 1967-1976
   Chairman Emeritus 1976-
ARTHUR B. HANSON 1967-
ELISHA HANSON 1936(d. 1962)
CARYL P. HASKINS 1964-
EVERETT HAYDEN 1890(r. 1898)
ANGELO HEILPRIN 1901(d. 1907)
ALFRED J. HENRY 1900(r. 1911)
J. R. HILDEBRAND 1946(d. 1951)
DAVID J. HILL 1899(r. 1903)
RUSSELL HINMAN 1901(r. 1905)
GARDINER GREENE
HUBBARD 1888(d. 1897)
CHARLES EVANS HUGHES 1930(d. 1948)
CARLISLE H. HUMELSINE 1972-
GEORGE W. HUTCHISON 1935(d. 1945)
JOHN HYDE 1892(r. 1901)
MRS. LYNDON B. JOHNSON 1974-
WILLARD D. JOHNSON 1888(r. 1891)
E. LESTER JONES 1921(d. 1929)
RUDOLPH KAUFFMANN 1906(d. 1927)
S. H. KAUFFMANN 1899(d. 1905)
C. A. KENASTON 1888(r. 1891)
GEORGE KENNAN 1888(r. 1889)
CHARLES F. KETTERING 1936(d. 1958)
JOHN OLIVER LA GORCE 1920(d. 1959)
EMORY S. LAND 1942(d. 1971)
FRANKLIN K. LANE 1911(d. 1921)
CURTIS E. LEMAY 1951-
LEROY A. LINCOLN 1938(d. 1957)
T. L. MACDONALD 1907(d. 1924)
W J MCGEE 1890(r. 1904)
BENJAMIN M. MCKELWAY 1955(d. 1976)
THOMAS W. MCKNEW 1949-
   Vice Chairman 1960-
   Chairman 1966-
   Advisory Chairman 1967-
H. RANDOLPH MADDOX 1951(d. 1977)
GEORGE C. MARSHALL 1949(d. 1959)
WM. MCCHESNEY
MARTIN, JR. 1964-
STEPHEN T. MATHER 1921(d. 1930)
GEORGE W. MELVILLE 1894(r. 1895)
T. C. MENDENHALL 1890(r. 1894)

C. HART MERRIAM 1888(d. 1942)
HENRY MITCHELL 1888(r. 1889)
WILLIS L. MOORE 1899(r. 1911)
WALTER K. MYERS 1960(d. 1964)
F. H. NEWELL 1892(r. 1899)
ERNEST E. NORRIS 1942(d. 1958)
S. N. D. NORTH 1906(d. 1924)
THEODORE W. NOYES 1927(d. 1946)
HERBERT G. OGDEN 1888(r. 1898)
RAYMOND S. PATTON 1930(d. 1937)
JOHN BARTON PAYNE 1923(d. 1935)
MELVIN M. PAYNE 1958-
   Chairman 1976-
ROBERT E. PEARY 1919(d. 1920)
JOHN J. PERSHING 1927(d. 1948)
JOHN E. PILLSBURY 1909(d. 1919)
GIFFORD PINCHOT 1901(r. 1904)
W. B. POWELL 1888(r. 1899)
WILLIAM V. PRATT 1933(d. 1957)
HENRY S. PRITCHETT 1898(r. 1901)
J. R. PROCTER 1895(r. 1896)
GEORGE R. PUTNAM 1912(d. 1953)
F. K. RICHTMYER 1938(d. 1939)
LAURANCE S.
ROCKEFELLER 1957-
W. W. ROCKHILL 1895(r. 1896)
ISRAEL C. RUSSELL 1902(d. 1906)
R. D. SALISBURY 1901(r. 1906)
E. R. SCIDMORE 1892(r. 1896)
ROBERT C. SEAMANS, JR. 1969-
GEORGE SHIRAS 3RD 1911(d. 1942)
GEORGE OTIS SMITH 1907(d. 1944)
GRANT SQUIRES 1911(d. 1928)
JOSEPH STANLEY-BROWN 1899(r. 1900)
WILLIAM HOWARD TAFT 1917(d. 1930)
A. H. THOMPSON 1888(r. 1891)
O. H. TITTMANN 1888(d. 1938)
JUAN T. TRIPPE 1942-
FREDERICK G. VOSBURGH 1962-
JAMES H. WAKELIN, JR. 1963-
B. H. WARDER 1890(r. 1891)
EARL WARREN 1955(d. 1974)
JAMES E. WEBB 1966-
J. C. WELLING 1888(r. 1891)
OSCAR WESTOVER 1936(d. 1938)
ALEXANDER WETMORE 1933-
HENRY WHITE 1915(d. 1927)
J. B. WIGHT 1896(r. 1897)
EDWIN WILLITTS 1892(d. 1895)
JOHN M. WILSON 1905(d. 1919)
LLOYD B. WILSON 1942-
CONRAD L. WIRTH 1957-
WILLIAM E. WRATHER 1951(d. 1963)
LOUIS B. WRIGHT 1964-

The Board of Trustees gathers at Society headquarters in Washington, D. C. on September 17, 1976. Seated clockwise from left: Carlisle H. Humelsine, President, The Colonial Williamsburg Foundation; Arthur B. Hanson, Society General Counsel; James H. Wakelin, Jr., former Assistant Secretary of Commerce for Science and Technology; J. Carter Brown, Director, National Gallery of Art; Melvin M. Payne, Chairman of the Board, National Geographic Society; Robert E. Doyle, Society President; Mrs. Lyndon B. Johnson; Melville Bell Grosvenor, Chairman Emeritus, and former Editor, NATIONAL GEOGRAPHIC MAGAZINE; Gen. Curtis E. LeMay, former Chief of Staff, USAF. Standing from left: Louis B. Wright, former Director, Folger Shakespeare Library; Caryl P. Haskins, former President, Carnegie Institution of Washington; Robert C. Seamans, Jr., former Administrator, Energy Research and Development Administration; Frederick G. Vosburgh, former Vice President and Editor, NATIONAL GEOGRAPHIC MAGAZINE; Lloyd H. Elliott, President, George Washington University; Gilbert M. Grosvenor, Vice President and Editor, NATIONAL GEOGRAPHIC MAGAZINE; James E. Webb, former Administrator, National Aeronautics and Space Administration; Wm. McChesney Martin, Jr., former Chairman, Federal Reserve Board; Conrad L. Wirth, former Director, National Park Service.

Not present at the September meeting (**facing page,** left to right): Thomas W. McKnew, Advisory Chairman of the Board; Frank Borman, President and Board Chairman, Eastern Air Lines; Warren E. Burger, United States Chief Justice; Crawford H. Greenewalt, Director, E. I. du Pont de Nemours & Company; H. Randolph Maddox, former Vice President, American Telephone & Telegraph Company (died May 19, 1977); Laurance S. Rockefeller, President, Rockefeller Brothers Fund; Juan T. Trippe, Honorary Chairman of the Board, Pan American World Airways; Alexander Wetmore, Research Associate, Smithsonian Institution; Lloyd B. Wilson, Honorary Chairman of the Board, Chesapeake & Potomac Telephone Company.

Geographical Distribution of the Society's Membership

AS OF DECEMBER 1976

United States	**7,778,450**
Alabama	84,385
Alaska	28,440
Arizona	99,833
Arkansas	46,639
California	1,007,810
Colorado	154,683
Connecticut	147,118
Delaware	25,785
District of Columbia	17,344
Florida	336,798
Georgia	133,659
Hawaii	45,204
Idaho	46,690
Illinois	388,178
Indiana	162,003
Iowa	101,861
Kansas	90,784
Kentucky	66,229
Louisiana	93,577
Maine	44,612
Maryland	160,821
Massachusetts	242,333
Michigan	319,630
Minnesota	179,051
Mississippi	43,621
Missouri	153,386
Montana	42,777
Nebraska	59,405
Nevada	32,211
New Hampshire	42,090
New Jersey	267,697
New Mexico	47,119
New York	528,464
North Carolina	132,114
North Dakota	23,411
Ohio	352,463
Oklahoma	92,584
Oregon	134,146
Pennsylvania	365,770
Rhode Island	33,831
South Carolina	58,432
South Dakota	24,924
Tennessee	103,163
Texas	443,053
Utah	62,320
Vermont	23,624
Virginia	184,758
Washington	213,648
West Virginia	36,159
Wisconsin	169,800
Wyoming	22,840
Possessions and territories	21,535
U. S. military and civilian personnel outside U. S.	39,638

Canada	**709,597**
Alberta	81,015
British Columbia	125,417
Manitoba	28,441
New Brunswick	14,097
Newfoundland	6,418
Northwest Terr.	1,605
Nova Scotia	23,180
Ontario	321,100
Prince Edward Is.	2,170
Quebec	81,491
Saskatchewan	23,253
Yukon Territory	1,410

Central and South America, Mexico	**85,007**
Argentina	6,694
Belize	297
Bolivia	868
Brazil	12,446
Chile	3,098
Colombia	4,313
Costa Rica	1,684
Ecuador	1,507
El Salvador	1,063
French Guiana	12
Guatemala	2,829
Guyana	342
Honduras	766
Mexico	34,759
Nicaragua	669
Panama	1,315
Paraguay	190
Peru	2,997
Surinam	255
Uruguay	821
Venezuela	8,082

Caribbean	**8,611**
Barbados	664
Cayman Islands	263
Cuba	13
Dominican Republic	888
Guadeloupe	84
Haiti	268
Jamaica	2,151
Leeward Islands	379
Martinique	106
Netherlands Antilles	1,418
Trinidad and Tobago	1,919
Turks Islands	16
Windward Islands	442

Atlantic Ocean	**6,207**
Ascension Island	7
Azores	167
Bahamas	1,868
Bermuda	2,389
Cape Verde Islands	7
Falkland Islands	24
Faeroe Islands	44
Greenland	100
Iceland	1,457
Madeira Islands	128
St. Helena	3
St. Pierre and Miquelon	13

Europe	**259,151**
Andorra	32
Austria	6,868
Belgium	14,086
Bulgaria	56
Czechoslovakia	2,949
Denmark	9,490
Finland	4,974

France	19,908	Egypt	633	Korea	1,263
German Democratic Republic	17	Ethiopia	321	Kuwait	873
		French Territory of the Afars and the Issas	11	Laos	13
German Federal Republic	44,187			Lebanon	4
Greece	4,768	Gabon	56	Macao	24
Hungary	4,667	Gambia	37	Malaysia	2,376
Ireland (Eire)	7,532	Ghana	534	Mongolia	1
Italy	19,139	Guinea	4	Nepal	140
Liechtenstein	111	Ivory Coast	246	Oman	186
Luxembourg	1,466	Kenya	1,369	Pakistan	737
Monaco	153	Liberia	625	Philippines	5,795
Netherlands	30,179	Libya	585	Qatar	145
Norway	15,238	Malawi	290	Saudi Arabia	945
Poland	1,193	Mali	34	Singapore	2,824
Portugal	3,487	Mauritania	8	Sri Lanka	519
Romania	774	Morocco	284	Syria	170
Spain	15,165	Mozambique	168	Taiwan	2,808
Sweden	20,737	Niger	33	Thailand	2,310
Switzerland	29,043	Nigeria	1,402	Turkey	3,303
U.S.S.R. (see Asia)		Rhodesia	3,583	United Arab Emirates	645
Vatican City	14	Rwanda	72	U.S.S.R.	1,412
Yugoslavia	2,919	Senegal	112	Yemen Arab Republic	30
		Sierra Leone	139	Yemen (People's Dem. Republic of)	10
United Kingdom	**164,770**	Somalia	12		
Channel Islands	1,306	South Africa	31,274	**Australasia**	**211,623**
England	136,814	South-West Africa	757	Australia and Tasmania	165,612
Northern Ireland	3,417	Sudan	104	New Zealand	46,011
Scotland	17,458	Tanzania	450		
Wales	5,775	Togo	37	**Pacific and Indian Oceans**	**4,145**
		Tunisia	119	Comoro Islands	3
Mediterranean	**1,081**	Uganda	95	Fiji	376
Cyprus	340	Upper Volta	39	French Polynesia	277
Gibraltar	99	Zaire	425	Gilbert Islands	50
Malta	642	Zambia	795	Madagascar	80
				Mauritius	183
Africa	**45,377**	**Asia**	**59,145**	Nauru	72
Algeria	218	Afghanistan	82	New Caledonia	198
Angola	47	Bahrain	334	New Hebrides	143
Benin	29	Bangladesh	102	Papua New Guinea	2,229
Botswana	193	Bhutan	8	Pitcairn Island	3
Burundi	57	Brunei	233	Réunion	35
Cameroon	113	Burma	106	Ryukyu Islands	118
Central African Empire	31	China (People's Republic of)	45	Seychelles	76
Chad	22	Hong Kong	3,589	Solomon Islands	127
Congo	14	India	7,422	Tonga	57
		Indonesia	1,055	Western Samoa	118
		Iran	2,198		
		Iraq	196	**Miscellaneous**	**2,947**
		Israel	7,176		
		Japan	9,847		
		Jordan	219	**Grand Total**	**9,336,112**

NATIONAL
GEOGRAPHIC
INDEX 1947-1976 INCLUSIVE

This index covers issues of January 1947 through December 1976. Its companion volume covers issues of October 1888 through December 1946.

The National Geographic Society publishes semiannually for each six-issue volume of the magazine a free detailed index, available on request to members.

A

ABACO (Island), Bahama Islands:
The Loyalists. By Kent Britt. Photos by Ted Spiegel. 510-539, Apr. 1975

ABALONE:
Goggle Fishing in California Waters. By David Hellyer. Photos by Lamar Boren. 615-632, May 1949

ABBOT, J. LLOYD, Jr.: Author:
Flight Into Antarctic Darkness. Photos by David S. Boyer. 732-738, Nov. 1967

ABBOTSBURY SWANNERY, England:
The Swans of Abbotsbury. By Michael Moynihan. Photos by Barnet Saidman. 563-570, Oct. 1959

ABDUL GHAFUR: Author-Photographer:
From America to Mecca on Airborne Pilgrimage. 1-60, July 1953

ABELL, GEORGE O.: Author:
Exploring the Farthest Reaches of Space. 782-790, Dec. 1956

ABELL, SAM: Photographer:
Newfoundland Trusts in the Sea. By Gary Jennings. 112-141, Jan. 1974
Yellowstone at 100: A Walk Through the Wilderness. By Karen and Derek Craighead. 579-603, May 1972

ABERCROMBIE, THOMAS J.:
National Geographic Photographers Win Top Magazine Awards. 830-831, June 1959
Author-Photographer
Afghanistan: Crossroad of Conquerors. 297-345, Sept. 1968
Algeria: Learning to Live With Independence. 200-233, Aug. 1973
Behind the Veil of Troubled Yemen. 403-445, Mar. 1964
Cambodia: Indochina's "Neutral" Corner. 514-551, Oct. 1964

ABERCROMBIE, THOMAS J.: Author-Photographer—
Continued
Ice Fishing's Frigid Charms. 861-872, Dec. 1958
Kansai, Japan's Historic Heartland. 295-339, Mar. 1970
Morocco, Land of the Farthest West. 834-865, June 1971
Nomad in Alaska's Outback. 540-567, Apr. 1969
Saudi Arabia: Beyond the Sands of Mecca. 1-53, Jan. 1966
Switzerland, Europe's High-rise Republic. 68-113, July 1969
The Sword and the Sermon. 3-45, July 1972
Venezuela Builds on Oil. 344-387, Mar. 1963
Young-old Lebanon Lives by Trade. 479-523, Apr. 1958

Photographer
Alaska Proudly Joins the Union. By Ernest Gruening. 43-83, July 1959
Brasília, Metropolis Made to Order. By Hernane Tavares de Sá. 704-724, May 1960
Captain Smith of Jamestown. By Bradford Smith. 581-620, May 1957
Easter Island and Its Mysterious Monuments. By Howard La Fay. 90-117, Jan. 1962
Enchantress! By Theodore H. Reed. 628-641, May 1961
Man's Deepest Dive. By Jacques Piccard. 224-239, Aug. 1960
Man's First Winter at the South Pole. By Paul A. Siple. 439-478, Apr. 1958
The Mighty *Enterprise*. By Nathaniel T. Kenney. 431-448, Mar. 1963
Old-New Iran, Next Door to Russia. By Edward J. Linehan. 44-85, Jan. 1961
Underwater Archeology: Key to History's Warehouse. By George F. Bass. Photos by Thomas J. Abercrombie and Robert B. Goodman. 138-156, July 1963
You and the Obedient Atom. By Allan C. Fisher,

The wintry mass of the Hindu Kush walls in a camel train crossing the frozen Wakhan River in Afghanistan.
SABRINA AND ROLAND MICHAUD

ABERCROMBIE, THOMAS J.: Photographer—*Continued*
Jr. Photos by B. Anthony Stewart and Thomas J. Abercrombie. 303-353, Sept. 1958

ABKHAZIAN A.S.S.R., U.S.S.R.:
"Every Day Is a Gift When You Are Over 100." By Alexander Leaf. Photos by John Launois. 93-119, Jan. 1973

ABOARD the N. S. *Savannah:* World's First Nuclear Merchantman. By Alan Villiers. Photos by John E. Fletcher. 280-298, Aug. 1962

"ABOMINABLE SNOWMAN":
Wintering on the Roof of the World. By Barry C. Bishop. 503-547, Oct. 1962

ABORIGINES, Australian:
"The Alice" in Australia's Wonderland. By Alan Villiers. Photos by Jeff Carter and David Moore. 230-257, Feb. 1966
An Arnhem Land Adventure. By Donald F. Thomson. 403-430, Mar. 1948
Arnhem Land Expedition of 1948. 430
Australia. By Alan Villiers. 309-385, Sept. 1963
I. The West and the South. 309-345
II. The Settled East, the Barrier Reef, the Center. 347-385
Cruise to Stone Age Arnhem Land. By Howell Walker. 417-430, Sept. 1949
Expedition to the Land of the Tiwi (Melville Island). By Charles P. Mountford. 417-440, Mar. 1956
Exploring Stone Age Arnhem Land. By Charles P. Mountford. Photos by Howell Walker. 745-782, Dec. 1949
From Spear to Hoe on Groote Eylandt. By Howell Walker. 131-142, Jan. 1953
In the Wake of Darwin's *Beagle.* By Alan Villiers. Photos by James L. Stanfield. 449-495, Oct. 1969
Queensland: Young Titan of Australia's Tropic North. By Kenneth MacLeish. Photos by Winfield Parks. 593-639, Nov. 1968
Rock Paintings of the Aborigines. By Kay and Stanley Breeden. 174-187, Feb. 1973
The Top End of Down Under. By Kenneth MacLeish. Photos by Thomas Nebbia. 145-174, Feb. 1973
Western Australia, the Big Country. By Kenneth MacLeish. Photos by James L. Stanfield. 150-187, Feb. 1975

ABRAHAM, the Friend of God. By Kenneth MacLeish. Photos by Dean Conger. 739-789, Dec. 1966

ABRAMS, AL: Author-Photographer:
Our Life on a Border Kibbutz. By Carol and Al Abrams. 364-391, Sept. 1970

ABRAMS, CAROL: Author:
Our Life on a Border Kibbutz. By Carol and Al Abrams. Photos by Al Abrams. 364-391, Sept. 1970

ABU DHABI, United Arab Emirates:
The Arab World, Inc. By John J. Putman. Photos by Winfield Parks. 494-533, Oct. 1975
Desert Sheikdoms of Arabia's Pirate Coast. By Ronald Codrai. 65-104, July 1956

ABU LATT (Island), Red Sea:
Fish Men Explore a New World Undersea. By Jacques-Yves Cousteau. 431-472, Oct. 1952

ABU SIMBEL, Egypt:
Abu Simbel's Ancient Temples Reborn. By Georg Gerster. 724-744, May 1969
Saving the Ancient Temples at Abu Simbel. By Georg Gerster. Paintings by Robert W. Nicholson. 694-742, May 1966
Threatened Treasures of the Nile. By Georg Gerster. 587-621, Oct. 1963

ABUNDANT Life in a Desert Land. By Walter Meayers Edwards. 424-436, Sept. 1973

ACADIA (Parish), Louisiana:
Cajunland, Louisiana's French-speaking Coast. By Bern Keating. Photos by Charles Harbutt and Franke Keating. 353-391, Mar. 1966

ACAPULCO, Mexico:
Mexico in Motion. By Bart McDowell. Photos by Kip Ross. 490-537, Oct. 1961
A New Riviera: Mexico's West Coast. By Nathaniel T. Kenney. Photos by Charles O'Rear. 670-699, Nov. 1973
The Two Acapulcos. By James Cerruti. Photos by Thomas Nebbia. 848-878, Dec. 1964

ACROPOLIS, Athens:
Athens: Her Golden Past Still Lights the World. By Kenneth F. Weaver. Photos by Phillip Harrington. 100-137, July 1963

ACROSS Canada by Mackenzie's Track. By Ralph Gray. 191-239, Aug. 1955

ACROSS the Alps in a Wicker Basket. By Phil Walker. 117-131, Jan. 1963

ACROSS the Frozen Desert to Byrd Station. By Paul W. Frazier. Photos by Calvin L. Larsen. 383-398, Sept. 1957

ACROSS the Potomac From Washington. By Albert W. Atwood. 1-33, Jan. 1953

ACROSS the Ridgepole of the Alps. By Walter Meayers Edwards. 410-419, Sept. 1960

ADAMS, ABIGAIL:
Patriots in Petticoats. By Lonnelle Aikman. Paintings by Louis S. Glanzman. 475-493, Oct. 1975

ADAMS, JOHN:
The Living White House. By Lonnelle Aikman. 593-643, Nov. 1966
Patriots in Petticoats. By Lonnelle Aikman. Paintings by Louis S. Glanzman. 475-493, Oct. 1975
Profiles of the Presidents: I. The Presidency and How It Grew. By Frank Freidel. 642-687, Nov. 1964

ADAMS, JOHN QUINCY:
The Living White House. By Lonnelle Aikman. 593-643, Nov. 1966
Profiles of the Presidents: I. The Presidency and How It Grew. By Frank Freidel. 642-687, Nov. 1964

ADAMS, SAMUEL:
Firebrands of the Revolution. By Eric F. Goldman. Photos by George F. Mobley. 2-27, July 1974

ADAMS FAMILY:
Literary Landmarks of Massachusetts. By William H. Nicholas. Photos by B. Anthony Stewart and John E. Fletcher. 279-310, Mar. 1950

ADDIS ABABA, Ethiopia:

Ethiopian Adventure. By Nathaniel T. Kenney. Photos by James P. Blair. 548-582, Apr. 1965

ADELAIDE, South Australia:

South Australia, Gateway to the Great Outback. By Howell Walker. Photos by Joseph J. Scherschel. 441-481, Apr. 1970

ADEN PROTECTORATE, now Democratic Yemen:

Along the Storied Incense Roads of Aden. By Hermann F. Eilts. Photos by Brian Brake. 230-254, Feb. 1957

Sailing with Sindbad's Sons. By Alan Villiers. 675-688, Nov. 1948

ADENA CULTURE. *See* Mound Builders

ADIRONDACK MOUNTAINS, New York:

My Backyard, the Adirondacks. By Anne LaBastille. Photos by David Alan Harvey. 616-639, May 1975

ADMIRAL of the Ends of the Earth. By Melville Bell Grosvenor. 36-48, July 1957

ADOBE New Mexico. By Mason Sutherland. Photos by Justin Locke. 783-830, Dec. 1949

"THE ADORATION OF THE MAGI," painting supplement. Jan. 1952

ADRIATIC REGION. *See* Trieste; Venice; Yugoslavia

ADRIFT on a Raft of Sargassum. Photos by Robert F. Sisson. 188-199, Feb. 1976

ADVENTURES in Lololand. By Rennold L. Lowy. 105-118, Jan. 1947

ADVENTURES in the Search for Man. By Louis S. B. Leakey. Photos by Hugo van Lawick. 132-152, Jan. 1963

ADVENTURES With South Africa's Black Eagles. By Jeanne Cowden. Photos by author and Arthur Bowland. 533-543, Oct. 1969

ADVENTURES with the Survey Navy. By Irving Johnson. 131-148, July 1947

ADVENTURING Along the South's Surprising Coast: Sea Islands. By James Cerruti. Photos by Thomas Nebbia and James L. Amos. 366-393, Mar. 1971

AEGEAN ISLANDS:

The Aegean Isles: Poseidon's Playground. By Gilbert M. Grosvenor. 733-781, Dec. 1958

Classical Lands of the Mediterranean, map supplement. Dec. 1949

Greece and the Aegean, Atlas series supplement. Dec. 1958

The Isles of Greece: Aegean Birthplace of Western Culture. By Melville Bell Grosvenor. Photos by Edwin Stuart Grosvenor and Winfield Parks. 147-193, Aug. 1972

On the Winds of the Dodecanese. By Jean and Franc Shor. 351-390, Mar. 1953

See also Thera

AEGEAN REGION. *See* Aegean Islands; Greece; Turkey

AEGEAN SEA:

New Tools for Undersea Archeology. By George F.

AEGEAN SEA—*Continued*

Bass. Photos by Charles R. Nicklin, Jr. 403-423, Sept. 1968

Thirty-three Centuries Under the Sea. By Peter Throckmorton. 682-703, May 1960

Underwater Archeology: Key to History's Warehouse. By George F. Bass. Photos by Thomas J. Abercrombie and Robert B. Goodman. 138-156, July 1963

AEPYORNIS (Extinct Bird):

Madagascar: Island at the End of the Earth. By Luis Marden. Photos by Albert Moldvay. 443-487, Oct. 1967

Re-creating Madagascar's Giant Extinct Bird. By Alexander Wetmore. 488-493, Oct. 1967

AERODYNAMICS. *See* Aeronautics; Wind-power Research

AERONAUTICS:

Alexander Graham Bell Museum: Tribute to Genius. By Jean Lesage. 227-256, Aug. 1956

Fact Finding for Tomorrow's Planes. By Hugh L. Dryden. Photos by Luis Marden. 757-780, Dec. 1953

Flying in the "Blowtorch" Era. By Frederick G. Vosburgh. 281-322, Sept. 1950

Happy Birthday, Otto Lilienthal! By Russell Hawkes. Photos by James Collison. 286-292, Feb. 1972

Our Air Age Speeds Ahead. By F. Barrows Colton. 249-272, Feb. 1948

Sailors of the Sky. By Gordon Young. Photos by Emory Kristof and Jack Fields. Paintings by Davis Meltzer. 49-73, Jan. 1967

See also Aviation; Balloons

AF CHAPMAN (Youth Hostel Ship):

Thumbs Up Round the North Sea's Rim. By Frances James. Photos by Erica Koch. 685-704, May 1952

AFAR TRIBE. *See* Danakil

AFGHANISTAN:

Afghanistan: Crossroad of Conquerors. By Thomas J. Abercrombie. 297-345, Sept. 1968

American Family in Afghanistan. By Rebecca Shannon Cresson. Photos by Osborne C. Cresson. 417-432, Sept. 1953

Bold Horsemen of the Steppes. By Sabrina and Roland Michaud. 634-669, Nov. 1973

In the Footsteps of Alexander the Great. By Helen and Frank Schreider. Paintings by Tom Lovell. 1-65, Jan. 1968

Sky Road East. By Tay and Lowell Thomas, Jr. 71-112, Jan. 1960

We Took the Highroad in Afghanistan. By Jean and Franc Shor. 673-706, Nov. 1950

West from the Khyber Pass. By William O. Douglas. Photos by Mercedes H. Douglas and author. 1-44, July 1958

When the President Goes Abroad (Eisenhower Tour). By Gilbert M. Grosvenor. 588-649, May 1960

Winter Caravan to the Roof of the World. By Sabrina and Roland Michaud. 435-465, Apr. 1972

AFO-A-KOM: A Sacred Symbol Comes Home. By William S. Ellis. Photos by James P. Blair. 141-148, July 1974

ALLMON, CHARLES: Author-Photographer—*Continued*

Shores and Sails in the South Seas (Marquesas Islands). 73-104, Jan. 1950

Photographer

Bermuda, Cradled in Warm Seas. By Beverley M. Bowie. 203-238, Feb. 1954

Martinique: A Tropical Bit of France. By Gwen Drayton Allmon. 255-283, Feb. 1959

Rubber-cushioned Liberia. By Henry S. Villard. 201-228, Feb. 1948

Spectacular Rio de Janeiro. By Hernane Tavares de Sá. 289-328, Mar. 1955

Virgin Islands: Tropical Playland, U.S.A. By John Scofield. 201-232, Feb. 1956

The *Yankee's* Wander-world. By Irving and Electa Johnson. 1-50, Jan. 1949

ALLMON, GWEN DRAYTON: Author:

Martinique: A Tropical Bit of France. Photos by Charles Allmon. 255-283, Feb. 1959

ALLYN, RUBE: Author:

Cruising Florida's Western Waterways. Photos by Bates Littlehales. 49-76, Jan. 1955

ALONE to Antarctica. By David Lewis. Drawings by Noel Sickles. 808-821, Dec. 1973

ALONG the Post Road Today. Photos by B. Anthony Stewart. 206-233, Aug. 1962

ALONG the Storied Incense Roads of Aden. By Hermann F. Eilts. Photos by Brian Brake. 230-254, Feb. 1957

ALONG the Yangtze, Main Street of China. By W. Robert Moore. 325-356, Mar. 1948

ALONG the Yukon Trail. By Amos Burg. 395-416, Sept. 1953

ALPS (Mountains), Europe:

Across the Alps in a Wicker Basket *(Bernina).* By Phil Walker. 117-131, Jan. 1963

Across the Ridgepole of the Alps. By Walter Meayers Edwards. 410-419, Sept. 1960
Included: Map of cableway between Chamonix, France, and La Palud, Italy

The Alps. Special Publication announced. 870-874, June 1972

The Alps—Europe's Backbone, double-sided Atlas series supplement. Sept. 1965

The Alps: Man's Own Mountains. By Ralph Gray. Photos by Walter Meayers Edwards and William Eppridge. 350-395, Sept. 1965
Included: Map of world's longest highway tunnel, Mont Blanc

The Great St. Bernard Hospice Today. By George Pickow. 49-62, Jan. 1957

Occupied Austria, Outpost of Democracy. By George W. Long. Photos by Volkmar Wentzel. 749-790, June 1951

Sheep Trek in the French Alps. By Maurice Moyal. Photos by Marcel Coen. 545-564, Apr. 1952

Soaring on Skis in the Swiss Alps. By Carolyn Bennett Patterson. Photos by Kathleen Revis. 94-121, Jan. 1961

Surprising Switzerland. By Jean and Franc Shor. 427-478, Oct. 1956

Switzerland, Europe's High-rise Republic. By Thomas J. Abercrombie. 68-113, July 1969

ALPS (Mountains), Europe—*Continued*

Switzerland Guards the Roof of Europe. By William H. Nicholas. Photos by Willard R. Culver. 205-246, Aug. 1950

See also Bavaria; Dolomites; Saint Véran; Salzkammergut; Tirol; Val d'Hérens

ALUMINUM:

Kitimat—Canada's Aluminum Titan. By David S. Boyer. 376-398, Sept. 1956

AL 'UQAYR, Saudi Arabia. *See* Gerrha

ALVIN (Research Submersible):

Project FAMOUS. 586-615, May 1975
I. Where the Earth Turns Inside Out. By J. R. Heirtzler. Photos by Emory Kristof. 586-603
II. Dive Into the Great Rift. By Robert D. Ballard. Photos by Emory Kristof. 604-615

Window on Earth's Interior. By Robert D. Ballard. Photos by Emory Kristof. 228-249, Aug. 1976

AMA, Sea Nymphs of Japan. By Luis Marden. 122-135, July 1971

AMA DABLAM (Mountain), Nepal:

Wintering on the Roof of the World. By Barry C. Bishop. 503-547, Oct. 1962

AMALFI, Italy's Divine Coast. By Luis Marden. 472-509, Oct. 1959

AMANA COLONIES, Iowa:

Iowa's Enduring Amana Colonies. By Laura Longley Babb. Photos by Steve Raymer. 863-878, Dec. 1975

AMARNATH CAVE, Kashmir:

Himalayan Pilgrimage. By Christopher Rand. 520-535, Oct. 1956

AMATEUR Gardener Creates a New Rose. By Elizabeth A. Moize. Photos by Farrell Grehan. 286-294, Aug. 1972

AMAZON BASIN INDIANS:

Amazon—The River Sea. By Loren McIntyre. 456-495, Oct. 1972

See also Cinta Larga; Erigbaagtsa; Kraho; Kreen-Akarores; Machiguenga; Suyá; Tchikao; Tukuna; Txukahameis; Waurá

AMAZON RIVER REGION, South America:

The Amazon. Photos by Loren McIntyre. 445-455, Oct. 1972

Amazon (Television film). 295A-295B, Feb. 1968

Amazon—The River Sea. By Loren McIntyre. 456-495, Oct. 1972

Exploring the Amazon. Special Publication announced. 880-884, June 1969

Giant Insects of the Amazon. By Paul A. Zahl. 632-669, May 1959

Jungle Jaunt on Amazon Headwaters. By Bernice M. Goetz. 371-388, Sept. 1952

Sea Fever. By John E. Schultz. 237-268, Feb. 1949

See also Brazil

AMBASSADORS of Good Will: The Peace Corps. By Sargent Shriver and Peace Corps Volunteers. 297-345, Sept. 1964

AMBER:

Exploring the World of Gems. By W. F. Foshag. 779-810, Dec. 1950

AMUSEMENT PARKS. *See* Disneyland; Tivoli; Walt Disney World

AN LAC, Viet Nam:

Viet Nam's Montagnards. By Howard Sochurek. 443-487, Apr. 1968

ANASAZI (Indians):

Ancient Cliff Dwellers of Mesa Verde. By Don Watson. Photos by Willard R. Culver. 349-376, Sept. 1948

Searching for Cliff Dwellers' Secrets. By Carroll A. Burroughs. 619-625, Nov. 1959

Solving the Riddles of Wetherill Mesa. By Douglas Osborne. Paintings by Peter V. Bianchi. 155-195, Feb. 1964

Your Society to Seek New Light on the Cliff Dwellers. 154-156, Jan. 1959

ANATOLIA (Region), Turkey:

Ancient Aphrodisias and Its Marble Treasures. By Kenan T. Erim. Photos by Jonathan S. Blair. 280-294, Aug. 1967

Aphrodisias, Awakened City of Ancient Art. By Kenan T. Erim. Photos by Jonathan Blair. 766-791, June 1972

Keeping House in a Cappadocian Cave. By Jonathan S. Blair. 127-146, July 1970

Peasants of Anatolia. By Alfred Marchionini. 57-72, July 1948

ANCHORAGE, Alaska:

An Alaskan Family's Night of Terror (Earthquake). By Tay Pryor Thomas. 142-156, July 1964

Earthquake! By William P. E. Graves. 112-139, July 1964

ANCIENT Aphrodisias and Its Marble Treasures. By Kenan T. Erim. Photos by Jonathan S. Blair. 280-294, Aug. 1967

ANCIENT Cliff Dwellers of Mesa Verde. By Don Watson. Photos by Willard R. Culver. 349-376, Sept. 1948

ANCIENT Mesopotamia: A Light That Did Not Fail. By E. A. Speiser. Paintings by H. M. Herget. 41-105, Jan. 1951

ANCIENT Shipwreck Yields New Facts—and a Strange Cargo. By Peter Throckmorton. Photos by Kim Hart and Joseph J. Scherschel. 282-300, Feb. 1969

ANCIENT "Skyscrapers" of the Yemen. Photos by Richard H. Sanger. 645-668, Nov. 1947

AND Now to Touch the Moon's Forbidding Face. By Kenneth F. Weaver. 633-635, May 1969

ANDALUSIA (Region), Spain:

Andalusia, the Spirit of Spain. By Howard La Fay. Photos by Joseph J. Scherschel. 833-857, June 1975

The Changing Face of Old Spain. By Bart McDowell. Photos by Albert Moldvay. 291-339, Mar. 1965

Gypsy Cave Dwellers of Andalusia. 572-582, Oct. 1957

Holy Week and the Fair in Sevilla. By Luis Marden. 499-530, Apr. 1951

Speaking of Spain. By Luis Marden. 415-456, Apr. 1950

ANDAMAN ISLANDS, India:

The Last Andaman Islanders. By Raghubir Singh. 66-91, July 1975

ANDEAN CONDORS:

The Condor, Soaring Spirit of the Andes. By Jerry McGahan. Photos by Libby McGahan. 684-709, May 1971

ANDEREGG, FRED: Photographer:

Mount Sinai's Holy Treasures (St. Catherine's Monastery). By Kurt Weitzmann. 109-127, Jan. 1964

ANDERS, WILLIAM A.:

Hubbard Medal recipient. 861, June 1970

"A Most Fantastic Voyage": The Story of Apollo 8's Rendezvous With the Moon. By Sam C. Phillips. 593-631, May 1969

ANDERSON, GEORGE W., Jr.: Author:

Our Nuclear Navy. 449-450, Mar. 1963

ANDERSON, NIKE: Author:

October Holiday on the Outer Banks. Photos by J. Baylor Roberts. 501-529, Oct. 1955

ANDERSON, RON J.: Author:

The Kiwi, New Zealand's Wonder Bird. 395-398, Sept. 1955

ANDERSON, STEWART: Author-Photographer:

The West Through Boston Eyes. 733-776, June 1949

ANDERSON, WILLIAM R.:

Submarine Through the North Pole. By William G. Lalor, Jr. Photos by John J. Krawczyk. 1-20, Jan. 1959

Author

The Arctic as a Sea Route of the Future. 21-24, Jan. 1959

ANDES (Mountains), South America:

At Home in the High Andes. By Harry Tschopik, Jr. 133-146, Jan. 1955

Avalanche! (Peru). By Bart McDowell. Photos by John E. Fletcher. 855-880, June 1962

El Sangay, Fire-breathing Giant of the Andes. By G. Edward Lewis. 117-138, Jan. 1950

In Quest of the Rarest Flamingo. By William G. Conway. Photos by Bates Littlehales. 91-105, July 1961

Parks, Plans, and People: How South America Guards Her Green Legacy. By Mary and Laurance Rockefeller. Photos by George F. Mobley. 74-119, Jan. 1967

Included: Christ of the Andes; Lake District; Moreno Glacier; Mount Aconcagua; Nahuel Huapí National Park

Peru, Homeland of the Warlike Inca. By Kip Ross. 421-462, Oct. 1950

Puya, the Pineapple's Andean Ancestor. By Mulford B. Foster. 463-480, Oct. 1950

Sky-high Bolivia. 481-496, Oct. 1950

To Torre Egger's Icy Summit. By Jim Donini. 813-823, Dec. 1976

ANDORRA:

The Enduring Pyrenees. By Robert Laxalt. Photos by Edwin Stuart Grosvenor. 794-819, Dec. 1974

ANTIGUA (Island), West Indies:

A Fresh Breeze Stirs the Leewards. By Carleton Mitchell. Photos by Winfield Parks. 488-537, Oct. 1966

ANTILLES, Greater. *See* Cuba; Haiti; Jamaica; Puerto Rico

ANTILLES, Lesser. *See* Barbados; Leeward Islands; Martinique; Netherlands Antilles; Tobago; Trinidad; Virgin Islands; Windward Islands

ANTI-LOCUST RESEARCH CENTRE, London:

Locusts: "Teeth of the Wind." By Robert A. M. Conley. Photos by Gianni Tortoli. 202-227, Aug. 1969

ANTIOCHUS I, King (Commagene):

Throne Above the Euphrates. By Theresa Goell. 390-405, Mar. 1961

ANTS:

At Home With the Bulldog Ant. By Robert F. Sisson. 62-75, July 1974
Face-to-Face With a World of Ants. 72-75

The Enigma of Bird Anting. By Hance Roy Ivor. 105-119, July 1956

Living Honey Jars of the Ant World. By Ross E. Hutchins. 405-411, Mar. 1962

ANTZE, PAUL: Author:

Round the World School. Photos by William Eppridge. 96-127, July 1962

APARTHEID:

The Zulus: Black Nation in a Land of Apartheid. By Joseph Judge. Photos by Dick Durrance II. 738-775, Dec. 1971

APES:

The Ape (Gibbon) With Friends in Washington. By Margaretta Burr Wells. 61-74, July 1953

Monkeys, Apes, and Man (Television film). 585A-585B, Oct. 1971

Search for the Great Apes (Television film). cover, Jan. 1976

See also Chimpanzees; Gorillas; Orangutans

APHIDS:

Following the Ladybug Home. By Kenneth S. Hagen. Photos by Robert F. Sisson. 543-553, Apr. 1970

Rose Aphids. By Treat Davidson. 851-859, June 1961

APHRODISIAS (Ancient City), Asia Minor:

Ancient Aphrodisias and Its Marble Treasures. By Kenan T. Erim. Photos by Jonathan S. Blair. 280-294, Aug. 1967

Aphrodisias, Awakened City of Ancient Art. By Kenan T. Erim. Photos by Jonathan Blair. 766-791, June 1972

APOLLO MISSIONS:

And Now to Touch the Moon's Forbidding Face. By Kenneth F. Weaver. 633-635, May 1969

Apollo 15 Explores the Mountains of the Moon. By Kenneth F. Weaver. Photos from NASA. 233-265, Feb. 1972

Apollo Missions. 289-331, Sept. 1973
I. Summing Up Mankind's Greatest Adventure. By Gilbert M. Grosvenor. 289

APOLLO MISSIONS—*Continued*

II. Exploring Taurus-Littrow. By Harrison H. Schmitt. Photos by the crew of Apollo 17. 290-307
III. Have We Solved the Mysteries of the Moon? By Kenneth F. Weaver. Paintings by William H. Bond. 309-325
IV. What Is It Like to Walk on the Moon? By David R. Scott. 326-331
V. "Teammates in Mankind's Greatest Adventure," painting supplement

Apollo 16 Brings Us Visions From Space (Photos). 856-865, Dec. 1972

The Climb Up Cone Crater (Apollo 14). By Alice J. Hall. Photos by Edgar D. Mitchell and Alan B. Shepard, Jr. 136-148, July 1971

First Explorers on the Moon: The Incredible Story of Apollo 11. 735-797, Dec. 1969
I. Man Walks on Another World. By Neil A. Armstrong, Edwin E. Aldrin, Jr., and Michael Collins. 738-749
II. Sounds of the Space Age, From Sputnik to Lunar Landing. A record narrated by Frank Borman. 750-751
III. The Flight of Apollo 11: "One giant leap for mankind." By Kenneth F. Weaver. 752-787
IV. What the Moon Rocks Tell Us. By Kenneth F. Weaver. 788-791

First Moon Explorers (Apollo 11) Receive the Society's Hubbard Medal. 859-861, June 1970
Included: Previous presentation of medal to Apollo 8 astronauts

Footprints on the Moon. By Hugh L. Dryden. Paintings by Davis Meltzer and Pierre Mion. 357-401, Mar. 1964

The Making of an Astronaut. By Robert R. Gilruth. 122-144, Jan. 1965

"A Most Fantastic Voyage": The Story of Apollo 8's Rendezvous With the Moon. By Sam C. Phillips. 593-631, May 1969

APOLLO-SOYUZ MISSION:

Apollo-Soyuz: Handclasp in Space. By Thomas Y. Canby. 183-187, Feb. 1976

APPALACHIA, U. S.:

Appalachian Valley Pilgrimage. By Catherine Bell Palmer. Photos by Justin Locke. 1-32, July 1949

The People of Cumberland Gap. By John Fetterman. Photos by Bruce Dale. 591-621, Nov. 1971

See also Cades Cove, Tennessee; West Virginia

APPALACHIAN MOUNTAINS, U. S.:

Skyline Trail from Maine to Georgia. By Andrew H. Brown. Photos by Robert F. Sisson. 219-251, Aug. 1949

See also Adirondack Mountains; Berkshires; Blue Ridge Mountains; Cumberland Country; Great Smoky Mountains; Green Mountains; White Mountains

APPALACHIAN TRAIL, U. S.:

The Appalachian Trail. Special Publication announced. 870-874, June 1972

Pack Trip Through the Smokies. By Val Hart. Photos by Robert F. Sisson. 473-502, Oct. 1952

Skyline Trail from Maine to Georgia. By Andrew H. Brown. Photos by Robert F. Sisson. 219-251, Aug. 1949

APPEL, FREDRIC C.: Author:

The Coming Revolution in Transportation. Photos by Dean Conger. 301-341, Sept. 1969

ARMADA. *See* Spanish Armada

ARMAGEDDON. *See* Megiddo, Israel

ARMSTRONG, NEIL A.:

First Explorers on the Moon: The Incredible Story of Apollo 11. 735-797, Dec. 1969
  I. Man Walks on Another World. By Neil A. Armstrong, Edwin E. Aldrin, Jr., and Michael Collins. 738-749
  II. Sounds of the Space Age, From Sputnik to Lunar Landing. A record narrated by Frank Borman. 750-751
  III. The Flight of Apollo 11: "One giant leap for mankind." By Kenneth F. Weaver. 752-787

First Moon Explorers (Apollo 11) Receive the Society's Hubbard Medal. 859-861, June 1970

ARNHEM LAND, Australia:

An Arnhem Land Adventure. By Donald F. Thomson. 403-430, Mar. 1948
  Arnhem Land Expedition of 1948. 430

Cruise to Stone Age Arnhem Land. By Howell Walker. 417-430, Sept. 1949

Exploring Stone Age Arnhem Land. By Charles P. Mountford. Photos by Howell Walker. 745-782, Dec. 1949

From Spear to Hoe on Groote Eylandt. By Howell Walker. 131-142, Jan. 1953

The Top End of Down Under. By Kenneth Mac-Leish. Photos by Thomas Nebbia. 145-174, Feb. 1973

ARNO (River), Italy:

Florence Rises From the Flood. By Joseph Judge. 1-43, July 1967

ARNOLD, DAVID L.: Photographer:

Yesterday Lingers Along the Connecticut. By Charles McCarry. 334-369, Sept. 1972

ARNOLD, HENRY H.:

Fledgling Wings of the Air Force. By Thomas W. McKnew. 266-271, Aug. 1957

Giant Effigies of the Southwest. By George C. Marshall. 389, Sept. 1952

Memorial Tribute to General of the Air Force H. H. Arnold. 400, Mar. 1950
Author

My Life in the Valley of the Moon. Photos by Willard R. Culver. 689-716, Dec. 1948

Wildlife In and Near the Valley of the Moon. Photos by Paul J. Fair. 401-414, Mar. 1950

ARNOLD, RUDY: Photographer:

Flying in the "Blowtorch" Era. By Frederick G. Vosburgh. 281-322, Sept. 1950

AROOSTOOK COUNTY, Maine, Source of Potatoes. By Howell Walker. 459-478, Oct. 1948

AROUND the "Great Lakes of the South." By Frederick Simpich. Photos by J. Baylor Roberts. 463-491, Apr. 1948

AROUND the World and the Calendar with the Geographic: The President's Annual Message. By Melville Bell Grosvenor. 832-866, Dec. 1959

"**AROUND** the World in Eighty Days." By Newman Bumstead. 705-750, Dec. 1951

ARRAN, Island of, Scotland:

Home to Arran, Scotland's Magic Isle. By J. Harvey Howells. 80-99, July 1965

ARROWS Speak Louder Than Words: The Last Andaman Islanders. By Raghubir Singh. 66-91, July 1975

ARROWSMITH, AARON:

Eight Maps of Discovery. 757-769, June 1953
  Included: George Washington's Travels, Traced on the Arrowsmith Map

ART. *See* Cave Art; Folk Art; Greek Art; Japanese Art; Mosaics; Painting Supplements; Renaissance; Rock Paintings; Sculpture; *and* Capitol, U. S.; Corcoran Gallery of Art; Hearst San Simeon State Historical Monument; Henry E. Huntington Library and Art Gallery; Hermitage; Kunsthistorisches Museum; The Louvre; National Gallery of Art; St. Catherine's Monastery; *and* Minoan Civilization; Pre-Hispanic Culture

ART RESTORATION:

Florence Rises From the Flood. By Joseph Judge. 1-43, July 1967

Venice Fights for Life. By Joseph Judge. Photos by Albert Moldvay. 591-631, Nov. 1972
  Venice's Golden Legacy. Photos by Victor R. Boswell, Jr. 609-619

ARTHUR, CHESTER A.:

Inside the White House. By Lonnelle Aikman. Photos by B. Anthony Stewart and Thomas Nebbia. 3-43, Jan. 1961

Profiles of the Presidents: III. The American Giant Comes of Age. By Frank Freidel. 660-711, May 1965

ARTISANS:

Gold, the Eternal Treasure. By Peter T. White. Photos by James L. Stanfield. 1-51, Jan. 1974
  Golden Masterpieces. 29-39

Human Treasures of Japan. By William Graves. Photos by James L. Stanfield. 370-379, Sept. 1972
  Contents: Ironcaster, Kabuki actor, Lacquer artist, Swordsmith, Wood sculptor

ARTISTS:

American Masters in the National Gallery. By John Walker. 295-324, Sept. 1948
  Contents: George Bellows, Mary Cassatt, William Merritt Chase, John Singleton Copley, Thomas Eakins, Chester Harding, Childe Hassam, Winslow Homer, George Inness, Rembrandt Peale, John Quidor, Edward Savage, Christian Schussele, Gilbert Stuart, Thomas Sully, James Abbott McNeill Whistler

American Processional: History on Canvas. By John and Blanche Leeper. 173-212, Feb. 1951
  Contents: John and Victor Audubon, George Caleb Bingham, David G. Blythe, James E. Butterworth, James H. Cafferty, Conrad Wise Chapman, John Singleton Copley, Robert Dudley, Thomas Eakins, J. G. Evans, Ambroise Louis Garneray, Henry Gilder, William Hahn, George Peter Alexander Healy, Winslow Homer, Thomas Hovenden, Frederick Kemmelmeyer, Edward Moran, Linton Park, Charles Willson Peale, Adrian Persac, Frederick Remington, C. Riess, Charles G. Rosenberg, John Searle, Dominique Serres, John Stevens, Louis Comfort Tiffany, John Trumbull, Charles F. Ulrich, Benjamin West

America's First Painters: Indians. By Dorothy Dunn. 349-377, Mar. 1955

Artists Look at Pennsylvania. By John Oliver La Gorce. 37-56, July 1948
  Contents: Aaron Bohrod, Adolf Dehn, Ernest Fiene, William Gropper, Fletcher Martin, Hobson Pittman, Paul Sample

ASTRONAUTS. *See* Apollo Missions; Apollo-Soyuz Mission; Gemini Missions; Mercury Missions; Skylab Missions

ASTRONOMY:

The Amazing Universe. Special Publication announced. 870-874, June 1975

Completing the Atlas of the Universe (National Geographic Society-Palomar Observatory Sky Survey). By Ira Sprague Bowen. 185-190, Aug. 1955
  Sky Survey Plates Unlock Secrets of the Stars. 186-187

Current Scientific Projects of the National Geographic Society. 143-144, July 1953
  Included: Cosmic ray research; Sky Survey

Exploring the Farthest Reaches of Space. By George O. Abell. 782-790, Dec. 1956

First Color Portraits of the Heavens. By William C. Miller. 670-679, May 1959

First Photographs of Planets and Moon Taken with Palomar's 200-inch Telescope. By Milton L. Humason. 125-130, Jan. 1953

The Incredible Universe. By Kenneth F. Weaver. Photos by James P. Blair. 589-625, May 1974
  Pioneers in Man's Search for the Universe. Paintings by Jean-Leon Huens. Text by Thomas Y. Canby. 627-633
    Contents: Seven men who solved riddles of the cosmos: Nicolaus Copernicus, Albert Einstein, Galileo Galilei, William Herschel, Edwin Hubble, Johannes Kepler, Isaac Newton

A Map of the Heavens, map supplement. Star charts on reverse. Dec. 1957

Map of the Heavens, map supplement. Star charts on reverse. Aug. 1970

Mapping the Unknown Universe. By F. Barrows Colton. 401-420, Sept. 1950

Our Universe Unfolds New Wonders (National Geographic-Palomar Sky Survey). By Albert G. Wilson. 245-260, Feb. 1952

Sky Survey Charts the Universe. By Ira Sprague Bowen. 780-781, Dec. 1956

Split-second Time Runs Today's World. By F. Barrows Colton and Catherine Bell Palmer. 399-428, Sept. 1947

Twelve National Geographic Society Scientific Projects Under Way. 869-870, June 1954
  Included: Aurora Borealis; Cosmic rays; Mars expedition; Sky Survey; Zodiacal light observations

See also Aurora Borealis; Comets; Moon; Planets; Stars; Sun

ASTRONOMY, Ancient. *See* Calendars (The Maya); Stonehenge

ASTROPHYSICS:

The Sun. By Herbert Friedman. 713-743, Nov. 1965

ASWÂN HIGH DAM, Nile River:

Threatened Treasures of the Nile. By Georg Gerster. 587-621, Oct. 1963

Yankee Cruises the Storied Nile. By Irving and Electa Johnson. Photos by Winfield Parks. 583-633, May 1965

AT Home in the High Andes. By Harry Tschopik, Jr. 133-146, Jan. 1955

AT Home in the Sea. By Jacques-Yves Cousteau. 465-507, Apr. 1964

AT Home With Right Whales. By Roger Payne. Photos by Des and Jen Bartlett. 322-339, Mar. 1976

AT Home With the Bulldog Ant. By Robert F. Sisson. 62-75, July 1974

AT World's End in Hunza. By Jean and Franc Shor. 485-518, Oct. 1953

ATACAMA DESERT, Chile:

Chile, Republic on a Shoestring. By Gordon Young. Photos by George F. Mobley. 437-477, Oct. 1973

ATATÜRK, KEMAL:

Turkey Paves the Path of Progress. By Maynard Owen Williams. 141-186, Aug. 1951

Yankee Cruises Turkey's History-haunted Coast. By Irving and Electa Johnson. Photos by Joseph J. Scherschel. 798-845, Dec. 1969

ATEN TEMPLE. *See* Akhenaten Temple Project

ATHAPASCAN LINGUISTIC STOCK:

Nomads of the Far North. By Matthew W. Stirling. 471-504, Oct. 1949
  Hearty Folk Defy Arctic Storms. Paintings by W. Langdon Kihn. 479-494

ATHENS, Greece:

"Around the World in Eighty Days." By Newman Bumstead. 705-750, Dec. 1951

Athens: Her Golden Past Still Lights the World. By Kenneth F. Weaver. Photos by Phillip Harrington. 100-137, July 1963

Athens to Istanbul. By Jean and Franc Shor. 37-76, Jan. 1956

Erosion, Trojan Horse of Greece. By F. G. Renner. 793-812, Dec. 1947

The Tower of the Winds. By Derek J. de Solla Price. Paintings by Robert C. Magis. 587-596, Apr. 1967

War-torn Greece Looks Ahead. By Maynard Owen Williams. 711-744, Dec. 1949

ATITLÁN, Lake, Guatemala:

Guatemala Revisited. By Luis Marden. 525-564, Oct. 1947

ATKA (Island), Alaska:

Atka, Rugged Home of My Aleut Friends. By Lael Morgan. 572-583, Oct. 1974

ATKESON, RAY: Photographer:

From Sagebrush to Roses on the Columbia. By Leo A. Borah. 571-611, Nov. 1952

ATKINSON, AGNES AKIN: Author:

Br'er Possum, Hermit of the Lowlands. Photos by Charles Philip Fox. 405-418, Mar. 1953

ATLANTA, Georgia:

Atlanta, Pacesetter City of the South. By William S. Ellis. Photos by James L. Amos. 246-281, Feb. 1969

The Greener Fields of Georgia. By Howell Walker. Photos by author and B. Anthony Stewart. 287-330, Mar. 1954

ATLANTIC COAST, U. S.:

Can We Save Our Salt Marshes? By Stephen W. Hitchcock. Photos by William R. Curtsinger. 729-765, June 1972

Our Changing Atlantic Coastline. By Nathaniel T.

B

BACKER, OLE FRIELE: Author-Photographer:
Seal Hunting Off Jan Mayen. 57-72, Jan. 1948
Photographer
Norway Cracks Her Mountain Shell. By Sydney Clark. Photos by Gilbert Grosvenor and Ole Friele Backer. 171-211, Aug. 1948

BACKER, WILLIAM SLADE: Author:
Down the Danube by Canoe. Photos by Richard S. Durrance and Christopher G. Knight. 34-79, July 1965

BACKPACK TRIPS:
Hiking the Backbone of the Rockies: Canada's Great Divide Trail. By Mike W. Edwards. Photos by Lowell Georgia. 795-817, June 1973
Mexico to Canada on the Pacific Crest Trail. By Mike W. Edwards. Photos by David Hiser. 741-779, June 1971
Yellowstone at 100: A Walk Through the Wilderness. By Karen and Derek Craighead. Photos by Sam Abell. 579-603, May 1972

BACKWOODS Japan During American Occupation. By M. A. Huberman. 491-518, Apr. 1947

BACON, EDMUND N.: Author:
Five Noted Thinkers Explore the Future. 74, July 1976

BAD Days for the Brown Pelican. By Ralph W. Schreiber. Photos by William R. Curtsinger and author. 111-123, Jan. 1975

BADDECK, Nova Scotia, Canada:
Canada's Winged Victory: the *Silver Dart*. By Gilbert M. Grosvenor. 254-267, Aug. 1959
Down East to Nova Scotia. By Winfield Parks. 853-879, June 1964
Miracle Men of the Telephone. By F. Barrows Colton. 273-316, Mar. 1947
Included: Photographs of Dr. Alexander Graham Bell and members of his family at their home in Baddeck
See also Bell Museum

BADLANDS, North Dakota:
North Dakota Comes into Its Own. By Leo A. Borah. Photos by J. Baylor Roberts. 283-322, Sept. 1951

BADLANDS, South Dakota:
Big Game Hunting (Paleontology) in the Land of Long Ago. By Joseph P. Connolly and James D. Bump. 589-605, May 1947
South Dakota Keeps Its West Wild. By Frederick Simpich. 555-588, May 1947
The West Through Boston Eyes. By Stewart Anderson. 733-776, June 1949

BAEKELAND, G. BROOKS: Author-Photographer:
By Parachute Into Peru's Lost World. Photos by author and Peter R. Gimbel. 268-296, Aug. 1964

BAFFIN ISLAND, Northwest Territories, Canada:
Far North with "Captain Mac." By Miriam MacMillan. 465-513, Oct. 1951
Included: Brevoort Island; Pond Inlet
I Live With the Eskimos. By Guy Mary-Rousseliere. 188-217, Feb. 1971
Milestones in My Arctic Journeys. By Willie Knutsen. 543-570, Oct. 1949
Included: Airfield at Frobisher Bay and the activities of the Arctic Search and Rescue section of the Air Force

BAGGARA (People):
With the Nuba Hillmen of Kordofan. By Robin Strachan. 249-278, Feb. 1951

BAGHDAD, Iraq:
"Around the World in Eighty Days." By Newman Bumstead. 705-750, Dec. 1951
Iraq—Where Oil and Water Mix. By Jean and Franc Shor. 443-489, Oct. 1958
Station Wagon Odyssey: Baghdad to İstanbul. By William O. Douglas. 48-87, Jan. 1959

BAHAMA ISLANDS, Atlantic Ocean:
The Bahamas, Isles of the Blue-green Sea. By Carleton Mitchell. Photos by B. Anthony Stewart. 147-203, Feb. 1958
Blue-water Plankton: Ghosts of the Gulf Stream. By William M. Hamner. 530-545, Oct. 1974
Cape Canaveral's 6,000-mile Shooting Gallery. By Allan C. Fisher, Jr. Photos by Luis Marden and Thomas Nebbia. 421-471, Oct. 1959
More of Sea Than of Land: The Bahamas. By Carleton Mitchell. Photos by James L. Stanfield. 218-267, Feb. 1967
See also Abaco; Andros Island; Bimini Islands; Great Bahama Bank; Great Inagua; Nassau

BAHREIN (Island), Persian Gulf:
In Search of Arabia's Past. By Peter Bruce Cornwall. 493-522, Apr. 1948
Troubled Waters East of Suez. By Ernest M. Eller. 483-522, Apr. 1954

BAILEY, ALFRED M.: Author-Photographer:
Desert River Through Navajo Land. Photos by author and Fred G. Brandenburg. 149-172, Aug. 1947

BAIT-FISHING ANIMALS:
Aha! It Really Works! (Heron). By Robert F. Sisson. 143-147, Jan. 1974
Something's Fishy About That Fin! (Decoy Fish). Photos by Robert J. Shallenberger and William D. Madden. 224-227, Aug. 1974

BAJA CALIFORNIA (Peninsula), Mexico:
Baja California's Rugged Outback. By Michael E. Long. 543-567, Oct. 1972
Hunting the Heartbeat of a Whale. By Paul Dudley White and Samuel W. Matthews. 49-64, July 1956
Rocks, Ruts, and Sand: Driving the Mexican 1000. By Michael E. Long. 569-575, Oct. 1972
See also Raza, Isla; Scammon Lagoon

BAJAUS (People):
Sea Gypsies of the Philippines. By Anne de Henning Singh. Photos by Raghubir Singh. 659-677, May 1976

BAKER, BETTY HAYNES: Artist:
Flags of the Americas. By Elizabeth W. King. 633-657, May 1949
Flags of the United Nations. By Elizabeth W. King. 213-238, Feb. 1951

BAKER, JOHN H.: Author:
Saving Man's Wildlife Heritage. Photos by Robert F. Sisson. 581-620, Nov. 1954

BAKHTIARI (Tribespeople):

I Become a Bakhtiari. By Paul Edward Case. 325-358, Mar. 1947

BALD EAGLES, American:

Eye to Eye With Eagles. By Frederick Kent Truslow. 123-148, Jan. 1961

BALEARIC ISLANDS, Mediterranean Sea:

The Balearics Are Booming. By Jean and Franc Shor. 621-660, May 1957

Spain's Sun-blest Pleasure Isles. By Ethel A. Starbird. Photos by James A . Sugar. 679-701, May 1976

BALI (Island), Indonesia:

Bali by the Back Roads. By Donna K. and Gilbert M. Grosvenor. 657-697, Nov. 1969

Bali's Sacred Mountain Blows Its Top. Photos by Robert F. Sisson. 436-458, Sept. 1963
I. Disaster in Paradise. By Windsor P. Booth. 436-447
II. Devastated Land and Homeless People. By Samuel W. Matthews. 447-458

Indonesia, the Young and Troubled Island Nation. By Helen and Frank Schreider. 579-625, May 1961

New Guinea to Bali in *Yankee.* By Irving and Electa Johnson. 767-815, Dec. 1959

Republican Indonesia Tries Its Wings. By W. Robert Moore. 1-40, Jan. 1951

This Young Giant, Indonesia. By Beverley M. Bowie. Photos by J. Baylor Roberts. 351-392, Sept. 1955

Yankee Roams the Orient. By Irving and Electa Johnson. 327-370, Mar. 1951

The **BALKANS:**

The Balkans, Atlas series supplement. Feb. 1962

Central Europe, including the Balkan States, map supplement. Sept. 1951

See also Bulgaria; Greece; Romania; Turkey (European); Yugoslavia

BALLARD, ROBERT D.: Author:

Dive Into the Great Rift (Project FAMOUS). Photos by Emory Kristof. 604-615, May 1975

Window on Earth's Interior. Photos by Emory Kristof. 228-249, Aug. 1976

BALLERINAS in Pink. By Carleton Mitchell. Photos by B. Anthony Stewart. 553-571, Oct. 1957

BALLOONS:

Across the Alps in a Wicker Basket *(Bernina).* By Phil Walker. 117-131, Jan. 1963

Braving the Atlantic by Balloon *(Small World).* By Arnold Eiloart. 123-146, July 1959

Hot-air Balloons Race on Silent Winds. By William R. Berry. Photos by Don W. Jones. 392-407, Mar. 1966

Laboratory in a Dirty Sky. By Rudolf J. Engelmann and Vera Simons. 616-621, Nov. 1976
Contents: Project Da Vinci's manned research balloon

The Long, Lonely Leap. By Joseph W. Kittinger, Jr. Photos by Volkmar Wentzel. 854-873, Dec. 1960

Rockets Explore the Air Above Us. By Newman Bumstead. 562-580, Apr. 1957

BALLOONS— *Continued*

To 76,000 Feet by *Strato-Lab* Balloon. By Malcolm D. Ross and M. Lee Lewis. 269-282, Feb. 1957

Trailing Cosmic Rays in Canada's North. By Martin A. Pomerantz. 99-115, Jan. 1953

We Saw the World From the Edge of Space. By Malcolm D. Ross. Photos by Walter Meayers Edwards. 671-685, Nov. 1961

BALTIC Cruise of the *Caribbee.* By Carleton Mitchell. 605-646, Nov. 1950

BALTIMORE, Maryland:

Baltimore: The Hidden City. By Fred Kline. Photos by Martin Rogers. 188-215, Feb. 1975

Chesapeake Country. By Nathaniel T. Kenney. Photos by Bates Littlehales. 370-411, Sept. 1964

Maryland on the Half Shell. By Stuart E. Jones. Photos by Robert W. Madden. 188-229, Feb. 1972

Spices, the Essence of Geography. By Stuart E. Jones. 401-420, Mar. 1949
Included: McCormick and Company

See also Sherwood Gardens; Sparrows Point

BALTISTAN (Region), Kashmir:

Trek to Lofty Hunza—and Beyond. By Sabrina and Roland Michaud. 644-669, Nov. 1975

BALUCHISTAN:

Pakistan, New Nation in an Old Land. By Jean and Franc Shor. 637-678, Nov. 1952

BANARAS, India:

The Ganges, River of Faith. By John J. Putman. Photos by Raghubir Singh. 445-483, Oct. 1971

BAND, GEORGE: Photographer:

Triumph on Everest. 1-63, July 1954
I. Siege and Assault. By Sir John Hunt. 1-43
II. The Conquest of the Summit. By Sir Edmund Hillary. 45-63

BANDELIER NATIONAL MONUMENT, New Mexico:

Adobe New Mexico. By Mason Sutherland. Photos by Justin Locke. 783-830, Dec. 1949

BANDING, Bird:

Tireless Voyager, the Whistling Swan. By William J. L. Sladen. Photos by Bianca Lavies. 134-147, July 1975

BANFF NATIONAL PARK, Alberta, Canada:

Canadian Rockies, Lords of a Beckoning Land. By Alan Phillips. Photos by James L. Stanfield. 353-393, Sept. 1966

Hiking the Backbone of the Rockies: Canada's Great Divide Trail. By Mike W. Edwards. Photos by Lowell Georgia. 795-817, June 1973

On the Ridgepole of the Rockies. By Walter Meayers Edwards. 745-780, June 1947

BANGKOK, Thailand:

"Around the World in Eighty Days." By Newman Bumstead. 705-750, Dec. 1951

Bangkok, City of Angels. By William Graves. Photos by John Launois. 96-129, July 1973

Hopes and Fears in Booming Thailand. By Peter T. White. Photos by Dean Conger. 76-125, July 1967

Operation Eclipse: 1948. By William A. Kinney. 325-372, Mar. 1949

BANGKOK, Thailand—*Continued*

Scintillating Siam. By W. Robert Moore. 173-200, Feb. 1947

Thailand Bolsters Its Freedom. By W. Robert Moore. 811-849, June 1961

Yankee Roams the Orient. By Irving and Electa Johnson. 327-370, Mar. 1951

BANGLADESH, People's Republic of:

Bangladesh: Hope Nourishes a New Nation. By William S. Ellis. Photos by Dick Durrance II. 295-333, Sept. 1972

Bangladesh: The Nightmare of Famine. Photos by Steve Raymer. 33-39, July 1975

The Peaceful Mrus of Bangladesh. By Claus-Dieter Brauns. 267-286, Feb. 1973

See also former name, East Pakistan

BANKS ISLAND, Northwest Territories, Canada:

Banks Island: Eskimo Life on the Polar Sea. By William O. Douglas. Photos by Clyde Hare. 703-735, May 1964

BANTU (Tribespeople):

My Life With Africa's Little People. By Anne Eisner Putnam. 278-302, Feb. 1960

BARBADOS (Island), Lesser Antilles:

Barbados, Outrider of the Antilles. By Charles Allmon. 363-392, Mar. 1952

Robin Sails Home. By Robin Lee Graham. 504-545, Oct. 1970

BARCELONA ZOO, Barcelona, Spain:

Growing Up With Snowflake (White Gorilla). By Arthur J. Riopelle. Photos by Michael Kuh. 491-503, Oct. 1970

BAREHANDED Battle to Cleanse the Bay. By Peter T. White. Photos by Jonathan S. Blair. 866-881, June 1971

BARGES:

Inside Europe Aboard *Yankee*. By Irving and Electa Johnson. Photos by Joseph J. Scherschel. 157-195, Aug. 1964

Paris to Antwerp with the Water Gypsies. By David S. Boyer. 530-559, Oct. 1955

That Dammed Missouri River. By Gordon Young. Photos by David Hiser. 374-413, Sept. 1971

See also Rhine (River); St. Louis (New Spirit)

BARNACLES:

Friendless Squatters of the Sea. By Ethel A. Starbird. Photos by Robert F. Sisson. 623-633, Nov. 1973

BARNUM & BAILEY CIRCUS. *See* Ringling Bros. and Barnum & Bailey Circus

BARRA (Island), Scotland:

From Barra to Butt in the Hebrides. By Isobel Wylie Hutchison. 559-580, Oct. 1954

Hunting Folk Songs in the Hebrides. By Margaret Shaw Campbell. 249-272, Feb. 1947

Isles on the Edge of the Sea: Scotland's Outer Hebrides. By Kenneth MacLeish. Photos by Thomas Nebbia. 676-711, May 1970
    The Thrush on the Island of Barra. By Archibald MacLeish. 692-693

Scotland From Her Lovely Lochs and Seas. By Alan Villiers. Photos by Robert F. Sisson. 492-541, Apr. 1961

BARROW, Alaska:

Will Oil and Tundra Mix? Alaska's North Slope Hangs in the Balance. By William S. Ellis. Photos by Emory Kristof. 485-517, Oct. 1971

BARTLETT, DES: Author-Photographer:

Beavers, Nature's Aquatic Engineers. By Des and Jen Bartlett. 716-732, May 1974

Beyond the North Wind With the Snow Goose. By Des and Jen Bartlett. 822-843, Dec. 1973
    ... And Then There was Fred. ... 843-847

Photographer

Finding the World's Earliest Man. By L. S. B. Leakey. 420-435, Sept. 1960

Patagonia. 290-339, Mar. 1976
    I. Argentina Protects Its Wildlife Treasures. By William G. Conway. 290-297
    II. Where Two Worlds Meet. 298-321
    III. At Home With Right Whales. By Roger Payne. 322-339

BARTLETT, JEN: Author-Photographer:

Beavers, Nature's Aquatic Engineers. By Des and Jen Bartlett. 716-732, May 1974

Beyond the North Wind With the Snow Goose. By Des and Jen Bartlett. 822-843, Dec. 1973
    ... And Then There was Fred. ... 843-847

Photographer

Patagonia. 290-339, Mar. 1976
    I. Argentina Protects Its Wildlife Treasures. By William G. Conway. 290-297
    II. Where Two Worlds Meet. 298-321
    III. At Home With Right Whales. By Roger Payne. 322-339

BARTLETT, LINDA: Photographer:

Benjamin Franklin, Philosopher of Dissent. By Alice J. Hall. 93-123, July 1975

Exploring England's Canals. By Bryan Hodgson. 76-111, July 1974

Irish Ways Live On in Dingle. By Bryan Hodgson. 551-576, Apr. 1976

Mountain Voices, Mountain Days (West Virginia). By Bryan Hodgson. 118-146, July 1972

Thomas Jefferson: Architect of Freedom. By Mike W. Edwards. 231-259, Feb. 1976

BARTLETT, ROBERT A.:

Newfoundland, Canada's New Province. By Andrew H. Brown. Photos by author and Robert F. Sisson. 777-812, June 1949

BARUNTSE (Peak), Himalayas:

Beyond Everest. By Sir Edmund Hillary. 579-610, Nov. 1955

BASEL, Switzerland:

The Rhine: Europe's River of Legend. By William Graves. Photos by Bruce Dale. 449-499, Apr. 1967

BASILIQUE DE LA SAINTE MARIE MADELEINE, Vézelay, France:

Vézelay, Hill of the Pilgrims. By Melvin Hall. 229-247, Feb. 1953

BASIN REGION, Utah-Nevada. *See* Great Basin

BASKET MAKERS (Indians):

Ancient Cliff Dwellers of Mesa Verde. By Don Watson. Photos by Willard R. Culver. 349-376, Sept. 1948

BEACH, EDWARD L.: Author—*Continued*

Wake. Photos by J. Baylor Roberts. 585-615, Nov. 1960

BEAGLE, H.M.S.:

In the Wake of Darwin's *Beagle.* By Alan Villiers. Photos by James L. Stanfield. 449-495, Oct. 1969

BEAN, ALAN L.:

Skylab, Outpost on the Frontier of Space. By Thomas Y. Canby. Photos by the nine mission astronauts. 441-469, Oct. 1974

BEAR MOUNTAIN, New York:

Skyline Trail (Appalachian Trail) from Maine to Georgia. By Andrew H. Brown. Photos by Robert F. Sisson. 219-251, Aug. 1949

BEAR RIVER MIGRATORY BIRD REFUGE, Utah:

The Dauntless Little Stilt. By Frederick Kent Truslow. 241-245, Aug. 1960

BEARD, DANIEL B.: Author:

Wildlife of Everglades National Park. Paintings by Walter A. Weber. 83-116, Jan. 1949

BEARS. *See* Black Bears; Brown Bears; Grizzly Bears; Polar Bear

La BEAUCE (Plain), France:

Chartres: Legacy from the Age of Faith. By Kenneth MacLeish. Photos by Dean Conger. 857-882, Dec. 1969

BEAUTY and Bounty of Southern State Trees. By William A. Dayton. Paintings by Walter A. Weber. 508-552, Oct. 1957

BEAVERS:

Arizona's Operation Beaver Lift. By Willis Peterson. 666-680, May 1955

Beavers, Nature's Aquatic Engineers. By Des and Jen Bartlett. 716-732, May 1974

The Romance of American Furs. By Wanda Burnett. 379-402, Mar. 1948

BECAUSE It Rains on Hawaii. By Frederick Simpich, Jr. 571-610, Nov. 1949

BECKER, JIM: Author:

Look What's Happened to Honolulu! Photos by Bates Littlehales. 500-531, Oct. 1969

BECKET, THOMAS À:

Canterbury Cathedral. By Kenneth MacLeish. Photos by Thomas Nebbia. 364-379, Mar. 1976

BEDI, NARESH: Photographer:

The Cobra, India's "Good Snake." By Harry Miller. 393-409, Sept. 1970

BEDI, RAJESH: Photographer:

The Cobra, India's "Good Snake." By Harry Miller. 393-409, Sept. 1970

India Struggles to Save Her Wildlife. By John J. Putman. 299-343, Sept. 1976

BEDOUIN:

Abraham, the Friend of God. By Kenneth MacLeish. Photos by Dean Conger. 739-789, Dec. 1966

Arab Land Beyond the Jordan. Photos by Frank Hurley. 753-768, Dec. 1947

Holy Land, My Country. By His Majesty King Hussein of Jordan. 784-789, Dec. 1964

BEDOUIN—*Continued*

In Search of Moses. By Harvey Arden. Photos by Nathan Benn. 2-37, Jan. 1976

Jerusalem, My Home. By Bertha Spafford Vester. 826-847, Dec. 1964

Morocco, Land of the Farthest West. By Thomas J. Abercrombie. 834-865, June 1971

The Other Side of Jordan. By Luis Marden. 790-825, Dec. 1964

Report from the Locust Wars. By Tony and Dickey Chapelle. 545-562, Apr. 1953

Saudi Arabia: Beyond the Sands of Mecca. By Thomas J. Abercrombie. 1-53, Jan. 1966

The Sword and the Sermon (Islam). By Thomas J. Abercrombie. 3-45, July 1972

BEEBE, WILLIAM: Author:

The High World of the Rain Forest. Paintings by Guy Neale. 838-855, June 1958

BEES:

Crossroads of the Insect World. By J. W. MacSwain. Photos by Edward S. Ross. 844-857, Dec. 1966

Inside the World of the Honeybee. By Treat Davidson. 188-217, Aug. 1959

Those Fiery Brazilian Bees. By Rick Gore. Photos by Bianca Lavies. 491-501, Apr. 1976

BEETLES:

Following the Ladybug Home. By Kenneth S. Hagen. Photos by Robert F. Sisson. 543-553, Apr. 1970

Larvae. *See* Glowworms; Railroad Worm

See also Fireflies

BEHIND New York's Window on Nature: The American Museum of Natural History. By James A. Oliver. Photos by Robert F. Sisson. 220-259, Feb. 1963

BEHIND the Headlines in Viet Nam. By Peter T. White. Photos by Winfield Parks. 149-189, Feb. 1967

BEHIND the Veil of Troubled Yemen. By Thomas J. Abercrombie. 403-445, Mar. 1964

BEHOLD the Computer Revolution. By Peter T. White. Photos by Bruce Dale and Emory Kristof. 593-633, Nov. 1970

BEINN BHREAGH, Cape Breton Island, Nova Scotia:

Down East to Nova Scotia. By Winfield Parks. 853-879, June 1964

BEIRUT, Lebanon:

Lebanon, Little Bible Land in the Crossfire of History. By William S. Ellis. Photos by George F. Mobley. 240-275, Feb. 1970

Young-old Lebanon Lives by Trade. By Thomas J. Abercrombie. 479-523, Apr. 1958

BELDEN, CHARLES J.: Author-Photographer:

Dinkelsbühl Rewards Its Children. 255-268, Feb. 1957

Photographer

The Palio of Siena. By Edgar Erskine Hume. 231-244, Aug. 1951

BELGIAN CONGO. *See* Zaire

The BENDS (Caisson Disease)—*Continued*

Underwater Archeology: Key to History's Warehouse. By George F. Bass. Photos by Thomas J. Abercrombie and Robert B. Goodman. 138-156, July 1963

BENELUX NATIONS. *See* Belgium; Luxembourg; Netherlands

BENJAMIN, GEORGE J.: Author-Photographer:

Diving Into the Blue Holes of the Bahamas. 347-363, Sept. 1970

BENJAMIN FRANKLIN, Philosopher of Dissent. By Alice J. Hall. Photos by Linda Bartlett. 93-123, July 1975

BENN, NATHAN: Photographer:

Cuba's Exiles Bring New Life to Miami. By Edward J. Linehan. 68-95, July 1973

In Search of Moses. By Harvey Arden. 2-37, Jan. 1976

The Pious Ones (Brooklyn's Hasidic Jews). By Harvey Arden. 276-298, Aug. 1975

Vermont—a State of Mind and Mountains. By Ethel A. Starbird. 28-61, July 1974

BENNETT, FLOYD:

Floyd Bennett awarded Gold Medal; presentation by President Coolidge. 868, Dec. 1957

BERBERS (Tribespeople):

Trek by Mule Among Morocco's Berbers. By Victor Englebert. 850-875, June 1968

BERGEN, Norway:

Norway, Land of the Generous Sea. By Edward J. Linehan. Photos by George F. Mobley. 1-43, July 1971

Norway Cracks Her Mountain Shell. By Sydney Clark. Photos by Gilbert Grosvenor and Ole Friele Backer. 171-211, Aug. 1948

BERING SEA PEOPLE. *See* Old Bering Sea People

BERING SEA REGION. *See* King Island; Pribilof Islands

BERING STRAIT:

Alaska's Russian Frontier: Little Diomede. Photos by Audrey and Frank Morgan. 551-562, Apr. 1951

Ice Age Man, the First American. By Thomas R. Henry. Paintings by Andre Durenceau. 781-806, Dec. 1955

BERKSHIRES (Mountains), Massachusetts:

Home to the Enduring Berkshires. By Charles McCarry. Photos by Jonathan S. Blair. 196-221, Aug. 1970

Massachusetts Builds for Tomorrow. By Robert de Roos. Photos by B. Anthony Stewart. 790-843, Dec. 1966

Mountains Top Off New England. By F. Barrows Colton. Photos by Robert F. Sisson. 563-602, May 1951

BERLIN, Germany:

Airlift to Berlin. 595-614, May 1949

Berlin, Island in a Soviet Sea. By Frederick G. Vosburgh. Photos by Volkmar Wentzel. 689-704, Nov. 1951

Berlin, on Both Sides of the Wall. By Howard So-

BERLIN, Germany—*Continued*

churek. 1-47, Jan. 1970

Modern Miracle, Made in Germany. By Robert Leslie Conly. Photos by Erich Lessing. 735-791, June 1959

What I Saw Across the Rhine. By J. Frank Dobie. 57-86, Jan. 1947

BERLIN, East, East Germany:

East Germany: The Struggle to Succeed. By John J. Putman. Photos by Gordon W. Gahan. 295-329, Sept. 1974

BERLIN, West:

Life in Walled-off West Berlin. By Nathaniel T. Kenney and Volkmar Wentzel. Photos by Thomas Nebbia. 735-767, Dec. 1961

BERMUDA (Islands), Atlantic Ocean:

Bermuda—Balmy, British, and Beautiful. By Peter Benchley. Photos by Emory Kristof. 93-121, July 1971

Bermuda, Cradled in Warm Seas. By Beverley M. Bowie. Photos by Charles Allmon. 203-238, Feb. 1954

By Square-rigger from Baltic to Bicentennial. By Kenneth Garrett. 824-857, Dec. 1976
  Included: Collision of tall ships in Bermuda waters

To Europe with a Racing Start. By Carleton Mitchell. 758-791, June 1958

BERN, Switzerland:

Surprising Switzerland. By Jean and Franc Shor. 427-478, Oct. 1956

Switzerland, Europe's High-rise Republic. By Thomas J. Abercrombie. 68-113, July 1969

Switzerland Guards the Roof of Europe. By William H. Nicholas. Photos by Willard R. Culver. 205-246, Aug. 1950

BERNINA (Balloon):

Across the Alps in a Wicker Basket. By Phil Walker. 117-131, Jan. 1963

BERRIES:

How Fruit Came to America. By J. R. Magness. Paintings by Else Bostelmann. 325-377, Sept. 1951

See also Cranberries

BERRY, WILLIAM R.: Author:

Hot-air Balloons Race on Silent Winds. Photos by Don W. Jones. 392-407, Mar. 1966

BESIDE the Persian Gulf. Photos by Maynard Owen Williams. 341-356, Mar. 1947

BETELGEUSE (Ketch):

Chesapeake Country. By Nathaniel T. Kenney. Photos by Bates Littlehales. 370-411, Sept. 1964

BETHLEHEM:

Hashemite Jordan, Arab Heartland. By John Scofield. 841-856, Dec. 1952

Pilgrims Follow the Christmas Star. By Maynard Owen Williams. 831-840, Dec. 1952

BETTER Days for the Navajos. By Jack Breed. Photos by Charles W. Herbert. 809-847, Dec. 1958

BEYOND Everest. By Sir Edmund Hillary. 579-610, Nov. 1955

BEYOND the Bight of Benin (Nigeria; Cameroons). By Jeannette and Maurice Fiévet. 221-253, Aug. 1959

BEYOND the North Wind With the Snow Goose. By Des and Jen Bartlett. 822-843, Dec. 1973

BHAVNANI, ENAKSHI: Author:

A Journey to "Little Tibet." Photos by Volkmar Wentzel. 603-634, May 1951

BHOTIAS (Tribespeople):

High Adventure in the Himalayas. By Thomas Weir. 193-234, Aug. 1952

BHUTAN:

Bhutan, Land of the Thunder Dragon. By Burt Kerr Todd. 713-754, Dec. 1952

Bhutan: Mountain Kingdom Between Tibet and India. By Desmond Doig. 384-415, Sept. 1961

Bhutan Crowns a New Dragon King. Photos by John Scofield. 546-571, Oct. 1974

Life Slowly Changes in Remote Bhutan. By John Scofield. 658-683, Nov. 1976

BIAMI (People):

Journey Into Stone Age New Guinea. By Malcolm S. Kirk. 568-592, Apr. 1969

BIANCHI, PETER V.: Artist:

Last Moments of the Pompeians. By Amedeo Maiuri. Photos by Lee E. Battaglia. 651-669, Nov. 1961

The Last Thousand Years Before Christ. By G. Ernest Wright. Paintings by H. J. Soulen and Peter V. Bianchi. 812-853, Dec. 1960

The Men Who Hid the Dead Sea Scrolls. By A. Douglas Tushingham. 785-808, Dec. 1958

Solving the Riddles of Wetherill Mesa. By Douglas Osborne. 155-195, Feb. 1964

BIBLE:

The British Way. By Sir Evelyn Wrench. 421-541, Apr. 1949
    Included: James I and the translation of the Bible

The Men Who Hid the Dead Sea Scrolls. By A. Douglas Tushingham. Paintings by Peter V. Bianchi. 785-808, Dec. 1958

BIBLE LANDS:

Abraham, the Friend of God. By Kenneth MacLeish. Photos by Dean Conger. 739-789, Dec. 1966

An Archeologist Looks at Palestine. By Nelson Glueck. 739-752, Dec. 1947

Bringing Old Testament Times to Life. By G. Ernest Wright. Paintings by Henry J. Soulen. 833-864, Dec. 1957

Crusader Lands Revisited. By Harold Lamb. Photos by David S. Boyer. 815-852, Dec. 1954
    Contents: Israel; Jordan; Lebanon; Syria; Turkey

Crusader Road to Jerusalem. By Franc Shor. Photos by Thomas Nebbia. 797-855, Dec. 1963
    I. Desert Ordeal of the Knights. 797-837
    II. Conquest of the Holy City. 839-855

Everyday Life in Bible Times. Book announced. 494-507, Oct. 1967

Eyewitness to War in the Holy Land. By Charles Harbutt. 782-795, Dec. 1967

Geographical Twins a World Apart. By David S. Boyer. 848-859, Dec. 1958

BIBLE LANDS—Continued
    Contents: Dead Sea, Sea of Galilee, Jordan River, and the caves at Qumrān compared with their counterparts in Utah

Holy Land, My Country. By His Majesty King Hussein of Jordan. 784-789, Dec. 1964

Holy Land Today, Atlas series supplement. Dec. 1963

Home to the Holy Land. By Maynard Owen Williams. 707-746, Dec. 1950

In Search of Moses. By Harvey Arden. Photos by Nathan Benn. 2-37, Jan. 1976

Israel: Land of Promise. By John Scofield. Photos by B. Anthony Stewart. 395-434, Mar. 1965

Jerusalem to Rome in the Path of St. Paul. By David S. Boyer. 707-759, Dec. 1956

Journey Into the Great Rift. By Helen and Frank Schreider. 254-290, Aug. 1965

The Land of Galilee. By Kenneth MacLeish. Photos by B. Anthony Stewart. 832-865, Dec. 1965

Lands of the Bible Today, map supplement. Dec. 1956

Lands of the Bible Today, map supplement. Dec. 1967

The Last Thousand Years Before Christ. By G. Ernest Wright. Paintings by H. J. Soulen and Peter V. Bianchi. 812-853, Dec. 1960

The Other Side of Jordan. By Luis Marden. 790-825, Dec. 1964

Pilgrims Follow the Christmas Star. By Maynard Owen Williams. 831-840, Dec. 1952

Sinai Sheds New Light on the Bible. By Henry Field. Photos by William B. and Gladys Terry. 795-815, Dec. 1948

Where Jesus Walked. By Howard La Fay. Photos by Charles Harbutt. 739-781, Dec. 1967

See also Jericho; Jerusalem; Jordan; Khirbat Qumrān; Mesopotamia; Petra, Jordan; St. Catherine's Monastery, Sinai

BICENTENNIAL, U. S.:

Benjamin Franklin, Philosopher of Dissent. By Alice J. Hall. Photos by Linda Bartlett. 93-123, July 1975

By Square-rigger from Baltic to Bicentennial (Operation Sail). By Kenneth Garrett. 824-857, Dec. 1976

Firebrands of the Revolution. By Eric F. Goldman. Photos by George F. Mobley. 2-27, July 1974

The Loyalists. By Kent Britt. Photos by Ted Spiegel. 510-539, Apr. 1975

The Nation's 200th Birthday. By Gilbert M. Grosvenor. 1, July 1974

Patriots in Petticoats. By Lonnelle Aikman. Paintings by Louis S. Glanzman. 475-493, Oct. 1975

This Land of Ours. 1-158, July 1976
    A Portfolio: "This land is your land . . ." 2-11
    A First American Views His Land. By N. Scott Momaday. 13-19
    This Land of Ours—How Are We Using It? By Peter T. White. Photos by Emory Kristof. 20-67
    Five Noted Thinkers Explore the Future. 68-75
    The Next Frontier? By Isaac Asimov. Paintings by Pierre Mion. 76-89
    George Washington: The Man Behind the Myths. By Howard La Fay. Photos by Ted Spiegel. 90-111

BLAIR, JAMES P.: Photographer—*Continued*
don Young. 234-259, Aug. 1975

Yugoslavia: Six Republics in One. By Robert Paul Jordan. 589-633, May 1970

BLAIR, JONATHAN S.: Author-Photographer:
Keeping House in a Cappadocian Cave. 127-146, July 1970

Photographer

Ancient Aphrodisias and Its Marble Treasures. By Kenan T. Erim. 280-294, Aug. 1967

Aphrodisias, Awakened City of Ancient Art. By Kenan T. Erim. 766-791, June 1972

Barehanded Battle to Cleanse the Bay. By Peter T. White. 866-881, June 1971

California, the Golden Magnet: II. Nature's North. By William Graves. Photos by James P. Blair and Jonathan S. Blair. 641-679, May 1966

Cyprus Under Four Flags: A Struggle for Unity. By Kenneth MacLeish. 356-383, Mar. 1973

Dry-land Fleet Sails the Sahara. By Jean du Boucher. 696-725, Nov. 1967

Florida's Booming—and Beleaguered—Heartland. By Joseph Judge. 585-621, Nov. 1973

Home to the Enduring Berkshires. By Charles McCarry. 196-221, Aug. 1970

Madeira, Like Its Wine, Improves With Age. By Veronica Thomas. 488-513, Apr. 1973

New Life for the Troubled Suez Canal. By William Graves. 792-817, June 1975

On the Road With an Old-time Circus. By John Fetterman. 410-434, Mar. 1972

Riding the Outlaw Trail. By Robert Redford. 622-657, Nov. 1976

Sicily, Where All the Songs Are Sad. By Howard La Fay. 407-436, Mar. 1976

Stockholm, Where "Kvalitet" Is a Way of Life. By James Cerruti. Photos by Albert Moldvay and Jonathan Blair. 43-69, Jan. 1976

Yellowstone at 100: The Pitfalls of Success. By William S. Ellis. 616-631, May 1972

BLESSING OF THE FLEET:
Gloucester Blesses Its Portuguese Fleet. By Luis Marden. 75-84, July 1953

BLIGH, WILLIAM:
Huzza for Otaheite! By Luis Marden. 435-459, Apr. 1962

I Found the Bones of the *Bounty*. By Luis Marden. 725-789, Dec. 1957

Tahiti, "Finest Island in the World." By Luis Marden. 1-47, July 1962

BLIZZARD of Birds: The Tortugas Terns. By Alexander Sprunt, Jr. 213-230, Feb. 1947

BLOOD, NED: Photographer:
Sheep Airlift in New Guinea. 831-844, Dec. 1949

BLOSSOMS That Defy the Seasons. By Geneal Condon. Photos by David S. Boyer. 420-427, Sept. 1958

BLOWGUN Hunters of the South Pacific. By Jane C. Goodale. Photos by Ann Chowning. 793-817, June 1966

BLUE CRABS:
Can We Save Our Salt Marshes? By Stephen W. Hitchcock. Photos by William R. Curtsinger. 729-765, June 1972

BLUE CRABS—*Continued*
This Is My Island, Tangier (Virginia). By Harold G. Wheatley. Photos by David Alan Harvey. 700-725, Nov. 1973

BLUE-EYED Indian: A City Boy's Sojourn with Primitive Tribesmen in Central Brazil. By Harald Schultz. 65-89, July 1961

BLUE HOLES, Great Bahama Bank:
Diving Into the Blue Holes of the Bahamas. By George J. Benjamin. 347-363, Sept. 1970

BLUE RIDGE (Mountains), U. S.:
Appalachian Valley Pilgrimage. By Catherine Bell Palmer. Photos by Justin Locke. 1-32, July 1949

My Neighbors Hold to Mountain Ways. By Malcolm Ross. Photos by Flip Schulke. 856-880, June 1958

Shenandoah, I Long to Hear You. By Mike W. Edwards. Photos by Thomas Anthony DeFeo. 554-588, Apr. 1970

Skyline Trail from Maine to Georgia. By Andrew H. Brown. Photos by Robert F. Sisson. 219-251, Aug. 1949

The Virginians. By Mike W. Edwards. Photos by David Alan Harvey. 588-617, Nov. 1974

BLUE-WATER Plankton: Ghosts of the Gulf Stream. By William M. Hamner. 530-545, Oct. 1974

BLUEBIRDS:
Seeing Birds as Real Personalities. By Hance Roy Ivor. 523-530, Apr. 1954
Bluebirds on the Wing in Color. Photos by Bernard Corby and author. 527-530

BLUEGRASS (Region), Kentucky:
Heart of the Bluegrass. By Charles McCarry. Photos by J. Bruce Baumann. 634-659, May 1974

BOAT RACES:
By Square-rigger from Baltic to Bicentennial. By Kenneth Garrett. 824-857, Dec. 1976

Down East to Nova Scotia. By Winfield Parks. 853-879, June 1964
Included: Marblehead-Halifax race; Bras d'Or Lakes 15-mile race for the McCurdy Cup; Jones Trophy for Canadian yachts

To Europe with a Racing Start. By Carleton Mitchell. 758-791, June 1958
Included: Newport-to-Bermuda race

See also Yachting

BOATS:
California's Surprising Inland Delta. By Judith and Neil Morgan. Photos by Charles O'Rear. 409-430, Sept. 1976

"Delmarva," Gift of the Sea. By Catherine Bell Palmer. 367-399, Sept. 1950
Included: Chesapeake Bay boats: Bugeyes, Hampton-class sloops, Log canoes, Skipjacks

Here's New York Harbor. By Stuart E. Jones. Photos by Robert F. Sisson and David S. Boyer. 773-813, Dec. 1954

Inflatable Ship *(Amphitrite)* Opens Era of Airborne Undersea Expeditions. By Jacques-Yves Cousteau. 142-148, July 1961

The Lower Mississippi. By Willard Price. Photos by W. D. Vaughn. 681-725, Nov. 1960

On the Winds of the Dodecanese. By Jean and Franc Shor. 351-390, Mar. 1953

BOOTH, WINDSOR P.: Author:

Disaster in Paradise (Bali). Photos by Robert F. Sisson. 436-447, Sept. 1963

BOOTHBAY HARBOR, Maine:

Seashore Summer. By Arline Strong. 436-444, Sept. 1960

BORAH, LEO A.: Author:

From Sagebrush to Roses on the Columbia. 571-611, Nov. 1952

Illinois—Healthy Heart of the Nation. Photos by B. Anthony Stewart and Willard R. Culver. 781-820, Dec. 1953

Landmarks of Literary England. Photos by Kathleen Revis. 295-350, Sept. 1955

Montana, Shining Mountain Treasureland. 693-736, June 1950

North Dakota Comes into Its Own. Photos by J. Baylor Roberts. 283-322, Sept. 1951

Ohio Makes Its Own Prosperity. Photos by B. Anthony Stewart. 435-484, Apr. 1955

BOREN, LAMAR: Photographer:

Goggle Fishing in California Waters. By David Hellyer. 615-632, May 1949

BORMAN, FRANK:

Hubbard Medal recipient. 861, June 1970

"A Most Fantastic Voyage": The Story of Apollo 8's Rendezvous With the Moon. By Sam C. Phillips. 593-631, May 1969

Sounds of the Space Age, from Sputnik to Lunar Landing. Record narrated by Frank Borman. 750-751, Dec. 1969

Space Rendezvous, Milestone on the Way to the Moon. By Kenneth F. Weaver. 539-553, Apr. 1966

BORN Hunters, the Bird Dogs. By Roland Kilbon. Paintings by Walter A. Weber. 369-398, Sept. 1947

BORNEO (Island). *See* Brunei; Sabah (North Borneo); Sarawak; Tanjung Puting Reserve

BORNHOLM (Island), Denmark:

Baltic Cruise of the *Caribbee*. By Carleton Mitchell. 605-646, Nov. 1950

2,000 Miles Through Europe's Oldest Kingdom. By Isobel Wylie Hutchison. Photos by Maynard Owen Williams. 141-180, Feb. 1949

BORTON, NAN and **JAMES W.:** Authors:

Ambassadors of Good Will: The Peace Corps. By Sargent Shriver and Peace Corps Volunteers. 297-345, Sept. 1964
Turkey. 331-333

BOSNIA-HERCEGOVINA (Republic), Yugoslavia:

Yugoslavia: Six Republics in One. By Robert Paul Jordan. Photos by James P. Blair. 589-633, May 1970

BOSTELMANN, ELSE: Artist:

How Fruit Came to America. By J. R. Magness. 325-377, Sept. 1951

Our Vegetable Travelers. By Victor R. Boswell. 145-217, Aug. 1949

The World in Your Garden (Flowers). By W. H. Camp. 1-65, July 1947

BOSTON, England:

The Original Boston: St. Botolph's Town. By Veronica Thomas. Photos by James L. Amos. 382-389, Sept. 1974

BOSTON, Massachusetts:

Benjamin Franklin, Philosopher of Dissent. By Alice J. Hall. Photos by Linda Bartlett. 93-123, July 1975

Firebrands of the Revolution. By Eric F. Goldman. Photos by George F. Mobley. 2-27, July 1974

Literary Landmarks of Massachusetts. By William H. Nicholas. Photos by B. Anthony Stewart and John E. Fletcher. 279-310, Mar. 1950

Massachusetts Builds for Tomorrow. By Robert de Roos. Photos by B. Anthony Stewart. 790-843, Dec. 1966

The Post Road Today. Photos by B. Anthony Stewart. 206-233, Aug. 1962

Those Proper and Other Bostonians. By Joseph Judge. Photos by Ted Spiegel. 352-381, Sept. 1974

The Wonder City That Moves by Night (Circus). By Francis Beverly Kelley. 289-324, Mar. 1948

BOSTON POST ROADS:

The Old Boston Post Roads. By Donald Barr Chidsey. 189-205, Aug. 1962

The Post Road Today. Photos by B. Anthony Stewart. 206-233, Aug. 1962

BOSWELL, VICTOR R.: Author:

Our Vegetable Travelers. Paintings by Else Bostelmann. 145-217, Aug. 1949

BOSWELL, VICTOR R., Jr.: Photographer:

The Magic Lure of Sea Shells. By Paul A. Zahl. Photos by Victor R. Boswell, Jr. and author. 386-429, Mar. 1969

900 Years Ago: the Norman Conquest. By Kenneth M. Setton. Photos by George F. Mobley. The complete Bayeux Tapestry photographed by Milton A. Ford and Victor R. Boswell, Jr. 206-251, Aug. 1966

Venice's Golden Legacy. 609-619, Nov. 1972

BOTANICAL EXPLORERS. *See* Agricultural and Botanical Explorers

BOTANICAL GARDENS. *See* Longwood Gardens; Royal Botanic Gardens

BOTTOM SCRATCHERS CLUB:

Goggle Fishing in California Waters. By David Hellyer. Photos by Lamar Boren. 615-632, May 1949

BOUCHAGE, LUC: Author:

Mysore Celebrates the Death of a Demon. Photos by Ylla. 706-711, May 1958

BOUCHER, JEAN DU: Author:

Dry-land Fleet Sails the Sahara. Photos by Jonathan S. Blair. 696-725, Nov. 1967

BOUNTY, H.M.S.:

Bounty Descendants Live on Remote Norfolk Island. By T. C. Roughley. Photos by J. Baylor Roberts. 559-584, Oct. 1960

Huzza for Otaheite! By Luis Marden. 435-459, Apr. 1962

I Found the Bones of the *Bounty*. By Luis Marden. 725-789, Dec. 1957

BOUNTY, H.M.S. (Replica):

Huzza for Otaheite! By Luis Marden. 435-459, Apr. 1962

Tahiti, "Finest Island in the World." By Luis Marden. 1-47, July 1962

BOURDILLON, TOM:

Triumph on Everest. 1-63, July 1954
I. Siege and Assault. By Sir John Hunt. 1-43
II. The Conquest of the Summit. By Sir Edmund Hillary. 45-63

BOW (River), Canada:

On the Ridgepole of the Rockies. By Walter Meayers Edwards. 745-780, June 1947

BOWDITCH, NATHANIEL:

Literary Landmarks of Massachusetts. By William H. Nicholas. Photos by B. Anthony Stewart and John E. Fletcher. 279-310, Mar. 1950

BOWEN, IRA SPRAGUE: Author:

Completing the Atlas of the Universe. 185-190, Aug. 1955
Sky Survey Plates Unlock Secrets of the Stars. 186-187

Sky Survey Charts the Universe. 780-781, Dec. 1956

BOWERBIRDS:

Australia's Amazing Bowerbirds. By Norman Chaffer. 866-873, Dec. 1961

BOWES, ANNE LaBASTILLE: Author:

The Quetzal, Fabulous Bird of Maya Land. Photos by David G. Allen. 141-150, Jan. 1969
See also LaBastille, Anne

BOWHEAD WHALES:

The Last U. S. Whale Hunters. By Emory Kristof. 346-355, Mar. 1973
"Ocean mammals are to us what the buffalo was to the Plains Indian." By Lael Morgan. 354-355

BOWIE, BEVERLEY M.:

Memorial Tribute to Beverley M. Bowie (1914-1958). 214, Feb. 1959

Author

Bermuda, Cradled in Warm Seas. Photos by Charles Allmon. 203-238, Feb. 1954

Building a New Austria. Photos by Volkmar Wentzel. 172-213, Feb. 1959

'Known but to God' (Unknown Heroes). 593-605, Nov. 1958

MATS: America's Long Arm of the Air. Photos by Robert F. Sisson. 283-317, Mar. 1957

New England, a Modern Pilgrim's Pride. 733-796, June 1955

Off the Beaten Track of Empire (Prince Philip's Tour). Photos by Michael Parker. 584-626, Nov. 1957

The Past Is Present in Greenfield Village (Henry Ford Museum). Photos by Neal P. Davis and Willard R. Culver. 96-127, July 1958

Salzkammergut, Austria's Alpine Playground. Photos by Volkmar Wentzel. 246-275, Aug. 1960

This Young Giant, Indonesia. Photos by J. Baylor Roberts. 351-392, Sept. 1955

Triumph on Everest: II. The Conquest of the Summit. By Sir Edmund Hillary. 45-63, July 1954

BOWIE, BEVERLEY M.: Author—*Continued*

Note: Sir Edmund related his personal narrative to Beverley M. Bowie.

The White Horses of Vienna. Photos by Volkmar Wentzel. 400-419, Sept. 1958

Williamsburg: Its College and Its Cinderella City. 439-486, Oct. 1954

Wisconsin, Land of the Good Life. Photos by Volkmar Wentzel. 141-187, Feb. 1957

BOWLAND, ARTHUR: Photographer:

Adventures With South Africa's Black Eagles. By Jeanne Cowden. Photos by author and Arthur Bowland. 533-543, Oct. 1969

BOY SCOUTS:

Philmont Scout Ranch Helps Boys Grow Up. By Andrew H. Brown. 399-416, Sept. 1956

Washington Lives Again at Valley Forge. By Howell Walker. 187-202, Feb. 1954
Included: Boy Scout Jamboree

BOYER, DAVID S.: Author:

Huntington Library, California Treasure House. 251-276, Feb. 1958

Micronesia: The Americanization of Eden. 702-744, May 1967

Portugal's Gem of the Ocean: Madeira. 364-394, Mar. 1959

Author-Photographer

Alberta Unearths Her Buried Treasures. 90-119, July 1960

British Columbia: Life Begins at 100. 147-189, Aug. 1958

The Canadian North: Emerging Giant. 1-43, July 1968

Geographical Twins (Holy Land and Utah) a World Apart. 848-859, Dec. 1958

The Glittering World of Rockhounds. 276-294, Feb. 1974

Jerusalem to Rome in the Path of St. Paul. 707-759, Dec. 1956

Kitimat—Canada's Aluminum Titan. 376-398, Sept. 1956

Minnesota, Where Water Is the Magic Word. Photos by author and David Brill. 200-229, Feb. 1976

Over and Under Chesapeake Bay. 593-612, Apr. 1964

Paris to Antwerp with the Water Gypsies. 530-559, Oct. 1955

Petra, Rose-red Citadel of Biblical Edom. 853-870, Dec. 1955

Powerhouse of the Northwest (Columbia River). 821-847, Dec. 1974

Rhododendron Glories of Southwest Scotland. Photos by B. Anthony Stewart and author. 641-664, May 1954

Wyoming: High, Wide, and Windy. 554-594, Apr. 1966

Year of Discovery Opens in Antarctica. 339-381, Sept. 1957

Photographer

Ambassadors of Good Will: The Peace Corps. By Sargent Shriver and Peace Corps Volunteers. 297-345, Sept. 1964

Blossoms That Defy the Seasons (Flower Preservation). By Geneal Condon. 420-427, Sept. 1958

Boom on San Francisco Bay. By Franc Shor. 181-

BROADSTAIRS, England:

The England of Charles Dickens. By Richard W. Long. Photos by Adam Woolfitt. 443-483, Apr. 1974

Included: Dickens Festival; "Bleak House," Dickens's summer home

BROMELIADS:

Hidden Worlds in the Heart of a Plant. By Paul A. Zahl. 389-397, Mar. 1975

Puya, the Pineapple's Andean Ancestor. By Mulford B. Foster. 463-480, Oct. 1950

BRONTOSAURS:

We Captured a 'Live' Brontosaur. By Roland T. Bird. 707-722, May 1954

BRONX ZOO. *See* New York Zoological Park

BRONZE AGE:

Oldest Known Shipwreck Yields Bronze Age Cargo. By Peter Throckmorton. 697-711, May 1962

Thirty-three Centuries Under the Sea (Shipwreck). By Peter Throckmorton. 682-703, May 1960

See also Hoabinhian Culture; Minoan Civilization

BRONZES:

China Unveils Her Newest Treasures. Photos by Robert W. Madden. 848-857, Dec. 1974

Mosaic of Cultures (Southeast Asia). By Peter T. White. Photos by W. E. Garrett. 296-329, Mar. 1971

See also Dreyfus Collection

BROOKFIELD, CHARLES M.: Author:

An Exotic New Oriole Settles in Florida. By Charles M. Brookfield and Oliver Griswold. 261-264, Feb. 1956

Key Largo Coral Reef: America's First Undersea Park. Photos by Jerry Greenberg. 58-69, Jan. 1962

BROOKLYN, New York:

Long Island Outgrows the Country. By Howell Walker. Photos by B. Anthony Stewart. 279-326, Mar. 1951

The Pious Ones (Brooklyn's Hasidic Jews). By Harvey Arden. Photos by Nathan Benn. 276-298, Aug. 1975

BROOKS, RHODA and EARLE: Authors:

Ambassadors of Good Will: The Peace Corps. By Sargent Shriver and Peace Corps Volunteers. 297-345, Sept. 1964

Ecuador. 339-345

BROWER, DAVID R.: Author:

Sierra High Trip. 844-868, June 1954

BROWER, WARD, Jr.:

Easter Egg Chickens. By Frederick G. Vosburgh. Photos by B. Anthony Stewart. 377-387, Sept. 1948

BROWN, ANDREW H.: Author:

Men Against the Hurricane. 537-560, Oct. 1950

New St. Lawrence Seaway Opens the Great Lakes to the World. 299-339, Mar. 1959

Newfoundland, Canada's New Province. Photos by Robert F. Sisson. 777-812, June 1949

Ontario, Pivot of Canada's Power. Photos by B. Anthony Stewart and Bates Littlehales. 823-852, Dec. 1953

BROWN, ANDREW H.: Author—*Continued*

Quebec's Forests, Farms, and Frontiers. 431-470, Oct. 1949

Skyline Trail from Maine to Georgia. Photos by Robert F. Sisson. 219-251, Aug. 1949

Sno-Cats Mechanize Oregon Snow Survey. Photos by John E. Fletcher. 691-710, Nov. 1949

Sweden, Quiet Workshop for the World. 451-491, Apr. 1963

Versatile Wood Waits on Man. 109-140, July 1951

Weather from the White North. Photos by John E. Fletcher. 543-572, Apr. 1955

Author-Photographer

Haunting Heart of the Everglades. Photos by author and Willard R. Culver. 145-173, Feb. 1948

Labrador Canoe Adventure. By Andrew Brown and Ralph Gray. 65-99, July 1951

Norway's Fjords Pit Men Against Mountains. 96-122, Jan. 1957

Philmont Scout Ranch Helps Boys Grow Up. 399-416, Sept. 1956

Saving Earth's Oldest Living Things (Sequoias). Photos by Raymond Moulin and author. 679-695, May 1951

Work-hard, Play-hard Michigan. 279-320, Mar. 1952

Photographer

All-out Assault on Antarctica. By Richard E. Byrd. 141-180, Aug. 1956

Native's Return to Norway. By Arnvid Nygaard. 683-691, Nov. 1953

Stop-and-Go Sail Around South Norway. By Edmond J. Moran. Photos by Randi Kjekstad Bull and Andrew H. Brown. 153-192, Aug. 1954

BROWN, JOHN:

History Awakens at Harpers Ferry. By Volkmar Wentzel. 399-416, Mar. 1957

BROWN, ROLAND W.: Author:

Fossils Lift the Veil of Time. By Harry S. Ladd and Roland W. Brown. 363-386, Mar. 1956

BROWN BEARS:

Among Alaska's Brown Bears. By Allan L. Egbert and Michael H. Luque. 428-442, Sept. 1975

When Giant Bears Go Fishing. By Cecil E. Rhode. 195-205, Aug. 1954

BROWN PELICANS:

Bad Days for the Brown Pelican. By Ralph W. Schreiber. Photos by William R. Curtsinger and author. 111-123, Jan. 1975

BRUCE, AILSA MELLON: Art Collection:

In Quest of Beauty. Text by Paul Mellon. 372-385, Mar. 1967

BRUGES, Belgium:

Belgium Comes Back. By Harvey Klemmer. Photos by Maynard Owen Williams. 575-614, May 1948

Belgium Welcomes the World (1958 World's Fair). By Howell Walker. 795-837, June 1958

Bruges, the City the Sea Forgot. By Luis Marden. 631-665, May 1955

BRUNEI (Sultanate), Borneo:

Brunei, Borneo's Abode of Peace. By Joseph Judge. Photos by Dean Conger. 207-225, Feb. 1974

In Storied Lands of Malaysia. By Maurice Shad-

BUTTERFLIES—*Continued*
Crane. Photos by M. Woodbridge Williams. 193-217, Aug. 1957
See also Monarch Butterfly

BUTTRICK GARDEN, Concord, Massachusetts:
History and Beauty Blend in a Concord Iris Garden. By Robert T. Cochran, Jr. Photos by M. Woodbridge Williams. 705-719, May 1959

BUZ KASHI:
Bold Horsemen of the Steppes (Turkomans). By Sabrina and Roland Michaud. 634-669, Nov. 1973

BY Cotswold Lanes to Wold's End. By Melville Bell Grosvenor. 615-654, May 1948

BY Full-rigged Ship to Denmark's Fairyland. By Alan Villiers. Photos by Alexander Taylor and author. 809-828, Dec. 1955

BY Parachute Into Peru's Lost World. By G. Brooks Baekeland. Photos by author and Peter R. Gimbel. 268-296, Aug. 1964

BY Square-rigger from Baltic to Bicentennial. By Kenneth Garrett. 824-857, Dec. 1976

BYRD, RICHARD EVELYN:
Admiral of the Ends of the Earth. By Melville Bell Grosvenor. 36-48, July 1957
The Nation Honors Admiral Richard E. Byrd. 567-578, Apr. 1962
The Society's Hubbard Medal Awarded to Commander MacMillan. 563-564, Apr. 1953
Note: Tribute was paid to the MacMillans by Admiral Byrd.
Author
All-out Assault on Antarctica. 141-180, Aug. 1956
Our Navy Explores Antarctica. U. S. Navy official photos. 429-522, Oct. 1974
To the Men at South Pole Station. 1-4, July 1957

BYZANTINE ART:
Athens to Istanbul. By Jean and Franc Shor. 37-76, Jan. 1956
Island of Faith in the Sinai Wilderness (St. Catherine's Monastery). By George H. Forsyth. Photos by Robert F. Sisson. 82-106, Jan. 1964
Mount Sinai's Holy Treasures (St. Catherine's Monastery). By Kurt Weitzmann. Photos by Fred Anderegg. 109-127, Jan. 1964

BYZANTINE EMPIRE:
Athens to Istanbul. By Jean and Franc Shor. 37-76, Jan. 1956
A New Look at Medieval Europe. By Kenneth M. Setton. Paintings by Andre Durenceau and Birney Lettick. 799-859, Dec. 1962
Yankee Cruises Turkey's History-haunted Coast. By Irving and Electa Johnson. Photos by Joseph J. Scherschel. 798-845, Dec. 1969

C

C & O CANAL. *See* Chesapeake and Ohio Canal

CABLEWAY:
Across the Ridgepole of the Alps. By Walter Meayers Edwards. 410-419, Sept. 1960

CABOT, JOHN:
The British Way. By Sir Evelyn Wrench. 421-541, Apr. 1949

CACAO:
Happy-go-lucky Trinidad and Tobago. By Charles Allmon. 35-75, Jan. 1953

CACTI:
Abundant Life in a Desert Land. By Walter Meayers Edwards. 424-436, Sept. 1973
American Wild Flower Odyssey. By P. L. Ricker. 603-634, May 1953

CADES COVE, Tennessee:
The People of Cades Cove. By William O. Douglas. Photos by Thomas Nebbia and Otis Imboden. 60-95, July 1962

CAERNARVON CASTLE, Caernarvonshire, Wales:
The Investiture of Great Britain's Prince of Wales. By Allan C. Fisher, Jr. Photos by James L. Stanfield and Adam Woolfitt. 698-715, Nov. 1969

CAFFERY, JEFFERSON: Author:
Fresh Treasures from Egypt's Ancient Sands. Photos by David S. Boyer. 611-650, Nov. 1955

CAIRNS, ROBERT: Author:
Sunny Corsica: French Morsel in the Mediterranean. Photos by Joseph J. Scherschel. 401-423, Sept. 1973

CAIRO, Egypt:
"Around the World in Eighty Days." By Newman Bumstead. 705-750, Dec. 1951
Cairo, Troubled Capital of the Arab World. By William S. Ellis. Photos by Winfield Parks. 639-667, May 1972
Safari from Congo to Cairo. By Elsie May Bell Grosvenor. Photos by Gilbert Grosvenor. 721-771, Dec. 1954
See also Akhenaten Temple Project

CAISSON DISEASE. *See* The Bends

CAJUNLAND, Louisiana's French-speaking Coast. By Bern Keating. Photos by Charles Harbutt and Franke Keating. 353-391, Mar. 1966

CALAVERAS BIG TREES STATE PARK, California:
Saving Earth's Oldest Living Things. By Andrew H. Brown. Photos by Raymond Moulin and author. 679-695, May 1951

CALCUTTA, India:
Calcutta, India's Maligned Metropolis. By Peter T. White. Photos by Raghubir Singh. 534-563, Apr. 1973
From the Hair of Siva. By Helen and Frank Schreider. 445-503, Oct. 1960
The Ganges, River of Faith. By John J. Putman. Photos by Raghubir Singh. 445-483, Oct. 1971

CALDY, the Monks' Island (Wales). By John E. H. Nolan. 564-578, Oct. 1955

CALENDARS:
A Bold New Look at Our Past. The Editor. 62-63, Jan. 1975
Exploring the Mind of Ice Age Man. By Alexander Marshack. 64-89, Jan. 1975
The Maya: Riddle of the Glyphs. By George E. Stuart. Photos by Otis Imboden. 768-791, Dec. 1975

CALGARY, Alberta, Canada:
Canada's Heartland, the Prairie Provinces. By W. E. Garrett. 443-489, Oct. 1970

CARONI SWAMP SANCTUARY, Trinidad:

New Scarlet Bird in Florida Skies. By Paul A. Zahl. 874-882, Dec. 1967

CARPATHIAN MOUNTAINS, Europe:

Americans Afoot in Rumania. By Dan Dimancescu. Photos by Dick Durrance II and Christopher G. Knight. 810-845, June 1969

CARR, ARCHIE: Author:

Alligators: Dragons in Distress. Photos by Treat Davidson and Laymond Hardy. 133-148, Jan. 1967

Imperiled Gift of the Sea: Caribbean Green Turtle. Photos by Robert E. Schroeder. 876-890, June 1967

CARR, GERALD P.:

Skylab, Outpost on the Frontier of Space. By Thomas Y. Canby. Photos by the nine mission astronauts. 441-469, Oct. 1974

CARRAO, Río, Venezuela:

Jungle Journey to the World's Highest Waterfall. By Ruth Robertson. 655-690, Nov. 1949

CARSON, Camp, Colorado:

School for Survival. By Curtis E. LeMay. 565-602, May 1953

CARTER, JEFF: Photographer:

"The Alice" in Australia's Wonderland. By Alan Villiers. Photos by Jeff Carter and David Moore. 230-257, Feb. 1966

CARTER, T. DONALD: Author:

Stalking Central Africa's Wildlife. Paintings by Walter A. Weber. 264-286, Aug. 1956

CARTHAGE (Ancient City), North Africa:

The Phoenicians, Sea Lords of Antiquity. By Samuel W. Matthews. Photos by Winfield Parks. Paintings by Robert C. Magis. 149-189, Aug. 1974

CARTIER, JACQUES:

North Through History Aboard *White Mist.* By Melville Bell Grosvenor. Photos by Edwin Stuart Grosvenor. 1-55, July 1970

CARTOGRAPHERS:

Eight Maps of Discovery. 757-769, June 1953

See also Bumstead, Newman; Chamberlin, Wellman; NGS: Cartographic Division

CARTOGRAPHY:

How We Mapped the Moon. By David W. Cook. 240-245, Feb. 1969

Landsat Looks at Hometown Earth. By Barry C. Bishop. 140-147, July 1976
     Contents: How the color photomosaic supplement *Portrait U.S.A.* was made from Landsat imagery

Remote Sensing: New Eyes to See the World. By Kenneth F. Weaver. 46-73, Jan. 1969

Science Explores the Monsoon Sea. By Samuel W. Matthews. Photos by Robert F. Sisson. 554-575, Oct. 1967

See also Globes; Inter-American Geodetic Survey; NGS: Cartographic Division; U. S. Coast and Geodetic Survey

CARTOONS:

Fun Helped Them Fight. By Stuart E. Jones. 95-104, Jan. 1948

CARTOONS—*Continued*

The Magic Worlds of Walt Disney. By Robert de Roos. Photos by Thomas Nebbia. 159-207, Aug. 1963

CASABLANCA, Morocco:

From Sea to Sahara in French Morocco. By Jean and Franc Shor. 147-188, Feb. 1955

Morocco, Land of the Farthest West. By Thomas J. Abercrombie. 834-865, June 1971

CASCADE RANGE, U. S.:

Forest Fire: The Devil's Picnic. By Stuart E. Jones and Jay Johnston. 100-127, July 1968

Mexico to Canada on the Pacific Crest Trail. By Mike W. Edwards. Photos by David Hiser. 741-779, June 1971

New National Park Proposed: The Spectacular North Cascades. By Nathaniel T. Kenney. Photos by James P. Blair. 642-667, May 1968

Sno-Cats Mechanize Oregon Snow Survey. By Andrew H. Brown. Photos by John E. Fletcher. 691-710, Nov. 1949

Washington Wilderness, the North Cascades. By Edwards Park. Photos by Kathleen Revis. 335-367, Mar. 1961

See also Rainier, Mount

CASE, LELAND D.: Author:

Back to the Historic Black Hills. Photos by Bates Littlehales. 479-509, Oct. 1956

CASE, PAUL EDWARD: Author:

Boom Time in Kuwait. 783-802, Dec. 1952

I Become a Bakhtiari. 325-358, Mar. 1947

CASH, J. ALLAN: Photographer:

From Barra to Butt in the Hebrides. By Isobel Wylie Hutchison. 559-580, Oct. 1954

Lundy, Treasure Island of Birds. By P. T. Etherton. 675-698, May 1947

CASSIDY, BUTCH:

Riding the Outlaw Trail. By Robert Redford. Photos by Jonathan Blair. 622-657, Nov. 1976

CASTE SYSTEM. *See* Hindus and Hinduism

CASTERET, NORBERT: Author:

Lascaux Cave, Cradle of World Art. Photos by Maynard Owen Williams. 771-794, Dec. 1948

Author-Photographer

Probing Ice Caves of the Pyrenees. 391-404, Mar. 1953
     Included: Casteret Grotto

CASTILLO DE SAN MARCOS, St. Augustine, Florida:

St. Augustine, Nation's Oldest City, Turns 400. By Robert L. Conly. 196-229, Feb. 1966

CASTLES:

Baltic Cruise of the *Caribbee.* By Carleton Mitchell. 605-646, Nov. 1950
     Included: Bohus, Hammershus, Kalmar Nyckel, Karlsten Fortress, and Stegeborg

The Britain That Shakespeare Knew. By Louis B. Wright. Photos by Dean Conger. 613-665, May 1964
     Included: Baynard's, Berkeley, Cawdor, Glamis, Middleham, Tower of London, Windsor

British Castles, History in Stone. By Norman Wil-

CHARTING Our Sea and Air Lanes. By Stuart E. Jones. Photos by J. Baylor Roberts. 189-209, Feb. 1957

CHARTRES, Cathedral of, France:
Chartres: Legacy From the Age of Faith. By Kenneth MacLeish. Photos by Dean Conger. 857-882, Dec. 1969

CHARYBDIS (Whirlpool and Legendary Monster). *See* Messina, Strait of

CHATEAUX:
France's Past Lives in Languedoc. By Walter Meayers Edwards. 1-43, July 1951
Included: Cité (Fortress), Carcassonne; Polignac
Lafayette's Homeland, Auvergne. By Howell Walker. 419-436, Sept. 1957
Included: Aix, Chavaniac, Du Motier, La Grange, St. Romain, Tournoël
River of Counts and Kings: The Loire. By Kenneth MacLeish. Photos by Dean Conger. 822-869, June 1966
Included: Amboise, Angers, Arlempdes, Azay-le-Rideau, Blois, Chambord, Chaumont, Chenonceaux, Cheverny, Chinon, Gien, Langeais, Saumur, Sully, Ussé

CHATURVEDI, M. D.: Author:
The Elephant and I. 489-507, Oct. 1957

CHAUCER, GEOFFREY:
The British Way. By Sir Evelyn Wrench. 421-541, Apr. 1949

CHEESE AND CHEESE MAKING:
Deep in the Heart of "Swissconsin." By William H. Nicholas. Photos by J. Baylor Roberts. 781-800, June 1947
Helping Holland Rebuild Her Land. By Gilbert M. Grosvenor and Charles Neave. 365-413, Sept. 1954
See also Goats of Thunder Hill; Switzerland (High-rise)

CHEKIANG (Province), China:
Operation Eclipse: 1948. By William A. Kinney. 325-372, Mar. 1949

CHELLEAN CULTURE:
Exploring 1,750,000 Years Into Man's Past. By L. S. B. Leakey. Photos by Robert F. Sisson. 564-589, Oct. 1961

CHELSEA, London's Haven of Individualists. By James Cerruti. Photos by Adam Woolfitt. 28-55, Jan. 1972

CHEMICAL INDUSTRY:
Today on the Delaware, Penn's Glorious River. By Albert W. Atwood. Photos by Robert F. Sisson. 1-40, July 1952

CHEMICAL POLLUTION:
Pollution, Threat to Man's Only Home. By Gordon Young. Photos by James P. Blair. 738-781, Dec. 1970
Quicksilver and Slow Death. By John J. Putman. Photos by Robert W. Madden. 507-527, Oct. 1972

CHEMISTRY:
The British Way. By Sir Evelyn Wrench. 421-541, Apr. 1949
The Romance of American Furs. By Wanda Burnett. 379-402, Mar. 1948

CHEMISTRY—*Continued*
Included: The plasticizing of furs, developed by Dr. José B. Calva
Uncle Sam's House of 1,000 Wonders (National Bureau of Standards). By Lyman J. Briggs and F. Barrows Colton. 755-784, Dec. 1951
See also Biochemistry; Perfume

CHEROKEE INDIANS:
Pack Trip Through the Smokies. By Val Hart. Photos by Robert F. Sisson. 473-502, Oct. 1952
See also Oklahoma, the Adventurous One

CHESAPEAKE AND OHIO CANAL:
Waterway to Washington, the C & O Canal. By Jay Johnston. 419-439, Mar. 1960

CHESAPEAKE BAY, and Region:
Chesapeake Country. By Nathaniel T. Kenney. Photos by Bates Littlehales. 370-411, Sept. 1964
"Delmarva," Gift of the Sea. By Catherine Bell Palmer. 367-399, Sept. 1950
Maryland on the Half Shell. By Stuart E. Jones. Photos by Robert W. Madden. 188-229, Feb. 1972
One Hundred Hours Beneath the Chesapeake. By Gilbert C. Klingel. Photos by Willard R. Culver. 681-696, May 1955
Round About the Nation's Capital, map supplement. Apr. 1956
Roving Maryland's Cavalier Country. By William A. Kinney. 431-470, Apr. 1954
The Sailing Oystermen of Chesapeake Bay. By Luis Marden. 798-819, Dec. 1967
This Is My Island, Tangier. By Harold G. Wheatley. Photos by David Alan Harvey. 700-725, Nov. 1973
See also Eastern Shore; Virginia (Captain Smith; History Keeps House); *and* Chesapeake Bay Bridge-Tunnel; Intracoastal Waterway

CHESAPEAKE BAY BRIDGE-TUNNEL:
Over and Under Chesapeake Bay. By David S. Boyer. 593-612, Apr. 1964

CHESSMEN Come to Life in Marostica. By Alexander Taylor. 658-668, Nov. 1956

CHESTER DALE COLLECTION:
Great Masters of a Brave Era in Art (Impressionist). By Hereward Lester Cooke, Jr. 661-697, May 1961

CHETELAT, ENZO DE: Author:
Roaming Korea South of the Iron Curtain. 777-808, June 1950

CHIANG KAI-SHEK:
Eyes on the China Coast. By George W. Long. 505-512, Apr. 1953
Taiwan: The Watchful Dragon. By Helen and Frank Schreider. 1-45, Jan. 1969

CHIAPAS (State), Mexico:
The Maya. 729-811, Dec. 1975
I. Children of Time. By Howard La Fay. Photos by David Alan Harvey. 729-767
Included: Bonampak; Chamula; Palenque
II. Riddle of the Glyphs. By George E. Stuart. Photos by Otis Imboden. 768-791
Included: Palenque; Yaxchilán
See also Piedra Parada

CHICAGO, Illinois:

The Great Lakes: Is It Too Late? By Gordon Young. Photos by James L. Amos and Martin Rogers. 147-185, Aug. 1973

Illinois—Healthy Heart of the Nation. By Leo A. Borah. Photos by B. Anthony Stewart and Willard R. Culver. 781-820, Dec. 1953

Illinois: The City and the Plain. By Robert Paul Jordan. Photos by James L. Stanfield and Joseph J. Scherschel. 745-797, June 1967

Mapping the Nation's Breadbasket. By Frederick Simpich. 831-849, June 1948

CHICHÉN ITZÁ, Yucatán, Mexico:

Into the Well of Sacrifice. 540-561, Oct. 1961
I. Return to the Sacred Cenote. By Eusebio Dávalos Hurtado. 540-549
II. Treasure Hunt in the Deep Past. By Bates Littlehales. 550-561

The Maya, Children of Time. By Howard La Fay. Photos by David Alan Harvey. 729-767, Dec. 1975

CHICHICASTENANGO, Guatemala:

Easter Week in Indian Guatemala. By John Scofield. 406-417, Mar. 1960

Guatemala Revisited. By Luis Marden. 525-564, Oct. 1947

CHICKENS:

Easter Egg Chickens. By Frederick G. Vosburgh. Photos by B. Anthony Stewart. 377-387, Sept. 1948

See also Onagadori

CHIDSEY, DONALD BARR: Author:

The Old Boston Post Roads. 189-205, Aug. 1962

CHIHUAHUA (State), Mexico:

The Tarahumaras: Mexico's Long Distance Runners. By James Norman. Photos by David Hiser. 702-718, May 1976

CHILDHOOD Summer on the Maine Coast. By Arline Strong. 436-444, Sept. 1960

CHILDREN:

Blue-eyed Indian: A City Boy's Sojourn with Primitive Tribesmen in Central Brazil. By Harald Schultz. 65-89, July 1961

Children's Art Around the World. By Newman Bumstead. 365-387, Mar. 1957

Dinkelsbühl Rewards Its Children. By Charles Belden. 255-268, Feb. 1957

The Family: A Mormon Shrine. 459-463, Apr. 1975

4-H Boys and Girls Grow More Food. By Frederick Simpich. 551-582, Nov. 1948

The GI and the Kids of Korea. By Robert H. Mosier. 635-664, May 1953

In Touch With Nature. Text by Elizabeth A. Moize. Photos by Steve Raymer. 537-543, Apr. 1974

Norway Cracks Her Mountain Shell. By Sydney Clark. Photos by Gilbert Grosvenor and Ole Friele Backer. 171-211, Aug. 1948

Passage to Freedom in Viet Nam. By Gertrude Samuels. 858-874, June 1955

Seashore Summer: One Mother's Recipe for Smallboy Bliss. By Arline Strong. 436-444, Sept. 1960

Uncle Sam Bends a Twig in Germany. By Frederick Simpich. Photos by J. Baylor Roberts. 529-550, Oct. 1948

CHILDREN—*Continued*

We Build a School for Sherpa Children. By Sir Edmund Hillary. 548-551, Oct. 1962

Zoo Animals Go to School. By Marion P. McCrane. Photos by W. E. Garrett. 694-706, Nov. 1956

See also Boy Scouts; Children's Village; Children's Zoo; Clarke School for the Deaf; Little Tibet in Switzerland; Spafford Memorial Children's Hospital

CHILDREN of the Sun and Moon. By Harald Schultz; translated from German by Curtis T. Everett. 340-363, Mar. 1959

CHILDREN'S BOOKS. *See* Books, NGS: Children's Books

CHILDREN'S MAGAZINES, NGS. *See* School Bulletin; *WORLD*

CHILDREN'S VILLAGE in Switzerland, Pestalozzi. Photos by Alfred Lammer. 268-282, Aug. 1959

CHILDREN'S ZOO, Regent's Park, London:

London's Zoo of Zoos. By Thomas Garner James. 771-786, June 1953

CHILE:

Atlantic Odyssey: Iceland to Antarctica. By Newman Bumstead. Photos by Volkmar Wentzel. 725-780, Dec. 1955

Chile, Republic on a Shoestring. By Gordon Young. Photos by George F. Mobley. 437-477, Oct. 1973

Chile, the Long and Narrow Land. By Kip Ross. 185-235, Feb. 1960

The Lost Empire of the Incas. By Loren McIntyre. Art by Ned and Rosalie Seidler. 729-787, Dec. 1973
A Pictorial Chronicle of the Incas. 747-753

Parks, Plans, and People: How South America Guards Her Green Legacy. By Mary and Laurance Rockefeller. Photos by George F. Mobley. 74-119, Jan. 1967

See also Easter Island; Patagonia; Torre Egger; Valparaíso

CHILIN (Kirin), China:

In Manchuria Now. By W. Robert Moore. 389-414, Mar. 1947

CHIMOR EMPIRE:

Chan Chan, Peru's Ancient City of Kings. By Michael E. Moseley and Carol J. Mackey. Photos by David Brill. 318-345, Mar. 1973

CHIMPANZEES:

Miss Goodall and the Wild Chimpanzees (Television film). 831A-831B, Dec. 1965

My Friends the Wild Chimpanzees. Special Publication announced. 408-417, Mar. 1966

My Life Among Wild Chimpanzees. By Jane Goodall. Photos by Baron Hugo van Lawick and author. 272-308, Aug. 1963

New Discoveries Among Africa's Chimpanzees. By Baroness Jane van Lawick-Goodall. Photos by Baron Hugo van Lawick. 802-831, Dec. 1965

School for Space Monkeys. 725-729, May 1961

CHIMU (People). *See* Chimor Empire

CHINA (People's Republic of China):

Adventures in Lololand. By Rennold L. Lowy. 105-118, Jan. 1947

CHINA (People's Republic of China)—*Continued*

Along the Yangtze, Main Street of China. By W. Robert Moore. 325-356, Mar. 1948

The Caves of the Thousand Buddhas. By Franc and Jean Shor. 383-415, Mar. 1951

China, Atlas series supplement. Nov. 1964

China Coast and Korea, map supplement. Oct. 1953

China Unveils Her Newest Treasures. Photos by Robert W. Madden. 848-857, Dec. 1974

Eyes on the China Coast. By George W. Long. 505-512, Apr. 1953

How Fruit Came to America. By J. R. Magness. Paintings by Else Bostelmann. 325-377, Sept. 1951

How the Kazakhs Fled to Freedom. By Milton J. Clark. 621-644, Nov. 1954

In Manchuria Now. By W. Robert Moore. 389-414, Mar. 1947

A Lady From China's Past. Photos from *China Pictorial*. Text by Alice J. Hall. 660-681, May 1974

Operation Eclipse: 1948. By William A. Kinney. 325-372, Mar. 1949

Our Vegetable Travelers. By Victor R. Boswell. Paintings by Else Bostelmann. 145-217, Aug. 1949

Return to Changing China. By Audrey Topping. 801-833, Dec. 1971

This Is the China I Saw. By Jørgen Bisch. 591-639, Nov. 1964
    Included: Canton; Hangchow; Peking; Shanghai; Sian; Tatung; Yun Kang Caves

Those Outlandish Goldfish! By Paul A. Zahl. 514-533, Apr. 1973
    Included: China's 1960 postage stamp series

Trawling the China Seas. Photos by J. Charles Thompson. 381-395, Mar. 1950

The World in Your Garden (Flowers). By W. H. Camp. Paintings by Else Bostelmann. 1-65, July 1947

See also Kunming; Peking

CHINA, Republic of. *See* Taiwan

CHINATOWN, the Gilded Ghetto. By William Albert Allard. 627-643, Nov. 1975

CHINCHILLAS:
The Romance of American Furs. By Wanda Burnett. 379-402, Mar. 1948

CHIRIQUÍ (Province), Panama:
Exploring Ancient Panama by Helicopter. By Matthew W. Stirling. Photos by Richard H. Stewart. 227-246, Feb. 1950

Panama, Link Between Oceans and Continents. By Jules B. Billard. Photos by Bruce Dale. 402-440, Mar. 1970

CHISOS MOUNTAINS, Texas:
Big Bend: Jewel in the Texas Desert. By Nathaniel T. Kenney. Photos by James L. Stanfield. 104-133, Jan. 1968

CHITTAGONG HILL TRACTS, Bangladesh:
Bangladesh: Hope Nourishes a New Nation. By William S. Ellis. Photos by Dick Durrance II. 295-333, Sept. 1972

The Peaceful Mrus of Bangladesh. By Claus-Dieter Brauns. 267-286, Feb. 1973

CHLOROPHYLL:
How the Sun Gives Life to the Sea (Photosynthesis). By Paul A. Zahl. 199-225, Feb. 1961

CHOCÓ (Region), Colombia:
Capturing Strange Creatures in Colombia. By Marte Latham. Photos by Tor Eigeland. 682-693, May 1966

CHOLLA CACTUS:
Abundant Life in a Desert Land. By Walter Meayers Edwards. 424-436, Sept. 1973

CHOLO INDIANS:
Capturing Strange Creatures in Colombia. By Marte Latham. Photos by Tor Eigeland. 682-693, May 1966

CHONG, JERRY: Photographer:
Saving the Nene, World's Rarest Goose. By S. Dillon Ripley. 745-754, Nov. 1965

CHOU EN-LAI:
Return to Changing China. By Audrey Topping. 801-833, Dec. 1971

CHOWNING, ANN: Photographer:
Blowgun Hunters of the South Pacific. By Jane C. Goodale. 793-817, June 1966

CHRISTCHURCH, New Zealand:
New Zealand, Pocket Wonder World. By Howell Walker. 419-460, Apr. 1952

New Zealand's Bountiful South Island. By Peter Benchley. Photos by James L. Amos. 93-123, Jan. 1972

CHRISTIANS AND CHRISTIANITY:
Hashemite Jordan, Arab Heartland. By John Scofield. 841-856, Dec. 1952

Jerusalem to Rome in the Path of St. Paul. By David S. Boyer. 707-759, Dec. 1956

The Land of Galilee. By Kenneth MacLeish. Photos by B. Anthony Stewart. 832-865, Dec. 1965

The Other Side of Jordan. By Luis Marden. 790-825, Dec. 1964

Pilgrimage to Holy Island and the Farnes. By John E. H. Nolan. 547-570, Oct. 1952

Pilgrims Follow the Christmas Star. By Maynard Owen Williams. 831-840, Dec. 1952

Searching Out Medieval Churches in Ethiopia's Wilds. By Georg Gerster. 856-884, Dec. 1970

Vézelay, Hill of the Pilgrims. By Melvin Hall. 229-247, Feb. 1953

Where Jesus Walked. By Howard La Fay. Photos by Charles Harbutt. 739-781, Dec. 1967

See also Amana Colonies; Churches; Crusades; Great St. Bernard Hospice; Greek Orthodox Church; Holy Week; Hutterites; Moravians; Mormons; Old Believers; Popes; Shakers

CHRISTIANSØ (Island), Denmark. *See* Baltic Cruise of the *Caribbee*

CHRISTMAS:
"The Adoration of the Magi," painting supplement. Jan. 1952

Christmas in Cookie Tree Land. By Louise Parker La Gorce. Photos by B. Anthony Stewart. 844-851, Dec. 1955

Old Salem, Morning Star of Moravian Faith. By Rowe Findley. Photos by Robert W. Madden. 818-837, Dec. 1970

CIVIL WAR, U. S. — *Continued*

With Honor a Century Ago. By Ulysses S. Grant 3rd. Photos by Bruce Dale. 435-469, Apr. 1965

Battlefields of the Civil War, double-sided Atlas series supplement. Apr. 1961

The Civil War. By Ulysses S. Grant 3rd. 437-449, Apr. 1961

The Civil War. Special Publication announced. 880-884, June 1969

Gettysburg and Vicksburg: the Battle Towns Today. By Robert Paul Jordan. Map notes by Carolyn Bennett Patterson. 4-57, July 1963

How We Found the *Monitor.* By John G. Newton. 48-61, Jan. 1975

Just a Hundred Years Ago. By Carl Sandburg. 1-3, July 1963

Lincoln, Man of Steel and Velvet. By Carl Sandburg. 239-241, Feb. 1960

Our Land Through Lincoln's Eyes. By Carolyn Bennett Patterson. Photos by W. D. Vaughn. 243-277, Feb. 1960

The Virginians. By Mike W. Edwards. Photos by David Alan Harvey. 588-617, Nov. 1974

Witness to a War: British Correspondent Frank Vizetelly. By Robert T. Cochran, Jr. 453-491, Apr. 1961

See also American Processional: History on Canvas; Atlanta; Harpers Ferry; Mobile; South Carolina Rediscovered

CLARK, DEENA: Author:

The Flowers That Say "Aloha." Photos by Robert B. Goodman. 121-131, Jan. 1967

Home Life in Paris Today. 43-72, July 1950

Iceland Tapestry. 599-630, Nov. 1951

La Jolla, a Gem of the California Coast. Photos by J. Baylor Roberts. 755-782, Dec. 1952

CLARK, EUGENIE: Author:

Into the Lairs of "Sleeping" Sharks. Photos by David Doubilet. 570-584, Apr. 1975

The Red Sea's Gardens of Eels. Photos by James L. Stanfield and David Doubilet. 724-735, Nov. 1972

The Red Sea's Sharkproof Fish. Photos by David Doubilet. 718-727, Nov. 1974

The Strangest Sea. Photos by David Doubilet. 338-343, Sept. 1975

CLARK, HARLAN B.: Author:

Yemen — Southern Arabia's Mountain Wonderland. 631-672, Nov. 1947

CLARK, LEWIS F.: Author:

Amid the Mighty Walls of Zion (Zion National Park). 37-70, Jan. 1954

CLARK, MILTON J.: Author-Photographer:

How the Kazakhs Fled to Freedom. 621-644, Nov. 1954

CLARK, ROBERT: Photographer:

Rafting Down the Yukon. By Keith Tryck. 830-861, Dec. 1975

CLARK, RONALD W.: Author:

Liechtenstein Thrives on Stamps. 105-112, July 1948

CLARK, SYDNEY: Author:

Luxembourg, Survivor of Invasions. Photos by Maynard Owen Williams. 791-810, June 1948

Mid-century Holland Builds Her Future. 747-778, Dec. 1950

Norway Cracks Her Mountain Shell. Photos by Gilbert Grosvenor and Ole Friele Backer. 171-211, Aug. 1948

CLARK, WILLIAM:

Following the Trail of Lewis and Clark. By Ralph Gray. 707-750, June 1953

CLARKE SCHOOL FOR THE DEAF, Northampton, Massachusetts:

Deaf Children Learn to Talk at Clarke School. By Lilian Grosvenor. Photos by Willard R. Culver. 379-397, Mar. 1955

CLASSICAL LANDS:

Classical Lands of the Mediterranean, map supplement. Dec. 1949

See also Greece; Roman Empire; Rome, Italy

CLEARWATER (River), Idaho:

Idaho Loggers Battle a River. 117-130, July 1951

CLEMENS, SAMUEL LANGHORNE. *See* Twain, Mark

CLEVELAND, GROVER:

Inside the White House. By Lonnelle Aikman. Photos by B. Anthony Stewart and Thomas Nebbia. 3-34, Jan. 1961

The Living White House. By Lonnelle Aikman. 593-643, Nov. 1966

Profiles of the Presidents: III. The American Giant Comes of Age. By Frank Freidel. 660-711, May 1965

CLIFF DWELLERS AND DWELLINGS:

Ancient Cliff Dwellers of Mesa Verde. By Don Watson. Photos by Willard R. Culver. 349-376, Sept. 1948

Cities of Stone in Utah's Canyonland. By W. Robert Moore. 653-677, May 1962

Cliff Dwellers of the Bering Sea. By Juan Muñoz. 129-146, Jan. 1954

Foxes Foretell the Future in Mali's Dogon Country. By Pamela Johnson Meyer. 431-448, Mar. 1969

Searching for Cliff Dwellers' Secrets (Wetherill Mesa). By Carroll A. Burroughs. 619-625, Nov. 1959

Solving the Riddles of Wetherill Mesa. By Douglas Osborne. Paintings by Peter V. Bianchi. 155-195, Feb. 1964

20th-century Indians Preserve Customs of the Cliff Dwellers. Photos by William Belknap, Jr. 196-211, Feb. 1964

Your Society to Seek New Light on the Cliff Dwellers. 154-156, Jan. 1959

CLIFF PAINTINGS. *See* Rock Paintings

CLIMATE:

Alaska's Mighty Rivers of Ice. By Maynard M. Miller. Photos by Christopher G. Knight. 194-217, Feb. 1967

What's Happening to Our Climate? By Samuel W. Matthews. 576-615, Nov. 1976

See also Weather

The CLIMB Up Cone Crater. By Alice J. Hall. Photos by Edgar D. Mitchell and Alan B. Shepard, Jr. 136-148, July 1971

CLIMBING Half Dome the Hard Way. By Galen Rowell. 782-791, June 1974

CLIMBING Our Northwest Glaciers. Photos by Bob and Ira Spring. 103-114, July 1953

CLINCH, NICHOLAS B.:
First La Gorce Medal Honors Antarctic Expedition. 864-867, June 1967
Author
First Conquest of Antarctica's Highest Peaks. 836-863, June 1967

A CLOCK for the Ages: Potassium-Argon. By Garniss H. Curtis. 590-592, Oct. 1961

CLOCKS AND CLOCKMAKING:
Split-second Time Runs Today's World. By F. Barrows Colton and Catherine Bell Palmer. 399-428, Sept. 1947
The Tower of the Winds. By Derek J. de Solla Price. Paintings by Robert C. Magis. 587-596, Apr. 1967

CLOUD FORMATIONS:
Historic Color Portrait of Earth From Space. By Kenneth F. Weaver. Photos by DODGE Satellite. 726-731, Nov. 1967

CLOUD Gardens in the Tetons. By Frank and John Craighead. 811-830, June 1948

CLOVE-SCENTED Zanzibar. By W. Robert Moore. 261-278, Feb. 1952

CLYDE, ROBERT, Family:
The Family: A Mormon Shrine. 459-463, Apr. 1975

COACHELLA VALLEY, California:
The Lure of the Changing Desert. 817-824, June 1954

COAL AND COAL MINING:
Coal Makes the Saar a Prize. By Franc Shor. 561-576, Apr. 1954
Illinois — Healthy Heart of the Nation. By Leo A. Borah. Photos by B. Anthony Stewart and Willard R. Culver. 781-820, Dec. 1953
In Manchuria Now. By W. Robert Moore. 389-414, Mar. 1947
Mountain Voices, Mountain Days (West Virginia). By Bryan Hodgson. Photos by Linda Bartlett. 118-146, July 1972
Pittsburgh: Workshop of the Titans. By Albert W. Atwood. 117-144, July 1949
The Search for Tomorrow's Power. By Kenneth F. Weaver. Photos by Emory Kristof. 650-681, Nov. 1972
Spitsbergen Mines Coal Again. 113-120, July 1948
This Land of Ours — How Are We Using It? By Peter T. White. Photos by Emory Kristof. 20-67, July 1976
Turnaround Time in West Virginia. By Elizabeth A. Moize. Photos by Jodi Cobb. 755-785, June 1976
Will Coal Be Tomorrow's "Black Gold"? By Gordon Young. Photos by James P. Blair. 234-259, Aug. 1975

COAST, U. S. See Atlantic Coast; Pacific Coast

COAST AND GEODETIC SURVEY. See U. S. Coast and Geodetic Survey

The COAST GUARD: Small Service With a Big Mission. By William S. Ellis. 113-139, July 1974
See also U. S. Coast Guard

COATS OF ARMS:
Flags of the Americas. By Elizabeth W. King. 633-657, May 1949
Included: Coats of arms of: Argentina; Bolivia; Brazil; Chile; Colombia; Costa Rica; Cuba; Dominican Republic; Ecuador; El Salvador; Guatemala; Haiti; Honduras; Mexico; Nicaragua; Panama; Paraguay; Peru; Uruguay; Venezuela
Flags of the United Nations. By Elizabeth W. King. 213-238, Feb. 1951
Included: Coats of arms of: Bolivia; Chile; Colombia; Costa Rica; Denmark; Dominican Republic; Ecuador; El Salvador; Greece; Guatemala; Haiti; Honduras; Iceland; Mexico; Nicaragua; Paraguay; Peru; Sweden; United Kingdom; Uruguay; Venezuela

COBB, JODI: Photographer:
California's Parched Oasis, the Owens Valley. By Judith and Neil Morgan. Photos by Jodi Cobb and Galen Rowell. 98-127, Jan. 1976
Turnaround Time in West Virginia. By Elizabeth A. Moize. 755-785, June 1976

COBRAS:
The Cobra, India's "Good Snake." By Harry Miller. Photos by author and Naresh and Rajesh Bedi. 393-409, Sept. 1970

COCHRAN, DORIS M.: Author:
Nature's Tank, the Turtle. Paintings by Walter A. Weber. 665-684, May 1952
Our Snake Friends and Foes. Paintings by Walter A. Weber. 334-364, Sept. 1954

COCHRAN, ROBERT T., Jr.: Author:
History and Beauty Blend in a Concord Iris Garden. Photos by M. Woodbridge Williams. 705-719, May 1959
Witness to a War: British Correspondent Frank Vizetelly. 453-491, Apr. 1961

COCK-OF-THE-ROCK:
Strange Courtship of the Cock-of-the-Rock. By E. Thomas Gilliard. 134-140, Jan. 1962

COCLÉ INDIAN CULTURE:
Exploring the Past in Panama. By Matthew W. Stirling. Photos by Richard H. Stewart. 373-399, Mar. 1949

COCOS (Keeling) ISLANDS, Indian Ocean:
Yankee Roams the Orient. By Irving and Electa Johnson. 327-370, Mar. 1951

COD, Cape, Massachusetts. See Cape Cod

COD FISHING:
Dory on the Banks: A Day in the Life of a Portuguese Fisherman. By James H. Pickerell. 573-583, Apr. 1968
Fishing in the Lofotens. Photos by Lennart Nilsson. 377-388, Mar. 1947
I Sailed with Portugal's Captains Courageous. By Alan Villiers. 565-596, May 1952
The Lonely Dorymen (Television film). 579A-579B, Apr. 1968

COMMAGENE (Ancient Country):

Throne Above the Euphrates. By Theresa Goell. 390-405, Mar. 1961

COMMERCE:

Behold the Computer Revolution. By Peter T. White. Photos by Bruce Dale and Emory Kristof. 593-633, Nov. 1970

COMMON TERNS:

Friend of the Wind: The Common Tern. By Ian Nisbet. Photos by Hope Alexander. 234-247, Aug. 1973

COMMONWEALTH OF NATIONS. *See* former name, British Commonwealth of Nations

COMMUNAL LIVING:

From Spear to Hoe on Groote Eylandt. By Howell Walker. 131-142, Jan. 1953

Old Salem, Morning Star of Moravian Faith. By Rowe Findley. Photos by Robert W. Madden. 818-837, Dec. 1970

Return to Changing China. By Audrey Topping. 801-833, Dec. 1971

See also Amana Colonies; Hutterites; Kibbutzim; Old Believers; Padanaram; Saint Véran; Shakers; Tasaday Tribe

COMMUNICATIONS:

The Flying Telegraph (Homing Pigeon). By Joseph F. Spears. Official U. S. Army Signal Corps photos. 531-554, Apr. 1947

Miracle Men of the Telephone. By F. Barrows Colton. 273-316, Mar. 1947

New Miracles of the Telephone Age. By Robert Leslie Conly. 87-120, July 1954

See also DEW Line; Satellites

COMMUNITY DEVELOPMENT PROGRAMS. *See* Bastar, India; *and* Peace Corps; YWCA

COMO, Lake, Italy:

Lombardy's Lakes, Blue Jewels in Italy's Crown. By Franc Shor. Photos by Joseph J. Scherschel. 58-99, July 1968

COMPUTERS:

Behold the Computer Revolution. By Peter T. White. Photos by Bruce Dale and Emory Kristof. 593-633, Nov. 1970

The Coming Revolution in Transportation. By Fredric C. Appel. Photos by Dean Conger. 301-341, Sept. 1969

Computer Helps Scholars Re-create an Egyptian Temple. By Ray Winfield Smith. Photos by Emory Kristof. 634-655, Nov. 1970

We're Doing Something About the Weather! By Walter Orr Roberts. 518-555, Apr. 1972

See also Integrated Circuits; Landsat; Space Flights and Research

CONCORD, Massachusetts:

History and Beauty Blend in a Concord Iris Garden. By Robert T. Cochran, Jr. Photos by M. Woodbridge Williams. 705-719, May 1959

Literary Landmarks of Massachusetts. By William H. Nicholas. Photos by B. Anthony Stewart and John E. Fletcher. 279-310, Mar. 1950

CONCORD, New Hampshire:

The Merrimack: River of Industry and Romance. By Albert W. Atwood. Photos by B. Anthony Stewart. 106-140, Jan. 1951

CONDON, GENEAL: Author:

Blossoms That Defy the Seasons (Flower Preservation). Photos by David S. Boyer. 420-427, Sept. 1958

The CONDOR, Soaring Spirit of the Andes. By Jerry McGahan. Photos by Libby McGahan. 684-709, May 1971

CONES AND CONE DWELLERS:

Cappadocia: Turkey's Country of Cones. Photos by Marc Riboud. 122-146, Jan. 1958

Keeping House in a Cappadocian Cave. By Jonathan S. Blair. 127-146, July 1970

CONGER, CLEMENT E.: Author-Photographer:

Portugal Is Different. 583-622, Nov. 1948

CONGER, DEAN: Author-Photographer:

Siberia: Russia's Frozen Frontier. 297-345, Mar. 1967

Photographer

Abraham, the Friend of God. By Kenneth MacLeish. 739-789, Dec. 1966

An American in Russia's Capital. By Thomas T. Hammond. 297-351, Mar. 1966

The Britain That Shakespeare Knew. By Louis B. Wright. 613-665, May 1964

Brunei, Borneo's Abode of Peace. By Joseph Judge. 207-225, Feb. 1974

Cape Cod, Where Sea Holds Sway Over Man and Land. By Nathaniel T. Kenney. 149-187, Aug. 1962

Chartres: Legacy From the Age of Faith. By Kenneth MacLeish. 857-882, Dec. 1969

The Coming Revolution in Transportation. By Fredric C. Appel. 301-341, Sept. 1969

Exploring Tomorrow With the Space Agency. By Allan C. Fisher, Jr. 48-89, July 1960

From Sea to Shining Sea: A Cross Section of the United States Along Historic Route 40. By Ralph Gray. Photos by Dean Conger and author. 1-61, July 1961

Help for Philippine Tribes in Trouble. By Kenneth MacLeish. 220-255, Aug. 1971

High-stepping Idaho. By William S. Ellis. 290-317, Mar. 1973

Hopes and Fears in Booming Thailand. By Peter T. White. 76-125, July 1967

I Fly the X-15. By Joseph A. Walker. 428-450, Sept. 1962

Java — Eden in Transition. By Kenneth MacLeish. 1-43, Jan. 1971

Journey to Outer Mongolia. By William O. Douglas. 289-345, Mar. 1962

Mr. Jefferson's Monticello. By Joseph Judge. Photos by Dean Conger and Richard S. Durrance. 426-444, Sept. 1966

The Other Yosemite. By Nathaniel T. Kenney. 762-781, June 1974

The Pilot's Story: Astronaut Shepard's Firsthand Account of His Flight. 432-444, Sept. 1961

River of Counts and Kings: The Loire. By Kenneth MacLeish. 822-869, June 1966

Siberia's Empire Road, the River Ob. By Robert Paul Jordan. 145-181, Feb. 1976

CONGO, Democratic Republic of the (formerly Belgian Congo, now Zaire):

Africa: The Winds of Freedom Stir a Continent. By

CRETAN CIVILIZATION. *See* Minoan Civilization

CRETE (Island), Greece:

The Aegean Isles: Poseidon's Playground. By Gilbert M. Grosvenor. 733-781, Dec. 1958

Crete, Cradle of Western Civilization. By Maynard Owen Williams. 693-706, Nov. 1953

War-torn Greece Looks Ahead. By Maynard Owen Williams. 711-744, Dec. 1949

CRICKETS, Nature's Expert Fiddlers. By Catherine Bell Palmer. 385-394, Sept. 1953

CRIME DETECTION:

The FBI: Public Friend Number One. By Jacob Hay. Photos by Robert F. Sisson. 860-886, June 1961

CRO-MAGNON MAN:

A Bold New Look at Our Past. The Editor. 62-63, Jan. 1975

Exploring the Mind of Ice Age Man. By Alexander Marshack. 64-89, Jan. 1975

CROATIA (Republic), Yugoslavia:

Yugoslavia: Six Republics in One. By Robert Paul Jordan. Photos by James P. Blair. 589-633, May 1970

CROCODILIANS:

Wildlife of Everglades National Park. By Daniel B. Beard. Paintings by Walter A. Weber. 83-116, Jan. 1949

Included: Alligators; Crocodiles

See also Alligators; Caymans

CROMWELL, EATON: Photographer:

Switzerland's Enchanted Val d'Hérens. By Georgia Engelhard Cromwell. 825-848, June 1955

CROMWELL, GEORGIA ENGELHARD: Author:

Switzerland's Enchanted Val d'Hérens. 825-848, June 1955

CROMWELL, OLIVER:

The British Way. By Sir Evelyn Wrench. 421-541, Apr. 1949

CROPP, BEN: Photographer:

Diving With Sea Snakes. By Kenneth MacLeish. 565-578, Apr. 1972

CROSS, JOHN W., Jr.: Author:

Westminster, World Series of Dogdom. 91-116, Jan. 1954

The CROSSING of Antarctica. By Sir Vivian Fuchs. Photos by George Lowe. 25-47, Jan. 1959

CROSSROADS of the Insect World. By J. W. MacSwain. Photos by Edward S. Ross. 844-857, Dec. 1966

CROWDER, WILLIAM: Artist:

Unlocking Secrets of the Northern Lights. By Carl W. Gartlein. 673-704, Nov. 1947

CROWLEY, DON: Artist:

Nature's Gifts to Medicine. By Lonnelle Aikman. Paintings by Lloyd K. Townsend and Don Crowley. 420-440, Sept. 1974

CROWN JEWELS:

Questing for Gems. By George S. Switzer. 835-863, Dec. 1971

CROWN JEWELS—*Continued*

Included: Great Britain; Iran; czarist Russia

See also Coronations (England; Iran)

CRUISE to Stone Age Arnhem Land. By Howell Walker. 417-430, Sept. 1949

CRUISES AND VOYAGES:

Adventures with the Survey Navy. By Irving Johnson. 131-148, July 1947

The Aegean Isles: Poseidon's Playground. By Gilbert M. Grosvenor. 733-781, Dec. 1958

Alone to Antarctica. By David Lewis. Drawings by Noel Sickles. 808-821, Dec. 1973

Atlantic Odyssey: Iceland to Antarctica. By Newman Bumstead. Photos by Volkmar Wentzel. 725-780, Dec. 1955

Baltic Cruise of the *Caribbee*. By Carleton Mitchell. 605-646, Nov. 1950

A Canoe Helps Hawaii Recapture Her Past. By Herb Kawainui Kane. Photos by David Hiser. 468-489, Apr. 1976

Captain Cook: The Man Who Mapped the Pacific. By Alan Villiers. Photos by Gordon W. Gahan. 297-349, Sept. 1971

Carib Cruises the West Indies. By Carleton Mitchell. 1-56, Jan. 1948

Channel Cruise to Glorious Devon. By Alan Villiers. Photos by Bates Littlehales. 208-259, Aug. 1963

Christopher Columbus and the New World He Found. By John Scofield. Photos by Adam Woolfitt. 584-625, Nov. 1975

Cowes to Cornwall. By Alan Villiers. Photos by Robert B. Goodman. 149-201, Aug. 1961

Cruising Colombia's "Ol' Man River." By Amos Burg. 615-660, May 1947

Cruising Florida's Western Waterways. By Rube Allyn. Photos by Bates Littlehales. 49-76, Jan. 1955

Cruising Japan's Inland Sea. By Willard Price. 619-650, Nov. 1953

Discoverers of the Pacific; Islands of the Pacific, double-sided map supplement. Dec. 1974

Down East to Nova Scotia. By Winfield Parks. 853-879, June 1964

Endeavour Sails the Inside Passage. By Amos Burg. 801-828, June 1947

Exploring England's Canals. By Bryan Hodgson. Photos by Linda Bartlett. 76-111, July 1974

Far North with "Captain Mac." By Miriam MacMillan. 465-513, Oct. 1951

Finisterre Sails the Windward Islands. By Carleton Mitchell. Photos by Winfield Parks. 755-801, Dec. 1965

French Riviera: Storied Playground on the Azure Coast. By Carleton Mitchell. Photos by Thomas Nebbia. 798-835, June 1967

A Fresh Breeze Stirs the Leewards. By Carleton Mitchell. Photos by Winfield Parks. 488-537, Oct. 1966

H.R.H. The Prince Philip, Duke of Edinburgh, Introduces to Members the Narrative of His Round-the-World Tour. 583-584, Nov. 1957

Hokule'a Follows the Stars to Tahiti. By David Lewis. Photos by Nicholas deVore III. 512-537, Oct. 1976

Homeward With Ulysses. By Melville Bell Grosve-

D

DARIUSLEUT (Sect):

The Hutterites, Plain People of the West. By William Albert Allard. 98-125, July 1970

DARLEY, JAMES M.:

Chief Cartographer, NGS. 875, Dec. 1961; 897, Dec. 1962; 108, 109, July 1964

DARWIN, CHARLES:

The British Way. By Sir Evelyn Wrench. 421-541, Apr. 1949

The Galapagos, Eerie Cradle of New Species. By Roger Tory Peterson. Photos by Alan and Joan Root. 541-585, Apr. 1967

In the Wake of Darwin's *Beagle*. By Alan Villiers. Photos by James L. Stanfield. 449-495, Oct. 1969

Lost World of the Galapagos. By Irving and Electa Johnson. 681-703, May 1959

DARWIN, Australia:

The Top End of Down Under. By Kenneth MacLeish. Photos by Thomas Nebbia. 145-174, Feb. 1973

DASARA (Festival): Mysore, India:

Mysore Celebrates the Death of a Demon. By Luc Bouchage. Photos by Ylla. 706-711, May 1958

DASSEN ISLAND, South Africa:

Oil and Penguins Don't Mix. Photos by Mike Holmes. 384-397, Mar. 1973

DATA PROCESSING, Electronic:

Behold the Computer Revolution. By Peter T. White. Photos by Bruce Dale and Emory Kristof. 593-633, Nov. 1970

Computer Helps Scholars Re-create an Egyptian Temple. By Ray Winfield Smith. Photos by Emory Kristof. 634-655, Nov. 1970

DATE LINE: United Nations, New York. By Carolyn Bennett Patterson. Photos by B. Anthony Stewart and John E. Fletcher. 305-331, Sept. 1961

DATE RAISING:

The Lure of the Changing Desert (California). 817-824, June 1954

DATING METHODS:

This Changing Earth. By Samuel W. Matthews. 1-37, Jan. 1973

Included: Carbon 14 dating, fossil dating, paleomagnetics, potassium-argon dating, radioactive-isotope dating

What's Happening to Our Climate? By Samuel W. Matthews. 576-615, Nov. 1976

Included: Ice-core dating, Sea-core dating, Tree-ring dating

See also Archeomagnetism Dating; Potassium-Argon Dating; Radiocarbon Dating; Tree-ring Dating

DAUFUSKIE (Island), South Carolina:

Sea Islands: Adventuring Along the South's Surprising Coast. By James Cerruti. Photos by Thomas Nebbia and James L. Amos. 366-393, Mar. 1971

DAUGHTERS OF THE AMERICAN REVOLUTION:

The DAR Story. By Lonnelle Aikman. Photos by B. Anthony Stewart and John E. Fletcher. 565-598, Nov. 1951

The DAUNTLESS Little Stilt. By Frederick Kent Truslow. 241-245, Aug. 1960

DÁVALOS HURTADO, EUSEBIO: Author:

Into the Well of Sacrifice. I. Return to the Sacred Cenote. 540-549, Oct. 1961

DAVENPORT, WILLIAM: Author:

Amiable Amsterdam. Photos by Adam Woolfitt. 683-705, May 1974

France's Wild, Watery South, the Camargue. 696-726, May 1973

Provence, Empire of the Sun. Photos by James A. Sugar. 692-715, May 1975

DAVIDSON, TREAT: Author-Photographer:

Bullfrog Ballet Filmed in Flight. 791-799, June 1963

Freezing the Trout's Lightning Leap. 525-530, Apr. 1958

Inside the World of the Honeybee. 188-217, Aug. 1959

Rose Aphids. 851-859, June 1961

Tree Snails, Gems of the Everglades. 372-387, Mar. 1965

Photographer

Alligators: Dragons in Distress. By Archie Carr. Photos by Treat Davidson and Laymond Hardy. 133-148, Jan. 1967

Moths That Behave Like Hummingbirds. 770-775, June 1965

DA VINCI, Project:

Laboratory in a Dirty Sky. By Rudolf J. Engelmann and Vera Simons. 616-621, Nov. 1976

DAVIS, MALCOLM: Author:

Nature's Clown, the Penguin. By David Hellyer and Malcolm Davis. 405-428, Sept. 1952

DAVIS, NEAL P.: Photographer:

The Past Is Present in Greenfield Village. By Beverley M. Bowie. Photos by Neal P. Davis and Willard R. Culver. 96-127, July 1958

DAVIS STRAIT, North America-Greenland:

I Sailed with Portugal's Captains Courageous. By Alan Villiers. 565-596, May 1952

DAVY, SIR HUMPHRY:

The British Way. By Sir Evelyn Wrench. 421-541, Apr. 1949

DAWSON, Canada:

Along the Yukon Trail. By Amos Burg. 395-416, Sept. 1953

DAYTON, WILLIAM A.: Author:

Beauty and Bounty of Southern State Trees. Paintings by Walter A. Weber. 508-552, Oct. 1957

Wealth and Wonder of Northern State Trees. Paintings by Walter A. Weber. 651-691, Nov. 1955

DEAD, Rites for the. *See* Burial Customs; Funerals

DEAD SEA, Israel-Jordan:

Abraham, the Friend of God. By Kenneth MacLeish. Photos by Dean Conger. 739-789, Dec. 1966

Geographical Twins (Holy Land and Utah) a World Apart. By David S. Boyer. 848-859, Dec. 1958

DEAD SEA SCROLLS:

The Men Who Hid the Dead Sea Scrolls. By A.

DEMOCRACY'S Fortress: Unsinkable Malta. By Ernle Bradford. Photos by Ted H. Funk. 852-879, June 1969

DENIS, ARMAND:
New Guinea's Rare Birds and Stone Age Men. By E. Thomas Gilliard. 421-488, Apr. 1953
Note: Armand Denis was the leader of the American Museum-Armand Denis Expedition.

DENISE (Diving Saucer):
Diving Saucer Takes to the Deep. By Jacques-Yves Cousteau. 571-586, Apr. 1960
See also Amphitrite (Denise Carrier)

DENMARK:
Baltic Cruise of the *Caribbee*. By Carleton Mitchell. 605-646, Nov. 1950
By Full-rigged Ship to Denmark's Fairyland. By Alan Villiers. Photos by Alexander Taylor and author. 809-828, Dec. 1955
Denmark, Field of the Danes. By William Graves. Photos by Thomas Nebbia. 245-275, Feb. 1974
Friendly Flight to Northern Europe. By Lyndon B. Johnson. Photos by Volkmar Wentzel. 268-293, Feb. 1964
Lifelike Man Preserved 2,000 Years in Peat. By P. V. Glob. 419-430, Mar. 1954
Thumbs Up Round the North Sea's Rim. By Frances James. Photos by Erica Koch. 685-704, May 1952
2,000 Miles Through Europe's Oldest Kingdom. By Isobel Wylie Hutchison. Photos by Maynard Owen Williams. 141-180, Feb. 1949
Under Canvas in the Atomic Age (U. S. Coast Guard). By Alan Villiers. 49-84, July 1955
The Vikings. By Howard La Fay. Photos by Ted Spiegel. 492-541, Apr. 1970
See also Copenhagen; Faeroe Islands; Greenland

DENNISON, EDWARD S.: Author:
Ambassadors of Good Will: The Peace Corps. By Sargent Shriver and Peace Corps Volunteers. 297-345, Sept. 1964
Bolivia. 315-319

DENTON, IVAN, Family:
An Ozark Family Carves a Living and a Way of Life. Photos by Bruce Dale. 124-133, July 1975

DENVER, Colorado:
Colorado, the Rockies' Pot of Gold. By Edward J. Linehan. Photos by James L. Amos. 157-201, Aug. 1969
Colorado by Car and Campfire. By Kathleen Revis. 207-248, Aug. 1954

DEOXYRIBONUCLEIC ACID (DNA):
The Awesome Worlds Within a Cell. By Rick Gore. Photos by Bruce Dale. Paintings by Davis Meltzer. 355-395, Sept. 1976
Included: The "Language of Life" foldout showing the replication of DNA and the manufacture of RNA and proteins

DEPARTMENT OF DEFENSE GRAVITY EXPERI-MENT. *See* DODGE Satellite

DE ROOS, ROBERT: Author:
Arizona: Booming Youngster of the West. Photos by Robert F. Sisson. 299-343, Mar. 1963
Costa Rica, Free of the Volcano's Veil. 125-152, July 1965

DE ROOS, ROBERT: Author—*Continued*
The Flower Seed Growers: Gardening's Color Merchants. Photos by Jack Fields. 720-738, May 1968
Los Angeles, City of the Angels. Photos by Thomas Nebbia. 451-501, Oct. 1962
The Magic Worlds of Walt Disney. Photos by Thomas Nebbia. 159-207, Aug. 1963
Massachusetts Builds for Tomorrow. Photos by B. Anthony Stewart. 790-843, Dec. 1966
New England's "Lively Experiment," Rhode Island. Photos by Fred Ward. 370-401, Sept. 1968
The Philippines, Freedom's Pacific Frontier. Photos by Ted Spiegel. 301-351, Sept. 1966

DESERT MUSEUM, Arizona:
Arizona's Window on Wildlife. By Lewis Wayne Walker. 240-250, Feb. 1958

DESERT Ordeal of the Knights (First Crusade). By Franc Shor. Photos by Thomas Nebbia. 797-837, Dec. 1963

DESERT River Through Navajo Land. By Alfred M. Bailey. Photos by author and Fred G. Brandenburg. 149-172, Aug. 1947

DESERT Sheikdoms of Arabia's Pirate Coast. By Ronald Codrai. 65-104, July 1956

DESERTS:
Abundant Life in a Desert Land. By Walter Meayers Edwards. 424-436, Sept. 1973
Great American Deserts. Special Publication announced. 870-874, June 1972
The Hohokam: First Masters of the American Desert. By Emil W. Haury. Photos by Helga Teiwes. 670-695, May 1967
In Search of Arabia's Past. By Peter Bruce Cornwall. 493-522, Apr. 1948
Lake Powell: Waterway to Desert Wonders. By Walter Meayers Edwards. 44-75, July 1967
The Lure of the Changing Desert. 817-824, June 1954
Magnetic Clues Help Date the Past. By Kenneth F. Weaver. 696-701, May 1967
Report from the Locust Wars. By Tony and Dickey Chapelle. 545-562, Apr. 1953
Scorpions: Living Fossils of the Sands. By Paul A. Zahl. 436-442, Mar. 1968
Wonders of the Desert World. Children's book announced. 718-720, Nov. 1976
See also Atacama Desert, Chile; Baja California; Chubut Province, Argentina; Colorado Desert; Coober Pedy, South Australia; Death Valley National Monument; Four Corners Country; Gobi; Great Rift Valley; Iran; Mazatzal Wilderness, Arizona; Mojave Desert; Oman; Organ Pipe Cactus National Monument; Sahara; Sinai; Sonoran Desert

DESERTS, Salt. *See* Danakil Depression, Ethiopia

DESIGN, Industrial:
Can We Harness the Wind? By Roger Hamilton. Photos by Emory Kristof. 812-829, Dec. 1975

DESPUJOLS, JEAN: Artist:
Portrait of Indochina. By W. Robert Moore and Maynard Owen Williams. 461-490, Apr. 1951

DETROIT, Michigan:

Work-hard, Play-hard Michigan. By Andrew H. Brown. 279-320, Mar. 1952

DETROIT (River), Michigan-Ontario:

J. W. Westcott, Postman for the Great Lakes. By Cy La Tour. 813-824, Dec. 1950

DETWILER, MARGARET M.: Author:

Hays, Kansas, at the Nation's Heart. Photos by John E. Fletcher. 461-490, Apr. 1952

DEVASTATED Land and Homeless People (Bali). By Samuel W. Matthews. Photos by Robert F. Sisson. 447-458, Sept. 1963

DEVEREUX, WALTER B.: Author:

New York Again Hails the Horse. 697-720, Nov. 1954

DEVIL DANCE:

A Journey to "Little Tibet." By Enakshi Bhavnani. Photos by Volkmar Wentzel. 603-634, May 1951

A Woman Paints the Tibetans. By Lafugie. 659-692, May 1949

DEVIL MOUNTAIN, Venezuela. *See* Auyán-tepuí

DEVIL'S ISLAND, Îles du Salut, French Guiana:

Yankee Roams the Orient. By Irving and Electa Johnson. 327-370, Mar. 1951

DEVONSHIRE, England:

Channel Cruise to Glorious Devon. By Alan Villiers. Photos by Bates Littlehales. 208-259, Aug. 1963

DeVORE, NICHOLAS, III: Photographer:

Hokule'a Follows the Stars to Tahiti. By David Lewis. 512-537, Oct. 1976

Should They Build a Fence Around Montana? By Mike W. Edwards. 614-657, May 1976
Growing Up in Montana. 650-657

Trek Across Arctic America. By Colin Irwin. 295-321, Mar. 1974

Wind, Wave, Star, and Bird. By David Lewis. 747-781, Dec. 1974

DEW LINE (Distant Early Warning Line), Sentry of the Far North. By Howard La Fay. 128-146, July 1958

DHAHRAN (Aẓ Ẓahrān), Saudi Arabia:

In Search of Arabia's Past. By Peter Bruce Cornwall. 493-522, Apr. 1948

Saudi Arabia: Beyond the Sands of Mecca. By Thomas J. Abercrombie. 1-53, Jan. 1966

DHANI NIVAT, Prince. *See* Sonakul, D.

DHOWS:

Sailing with Sindbad's Sons. By Alan Villiers. 675-688, Nov. 1948
Contents: *Bayan; Sheikh Mansur;* and Baggalas, Booms, Sambuks, Zarooks

Twilight of the Arab Dhow. By Marion Kaplan. 330-351, Sept. 1974

DIABLE, Île du, French Guiana. *See* Devil's Island

DIAMOND JUBILEE:

Weighing the Aga Khan in Diamonds. Photos by David J. Carnegie. 317-324, Mar. 1947

DIAMOND ROCK ("H.M.S. Diamond Rock"), Martinique:

Carib Cruises the West Indies. By Carleton Mitchell. 1-56, Jan. 1948

DIAMONDS:

Britain Tackles the East African Bush. By W. Robert Moore. 311-352, Mar. 1950
Included: Williamson mine in Tanganyika

Exploring the World of Gems. By W. F. Foshag. 779-810, Dec. 1950

The Jungle Was My Home. By Sasha Siemel. 695-712, Nov. 1952

The Many-sided Diamond. By George S. Switzer. 568-586, Apr. 1958

Questing for Gems. By George S. Switzer. 835-863, Dec. 1971

Weighing the Aga Khan in Diamonds. Photos by David J. Carnegie. 317-324, Mar. 1947

White Magic in the Belgian Congo. By W. Robert Moore. 321-362, Mar. 1952

DIARY of the President's Daughter: I See America First. By Lynda Bird Johnson. Photos by William Albert Allard. 874-904, Dec. 1965

DICKENS, CHARLES:

The British Way. By Sir Evelyn Wrench. 421-541, Apr. 1949

The England of Charles Dickens. By Richard W. Long. Photos by Adam Woolfitt. 443-483, Apr. 1974

DICKEY CHAPELLE Killed in Action. By W. E. Garrett. 270-271, Feb. 1966

DICKINSON, EMILY:

Literary Landmarks of Massachusetts. By William H. Nicholas. Photos by B. Anthony Stewart and John E. Fletcher. 279-310, Mar. 1950

DIETZ, ROBERT S.: Author:

The Explosive Birth of Myojin Island. 117-128, Jan. 1954

DIFFENDERFER, HOPE A.: Author:

Okinawa, the Island Rebuilt. 265-288, Feb. 1955

The DIFFIDENT Truffle, France's Gift to Gourmets. 419-426, Sept. 1956

DIKES AND LEVEES:

California's Surprising Inland Delta. By Judith and Neil Morgan. Photos by Charles O'Rear. 409-430, Sept. 1976
Included: Map showing the 1,100 miles of levees that rim the 55 islands reclaimed from marshland

Helping Holland Rebuild Her Land. By Gilbert M. Grosvenor and Charles Neave. 365-413, Sept. 1954

The Lower Mississippi. By Willard Price. Photos by W. D. Vaughn. 681-725, Nov. 1960

DIMANCESCU, DAN: Author:

Americans Afoot in Rumania. Photos by Dick Durrance II and Christopher G. Knight. 810-845, June 1969

Kayak Odyssey: From the Inland Sea to Tokyo. Photos by Christopher G. Knight. 295-337, Sept. 1967

DINGLE PENINSULA, Ireland:

Irish Ways Live On in Dingle. By Bryan Hodgson. Photos by Linda Bartlett. 551-576, Apr. 1976

DRAKE, SIR FRANCIS — *Continued*

don W. Gahan. 216-253, Feb. 1975

The World of Elizabeth I. By Louis B. Wright. Photos by Ted Spiegel. 668-709, Nov. 1968

Included: Historical map based on the Hondius Map of 1589, showing Drake's voyage around the world

DRAKENSBERG RANGE, South Africa. See Black Eagles; *and* Africa's Bushman Art Treasures

DRAMA. *See* Theater

DRESDEN, DONALD WILLIAM: Author:

Paris, Home Town of the World. Photos by Justin Locke. 767-804, June 1952

DREYFUS COLLECTION (Renaissance Bronzes):

Your National Gallery of Art After 10 Years. By John Walker. 73-103, Jan. 1952

DRILLING, Undersea. *See Glomar Challenger;* Mohole, Project

DRIVING the Mexican 1000: Rocks, Ruts, and Sand. By Michael E. Long. 569-575, Oct. 1972

DROUGHT:

Drought Bedevils Brazil's Sertão. By John Wilson. Photos by Gordon W. Gahan. 704-723, Nov. 1972

Drought Threatens the Tuareg World. By Victor Englebert. 544-571, Apr. 1974

The Imperiled Everglades. By Fred Ward. 1-27, Jan. 1972

The Niger: River of Sorrow, River of Hope. By Georg Gerster. 152-189, Aug. 1975

Oklahoma, the Adventurous One. By Robert Paul Jordan. Photos by Robert W. Madden. 149-189, Aug. 1971

The Top End of Down Under. By Kenneth MacLeish. Photos by Thomas Nebbia. 145-174, Feb. 1973

What's Happening to Our Climate? By Samuel W. Matthews. 576-615, Nov. 1976

DROWNED Galleons Yield Spanish Gold. By Kip Wagner. Photos by Otis Imboden. 1-37, Jan. 1965

DRUCKER, PHILIP: Author:

Gifts for the Jaguar God. By Philip Drucker and Robert F. Heizer. 367-375, Sept. 1956

DRUGS:

Nature's Gifts to Medicine. By Lonnelle Aikman. Paintings by Lloyd K. Townsend and Don Crowley. 420-440, Sept. 1974

See also Medicine and Health

DRUIDS. *See* Stonehenge

DRUMS to Dynamos on the Mohawk. By Frederick G. Vosburgh. Photos by B. Anthony Stewart. 67-110, July 1947

DRY-LAND Fleet Sails the Sahara. By Jean du Boucher. Photos by Jonathan S. Blair. 696-725, Nov. 1967

DRY TORTUGAS (Islands), Florida:

Blizzard of Birds: The Tortugas Terns. By Alexander Sprunt, Jr. 213-230, Feb. 1947

See also Shrimp (Shrimp Nursery)

DRYDEN, HUGH L.: Author:

Fact Finding for Tomorrow's Planes. Photos by Luis Marden. 757-780, Dec. 1953

Footprints on the Moon. Paintings by Davis Meltzer and Pierre Mion. 357-401, Mar. 1964

The International Geophysical Year: Man's Most Ambitious Study of His Environment. 285-298, Feb. 1956

DUBAI, United Arab Emirates:

The Arab World, Inc. By John J. Putman. Photos by Winfield Parks. 494-533, Oct. 1975

DUBLIN, Ireland:

Dublin's Historic Horse Show. By Maynard Owen Williams. 115-132, July 1953

The Friendly Irish. By John Scofield. Photos by James A. Sugar. 354-391, Sept. 1969

I Walked Some Irish Miles. By Dorothea Sheats. 653-678, May 1951

DU BOUCHER, JEAN: Author:

Dry-land Fleet Sails the Sahara. Photos by Jonathan S. Blair. 696-725, Nov. 1967

DUBROVNIK (Ragusa), Yugoslavia:

Yugoslavia's Window on the Adriatic. By Gilbert M. Grosvenor. 219-247, Feb. 1962

DUCK RAISING:

Long Island Outgrows the Country. By Howell Walker. Photos by B. Anthony Stewart. 279-326, Mar. 1951

DUCKBILLS. *See* Platypuses

DUCKS:

Duck Hunting with a Color Camera. By Arthur A. Allen. 514-539, Oct. 1951

Contents: Baldpates; Black Ducks; Buffleheads; Canvasbacks; Eiders; Gadwalls; Golden-eyes; Mallards; Mergansers; Muscovy Ducks; Old-squaws; Pintails; Redheads; Ringnecks; Ruddy Ducks; Scaups, Greater and Lesser; Shovellers; Teals, Blue-winged, and Cinnamon; Widgeons, European; Wood Ducks

DUFEK, GEORGE J.:

Hubbard Medal recipient. 589-590, Apr. 1959; 530, Oct. 1959

Author

Nuclear Power for the Polar Regions. 712-730, May 1962

What We've Accomplished in Antarctica. 527-557, Oct. 1959

DUGOUT CANOES:

Jungle Journey to the World's Highest Waterfall. By Ruth Robertson. 655-690, Nov. 1949

Sea Fever. By John E. Schultz. 237-268, Feb. 1949

DULUTH, Minnesota:

Minnesota Makes Ideas Pay. By Frederick G. Vosburgh. Photos by John E. Fletcher and B. Anthony Stewart. 291-336, Sept. 1949

DUMAS, FRÉDÉRIC:

Fish Men Explore a New World Undersea. By Jacques-Yves Cousteau. 431-472, Oct. 1952

DUNCAN, DAVID D.: Photographer:

Power Comes Back to Peiping. By Nelson T. Johnson and W. Robert Moore. 337-368, Sept. 1949

E

ELLIS, MELVIN R.: Author—*Continued*

Skunks Want Peace—or Else! Photos by Charles Philip Fox. 279-294, Aug. 1955

ELLIS, WILLIAM S.: Author:

Afo-A-Kom: A Sacred Symbol Comes Home. Photos by James P. Blair. 141-148, July 1974

Atlanta, Pacesetter City of the South. Photos by James L. Amos. 246-281, Feb. 1969

Bangladesh: Hope Nourishes a New Nation. Photos by Dick Durrance II. 295-333, Sept. 1972

Cairo, Troubled Capital of the Arab World. Photos by Winfield Parks. 639-667, May 1972

The Coast Guard: Small Service With a Big Mission. 113-139, July 1974

High-stepping Idaho. Photos by Dean Conger. 290-317, Mar. 1973

Istanbul, the City That Links Europe and Asia. Photos by Winfield Parks. 501-533, Oct. 1973

Lebanon, Little Bible Land in the Crossfire of History. Photos by George F. Mobley. 240-275, Feb. 1970

Lonely Cape Hatteras, Besieged by the Sea. Photos by Emory Kristof. 393-421, Sept. 1969

Romania: Maverick on a Tightrope. Photos by Winfield Parks. 688-713, Nov. 1975

Tracking Danger With the Ice Patrol. Photos by James R. Holland. 780-793, June 1968

Will Oil and Tundra Mix? Alaska's North Slope Hangs in the Balance. Photos by Emory Kristof. 485-517, Oct. 1971

Wisconsin's Door Peninsula. Photos by Ted Rozumalski. 347-371, Mar. 1969

Yellowstone at 100: The Pitfalls of Success. Photos by Jonathan Blair. 616-631, May 1972

ELLSWORTH HIGHLAND TRAVERSE:

Exploring Antarctica's Phantom Coast. By Edwin A. McDonald. Photos by W. D. Vaughn. 251-273, Feb. 1962

ELLSWORTH MOUNTAINS, Antarctica. *See* Sentinel Range

EL MORRO: Story in Stone (New Mexico). By Edwards Park. 237-244, Aug. 1957

EL SANGAY, Fire-breathing Giant of the Andes. By G. Edward Lewis. 117-138, Jan. 1950

ELSIE (Yawl):

Down East to Nova Scotia. By Winfield Parks. 853-879, June 1964

EMBROIDERY:

Madeira, Like Its Wine, Improves With Age. By Veronica Thomas. Photos by Jonathan Blair. 488-513, Apr. 1973

EMERALDS:

Questing for Gems. By George S. Switzer. 835-863, Dec. 1971

EMERSON, GILBERT: Artist:

How Man-made Satellites Can Affect Our Lives. By Joseph Kaplan. 791-810, Dec. 1957

EMERSON, GUY: Author:

The Kress Collection: A Gift to the Nation. 823-865, Dec. 1961

EMERSON, RALPH WALDO:

Literary Landmarks of Massachusetts. By William

EMERSON, RALPH WALDO—*Continued*

H. Nicholas. Photos by B. Anthony Stewart and John E. Fletcher. 279-310, Mar. 1950

EMORY, KENNETH P.: Author:

The Coming of the Polynesians. 732-745, Dec. 1974

The EMPEROR'S Private Garden: Kashmir. By Nigel Cameron. Photos by Brian Brake. 606-647, Nov. 1958

ENCHANTRESS! (White Tigress). By Theodore H. Reed. Photos by Thomas J. Abercrombie. 628-641, May 1961

ENCYCLOPAEDIA BRITANNICA EDUCATIONAL CORPORATION:

The World in Geographic Filmstrips. By Melvin M. Payne. 134-137, Jan. 1968

ENDANGERED SPECIES:

African Wildlife: Man's Threatened Legacy. By Allan C. Fisher, Jr. Photos by Thomas Nebbia. Paintings by Ned Seidler. 147-187, Feb. 1972

India Struggles to Save Her Wildlife. By John J. Putman. Paintings by Ned Seidler. 299-343, Sept. 1976

Vanishing Wildlife of North America. Special Publication announced. 865-868, June 1973

See also Andean Condors; Bighorn Sheep; Brown Pelicans; Giant Tortoises; Gorillas; Grizzly Bears; Harp Seals; Horses, Wild; Polar Bear; Snow Leopards; Vicuñas; Whales; *and* Everglades

ENDEAVOUR (Bark):

Captain Cook: The Man Who Mapped the Pacific. By Alan Villiers. Photos by Gordon W. Gahan. 297-349, Sept. 1971

ENDEAVOUR (Cutter) Sails the Inside Passage. By Amos Burg. 801-828, June 1947

The ENDURING Pyrenees. By Robert Laxalt. Photos by Edwin Stuart Grosvenor. 794-819, Dec. 1974

ENERGY RESEARCH AND DEVELOPMENT ADMINISTRATION. *See* listing under former name, Atomic Energy Commission

ENERGY SOURCES:

Can We Harness the Wind? By Roger Hamilton. Photos by Emory Kristof. 812-829, Dec. 1975

The Fire of Heaven: Electricity Revolutionizes the Modern World. By Albert W. Atwood. 655-674, Nov. 1948

Five Noted Thinkers Explore the Future. 68-75, July 1976

Included: Isaac Asimov, Richard F. Babcock, Edmund N. Bacon, Buckminster Fuller, Gerard Piel

Hunting Uranium Around the World. By Robert D. Nininger. Photos by Volkmar Wentzel. 533-558, Oct. 1954

The Search for Tomorrow's Power. By Kenneth F. Weaver. Photos by Emory Kristof. 650-681, Nov. 1972

This Land of Ours—How Are We Using It? By Peter T. White. Photos by Emory Kristof. 20-67, July 1976

See also Coal; Hydroelectric Power; Natural Gas; Nuclear Energy; Oil; Solar Energy

ENGELMANN, RUDOLF J.: Author:

Laboratory in a Dirty Sky. By Rudolf J. Engelmann and Vera Simons. 616-621, Nov. 1976

ERIGBAAGTSA (Indians):

Indians of the Amazon Darkness. By Harald Schultz. 737-758, May 1964

ERIM, KENAN T.: Author:

Ancient Aphrodisias and Its Marble Treasures. Photos by Jonathan S. Blair. 280-294, Aug. 1967

Aphrodisias, Awakened City of Ancient Art. Photos by Jonathan Blair. 766-791, June 1972

ERONGARÍCUARO, Mexico:

Lost Kingdom in Indian Mexico (Tarascan). By Justin Locke. 517-546, Oct. 1952

EROSION:

Erosion, Trojan Horse of Greece. By F. G. Renner. 793-812, Dec. 1947

Water for the World's Growing Needs. By Herbert B. Nichols and F. Barrows Colton. 269-286, Aug. 1952

See also Forests and Reforestation; Mud Slides; This Land of Ours; U. S. Soil Conservation Service

ERTAUD, JACQUES: Photographer:

Fish Men Discover a 2,200-year-old Greek Ship. By Jacques-Yves Cousteau. 1-36, Jan. 1954

Fish Men Explore a New World Undersea. By Jacques-Yves Cousteau. 431-472, Oct. 1952

ERZURUM, Turkey:

Turkey Paves the Path of Progress. By Maynard Owen Williams. 141-186, Aug. 1951

Where Turk and Russian Meet. By Ferdinand Kuhn. 743-766, June 1952

ESCALANTE CANYON, Utah:

Escalante: Utah's River of Arches. By W. Robert Moore. 399-425, Sept. 1955

Escalante Canyon—Wilderness at the Crossroads. By Jon Schneeberger. 270-285, Aug. 1972

First Motor Sortie into Escalante Land. By Jack Breed. 369-404, Sept. 1949

ESCORTING Mona Lisa to America. By Edward T. Folliard. 838-847, June 1963

ESKIMAUAN LINGUISTIC STOCK:

Nomads of the Far North. By Matthew W. Stirling. 471-504, Oct. 1949
    Hearty Folk Defy Arctic Storms. Paintings by W. Langdon Kihn. 479-494

ESKIMOS:

Alaska: Rising Northern Star. By Joseph Judge. Photos by Bruce Dale. 730-767, June 1975
    Included: Inupiat and Nunamiut Eskimos; also Eskimos of Nunapitchuk, Selawik, and Wainwright

Alaska Proudly Joins the Union. By Ernest Gruening. Photos by Thomas J. Abercrombie. 43-83, July 1959

Alaska's Russian Frontier: Little Diomede. Photos by Audrey and Frank Morgan. 551-562, Apr. 1951

Banks Island: Eskimo Life on the Polar Sea. By William O. Douglas. Photos by Clyde Hare. 703-735, May 1964

Canada Counts Its Caribou. 261-268, Aug. 1952

Canada's Caribou Eskimos. By Donald B. Marsh. 87-104, Jan. 1947

The Canadian North: Emerging Giant. By David S. Boyer. 1-43, July 1968

Caribou: Hardy Nomads of the North. By Jim

ESKIMOS—Continued

Rearden. 858-878, Dec. 1974

Cliff Dwellers of the Bering Sea. By Juan Muñoz. 129-146, Jan. 1954

Domesticating the Wild and Woolly Musk Ox. By John J. Teal, Jr. Photos by Robert W. Madden. 862-879, June 1970

Far North with "Captain Mac." By Miriam MacMillan. 465-513, Oct. 1951
    Included: Eskimos of Baffin Island, Greenland, Labrador; Polar Eskimos

Greenland Feels the Winds of Change. By John J. Putman. Photos by George F. Mobley. 366-393, Sept. 1975
    Included: Polar Eskimos of northwest Greenland, last of the true Eskimos

I Live With the Eskimos (Canadian). By Guy Mary-Rousseliere. 188-217, Feb. 1971

Indians of North America, double-sided map supplement. Dec. 1972
    Included: Central Eskimos; Copper Eskimos

The Last U. S. Whale Hunters. By Emory Kristof. 346-355, Mar. 1973
    "Ocean mammals are to us what the buffalo was to the Plains Indian." By Lael Morgan. 354-355

Milestones in My Arctic Journeys. By Willie Knutsen. 543-570, Oct. 1949

Nomad in Alaska's Outback. By Thomas J. Abercrombie. 540-567, Apr. 1969

Nomads of the Far North. By Matthew W. Stirling. 471-504, Oct. 1949
    Hearty Folk Defy Arctic Storms. Paintings by W. Langdon Kihn. 479-494

North Star Cruises Alaska's Wild West. By Amos Burg. 57-86, July 1952

Trek Across Arctic America. By Colin Irwin. 295-321, Mar. 1974

Vanished Mystery Men of Hudson Bay. By Henry B. Collins. 669-687, Nov. 1956

A Visit to the Living Ice Age. By Rutherford Platt. 525-545, Apr. 1957

Weather from the White North. By Andrew H. Brown. Photos by John E. Fletcher. 543-572, Apr. 1955

Will Oil and Tundra Mix? Alaska's North Slope Hangs in the Balance. By William S. Ellis. Photos by Emory Kristof. 485-517, Oct. 1971

ESSENES:

The Men Who Hid the Dead Sea Scrolls. By A. Douglas Tushingham. Paintings by Peter V. Bianchi. 785-808, Dec. 1958

ESTATES AND PLANTATIONS:

Land of Louisiana Sugar Kings. By Harnett T. Kane. Photos by Willard R. Culver. 531-567, Apr. 1958

Philadelphia Houses a Proud Past. By Harold Donaldson Eberlein. Photos by Thomas Nebbia. 151-191, Aug. 1960

Rhododendron Glories of Southwest Scotland. By David S. Boyer. Photos by B. Anthony Stewart and author. 641-664, May 1954

South Carolina Rediscovered. By Herbert Ravenel Sass. Photos by Robert F. Sisson. 281-321, Mar. 1953

See also Buttrick Garden; Georgia (Greener Fields); Hearst San Simeon State Historical Monument; Henry E. Huntington Library and Art Gallery;

EXTRAORDINARY Photographs of Earth Taken by Satellite *Tiros*. By W. G. Stroud. 293-302, Aug. 1960

EXUMA CAYS, Bahama Islands:

The Bahamas, Isles of the Blue-green Sea. By Carleton Mitchell. Photos by B. Anthony Stewart. 147-203, Feb. 1958

More of Sea Than of Land: The Bahamas. By Carleton Mitchell. Photos by James L. Stanfield. 218-267, Feb. 1967

EYE to Eye With Eagles. By Frederick Kent Truslow. 123-148, Jan. 1961

EYES:

Nature's Alert Eyes (Animal Eyes). By Constance P. Warner. 558-569, Apr. 1959

EYES on the China Coast. By George W. Long. 505-512, Apr. 1953

EYEWITNESS to War in the Holy Land. By Charles Harbutt. 782-795, Dec. 1967

F

FAO. *See* United Nations Food and Agriculture Organization

The **FBI**: Public Friend Number One. By Jacob Hay. Photos by Robert F. Sisson. 860-886, June 1961

F.N.R.S. 3 (Bathyscaph):

Deep Diving off Japan. By Georges S. Houot. 138-150, Jan. 1960

Diving Through an Undersea Avalanche. By Jacques-Yves Cousteau. 538-542, Apr. 1955

Four Years of Diving to the Bottom of the Sea. By Georges S. Houot. 715-731, May 1958

Photographing the Sea's Dark Underworld. By Harold E. Edgerton. 523-537, Apr. 1955

To the Depths of the Sea by Bathyscaphe. By Jacques-Yves Cousteau. 67-79, July 1954

Two and a Half Miles Down. By Georges S. Houot. 80-86, July 1954

FABLED Mount of St. Michael. By Alan Villiers. Photos by Bates Littlehales. 880-898, June 1964

The **FABULOUS** Sierra Nevada. By J. R. Challacombe. 825-843, June 1954

The **FABULOUS** State of Texas. By Stanley Walker. Photos by B. Anthony Stewart and Thomas Nebbia. 149-195, Feb. 1961

FACE to Face With Gorillas in Central Africa. By Paul A. Zahl. 114-137, Jan. 1960

FACT Finding for Tomorrow's Planes. By Hugh L. Dryden. Photos by Luis Marden. 757-780, Dec. 1953

FAEROE ISLANDS, North Atlantic Ocean:

The Faeroes, Isles of Maybe. By Ernle Bradford. Photos by Adam Woolfitt. 410-422, Sept. 1970

The Last Vikings (Television film). 434A-434B, Mar. 1972

FAIR, PAUL J.: Photographer:

Wildlife In and Near the Valley of the Moon. By H. H. Arnold. 401-414, Mar. 1950

FAIRBANKS, Alaska:

Busy Fairbanks Sets Alaska's Pace. By Bruce A. Wilson. 505-523, Oct. 1949

FAIRS:

America Goes to the Fair. By Samuel W. Matthews. 293-333, Sept. 1954

Australian New Guinea. By John Scofield. 604-637, May 1962
Included: Intertribal Fair

Belgium Welcomes the World (World's Fair). By Howell Walker. 795-837, June 1958

The Fair Reopens (New York World's Fair). Photos by James P. Blair. Text by Carolyn Bennett Patterson. 505-529, Apr. 1965
Included: Visitors' guide

4-H Boys and Girls Grow More Food. By Frederick Simpich. 551-582, Nov. 1948

Holy Week and the Fair in Sevilla (Spain). By Luis Marden. 499-530, Apr. 1951

I Walked Some Irish Miles. By Dorothea Sheats. 653-678, May 1951
Included: Galway Fair; Killorglin's Puck Fair

Kansai, Japan's Historic Heartland. By Thomas J. Abercrombie. 295-339, Mar. 1970
Included: Expo '70

Montreal Greets the World. By Jules B. Billard. 600-621, May 1967
Included: Expo 67

Russia as I Saw It. By Richard M. Nixon. Photos by B. Anthony Stewart. 715-750, Dec. 1959
Included: American National Exhibition at Sokolniki Park in Moscow

Seattle Fair Looks to the 21st Century (World's Fair). By Carolyn Bennett Patterson. Photos by Thomas Nebbia. 402-427, Sept. 1962

When Gypsies Gather at Appleby Fair. Photos by Bruce Dale. 848-869, June 1972

A Woman Paints the Tibetans. By Lafugie. 659-692, May 1949
Included: Himis Fair

See also Dog Shows; Horse Shows; Pennsylvania Dutch (Folk Festival); Sing-Sing

FAIRY TERNS:

What a Place to Lay an Egg! By Thomas R. Howell. 414-419, Sept. 1971

FALCONRY:

A New Light Dawns on Bird Photography. By Arthur A. Allen. 774-790, June 1948

FALI (Tribespeople):

Carefree People of the Cameroons. Photos by Pierre Ichac. 233-248, Feb. 1947

FALKLAND ISLANDS AND DEPENDENCIES:

Off the Beaten Track of Empire (Prince Philip's Tour). By Beverley M. Bowie. Photos by Michael Parker. 584-626, Nov. 1957

People and Penguins of the Faraway Falklands. By Olin Sewall Pettingill, Jr. 387-416, Mar. 1956

'Round the Horn by Submarine. By Paul C. Stimson. 129-144, Jan. 1948

The **FAMILY FARM** Ain't What It Used To Be. By James A. Sugar. 391-411, Sept. 1974

FAMILY in Search of Prehistoric Man: The Leakeys of Africa. By Melvin M. Payne. 194-231, Feb. 1965

FAMILY LIFE:

The Family: a Mormon Shrine. 459-463, Apr. 1975

FIRST Lady of the National Geographic (Elsie May Bell Grosvenor). By Gilbert Hovey Grosvenor. 101-121, July 1965

FIRST La Gorce Medal Honors Antarctic Expedition. 864-867, June 1967

FIRST Masters of the American Desert: The Hohokam. By Emil W. Haury. Photos by Helga Teiwes. 670-695, May 1967

FIRST Moon Explorers (Apollo 11) Receive the Society's Hubbard Medal. 859-861, June 1970

FIRST Motor Sortie into Escalante Land. By Jack Breed. 369-404, Sept. 1949

FIRST Photographs of Planets and Moon Taken With Palomar's 200-inch Telescope. By Milton L. Humason. 125-130, Jan. 1953

FIRST Photographs of Snow Leopards in the Wild. By George B. Schaller. 702-707, Nov. 1971

The **FIRST** Traverse (Mount Everest). By Thomas F. Hornbein and William F. Unsoeld. 509-513, Oct. 1963

FIRST Voyage Around the World (Magellan). By Alan Villiers. Photos by Bruce Dale. 721-753, June 1976

FIRST Woman Across Greenland's Ice. By Myrtle Simpson. Photos by Hugh Simpson. 264-279, Aug. 1967

FIRSTHAND Look at the Soviet Union. By Thomas T. Hammond. Photos by Erich Lessing. 352-407, Sept. 1959

FISH-BAITING ANIMALS:

Aha! It Really Works! (Heron). By Robert F. Sisson. 143-147, Jan. 1974

Something's Fishy About That Fin! (Decoy Fish). Photos by Robert J. Shallenberger and William D. Madden. 224-227, Aug. 1974

FISH FARMING. *See* Shrimp (Shrimp Nursery)

FISH Men Discover a 2,200-year-old Greek Ship. By Jacques-Yves Cousteau. 1-36, Jan. 1954

FISH Men Explore a New World Undersea. By Jacques-Yves Cousteau. 431-472, Oct. 1952

FISHER, ALLAN C., Jr.: Author:

African Wildlife: Man's Threatened Legacy. Photos by Thomas Nebbia. Paintings by Ned Seidler. 147-187, Feb. 1972

Australia's Pacesetter State, Victoria. Photos by Thomas Nebbia. 218-253, Feb. 1971

Aviation Medicine on the Threshold of Space. Photos by Luis Marden. 241-278, Aug. 1955

Cape Canaveral's 6,000-mile Shooting Gallery. Photos by Luis Marden and Thomas Nebbia. 421-471, Oct. 1959

"The City"—London's Storied Square Mile. 735-777, June 1961

Eastman of Rochester: Photographic Pioneer. 423-438, Sept. 1954

Everyone's Servant, the Post Office. Photos by Volkmar Wentzel. 121-152, July 1954

Exploring Tomorrow With the Space Agency. Photos by Dean Conger. 48-89, July 1960

The Investiture of Great Britain's Prince of Wales. Photos by James L. Stanfield and Adam Woolfitt. 698-715, Nov. 1969

FISHER, ALLAN C., Jr.: Author—*Continued*

Kenya Says *Harambee!* Photos by Bruce Dale. 151-205, Feb. 1969

Minutemen of the Civil Air Patrol. Photos by John E. Fletcher. 637-665, May 1956

The Nation's River. Photos by James L. Stanfield. 432-469, Oct. 1976

One Man's London. Photos by James P. Blair. 743-791, June 1966

Our Navy's Long Submarine Arm. 613-636, Nov. 1952

Reaching for the Moon. Photos by Luis Marden. 157-171, Feb. 1959

Rhodesia, a House Divided. Photos by Thomas Nebbia. 641-671, May 1975

San Diego, California's Plymouth Rock. Photos by James L. Amos. 114-147, July 1969

You and the Obedient Atom. 303-353, Sept. 1958

FISHER, FRANKLIN L.:

Memorial Tribute to Franklin L. Fisher. 692, Nov. 1953

Author

Our Search for British Paintings. 543-550, Apr. 1949

FISHER, MELVIN A.:

Atocha, Tragic Treasure Galleon of the Florida Keys. By Eugene Lyon. 787-809, June 1976

FISHER TOWERS, Utah:

We Climbed Utah's Skyscraper Rock. By Huntley Ingalls. Photos by author and Barry C. Bishop. 705-721, Nov. 1962

FISHERMEN:

Dory on the Banks: A Day in the Life of a Portuguese Fisherman. By James H. Pickerell. 573-583, Apr. 1968

Fishing in the Lofotens. Photos by Lennart Nilsson. 377-388, Mar. 1947

Gloucester Blesses Its Portuguese Fleet. By Luis Marden. 75-84, July 1953

I Sailed with Portugal's Captains Courageous. By Alan Villiers. 565-596, May 1952

The Lonely Dorymen (Television film). 579A-579B, Apr. 1968

The Sailing Oystermen of Chesapeake Bay. By Luis Marden. 798-819, Dec. 1967

Shad in the Shadow of Skyscrapers. By Dudley B. Martin. Photos by Luis Marden. 359-376, Mar. 1947

Trawling the China Seas. Photos by J. Charles Thompson. 381-395, Mar. 1950

See also Basques (Land of the Ancient; Life in the Land); Goggle Fishing; Lobsters and Lobstering; Sea Gypsies; Sponge Fishing Industry; Tuna

FISHERWOMEN:

Ama, Sea Nymphs of Japan. By Luis Marden. 122-135, July 1971

FISHES:

An Artist's Glimpses of Our Roadside Wildlife. Paintings by Walter A. Weber. 16-32, July 1950
Included: Black bass, Cutthroat trout, Eastern brook trout, Golden trout, Northern pike, Rainbow trout, Yellow perch

The Book of Fishes (1952). 418, Mar. 1957; 440, Mar. 1960; 563, Aug. 1961

Exploring Stone Age Arnhem Land. By Charles P.

FORT DE FRANCE, Martinique:

Martinique: Liberté, Egalité, and Uncertainty in the Caribbean. By Kenneth MacLeish. Photos by John Launois. 124-148, Jan. 1975

FORT JEFFERSON NATIONAL MONUMENT, Florida:

The Lower Keys, Florida's "Out Islands." By John Scofield. Photos by Emory Kristof and Bates Littlehales. 72-93, Jan. 1971

FORT TERNAN, Kenya:

Adventures in the Search for Man. By Louis S. B. Leakey. Photos by Hugo van Lawick. 132-152, Jan. 1963

FORT TICONDEROGA, New York:

From Sword to Scythe in Champlain Country. By Ethel A. Starbird. Photos by B. Anthony Stewart and Emory Kristof. 153-201, Aug. 1967

North Through History Aboard *White Mist*. By Melville Bell Grosvenor. Photos by Edwin Stuart Grosvenor. 1-55, July 1970

FORTRESSES. *See* Alhambra; Castillo de San Marcos; Castles; Kremlin; Louisbourg; St. Catherine's Monastery; St. Michael's Mount; Vizcaya (Fortress-Palace); *and* Jaisalmer; Languedoc (Region), France, for Cité; Luxembourg; Peru (The Five Worlds), for Sacsahuamán; Quebec (City)

FORTUNATE ISLANDS. *See* Canary Islands

FORTUNATE ISLES. *See* Scilly, Isles of

FORTUNE TELLING. *See* Dogon

FORTY-NINERS. *See* Golden Ghosts; *and* Death Valley National Monument

FOSFORESCÉNTE, Bahía, Puerto Rico. *See* Phosphorescent Bay

FOSHAG, W. F.: Author:

Exploring the World of Gems. 779-810, Dec. 1950

FOSSEY, DIAN: Author:

Making Friends With Mountain Gorillas. Photos by Robert M. Campbell. 48-67, Jan. 1970

More Years With Mountain Gorillas. Photos by Robert M. Campbell. 574-585, Oct. 1971

FOSSILS:

Fossils Lift the Veil of Time. By Harry S. Ladd and Roland W. Brown. 363-386, Mar. 1956

See also Evolution (In the Wake of Darwin's *Beagle*); Paleontology

FOSTER, JOSEPH T.: Author:

Folger: Biggest Little Library in the World. Photos by B. Anthony Stewart and John E. Fletcher. 411-424, Sept. 1951

FOSTER, MULFORD B.: Author-Photographer:

Puya, the Pineapple's Andean Ancestor. 463-480, Oct. 1950

FOUND at Last: the Monarch's Winter Home. By Fred A. Urquhart. Photos by Bianca Lavies. 161-173, Aug. 1976

FOUNDERS of New England. By Sir Evelyn Wrench. Photos by B. Anthony Stewart. 803-838, June 1953

FOUNDERS of Virginia. By Sir Evelyn Wrench. Photos by B. Anthony Stewart. 433-462, Apr. 1948

FOUNTAIN of Fire in Hawaii. By Frederick Simpich, Jr. Photos by Robert B. Goodman and Robert Wenkam. 303-327, Mar. 1960

FOUR CORNERS COUNTRY (Utah-Colorado-Arizona-New Mexico):

Roaming the West's Fantastic Four Corners. By Jack Breed. 705-742, June 1952

Stalking the West's Wild Foods. By Euell Gibbons. Photos by David Hiser. 186-199, Aug. 1973

See also Mesa Verde National Park; Rainbow Bridge National Monument; *and* Navajos

4-H CLUBS:

America Goes to the Fair. By Samuel W. Matthews. 293-333, Sept. 1954

4-H Boys and Girls Grow More Food. By Frederick Simpich. 551-582, Nov. 1948

FOUR-OCEAN Navy in the Nuclear Age. By Thomas W. McKnew. 145-187, Feb. 1965

A FOUR-PART Look at the Isles of the Pacific. 732-793, Dec. 1974

FOUR Years of Diving to the Bottom of the Sea. By Georges S. Houot. 715-731, May 1958

"1470 MAN." *See* Skull 1470

FOWL:

Scientist Studies Japan's Fantastic Long-tailed Fowl. By Frank X. Ogasawara. Photos by Eiji Miyazawa. 845-855, Dec. 1970

See also Poultry; Sea Birds

FOX, CHARLES J.:

Portrait of Gilbert H. Grosvenor. 252, 258, Aug. 1949

FOX, CHARLES PHILIP: Photographer:

Br'er Possum, Hermit of the Lowlands. By Agnes Akin Atkinson. 405-418, Mar. 1953

Skunks Want Peace — or Else! By Melvin R. Ellis. 279-294, Aug. 1955

FOXES:

Foxes Foretell the Future in Mali's Dogon Country. By Pamela Johnson Meyer. 431-448, Mar. 1969

The Romance of American Furs. By Wanda Burnett. 379-402, Mar. 1948

The FRAGILE Beauty All About Us. Photos by Harry S. C. Yen. 785-795, Dec. 1970

FRAGILE Nurseries of the Sea: Can We Save Our Salt Marshes? By Stephen W. Hitchcock. Photos by William R. Curtsinger. 729-765, June 1972

FRANCE:

Across the Ridgepole of the Alps. By Walter Meayers Edwards. 410-419, Sept. 1960

The Alps: Man's Own Mountains. By Ralph Gray. Photos by Walter Meayers Edwards and William Eppridge. 350-395, Sept. 1965
Included: Mont Blanc highway tunnel, from Haute Savoie, France, to Valle d'Aosta, Italy

"Around the World in Eighty Days." By Newman Bumstead. 705-750, Dec. 1951
Included: Avignon; Corsica; Lyon; Marseille; Mont Blanc; Montpellier; Paris

The Diffident Truffle, France's Gift to Gourmets. 419-426, Sept. 1956

The Enduring Pyrenees. By Robert Laxalt. Photos by Edwin Stuart Grosvenor. 794-819, Dec. 1974

G

GABON:

Ambassadors of Good Will: The Peace Corps. By Sargent Shriver and Peace Corps Volunteers. 297-345, Sept. 1964

Gabon. By John F. Murphy, Jr. 325-329

GAELS:

The Highlands, Stronghold of Scottish Gaeldom. By Kenneth MacLeish. Photos by Winfield Parks. 398-435, Mar. 1968

Isles on the Edge of the Sea: Scotland's Outer Hebrides. By Kenneth MacLeish. Photos by Thomas Nebbia. 676-711, May 1970

Scotland's Inner Hebrides: Isles of the Western Sea. By Kenneth MacLeish. Photos by R. Stephen Uzzell III. 690-717, Nov. 1974

GAHAN, GORDON W.: Photographer:

Captain Cook: The Man Who Mapped the Pacific. By Alan Villiers. 297-349, Sept. 1971

Drought Bedevils Brazil's Sertão. By John Wilson. 704-723, Nov. 1972

East Germany: The Struggle to Succeed. By John J. Putman. 295-329, Sept. 1974

In Search of Man's Past at Lake Rudolf. By Richard E. Leakey. 712-734, May 1970

Israel—The Seventh Day. By Joseph Judge. 816-855, Dec. 1972

Maui, Where Old Hawaii Still Lives. By Kenneth F. Weaver. 514-543, Apr. 1971

The More Paris Changes. . . . By Howell Walker. 64-103, July 1972

Nova Scotia, the Magnificent Anchorage. By Charles McCarry. 334-363, Mar. 1975

Sir Francis Drake. By Alan Villiers. 216-253, Feb. 1975

GALAPAGOS ISLANDS, Pacific Ocean:

The Galapagos, Eerie Cradle of New Species. By Roger Tory Peterson. Photos by Alan and Joan Root. 541-585, Apr. 1967

Giant Tortoises: Goliaths of the Galapagos. By Craig MacFarland. Photos by author and Jan MacFarland. 632-649, Nov. 1972
    Included: Española; Isabela; Pinzón; Santa Cruz

In the Wake of Darwin's *Beagle*. By Alan Villiers. Photos by James L. Stanfield. 449-495, Oct. 1969

Lost World of the Galapagos. By Irving and Electa Johnson. 681-703, May 1959

Robin Sails Home. By Robin Lee Graham. 504-545, Oct. 1970

The *Yankee*'s Wander-world. By Irving and Electa Johnson. 1-50, Jan. 1949

GALDIKAS-BRINDAMOUR, BIRUTÉ: Author:

Orangutans, Indonesia's "People of the Forest." Photos by Rod Brindamour. 444-473, Oct. 1975

GALILEE (Region), Israel:

The Land of Galilee. By Kenneth MacLeish. Photos by B. Anthony Stewart. 832-865, Dec. 1965

Where Jesus Walked. By Howard La Fay. Photos by Charles Harbutt. 739-781, Dec. 1967

GALILEO GALILEI:

The Renaissance Lives On in Tuscany. By Luis Marden. Photos by Albert Moldvay. 626-659, Nov. 1974

GALLATIN COUNTY, Illinois. *See* Shawneetown

GALLEONS AND GALLEASSES:

Drowned Galleons Yield Spanish Gold. By Kip Wagner. Photos by Otis Imboden. 1-37, Jan. 1965

See also Atocha; Girona

GALLINAZO CULTURE:

Finding the Tomb of a Warrior-God. By William Duncan Strong. Photos by Clifford Evans, Jr. 453-482, Apr. 1947

The **GAMBIA:**

Freedom Speaks French in Ouagadougou. By John Scofield. 153-203, Aug. 1966

GAME FISH. *See* Sailfish; Salmon; Trout

GAME PRESERVES:

Roaming Africa's Unfenced Zoos. By W. Robert Moore. 353-380, Mar. 1950

Safari from Congo to Cairo. By Elsie May Bell Grosvenor. Photos by Gilbert Grosvenor. 721-771, Dec. 1954

Safari Through Changing Africa. By Elsie May Bell Grosvenor. Photos by Gilbert Grosvenor. 145-198, Aug. 1953

White Magic in the Belgian Congo. By W. Robert Moore. 321-362, Mar. 1952

See also National Parks; *and* listing under Wildlife Refuges

GAMES. *See* Highland Games; Olympic Games; Sports; *and* Marostica, Italy, for Chess; Pennsylvania Dutch (Folk Festival)

GANDHI, MOHANDAS KARAMCHAND:

Delhi, Capital of a New Dominion. By Phillips Talbot. Photos by Volkmar Wentzel. 597-630, Nov. 1947

GANGES (River), India-Pakistan:

From the Hair of Siva. By Helen and Frank Schreider. 445-503, Oct. 1960

The Ganges, River of Faith. By John J. Putman. Photos by Raghubir Singh. 445-483, Oct. 1971

GANGTOK, Sikkim:

Gangtok, Cloud-wreathed Himalayan Capital. By John Scofield. 689-713, Nov. 1970

Sikkim. By Desmond Doig. 398-429, Mar. 1963

Wedding of Two Worlds. By Lee E. Battaglia. 708-727, Nov. 1963

GANNETS:

Sea Bird Cities Off Audubon's Labrador. By Arthur A. Allen. 755-774, June 1948

GARBISCH COLLECTION:

Early America Through the Eyes of Her Native Artists. By Hereward Lester Cooke, Jr. Paintings by American primitive artists. 356-389, Sept. 1962

GARDENING'S Color Merchants: The Flower Seed Growers. By Robert de Roos. Photos by Jack Fields. 720-738, May 1968

GARDENS:

Nautical Norfolk Turns to Azaleas. By William H. Nicholas. Photos by B. Anthony Stewart. 606-614, May 1947

Our Vegetable Travelers. By Victor R. Boswell. Paintings by Else Bostelmann. 145-217, Aug. 1949

GERMANY, Federal Republic of (West Germany):

The Alps: Man's Own Mountains. By Ralph Gray. Photos by Walter Meayers Edwards and William Eppridge. 350-395, Sept. 1965

"Around the World in Eighty Days." By Newman Bumstead. 705-750, Dec. 1951
Included: Darmstadt; Frankfurt; Rothenburg

Bavaria: Mod, Medieval—and Bewitching. By Gary Jennings. Photos by George F. Mobley. 409-431, Mar. 1974

Down the Danube by Canoe. By William Slade Backer. Photos by Richard S. Durrance and Christopher G. Knight. 34-79, July 1965

Modern Miracle, Made in Germany. By Robert Leslie Conly. Photos by Erich Lessing. 735-791, June 1959

The Rhine: Europe's River of Legend. By William Graves. Photos by Bruce Dale. 449-499, Apr. 1967

See also Berlin, West; Dinkelsbühl

GERRHA (Ancient City), Saudi Arabia:

In Search of Arabia's Past. By Peter Bruce Cornwall. 493-522, Apr. 1948

GERSTER, GEORG: Author-Photographer:

Abu Simbel's Ancient Temples Reborn. 724-744, May 1969

The Niger: River of Sorrow, River of Hope. 152-189, Aug. 1975

Saving the Ancient Temples at Abu Simbel. Paintings by Robert W. Nicholson. 694-742, May 1966

Searching Out Medieval Churches in Ethiopia's Wilds. 856-884, Dec. 1970

Threatened Treasures of the Nile. 587-621, Oct. 1963

GETTING to Know the Wild Burros of Death Valley. By Patricia des Roses Moehlman. Photos by Ira S. Lerner and author. 502-517, Apr. 1972

GETTYSBURG, Pennsylvania:

Gettysburg and Vicksburg: the Battle Towns Today. By Robert Paul Jordan. Map notes by Carolyn Bennett Patterson. 4-57, July 1963

GHANA:

Africa: The Winds of Freedom Stir a Continent. By Nathaniel T. Kenney. Photos by W. D. Vaughn. 303-359, Sept. 1960

See also former name, Gold Coast

GHOST From the Depths: the Warship *Vasa*. By Anders Franzén. 42-57, Jan. 1962

The GHOSTS of Jericho. By James L. Kelso. 825-844, Dec. 1951

GHOSTS of the Gulf Stream: Blue-water Plankton. By William M. Hamner. 530-545, Oct. 1974

GIANT AFRICAN LAND SNAILS:

Formosa—Hot Spot of the East. By Frederick G. Vosburgh. Photos by J. Baylor Roberts. 139-176, Feb. 1950

GIANT BRAZIL. By Peter T. White. Photos by Winfield Parks. 299-353, Sept. 1962

GIANT COMET Grazes the Sun. By Kenneth F. Weaver. 259-261, Feb. 1966

GIANT EARTHWORMS:

Capturing Strange Creatures in Colombia. By

GIANT EARTHWORMS—*Continued*

Marte Latham. Photos by Tor Eigeland. 682-693, May 1966

GIANT EFFIGIES of the Southwest. By George C. Marshall. 389, Sept. 1952

GIANT FOREST, Sequoia National Park, California:

Giant Sequoias Draw Millions to California Parks. By John Michael Kauffmann. Photos by B. Anthony Stewart. 147-187, Aug. 1959

Saving Earth's Oldest Living Things. By Andrew H. Brown. Photos by Raymond Moulin and author. 679-695, May 1951

GIANT FROGS:

In Quest of the World's Largest Frog. By Paul A. Zahl. 146-152, July 1967

GIANT INSECTS of the Amazon. By Paul A. Zahl. 632-669, May 1959

GIANT KELP, Sequoias of the Sea. By Wheeler J. North. Photos by Bates Littlehales. 251-269, Aug. 1972

GIANT SEQUOIAS Draw Millions to California Parks. By John Michael Kauffmann. Photos by B. Anthony Stewart. 147-187, Aug. 1959

The GIANT TIDES of Fundy. By Paul A. Zahl. 153-192, Aug. 1957

GIANT TORTOISES: Goliaths of the Galapagos. By Craig MacFarland. Photos by author and Jan MacFarland. 632-649, Nov. 1972

GIBBONS, EUELL: Author:

Stalking the West's Wild Foods. Photos by David Hiser. 186-199, Aug. 1973

Stalking Wild Foods on a Desert Isle. Photos by David Hiser. 47-63, July 1972

GIBBONS:

The Ape With Friends in Washington. By Margaretta Burr Wells. 61-74, July 1953

GIBRALTAR:

Gibraltar—Rock of Contention. By Howard La Fay. Photos by Bates Littlehales. 102-121, July 1966

GIBSON, EDWARD G.:

Skylab, Outpost on the Frontier of Space. By Thomas Y. Canby. Photos by the nine mission astronauts. 441-469, Oct. 1974
Author
The Sun As Never Seen Before. 494-503, Oct. 1974

GIDDINGS, AL: Photographer:

Life Springs From Death in Truk Lagoon. By Sylvia A. Earle. 578-613, May 1976
From Graveyard to Garden. 604-613

GIFTS for the Jaguar God. By Philip Drucker and Robert F. Heizer. 367-375, Sept. 1956

GILBERT, SIR WILLIAM:

The British Way. By Sir Evelyn Wrench. 421-541, Apr. 1949

GILBERT GROSVENOR Is Elected Chairman of the Board, John Oliver La Gorce Chosen President and Editor of the National Geographic Society. 65, 65A-65H, 66, July 1954

See also Grosvenor, Gilbert Hovey

GLASS Menageries of the Sea. By Paul A. Zahl. 797-822, June 1955

GLEN CANYON NATIONAL RECREATION AREA, Arizona-Utah:
Lake Powell: Waterway to Desert Wonders. By Walter Meayers Edwards. 44-75, July 1967

GLENDORA, California:
Southern California's Trial by Mud and Water. By Nathaniel T. Kenney. Photos by Bruce Dale. 552-573, Oct. 1969

GLENN, JOHN H., Jr.:
John Glenn Receives the Society's Hubbard Medal. 827, June 1962
John Glenn's Three Orbits in *Friendship 7:* A Minute-by-Minute Account of America's First Orbital Space Flight. By Robert B. Voas. 792-827, June 1962

GLIDERS. *See* Sailplanes

The GLITTERING World of Rockhounds. By David S. Boyer. 276-294, Feb. 1974

GLOB, P. V.: Author:
Lifelike Man Preserved 2,000 Years in Peat. 419-430, Mar. 1954

GLOBE, Great: Explorers Hall, NGS:
12-foot globe. 673-675, 677, 679, May 1964; 880, Dec. 1964; 578-579, Oct. 1967

GLOBES, NGS:
First. 698-701, 716, May 1961; 580, 581, Oct. 1967
Manufacturer of NGS globes. 874-875, 876-878, Dec. 1961
National Geographic Physical Globe announced. 736, Nov. 1971
Number sold (265,000). 585, Oct. 1967
16-inch globe and 12-inch globe. 897, Dec. 1962
16-inch globe presented to Mrs. Lyndon B. Johnson. 676, 679, May 1964; 584, Oct. 1967

GLOMAR CHALLENGER (Deep Sea Drilling Project Ship):
This Changing Earth. By Samuel W. Matthews. 1-37, Jan. 1973

GLOUCESTER, Massachusetts:
Gloucester Blesses Its Portuguese Fleet. By Luis Marden. 75-84, July 1953
Windjamming Around New England. By Tom Horgan. Photos by Robert F. Sisson. 141-169, Aug. 1950

GLOWWORMS (Beetle Larvae):
Nature's Night Lights: Probing the Secrets of Bioluminescence. By Paul A. Zahl. 45-69, July 1971

GLUECK, NELSON: Author:
An Archeologist Looks at Palestine. 739-752, Dec. 1947

GLYPHS:
The Maya. 729-811, Dec. 1975
I. Children of Time. By Howard La Fay. Photos by David Alan Harvey. 729-767
II. Riddle of the Glyphs. By George E. Stuart. Photos by Otis Imboden. 768-791

GOATS:
The Goats of Thunder Hill. By Elizabeth Nicholds.

GOATS—*Continued*
Photos by Robert F. Sisson. 625-640, May 1954
Sheep Trek in the French Alps. By Maurice Moyal. Photos by Marcel Coen. 545-564, Apr. 1952

GOBI (Desert), Asia:
The Caves of the Thousand Buddhas. By Franc and Jean Shor. 383-415, Mar. 1951
Journey to Outer Mongolia. By William O. Douglas. Photos by Dean Conger. 289-345, Mar. 1962

GODDARD, JOHN M.: Author:
Kayaks Down the Nile. 697-732, May 1955

GODIVA, LADY:
The British Way. By Sir Evelyn Wrench. 421-541, Apr. 1949

GODLEY, JOHN, Third Baron Kilbracken. *See* Kilbracken, Lord

GOELL, THERESA: Author-Photographer:
Throne Above the Euphrates. 390-405, Mar. 1961

GOETZ, BERNICE M.: Author-Photographer:
Jungle Jaunt on Amazon Headwaters. 371-388, Sept. 1952

GOGGLE FISHING in California Waters. By David Hellyer. Photos by Lamar Boren. 615-632, May 1949

GOLD AND GOLD MINING:
Along the Yukon Trail. By Amos Burg. 395-416, Sept. 1953
Busy Fairbanks Sets Alaska's Pace. By Bruce A. Wilson. Photos by O. C. Sweet. 505-523, Oct. 1949
Gold, the Eternal Treasure. By Peter T. White. Photos by James L. Stanfield. 1-51, Jan. 1974
Golden Masterpieces. 29-39
Golden Ghosts of the Lost Sierra. By Robert Laxalt. Photos by David Hiser. 332-353, Sept. 1973
Nevada's Mountain of Invisible Gold. By Samuel W. Matthews. Photos by David F. Cupp. 668-679, May 1968
See also Spanish Treasure

GOLD COAST, West Africa:
Hunting Musical Game in West Africa. By Arthur S. Alberts. 262-282, Aug. 1951
See also Ghana

GOLD MEDAL, NGS. *See* Special Gold Medal

GOLD Medal Awarded to Mrs. Robert E. Peary. 148, Jan. 1956

GOLDEN Beaches of Portugal. By Alan Villiers. 673-696, Nov. 1954

GOLDEN COCK-OF-THE-ROCK:
Strange Courtship of the Cock-of-the-Rock. By E. Thomas Gilliard. 134-140, Jan. 1962

GOLDEN EAGLES:
Scotland's Golden Eagles at Home. By C. Eric Palmar. 273-286, Feb. 1954
Sharing the Lives of Wild Golden Eagles. By John Craighead. Photos by Charles and Derek Craighead. 420-439, Sept. 1967

GOLDEN Ghosts of the Lost Sierra. By Robert Laxalt. Photos by David Hiser. 332-353, Sept. 1973

's GRAVENHAGE (The Hague), Netherlands:

Mid-century Holland Builds Her Future. By Sydney Clark. 747-778, Dec. 1950

GRAVES, WILLIAM: Author:

Bangkok, City of Angels. Photos by John Launois. 96-129, July 1973

California, the Golden Magnet. 595-679, May 1966
I. The South. Photos by Thomas Nebbia. 595-639
II. Nature's North. Photos by James P. Blair and Jonathan S. Blair. 641-679

Denmark, Field of the Danes. Photos by Thomas Nebbia. 245-275, Feb. 1974

Earthquake! (Alaska, 1964). 112-139, July 1964

Finland: Plucky Neighbor of Soviet Russia. Photos by George F. Mobley. 587-629, May 1968

Human Treasures of Japan. Photos by James L. Stanfield. 370-379, Sept. 1972

The Imperiled Giants (Whales). 722-751, Dec. 1976

Iran: Desert Miracle. Photos by James P. Blair. 2-47, Jan. 1975

Living in a Japanese Village. Photos by James L. Stanfield. 668-693, May 1972

Maine's Lobster Island, Monhegan. Photos by Kosti Ruohomaa. 285-298, Feb. 1959

Martha's Vineyard. Photos by James P. Blair. 778-809, June 1961

Mobile, Alabama's City in Motion. Photos by Joseph J. Scherschel and Robert W. Madden. 368-397, Mar. 1968

New Life for the Troubled Suez Canal. Photos by Jonathan Blair. 792-817, June 1975

The Rhine: Europe's River of Legend. Photos by Bruce Dale. 449-499, Apr. 1967

San Francisco Bay, the Westward Gate. Photos by James L. Stanfield. 593-637, Nov. 1969

Tokyo, the Peaceful Explosion. Photos by Winfield Parks. 445-487, Oct. 1964

Washington: The City Freedom Built. Photos by Bruce Dale and Thomas Nebbia. 735-781, Dec. 1964

World's Last Salute to a Great American (Dwight D. Eisenhower). By William Graves and other members of the National Geographic staff. 40-51, July 1969

GRAY, RALPH: Author:

The Alps: Man's Own Mountains. Photos by Walter Meayers Edwards and William Eppridge. 350-395, Sept. 1965

Down the Potomac by Canoe. Photos by Walter Meayers Edwards. 213-242, Aug. 1948

Down the Susquehanna by Canoe. Photos by Walter Meayers Edwards. 73-120, July 1950

From Sun-clad Sea to Shining Mountains. Photos by James P. Blair. 542-589, Apr. 1964

Rhododendron Time on Roan Mountain. 819-828, June 1957

Author-Photographer

Across Canada by Mackenzie's Track. 191-239, Aug. 1955

Following the Trail of Lewis and Clark. 707-750, June 1953

From Sea to Shining Sea: A Cross Section of the United States Along Historic Route 40. Photos by Dean Conger and author. 1-61, July 1961

Labrador Canoe Adventure. By Andrew Brown and Ralph Gray. 65-99, July 1951

GRAY, RALPH: Author-Photographer—*Continued*

Three Roads to Rainbow. 547-561, Apr. 1957

Vacation Tour Through Lincoln Land. 141-184, Feb. 1952

GRAY WHALES:

The California Gray Whale Comes Back. By Theodore J. Walker. 394-415, Mar. 1971

GREAT ANDAMANESE (Negrito Tribe):

The Last Andaman Islanders. By Raghubir Singh. 66-91, July 1975

GREAT BAHAMA BANK, Bahama Islands:

Diving Into the Blue Holes of the Bahamas. By George J. Benjamin. 347-363, Sept. 1970

Strange March of the Spiny Lobster. By William F. Herrnkind. Photos by Rick Frehsee and Bruce Mounier. 819-831, June 1975

GREAT BARRIER REEF, Australia:

Australia. II. The Settled East, the Barrier Reef, the Center. By Alan Villiers. 347-385, Sept. 1963

Australia's Great Barrier Reef. Photos by Valerie and Ron Taylor. 728-741, June 1973

Exploring Australia's Coral Jungle. By Kenneth MacLeish. 743-779, June 1973

Life Cycle of a Coral. By Robert F. Sisson. 780-793, June 1973

On Australia's Coral Ramparts. By Paul A. Zahl. 1-48, Jan. 1957

Queensland: Young Titan of Australia's Tropic North. By Kenneth MacLeish. Photos by Winfield Parks. 593-639, Nov. 1968

GREAT BASIN, U. S.:

Indians of the Far West. By Matthew W. Stirling. Paintings by W. Langdon Kihn. 175-200, Feb. 1948

See also Death Valley National Monument; Great Salt Lake; Mojave Desert

GREAT BRITAIN:

"Be Ye Men of Valour" (Churchill's Life and Funeral). By Howard La Fay. 159-197, Aug. 1965

The Britain That Shakespeare Knew. By Louis B. Wright. Photos by Dean Conger. 613-665, May 1964

British Castles, History in Stone. By Norman Wilkinson. 111-129, July 1947

British Isles, Atlas series supplement. July 1958

The British Isles, map supplement. Apr. 1949

The British Way: Great Britain's Major Gifts to Freedom, Democratic Government, Science, and Society. By Sir Evelyn Wrench. 421-541, Apr. 1949

The Final Tribute (Churchill Funeral). By Carolyn Bennett Patterson. 199-225, Aug. 1965

The Investiture of Great Britain's Prince of Wales. By Allan C. Fisher, Jr. Photos by James L. Stanfield and Adam Woolfitt. 698-715, Nov. 1969

Our Search for British Paintings. By Franklin L. Fisher. 543-550, Apr. 1949

Shakespeare's Britain, map supplement. May 1964

This Britain (Television film). 583, Nov. 1975; cover, Dec. 1975

A Traveler's Map of the British Isles, map supplement. Text on reverse. Apr. 1974

See also England; Scotland; Wales; *and* Arran, Island of; Caldy (Island); Channel Islands; Hebri-

H

H.R.H. The Prince Philip, Duke of Edinburgh—*Continued*
the-World Tour. 583-584, Nov. 1957
See also Philip, H.R.H. The Prince

HA ON (Kibbutz), Israel:
Our Life on a Border Kibbutz. By Carol and Al Abrams. Photos by Al Abrams. 364-391, Sept. 1970

HÂ-ÅK VÂ-ÅK (Hâ-âk Lying Site), Arizona:
Seeking the Secret of the Giants. By Frank M. Setzler. Photos by Richard H. Stewart. 390-404, Sept. 1952

HABER, HEINZ: Author:
Space Satellites, Tools of Earth Research. Paintings by William N. Palmstrom. 487-509, Apr. 1956

HADAR, Ethiopia:
Ethiopia Yields First "Family" of Early Man. By Donald C. Johanson. Photos by David Brill. 790-811, Dec. 1976

HADJ (Moslem Pilgrimage to Mecca):
From America to Mecca on Airborne Pilgrimage. By Abdul Ghafur. 1-60, July 1953
Saudi Arabia: Beyond the Sands of Mecca. By Thomas J. Abercrombie. 1-53, Jan. 1966
The Sword and the Sermon. By Thomas J. Abercrombie. 3-45, July 1972

HAGEN, KENNETH S.: Author:
Following the Ladybug Home. Photos by Robert F. Sisson. 543-553, Apr. 1970

HAGEN, TONI: Author-Photographer:
Afoot in Roadless Nepal. 361-405, Mar. 1960

HAGERSTOWN VALLEY, Maryland:
Appalachian Valley Pilgrimage. By Catherine Bell Palmer. Photos by Justin Locke. 1-32, July 1949

The **HAGUE** ('s Gravenhage), Netherlands:
Mid-century Holland Builds Her Future. By Sydney Clark. 747-778, Dec. 1950
The Netherlands: Nation at War With the Sea. By Alan Villiers. Photos by Adam Woolfitt. 530-571, Apr. 1968

HAIFA, Israel:
An Archeologist Looks at Palestine. By Nelson Glueck. 739-752, Dec. 1947

HAILE SELASSIE I, Emperor (Ethiopia):
Ethiopian Adventure. By Nathaniel T. Kenney. Photos by James P. Blair. 548-582, Apr. 1965

HAITI, Republic of:
Haiti: Beyond Mountains, More Mountains. By Carolyn Bennett Patterson. Photos by Thomas Nebbia. 70-97, Jan. 1976
Haiti—West Africa in the West Indies. By John Scofield. 226-259, Feb. 1961

HAKLUYT, RICHARD:
Founders of Virginia. By Sir Evelyn Wrench. Photos by B. Anthony Stewart. 433-462, Apr. 1948

HALE, SARAH JOSEPHA:
Literary Landmarks of Massachusetts. By William H. Nicholas. Photos by B. Anthony Stewart and John E. Fletcher. 279-310, Mar. 1950

HALEAKALA NATIONAL PARK, Hawaii:
Maui, Where Old Hawaii Still Lives. By Kenneth F. Weaver. Photos by Gordon W. Gahan. 514-543, Apr. 1971

HALF DOME (Massif), Yosemite National Park, California:
Climbing Half Dome the Hard Way. By Galen Rowell. 782-791, June 1974

HALIFAX RACE (Marblehead-Halifax Yacht Race):
Down East to Nova Scotia. By Winfield Parks. 853-879, June 1964

HALL, ALICE J.: Author:
Benjamin Franklin, Philosopher of Dissent. Photos by Linda Bartlett. 93-123, July 1975
The Climb Up Cone Crater. Photos by Edgar D. Mitchell and Alan B. Shepard, Jr. 136-148, July 1971
A Lady From China's Past. Photos from *China Pictorial.* 660-681, May 1974
A Traveler's Tale of Ancient Tikal. Paintings by Peter Spier. 799-811, Dec. 1975

HALL, MELVIN: Author-Photographer:
Vézelay, Hill of the Pilgrims. 229-247, Feb. 1953

HALL, ROSS: Photographer:
Idaho Loggers Battle a River. 117-130, July 1951

HALLSTROM, E. J. L.:
Sheep Airlift in New Guinea. Photos by Ned Blood. 831-844, Dec. 1949

HAMI, Sinkiang:
The Caves of the Thousand Buddhas. By Franc and Jean Shor. 383-415, Mar. 1951

HAMILL, HUGH M., Jr.: Author-Photographer:
Experiment in International Living. 323-350, Mar. 1953

HAMILTON, ROGER: Author:
Can We Harness the Wind? Photos by Emory Kristof. 812-829, Dec. 1975

HAMILTON (River), Labrador, Newfoundland:
Labrador Canoe Adventure. By Andrew Brown and Ralph Gray. 65-99, July 1951

HAMMARSKJÖLD, DAG: Author-Photographer:
A New Look at Everest. 87-93, Jan. 1961

HAMMOND, THOMAS T.: Author:
An American in Russia's Capital. Photos by Dean Conger. 297-351, Mar. 1966
Firsthand Look at the Soviet Union. Photos by Erich Lessing. 352-407, Sept. 1959

HAMMURABI, King (Babylon):
Ancient Mesopotamia: A Light That Did Not Fail. By E. A. Speiser. Paintings by H. M. Herget. 41-105, Jan. 1951

HAMNER, WILLIAM M.: Author:
Blue-water Plankton: Ghosts of the Gulf Stream. 530-545, Oct. 1974

HAN DYNASTY TOMBS:
China Unveils Her Newest Treasures. Photos by Robert W. Madden. 848-857, Dec. 1974

HELSINKI, Finland:

Baltic Cruise of the *Caribbee*. By Carleton Mitchell. 605-646, Nov. 1950

Finland: Plucky Neighbor of Soviet Russia. By William Graves. Photos by George F. Mobley. 587-629, May 1968

HENLOPEN DUNES, Delaware:

The Living Sand. By William H. Amos. 820-833, June 1965

HENRY VIII, King (England):

The British Way. By Sir Evelyn Wrench. 421-541, Apr. 1949

HENRY, Prince, the Navigator:

Prince Henry, the Explorer Who Stayed Home. By Alan Villiers. Photos by Thomas Nebbia. 616-656, Nov. 1960

HENRY, PATRICK:

Firebrands of the Revolution. By Eric F. Goldman. Photos by George F. Mobley. 2-27, July 1974

HENRY, THOMAS R.: Author:

Ice Age Man, the First American. Paintings by Andre Durenceau. 781-806, Dec. 1955

The Smithsonian Institution. 325-348, Sept. 1948

HENRY, Cape, Virginia:

Exploring America's Great Sand Barrier Reef. By Eugene R. Guild. Photos by John E. Fletcher and author. 325-350, Sept. 1947

HENRY E. HUNTINGTON LIBRARY AND ART GALLERY, San Marino, California:

Huntington Library, California Treasure House. By David S. Boyer. 251-276, Feb. 1958

HENRY FORD MUSEUM, Dearborn, Michigan:

The Past Is Present in Greenfield Village. By Beverley M. Bowie. Photos by Neal P. Davis and Willard R. Culver. 96-127, July 1958

HENRY HUDSON'S River. By Willard Price. Photos by Wayne Miller. 364-403, Mar. 1962

HERALDRY. *See* Coats of Arms

HERBAL MEDICINE:

Karnali, Roadless World of Western Nepal. By Lila M. and Barry C. Bishop. 656-689, Nov. 1971

Nature's Gifts to Medicine. By Lonnelle Aikman. Paintings by Lloyd K. Townsend and Don Crowley. 420-440, Sept. 1974

The People of Cumberland Gap. By John Fetterman. Photos by Bruce Dale. 591-621, Nov. 1971

HERBERT, CHARLES W.: Photographer:

Better Days for the Navajos. By Jack Breed. 809-847, Dec. 1958

Californians Escape to the Desert. By Mason Sutherland. 675-724, Nov. 1957

Sonora Is Jumping. By Mason Sutherland. 215-246, Feb. 1955

HERBS. *See* Bromeliads; Herbal Medicine; *and* Kew

HERE Come the Marines. By Frederick Simpich. 647-672, Nov. 1950

HERE Rest in Honored Glory . . . (War Memorials). By Howell Walker. 739-768, June 1957

HÉRENS, Val d', Switzerland:

Switzerland's Enchanted Val d'Hérens. By Georgia Engelhard Cromwell. 825-848, June 1955

HERE'S New York Harbor. By Stuart E. Jones. Photos by Robert F. Sisson and David S. Boyer. 773-813, Dec. 1954

HERGET, H. M.: Artist:

Ancient Mesopotamia: A Light That Did Not Fail. By E. A. Speiser. 41-105, Jan. 1951
   How the Herget Paintings Were Composed. 57

HERITAGE of Beauty and History (U. S. National Parks). By Conrad L. Wirth. 587-661, May 1958

HERM (Island), English Channel:

Britain's "French" Channel Islands. By James Cerruti. Photos by James L. Amos. 710-740, May 1971

HERMES, R. C.: Photographer:

The Solemn, Sociable Puffins. By R. M. Lockley. 414-422, Sept. 1954

HERMITAGE (State Museum), Leningrad, U.S.S.R.:

Leningrad, Russia's Window on the West. By Howard La Fay. Photos by Dick Durrance II. 636-673, May 1971

HERO (Research Vessel):

Antarctica's Nearer Side. By Samuel W. Matthews. Photos by William R. Curtsinger. 622-655, Nov. 1971

HEROD THE GREAT, King (Judea):

The Ghosts of Jericho. By James L. Kelso. 825-844, Dec. 1951

HERONS:

Aha! It Really Works! By Robert F. Sisson. 143-147, Jan. 1974
   Contents: Green heron that fishes with bait

Wildlife of Everglades National Park. By Daniel B. Beard. Paintings by Walter A. Weber. 83-116, Jan. 1949

HERRING:

Scenes of Postwar Finland. By La Verne Bradley. Photos by Jerry Waller. 233-264, Aug. 1947
See also Menhaden

HERRNKIND, WILLIAM F.: Author:

Strange March of the Spiny Lobster. Photos by Rick Frehsee and Bruce Mounier. 819-831, June 1975

HEYDEN, FRANCIS J.:

Eclipse Hunting in Brazil's Ranchland. By F. Barrows Colton. Photos by Richard H. Stewart and Guy W. Starling. 285-324, Sept. 1947

HEYERDAHL, THOR: Author:

The Voyage of *Ra II*. Photos by Carlo Mauri and Georges Sourial. 44-71, Jan. 1971

HIBERNATION. *See* Grizzly Bears; Poorwill

HIDDEN Worlds in the Heart of a Plant (Bromeliad). By Paul A. Zahl. 389-397, Mar. 1975

HIEROGLYPHS:

Computer Helps Scholars Re-create an Egyptian Temple. By Ray Winfield Smith. Photos by Emory Kristof. 634-655, Nov. 1970
See also Glyphs, for Maya glyphs

HIERONYMUS, REX E.: Author:

Down Mark Twain's River on a Raft. 551-574, Apr. 1948

HIGAONON TRIBE:

Help for Philippine Tribes in Trouble. By Kenneth MacLeish. Photos by Dean Conger. 220-255, Aug. 1971

HIGDON, HAL: Author:

New Tricks Outwit Our Insect Enemies. Photos by Robert F. Sisson and Emory Kristof. 380-399, Sept. 1972

HIGH, Wild World of the Vicuña. By William L. Franklin. 77-91, Jan. 1973

HIGH Adventure in the Himalayas. By Thomas Weir. 193-234, Aug. 1952

HIGH ATLAS (Mountains), Africa:

Morocco, Land of the Farthest West. By Thomas J. Abercrombie. 834-865, June 1971

Trek by Mule Among Morocco's Berbers. By Victor Englebert. 850-875, June 1968

HIGH Road in the Pyrenees. By H. V. Morton. Photos by Justin Locke. 299-334, Mar. 1956

HIGH-STEPPING Idaho. By William S. Ellis. Photos by Dean Conger. 290-317, Mar. 1973

HIGH Trail Through the Canadian Rockies. By Mike W. Edwards. Photos by Lowell Georgia. 795-817, June 1973

The **HIGH** World of the Rain Forest. By William Beebe. Paintings by Guy Neale. 838-855, June 1958

HIGHLAND GAMES:

Over the Sea to Scotland's Skye. By Robert J. Reynolds. 87-112, July 1952

The **HIGHLANDS,** Stronghold of Scottish Gaeldom. By Kenneth MacLeish. Photos by Winfield Parks. 398-435, Mar. 1968

HIGHWAYS AND ROADS:

Amalfi, Italy's Divine Coast. By Luis Marden. 472-509, Oct. 1959

California's Wonderful One (State Highway No. 1). By Frank Cameron. Photos by B. Anthony Stewart. 571-617, Nov. 1959

From Sea to Shining Sea: A Cross Section of the United States Along Historic Route 40. By Ralph Gray. Photos by Dean Conger and author. 1-61, July 1961

From Sun-clad Sea to Shining Mountains. By Ralph Gray. Photos by James P. Blair. 542-589, Apr. 1964

Contents: "International 89": Mexico's West Coast Highway; U. S. 89; Canada's Coleman-Kananaskis Road and Banff-Jasper Highway

The Old Boston Post Roads. By Donald Barr Chidsey. 189-205, Aug. 1962

Our Growing Interstate Highway System. By Robert Paul Jordan. 195-219, Feb. 1968

The Post Road Today. Photos by B. Anthony Stewart. 206-233, Aug. 1962

Trucks Race the Clock From Coast to Coast. By James A. Sugar. 226-243, Feb. 1974

See also Natchez Trace; New York State Thruway; Pan American Highway

HIKING:

Afoot in Roadless Nepal. By Toni Hagen. 361-405, Mar. 1960

Americans Afoot in Rumania. By Dan Dimancescu. Photos by Dick Durrance II and Christopher G. Knight. 810-845, June 1969

The Friendly Huts of the White Mountains. By William O. Douglas. Photos by Kathleen Revis. 205-239, Aug. 1961

Hiking the Backbone of the Rockies: Canada's Great Divide Trail. By Mike W. Edwards. Photos by Lowell Georgia. 795-817, June 1973

Karnali, Roadless World of Western Nepal. By Lila M. and Barry C. Bishop. 656-689, Nov. 1971

Mexico to Canada on the Pacific Crest Trail. By Mike W. Edwards. Photos by David Hiser. 741-779, June 1971

Pack Trip Through the Smokies. By Val Hart. Photos by Robert F. Sisson. 473-502, Oct. 1952

Sierra High Trip. By David R. Brower. 844-868, June 1954

Skyline Trail from Maine to Georgia. By Andrew H. Brown. Photos by Robert F. Sisson. 219-251, Aug. 1949

Thumbs Up Round the North Sea's Rim. By Frances James. Photos by Erica Koch. 685-704, May 1952

Yellowstone at 100: A Walk Through the Wilderness. By Karen and Derek Craighead. Photos by Sam Abell. 579-603, May 1972

See also Pilgrimages; Walking Tours

HILDEBRAND, JESSE RICHARDSON:

Memorial Tribute to Jesse Richardson Hildebrand. 104, Jan. 1952

HILGER, MARY INEZ: Author:

Japan's "Sky People," the Vanishing Ainu. Photos by Eiji Miyazawa. 268-296, Feb. 1967

HILLARY, SIR EDMUND:

The Crossing of Antarctica. By Sir Vivian Fuchs. Photos by George Lowe. 25-47, Jan. 1959

President Eisenhower Presents the Hubbard Medal to Everest's Conquerors. 64, July 1954

Triumph on Everest. 1-63, July 1954

Author

Beyond Everest. 579-610, Nov. 1955

The Conquest of the Summit. 45-63, July 1954

We Build a School for Sherpa Children. 548-551, Oct. 1962

HILO, Hawaii:

Hawaii, Island of Fire and Flowers. By Gordon Young. Photos by Robert W. Madden. 399-425, Mar. 1975

HILTON HEAD (Island), South Carolina:

Sea Islands: Adventuring Along the South's Surprising Coast. By James Cerruti. Photos by Thomas Nebbia and James L. Amos. 366-393, Mar. 1971

HIMALAYAS (Mountains), Asia:

American and Geographic Flags Top Everest. By Melvin M. Payne. Photos by Barry C. Bishop. 157-157C, Aug. 1963

Americans on Everest (Television film). 448-452, Sept. 1965; 575, Nov. 1976

Beyond Everest. By Sir Edmund Hillary. 579-610, Nov. 1955

HOLMES, MIKE: Photographer — *Continued*
Oil and Penguins Don't Mix. 384-397, Mar. 1973

HOLY ISLAND (Lindisfarne), England:
Pilgrimage to Holy Island and the Farnes. By John E. H. Nolan. 547-570, Oct. 1952

HOLY LAND. *See* Bible Lands

HOLY Land, My Country. By His Majesty King Hussein of Jordan. 784-789, Dec. 1964

HOLY WEEK:
Andalusia, the Spirit of Spain. By Howard La Fay. Photos by Joseph J. Scherschel. 833-857, June 1975

Easter Week in Indian Guatemala. By John Scofield. 406-417, Mar. 1960

Guatemala, Maya and Modern. By Louis de la Haba. Photos by Joseph J. Scherschel. 661-689, Nov. 1974

Holy Week and the Fair in Sevilla (Spain). By Luis Marden. 499-530, Apr. 1951

Mesa del Nayar's Strange Holy Week. By Guillermo Aldana E. 780-795, June 1971

HOME Life in Paris Today. By Deena Clark. 43-72, July 1950

HOME to Arran, Scotland's Magic Isle. By J. Harvey Howells. 80-99, July 1965

HOME to Lonely Tristan da Cunha. By James P. Blair. 60-81, Jan. 1964

HOME to the Enduring Berkshires. By Charles McCarry. Photos by Jonathan S. Blair. 196-221, Aug. 1970

HOME to the Holy Land. By Maynard Owen Williams. 707-746, Dec. 1950

HOMER:
Homeward With Ulysses. By Melville Bell Grosvenor. Photos by Edwin Stuart Grosvenor. 1-39, July 1973

HOMESTEADING:
Alaskan Family Robinson. By Nancy Robinson. Photos by John Metzger and Peter Robinson. 55-75, Jan. 1973

HOMEWARD With Ulysses. By Melville Bell Grosvenor. Photos by Edwin Stuart Grosvenor. 1-39, July 1973

HONDURAS, British. *See* Belize

HONEY ANTS:
Living Honey Jars of the Ant World. By Ross E. Hutchins. 405-411, Mar. 1962

HONEY EATERS of Currumbin (Lorikeets). By Paul A. Zahl. 510-519, Oct. 1956

HONEY-GUIDE: The Bird That Eats Wax. By Herbert Friedmann. Paintings by Walter A. Weber. 551-560, Apr. 1954

HONEYBEES:
Honeybees. Children's book announced. 726-728, Nov. 1973

Inside the World of the Honeybee. By Treat Davidson. 188-217, Aug. 1959

Those Fiery Brazilian Bees. By Rick Gore. Photos

HONEYBEES — *Continued*
by Bianca Lavies. 491-501, Apr. 1976

HONEYCUTT, BROOKS: Photographer:
Life 8,000 Years Ago Uncovered in an Alabama Cave. By Carl F. Miller. 542-558, Oct. 1956

HONG KONG:
Eyes on the China Coast. By George W. Long. 505-512, Apr. 1953

Hong Kong, Saturday's Child. By Joseph Judge. Photos by Bruce Dale. 541-573, Oct. 1971

Hong Kong Hangs On. By George W. Long. Photos by J. Baylor Roberts. 239-272, Feb. 1954

Hong Kong Has Many Faces. By John Scofield. 1-41, Jan. 1962

Hong Kong Restored. 483-490, Apr. 1947

Round the World School (ISA). By Paul Antze. Photos by William Eppridge. 96-127, July 1962

Those Outlandish Goldfish! By Paul A. Zahl. 514-533, Apr. 1973

Trawling the China Seas. Photos by J. Charles Thompson. 381-395, Mar. 1950

YWCA: International Success Story. By Mary French Rockefeller. Photos by Otis Imboden. 904-933, Dec. 1963

See also Pacific Fleet, U. S.

HONOLULU, Oahu, Hawaii:
Because It Rains on Hawaii. By Frederick Simpich, Jr. 571-610, Nov. 1949

Honolulu, Mid-ocean Capital. By Frederick Simpich, Jr. Photos by B. Anthony Stewart. 577-624, May 1954

Look What's Happened to Honolulu! By Jim Becker. Photos by Bates Littlehales. 500-531, Oct. 1969

HONSHU (Island), Japan:
Backwoods Japan During American Occupation. By M. A. Huberman. 491-518, Apr. 1947

Kayak Odyssey: From the Inland Sea to Tokyo. By Dan Dimancescu. Photos by Christopher G. Knight. 295-337, Sept. 1967

HOOGSTRAAL, HARRY: Author:
South in the Sudan. 249-272, Feb. 1953

Yemen Opens the Door to Progress. 213-244, Feb. 1952

HOOVER, HERBERT:
The Living White House. By Lonnelle Aikman. 593-643, Nov. 1966

Profiles of the Presidents: IV. America Enters the Modern Era. By Frank Freidel. 537-577, Oct. 1965

HOPE DIAMOND:
Questing for Gems. By George S. Switzer. 835-863, Dec. 1971

HOPE for Big Cypress Swamp. By Rick Gore. Photos by Patricia Caulfield. 251-273, Aug. 1976

HOPE-TAYLOR, BRIAN: Artist:
Stonehenge — New Light on an Old Riddle. By Harold E. Edgerton. 846-866, June 1960

HOPEH (Province), China. *See* Peking

HOPES and Fears in Booming Thailand. By Peter T. White. Photos by Dean Conger. 76-125, July 1967

HUNTING Mexico's Buried Temples. Photos by Richard H. Stewart. 145-168, Feb. 1947

HUNTING Musical Game in West Africa. By Arthur S. Alberts. 262-282, Aug. 1951

HUNTING Prehistory in Panama Jungles. By Matthew W. Stirling. Photos by Richard H. Stewart. 271-290, Aug. 1953

HUNTING the Heartbeat of a Whale. By Paul Dudley White and Samuel W. Matthews. 49-64, July 1956

HUNTING Uranium Around the World. By Robert D. Nininger. Photos by Volkmar Wentzel. 533-558, Oct. 1954

HUNTINGTON, HENRY E., LIBRARY AND ART GALLERY, San Marino, California:

Huntington Library, California Treasure House. By David S. Boyer. 251-276, Feb. 1958

HUNZA:

At World's End in Hunza. By Jean and Franc Shor. 485-518, Oct. 1953

"Every Day Is a Gift When You Are Over 100." By Alexander Leaf. Photos by John Launois. 93-119, Jan. 1973

Sky Road East. By Tay and Lowell Thomas, Jr. 71-112, Jan. 1960

Trek to Lofty Hunza—and Beyond. By Sabrina and Roland Michaud. 644-669, Nov. 1975

HUPEH (Province), China. *See* Hankow

HURLEY, FRANK: Photographer:
Arab Land Beyond the Jordan. 753-768, Dec. 1947

HURON, Lake, Canada-U. S.:

The Great Lakes: Is It Too Late? By Gordon Young. Photos by James L. Amos and Martin Rogers. 147-185, Aug. 1973

HURRICANES:

Cajunland, Louisiana's French-speaking Coast. By Bern Keating. Photos by Charles Harbutt and Franke Keating. 353-391, Mar. 1966
    Included: Hurricane Audrey (1957); Hurricane Betsy (1965)

Men Against the Hurricane. By Andrew H. Brown. 537-560, Oct. 1950

We're Doing Something About the Weather! By Walter Orr Roberts. 518-555, Apr. 1972

HURTADO, EUSEBIO DÁVALOS. *See* Dávalos Hurtado, Eusebio

HUSSEIN, King (Jordan):

The Other Side of Jordan. By Luis Marden. 790-825, Dec. 1964

Author

Holy Land, My Country. 784-789, Dec. 1964

HUTCHINS, ROSS E.: Author-Photographer:
Living Honey Jars of the Ant World. 405-411, Mar. 1962

HUTCHISON, BRUCE: Author:
Exploring Ottawa. 565-596, Nov. 1947

HUTCHISON, ISOBEL WYLIE: Author:
From Barra to Butt in the Hebrides. 559-580, Oct. 1954

HUTCHISON, ISOBEL WYLIE: Author—*Continued*

Poets' Voices Linger in Scottish Shrines. Photos by Kathleen Revis. 437-488, Oct. 1957

Shetland and Orkney, Britain's Far North. 519-536, Oct. 1953

A Stroll to John o'Groat's. 1-48, July 1956

A Stroll to London. Photos by B. Anthony Stewart. 171-204, Aug. 1950

A Stroll to Venice. 378-410, Sept. 1951

2,000 Miles Through Europe's Oldest Kingdom. Photos by Maynard Owen Williams. 141-180, Feb. 1949

HUTSON, PAT: Author:
Snow-mantled Stehekin: Where Solitude Is in Season. Photos by Bruce Dale. 572-588, Apr. 1974

The **HUTTERITES,** Plain People of the West. By William Albert Allard. 98-125, July 1970

HUTTON, JACQUELINE: Artist:
Strange Babies of the Sea. By Hilary B. Moore. Paintings by Craig Phillips and Jacqueline Hutton. 41-56, July 1952

HUZZA for Otaheite! By Luis Marden. 435-459, Apr. 1962

HYBRIDS:

Amateur Gardener Creates a New Rose. By Elizabeth A. Moize. Photos by Farrell Grehan. 286-294, Aug. 1972

The Exquisite Orchids. By Luis Marden. 485-513, Apr. 1971

See also Africanized Honeybees

HYDROELECTRIC POWER:

The Fire of Heaven. By Albert W. Atwood. 655-674, Nov. 1948

New St. Lawrence Seaway Opens the Great Lakes to the World. By Andrew H. Brown. 299-339, Mar. 1959

Niagara Falls, Servant of Good Neighbors. Photos by Walter Meayers Edwards. 574-587, Apr. 1963

Powerhouse of the Northwest (Columbia River). By David S. Boyer. 821-847, Dec. 1974

See also Cooper River Water Project; Kemano Power Development

HYDROFOIL BOATS:

Hydrofoil, *HD-4,* designed by Alexander Graham Bell. 493, 495, 496, Apr. 1957; 257, 264, Aug. 1959; 554-555, Oct. 1963

Hydrofoil Ferry "Flies" the Strait of Messina. By Gilbert Grosvenor. 493-496, Apr. 1957
    Contents: *Arrow of the Sun, HD-4*

HYENAS:

The Flamingo Eaters of Ngorongoro. By Richard D. Estes. 535-539, Oct. 1973

Hyenas, the Hunters Nobody Knows. By Hans Kruuk. Photos by Baron Hugo van Lawick. 44-57, July 1968

I

IC. *See* Integrated Circuits

IGY. *See* International Geophysical Year

ISA. *See* International School of America

ICONS:

Mount Sinai's Holy Treasures (St. Catherine's Monastery). By Kurt Weitzmann. Photos by Fred Anderegg. 109-127, Jan. 1964

IDAHO:

Following the Trail of Lewis and Clark. By Ralph Gray. 707-750, June 1953

Forest Fire: The Devil's Picnic. By Stuart E. Jones and Jay Johnston. 100-127, July 1968
   Included: Blazes in Kaniksu National Forest and Nezperce National Forest

High-stepping Idaho. By William S. Ellis. Photos by Dean Conger. 290-317, Mar. 1973

Idaho Loggers Battle a River. 117-130, July 1951

Man on the Moon in Idaho. By William Belknap, Jr. 505-525, Oct. 1960

A Map Maker Looks at the United States. By Newman Bumstead. 705-748, June 1951
   Included: Coeur d'Alene; Lewiston; Pleasant Valley Rapids; Pocatello; Seven Devils country; Snake River; Weiser

White-water Adventure on Wild Rivers of Idaho. By Frank Craighead, Jr. and John Craighead. 213-239, Feb. 1970

See also Morgan Creek

IDYLL, CLARENCE P.: Author:

The Crab That Shakes Hands. Photos by Robert F. Sisson. 254-271, Feb. 1971

Grunion, the Fish That Spawns on Land. Photos by Robert F. Sisson. 714-723, May 1969

The Incredible Salmon. Photos by Robert F. Sisson. Paintings by Walter A. Weber. 195-219, Aug. 1968

New Florida Resident, the Walking Catfish. Photos by Robert F. Sisson. 847-851, June 1969

Shrimp Nursery: Science Explores New Ways to Farm the Sea. Photos by Robert F. Sisson. 636-659, May 1965

Shrimpers Strike Gold in the Gulf. Photos by Robert F. Sisson. 699-707, May 1957

The **IDYLLIC** Vale of Kashmir. By Volkmar Wentzel. 523-550, Apr. 1948

IFALIK, Lonely Paradise of the South Seas. By Marston Bates. 547-571, Apr. 1956

IGLOOLIK, Northwest Territories, Canada:

I Live With the Eskimos. By Guy Mary-Rousseliere. 188-217, Feb. 1971

IGUANAS:

The Galapagos, Eerie Cradle of New Species. By Roger Tory Peterson. Photos by Alan and Joan Root. 541-585, Apr. 1967

In the Wilds of a City Parlor. By Paul A. Zahl. 645-672, Nov. 1954

Lost World of the Galapagos. By Irving and Electa Johnson. 681-703, May 1959

IKEYA-SEKI COMET:

Giant Comet Grazes the Sun. By Kenneth F. Weaver. 259-261, Feb. 1966

ÎLE DE LA CITÉ, Birthplace of Paris. By Kenneth MacLeish. Photos by Bruce Dale. 680-719, May 1968

ILHA NOVA, Azores:

A New Volcano Bursts from the Atlantic. By John

ILHA NOVA, Azores—*Continued*

Scofield. Photos by Robert F. Sisson. 735-757, June 1958

ILLINOIS:

Following the Trail of Lewis and Clark. By Ralph Gray. 707-750, June 1953

Illinois—Healthy Heart of the Nation. By Leo A. Borah. Photos by B. Anthony Stewart and Willard R. Culver. 781-820, Dec. 1953

Illinois: The City and the Plain. By Robert Paul Jordan. Photos by James L. Stanfield and Joseph J. Scherschel. 745-797, June 1967

Mapping the Nation's Breadbasket. By Frederick Simpich. 831-849, June 1948

The Upper Mississippi. By Willard Price. 651-699, Nov. 1958

Vacation Tour Through Lincoln Land. By Ralph Gray. 141-184, Feb. 1952

Who Were the "Mound Builders"? By George E. Stuart. 783-801, Dec. 1972

See also Cairo; East St. Louis; Shawneetown

ILLINOIS (River), Illinois:

Down Mark Twain's River on a Raft. By Rex E. Hieronymus. 551-574, Apr. 1948
   Included: Illinois River; Mississippi River

ILLUSTRATED LONDON NEWS:

Witness to a War (U. S. Civil War): British Correspondent Frank Vizetelly. By Robert T. Cochran, Jr. 453-491, Apr. 1961

ILULÍSSAT, Greenland. *See* Jakobshavn

I'M From New Jersey. By John T. Cunningham. Photos by Volkmar Wentzel. 1-45, Jan. 1960

IMBODEN, OTIS: Photographer:

Drowned Galleons Yield Spanish Gold. By Kip Wagner. 1-37, Jan. 1965

First Flight Across the Bottom of the World. By James R. Reedy. 454-464, Mar. 1964

Florida's Emerging Seminoles. By Louis Capron. 716-734, Nov. 1969

The Maya: Riddle of the Glyphs. By George E. Stuart. 768-791, Dec. 1975

The People of Cades Cove. By William O. Douglas. Photos by Thomas Nebbia and Otis Imboden. 60-95, July 1962

Thera, Key to the Riddle of Minos. By Spyridon Marinatos. 702-726, May 1972

Threatened Glories of Everglades National Park. By Frederick Kent Truslow and Frederick G. Vosburgh. Photos by Frederick Kent Truslow and Otis Imboden. 508-553, Oct. 1967

YWCA: International Success Story. By Mary French Rockefeller. 904-933, Dec. 1963

IMMIGRANTS:

Australia

Coober Pedy: Opal Capital of Australia's Outback. By Kenny Moore. Photos by Penny Tweedie. 560-571, Oct. 1976

The Making of a New Australia. By Howell Walker. 233-259, Feb. 1956

South Australia, Gateway to the Great Outback. By Howell Walker. Photos by Joseph J. Scherschel. 441-481, Apr. 1970

Israel

Israel—The Seventh Day. By Joseph Judge. Photos by Gordon W. Gahan. 816-855, Dec. 1972

INSIDE a Hornbill's Walled-up Nest. Photos by Joan and Alan Root. 846-855, Dec. 1969

INSIDE Europe Aboard *Yankee*. By Irving and Electa Johnson. Photos by Joseph J. Scherschel. 157-195, Aug. 1964

INSIDE PASSAGE (Washington-British Columbia-Alaska):

Alaska's Marine Highway: Ferry Route to the North. By W. E. Garrett. 776-819, June 1965

Alaska's Warmer Side. By Elsie May Bell Grosvenor. 737-775, June 1956

Endeavour Sails the Inside Passage. By Amos Burg. 801-828, June 1947

Making Friends With a Killer Whale. By Edward I. Griffin. 418-446, Mar. 1966

INSIDE the White House. By Lonnelle Aikman. Photos by B. Anthony Stewart and Thomas Nebbia. 3-43, Jan. 1961

INSIDE the World of the Honeybee. By Treat Davidson. 188-217, Aug. 1959

INTEGRATED CIRCUITS:

Crystals, Magical Servants of the Space Age. By Kenneth F. Weaver. Photos by James P. Blair. 278-296, Aug. 1968

INTER-AMERICAN GEODETIC SURVEY (IAGS):

Expedition to Amazon source. 445, 459, 460, Oct. 1972

Men Who Measure the Earth. By Robert Leslie Conly. Photos by John E. Fletcher. 335-362, Mar. 1956

INTER-AMERICAN HIGHWAY. See Pan American Highway

INTERNATIONAL GEOPHYSICAL YEAR (IGY):

The International Geophysical Year. By Hugh L. Dryden. 285-298, Feb. 1956

Man's First Winter at the South Pole. By Paul A. Siple. 439-478, Apr. 1958

To the Men at South Pole Station. By Richard E. Byrd. 1-4, July 1957

We Are Living at the South Pole. By Paul A. Siple. Photos by David S. Boyer. 5-35, July 1957

Year of Discovery Opens in Antarctica. By David S. Boyer. 339-381, Sept. 1957

See also Expéditions Polaires Françaises; Operation Deep Freeze; Rockets Explore the Air; Satellites (How Man-made Satellites Can Affect Our Lives; Space Satellites)

INTERNATIONAL ICE PATROL:

Tracking Danger With the Ice Patrol. By William S. Ellis. Photos by James R. Holland. 780-793, June 1968

INTERNATIONAL INDIAN OCEAN EXPEDITION:

Science Explores the Monsoon Sea. By Samuel W. Matthews. Photos by Robert F. Sisson. 554-575, Oct. 1967

INTERNATIONAL PARK. See Waterton-Glacier International Peace Park

INTERNATIONAL SCHOOL OF AMERICA (ISA):

Round the World School. By Paul Antze. Photos by William Eppridge. 96-127, July 1962

INTERSTATE HIGHWAY SYSTEM:

Our Growing Interstate Highway System. By Rob-

INTERSTATE HIGHWAY SYSTEM—*Continued*

ert Paul Jordan. 195-219, Feb. 1968

Trucks Race the Clock From Coast to Coast. By James A. Sugar. 226-243, Feb. 1974

INTERSTATE PARK. *See* Palisades Interstate Park

INTHA (People):

Burma's Leg Rowers and Floating Farms. Photos by W. E. Garrett. Text by David Jeffery. 826-845, June 1974

INTO the Heart of Africa. By Gertrude S. Weeks. 257-263, Aug. 1956

INTO the Lairs of "Sleeping" Sharks. By Eugenie Clark. Photos by David Doubilet. 570-584, Apr. 1975

INTO the Well of Sacrifice (Chichén Itzá). By Eusebio Dávalos Hurtado and Bates Littlehales. Photos by Bates Littlehales. 540-561, Oct. 1961

INTRACOASTAL WATERWAY, Atlantic Coast, U. S.:

America's Inland Waterway. Special Publication announced. 865-868, June 1973

Slow Boat to Florida. By Dorothea and Stuart E. Jones. 1-65, Jan. 1958

See also Florida Keys; Sea Islands

INVENTORS AND INVENTIONS:

Alexander Graham Bell Museum: Tribute to Genius. By Jean Lesage. 227-256, Aug. 1956

Behold the Computer Revolution. By Peter T. White. Photos by Bruce Dale and Emory Kristof. 593-633, Nov. 1970

The British Way: Great Britain's Major Gifts to Freedom, Democratic Government, Science, and Society. By Sir Evelyn Wrench. 421-541, Apr. 1949

Cities Like Worcester Make America. By Howell Walker. 189-214, Feb. 1955

Included: Bigelow's power carpet loom; Blanchard's lathe; Goddard's liquid-fueled rocket; Hawes's envelope-folding machine; Howe's sewing machine; piano wire; the steam calliope; Whitney's cotton gin

Miracle Men of the Telephone. By F. Barrows Colton. 273-316, Mar. 1947

Those Inventive Americans. Special Publication announced. 880-884, June 1970

Yesterday Lingers Along the Connecticut. By Charles McCarry. Photos by David L. Arnold. 334-369, Sept. 1972

Included: Samuel Colt (six-shooter); John C. Garand (M-1 rifle); Samuel Morey (steamboat); James F. Tasker (bridges); Eli Whitney (interchangeable parts)

See also Bell, Alexander Graham; Ford, Henry, Museum; Franklin, Benjamin; Jefferson, Thomas; Wright, Orville and Wilbur; *and* NGS: Inventions

The INVESTITURE of Great Britain's Prince of Wales. By Allan C. Fisher, Jr. Photos by James L. Stanfield and Adam Woolfitt. 698-715, Nov. 1969

INYO NATIONAL FOREST, California:

Bristlecone Pine, Oldest Known Living Thing. By Edmund Schulman. Photos by W. Robert Moore. 355-372, Mar. 1958

IONIAN ISLANDS, Greece:

Homeward With Ulysses. By Melville Bell Grosvenor. Photos by Edwin Stuart Grosvenor. 1-39, July 1973

K

KING ISLAND, Alaska:

Cliff Dwellers of the Bering Sea. By Juan Muñoz. 129-146, Jan. 1954

North Star Cruises Alaska's Wild West. By Amos Burg. 57-86, July 1952

KING RANCH, Texas:

America's "Meat on the Hoof." By William H. Nicholas. 33-72, Jan. 1952
King Ranch, Cattle Empire in Texas. 41-64

KINGDON-WARD, F.: Author-Photographer:

Caught in the Assam-Tibet Earthquake. 403-416, Mar. 1952

KINGFISHERS:

The Shy and Spectacular Kingfisher (European). Photos by Carl-Johan Junge and Emil Lütken. 413-419, Sept. 1974

KINGS CANYON NATIONAL PARK, California:

Giant Sequoias Draw Millions to California Parks. By John Michael Kauffmann. Photos by B. Anthony Stewart. 147-187, Aug. 1959

KINGS POINT, New York: U. S. Merchant Marine Academy:

Kings Point: Maker of Mariners. By Nathaniel T. Kenney. Photos by Volkmar Wentzel. 693-706, Nov. 1955

KINGSTON, Massachusetts:

Land of the Pilgrims' Pride. By George W. Long. Photos by Robert F. Sisson. 193-219, Aug. 1947

KINGSTON, Ontario, Canada:

Sea to Lakes on the St. Lawrence. By George W. Long. Photos by B. Anthony Stewart and John E. Fletcher. 323-366, Sept. 1950

KINLOCH, BRUCE G.: Author-Photographer:

Orphans of the Wild. 683-699, Nov. 1962

KINNEY, WILLIAM A.: Author:

Operation Eclipse: 1948. 325-372, Mar. 1949

Roving Maryland's Cavalier Country. 431-470, Apr. 1954

Washington's Historic Georgetown. 513-544, Apr. 1953

KIRGHIZ (People):

We Took the Highroad in Afghanistan. By Jean and Franc Shor. 673-706, Nov. 1950

Winter Caravan to the Roof of the World. By Sabrina and Roland Michaud. 435-465, Apr. 1972

KIRIN (Chilin), Manchuria:

In Manchuria Now. By W. Robert Moore. 389-414, Mar. 1947

KIRK, MALCOLM S.: Author-Photographer:

The Asmat of New Guinea, Headhunters in Today's World. 376-409, Mar. 1972

Change Ripples New Guinea's Sepik River. 354-381, Sept. 1973

Journey Into Stone Age New Guinea. 568-592, Apr. 1969

New Guinea Festival of Faces. 148-156, July 1969

KIRKJUFELL (Volcano), Heimaey, Iceland:

A Village Fights for Its Life. By Noel Grove. 40-67, July 1973

KITES:

Alexander Graham Bell Museum: Tribute to Genius. By Jean Lesage. 227-256, Aug. 1956

Miracle Men of the Telephone. By F. Barrows Colton. 273-316, Mar. 1947
Included: Illustrations of Alexander Graham Bell's multicelled and tetrahedral kites

KITES (Birds):

The Swallow-tailed Kite: Graceful Aerialist of the Everglades. Photos by Ray O. Green, Jr., Norman D. Reed, and Myron H. Wright, Jr. 496-505, Oct. 1972

KITIMAT – Canada's Aluminum Titan. By David S. Boyer. 376-398, Sept. 1956

KITTINGER, JOSEPH W., Jr.: Author:

The Long, Lonely Leap. Photos by Volkmar Wentzel. 854-873, Dec. 1960

The **KIWI**, New Zealand's Wonder Bird. By Ron J. Anderson. 395-398, Sept. 1955

KLEMMER, HARVEY: Author:

Belgium Comes Back. Photos by Maynard Owen Williams. 575-614, May 1948

KLEMPERER, WOLFGANG B.: Author:

The Solar Eclipse From a Jet. 785-796, Nov. 1963

KLINE, FRED: Author:

Baltimore: The Hidden City. Photos by Martin Rogers. 188-215, Feb. 1975

Library of Congress: The Nation's Bookcase. Photos by Dick Durrance II. 671-687, Nov. 1975

San Antonio: "Texas, Actin' Kind of Natural." Photos by David Hiser. 524-549, Apr. 1976

KLINGEL, GILBERT C.: Author:

One Hundred Hours Beneath the Chesapeake. Photos by Willard R. Culver. 681-696, May 1955

KLINGMAN, LAWRENCE L.: Author:

Incredible Andorra. Photos by B. Anthony Stewart. 262-290, Aug. 1949

KNEEN, ORVILLE H.: Author:

Patent Plants Enrich Our World. 357-378, Mar. 1948

KNIGHT, CHRISTOPHER G.: Photographer:

Alaska's Mighty Rivers of Ice. By Maynard M. Miller. 194-217, Feb. 1967

Americans Afoot in Rumania. By Dan Dimancescu. Photos by Dick Durrance II and Christopher G. Knight. 810-845, June 1969

Down the Danube by Canoe. By William Slade Backer. Photos by Richard S. Durrance and Christopher G. Knight. 34-79, July 1965

Kayak Odyssey: From the Inland Sea to Tokyo. By Dan Dimancescu. 295-337, Sept. 1967

KNIK GLACIER AND RIVER, Alaska:

Alaska's Automatic Lake Drains Itself (Lake George). 835-844, June 1951

KNOCKING Out Grizzly Bears for Their Own Good. By Frank and John Craighead. 276-291, Aug. 1960

'KNOWN but to God' (Unknown Heroes). By Beverley M. Bowie. 593-605, Nov. 1958

KNUDSEN, DON C.: Photographer:

Alaska's Automatic Lake Drains Itself (Lake

KYUSHU (Island), Japan:
Backwoods Japan During American Occupation. By M. A. Huberman. 491-518, Apr. 1947

L

L-5 (Space Colony, A.D. 2026):
The Next Frontier? By Isaac Asimov. Paintings by Pierre Mion. 76-89, July 1976

L. S. B. LEAKEY FOUNDATION:
Contributions invited; address given. 144, Jan. 1973
Early-man research in Ethiopia sponsored. 805, Dec. 1976

LaBASTILLE, ANNE: Author:
My Backyard, the Adirondacks. Photos by David Alan Harvey. 616-639, May 1975
See also Bowes, Anne LaBastille

LA BEAUCE (Plain), France:
Chartres: Legacy From the Age of Faith. By Kenneth MacLeish. Photos by Dean Conger. 857-882, Dec. 1969

LABORATORY in a Dirty Sky. By Rudolf J. Engelmann and Vera Simons. 616-621, Nov. 1976

LABRADOR (Region), Newfoundland:
Far North with "Captain Mac." By Miriam MacMillan. 465-513, Oct. 1951
Labrador Canoe Adventure. By Andrew Brown and Ralph Gray. 65-99, July 1951
Milestones in My Arctic Journeys. By Willie Knutsen. 543-570, Oct. 1949
   Included: Activities of the Search and Rescue section of the Air Force at Goose Bay
Newfoundland, Canada's New Province. By Andrew H. Brown. Photos by author and Robert F. Sisson. 777-812, June 1949
School for Survival. By Curtis E. LeMay. 565-602, May 1953

LACQUER WARE:
Human Treasures of Japan. By William Graves. Photos by James L. Stanfield. 370-379, Sept. 1972
A Lady From China's Past. Photos from *China Pictorial*. Text by Alice J. Hall. 660-681, May 1974

LA CRAU (Plain), France:
Sheep Trek in the French Alps. By Maurice Moyal. Photos by Marcel Coen. 545-564, Apr. 1952

LADAKH (District), Jammu and Kashmir:
A Journey to "Little Tibet." By Enakshi Bhavnani. Photos by Volkmar Wentzel. 603-634, May 1951
Mountaintop War in Remote Ladakh. By W. E. Garrett. 664-687, May 1963
A Woman Paints the Tibetans. By Lafugie. 659-692, May 1949

LADD, HARRY S.: Author:
Fossils Lift the Veil of Time. By Harry S. Ladd and Roland W. Brown. 363-386, Mar. 1956

A LADY From China's Past. Photos from *China Pictorial*. Text by Alice J. Hall. 660-681, May 1974

LADYBUGS:
Following the Ladybug Home. By Kenneth S. Ha-

LADYBUGS — *Continued*
gen. Photos by Robert F. Sisson. 543-553, Apr. 1970
New Tricks Outwit Our Insect Enemies. By Hal Higdon. Photos by Robert F. Sisson and Emory Kristof. 380-399, Sept. 1972

LA FAY, HOWARD: Author:
Alabama, Dixie to a Different Tune. Photos by Dick Durrance II. 534-569, Oct. 1975
Algeria: France's Stepchild, Problem and Promise. Photos by Robert F. Sisson. 768-795, June 1960
Andalusia, the Spirit of Spain. Photos by Joseph J. Scherschel. 833-857, June 1975
"Be Ye Men of Valour" (Churchill's Life and Funeral). 159-197, Aug. 1965
Carnival in Trinidad. Photos by Winfield Parks. 693-701, Nov. 1971
DEW Line, Sentry of the Far North. 128-146, July 1958
Easter Island and Its Mysterious Monuments. Photos by Thomas J. Abercrombie. 90-117, Jan. 1962
The Eisenhower Story. 1-39, July 1969
Freedom's Progress South of the Sahara. Photos by Joseph J. Scherschel. 603-637, Nov. 1962
George Washington: The Man Behind the Myths. Photos by Ted Spiegel. 90-111, July 1976
Gibraltar — Rock of Contention. Photos by Bates Littlehales. 102-121, July 1966
Leningrad, Russia's Window on the West. Photos by Dick Durrance II. 636-673, May 1971
The Maya, Children of Time. Photos by David Alan Harvey. 729-767, Dec. 1975
Portugal at the Crossroads. Photos by Volkmar Wentzel. 453-501, Oct. 1965
The St. Lawrence, River Key to Canada. Photos by John Launois. 622-667, May 1967
Sicily, Where All the Songs Are Sad. Photos by Jonathan Blair. 407-436, Mar. 1976
Uganda, Africa's Uneasy Heartland. Photos by George F. Mobley. 708-735, Nov. 1971
The Vikings. Photos by Ted Spiegel. 492-541, Apr. 1970
Where Jesus Walked. Photos by Charles Harbutt. 739-781, Dec. 1967

LAFAYETTE, Marquis de:
Lafayette's Homeland, Auvergne. By Howell Walker. 419-436, Sept. 1957

LAFUGIE, Madame: Author-Artist:
A Woman Paints the Tibetans. 659-692, May 1949

LA GORCE, GILBERT GROSVENOR:
NGM advertising director. 442, 444, Mar. 1960
Author
Marineland, Florida's Giant Fish Bowl. Photos by Luis Marden. 679-694, Nov. 1952

LA GORCE, JOHN OLIVER:
Board of Trustees, Vice Chairman. 419-423, Mar. 1957; 98, Jan. 1966
Colleague of the Golden Years: John Oliver La Gorce (Memorial Tribute). By Gilbert Grosvenor. 440-444, Mar. 1960
Editor (1954-1957). 65, 65D, July 1954; 441, 442, 444, Mar. 1960; 46-47, 67, July 1967
Editor, Assistant. 418, Mar. 1957
Editor, Associate. 65, 65C, July 1954; 418, Mar.

LA PITA, Panama:

Exploring Ancient Panama by Helicopter. By Matthew W. Stirling. Photos by Richard H. Stewart. 227-246, Feb. 1950

LAPLAND:

Friendly Flight to Northern Europe. By Lyndon B. Johnson. Photos by Volkmar Wentzel. 268-293, Feb. 1964

Lapland's Reindeer Roundup. 109-116, July 1949

North with Finland's Lapps. By Jean and Franc Shor. 249-280, Aug. 1954

Norway, Land of the Generous Sea. By Edward J. Linehan. Photos by George F. Mobley. 1-43, July 1971

LARSEN, CALVIN L.: Photographer:

Across the Frozen Desert to Byrd Station. By Paul W. Frazier. 383-398, Sept. 1957

LARSEN, THOR: Author-Photographer:

Polar Bear: Lonely Nomad of the North. 574-590, Apr. 1971

LASCAUX CAVE, Cradle of World Art (France). By Norbert Casteret. Photos by Maynard Owen Williams. 771-794, Dec. 1948

LASERS:

The Laser's Bright Magic. By Thomas Meloy. Photos by Howard Sochurek. 858-881, Dec. 1966

LAS MARISMAS (Marshes), Spain:

Rare Birds Flock to Spain's Marismas. By Roger Tory Peterson. 397-425, Mar. 1958

The **LAST** Andaman Islanders. By Raghubir Singh. 66-91, July 1975

The **LAST** Full Measure. By Melville Bell Grosvenor. 307-355, Mar. 1964

The **LAST** Great Animal Kingdom: A Portfolio of Africa's Vanishing Wildlife. 390-409, Sept. 1960

LAST Harbor for the Oldest Ship. By Susan W. and Michael L. Katzev. 618-625, Nov. 1974

LAST Moments of the Pompeians. By Amedeo Maiuri. Photos by Lee E. Battaglia. Paintings by Peter V. Bianchi. 651-669, Nov. 1961

LAST of the Cape Horners (*Pamir*). By Alan Villiers. 701-710, May 1948

LAST Stand for the Bighorn. By James K. Morgan. 383-399, Sept. 1973

The **LAST** Thousand Years Before Christ. By G. Ernest Wright. Paintings by H. J. Soulen and Peter V. Bianchi. 812-853, Dec. 1960

The **LAST** U. S. Whale Hunters. By Emory Kristof. 346-353, Mar. 1973

LAS VEGAS, Nevada:

The Other Nevada. By Robert Laxalt. Photos by J. Bruce Baumann. 733-761, June 1974

LATHAM, MARTE: Author:

Capturing Strange Creatures in Colombia. Photos by Tor Eigeland. 682-693, May 1966

LA TOUR, CY: Author-Photographer:

J. W. Westcott, Postman for the Great Lakes. 813-824, Dec. 1950

LAUNOIS, JOHN: Photographer:

Bangkok, City of Angels. By William Graves. 96-129, July 1973

"Every Day Is a Gift When You Are Over 100." By Alexander Leaf. 93-119, Jan. 1973

Japan, the Exquisite Enigma. By Franc Shor. 733-777, Dec. 1960

Martinique: Liberté, Egalité, and Uncertainty in the Caribbean. By Kenneth MacLeish. 124-148, Jan. 1975

The St. Lawrence, River Key to Canada. By Howard La Fay. 622-667, May 1967

The Tasadays, Stone Age Cavemen of Mindanao. By Kenneth MacLeish. 219-249, Aug. 1972

Vienna, City of Song. By Peter T. White. 739-779, June 1968

LA VENTA, Mexico:

Gifts for the Jaguar God. By Philip Drucker and Robert F. Heizer. 367-375, Sept. 1956

On the Trail of La Venta Man. By Matthew W. Stirling. Photos by Richard H. Stewart. 137-172, Feb. 1947

Hunting Mexico's Buried Temples. 145-168

LAVIES, BIANCA: Photographer:

Found at Last: the Monarch's Winter Home. By Fred A. Urquhart. 161-173, Aug. 1976

Manitoba's Fantastic Snake Pits. By Michael Aleksiuk. 715-723, Nov. 1975

Those Fiery Brazilian Bees. By Rick Gore. 491-501, Apr. 1976

Tireless Voyager, the Whistling Swan. By William J. L. Sladen. 134-147, July 1975

LAVIGNE, DAVID M.: Author:

Life or Death for the Harp Seal. Photos by William R. Curtsinger. 129-142, Jan. 1976

LAW:

Ancient Mesopotamia: A Light That Did Not Fail. By E. A. Speiser. Paintings by H. M. Herget. 41-105, Jan. 1951

Included: The Law Protects Zealously the Institution of Marriage.—Justice Catches Up With a Corrupt Magistrate

The British Way. By Sir Evelyn Wrench. 421-541, Apr. 1949

Included: Jury System (1066-1086); Magna Carta (1215); The Mother of Parliaments (1295); William Blackstone (1723-1780)

LAW ENFORCEMENT:

The FBI: Public Friend Number One. By Jacob Hay. Photos by Robert F. Sisson. 860-886, June 1961

LAWA (People). *See* Lua

LAWICK, HUGO VAN: Photographer:

Adventures in the Search for Man. By Louis S. B. Leakey. 132-152, Jan. 1963

Hyenas, the Hunters Nobody Knows. By Hans Kruuk. 44-57, July 1968

The Leakeys of Africa: Family in Search of Prehistoric Man. By Melvin M. Payne. 194-231, Feb. 1965

My Life Among Wild Chimpanzees. By Jane Goodall. Photos by Baron Hugo van Lawick and author. 272-308, Aug. 1963

New Discoveries Among Africa's Chimpanzees. By

LENDOMBWEY. *See* Malekula (Island)

LENINGRAD, U.S.S.R.:

Leningrad, Russia's Window on the West. By Howard La Fay. Photos by Dick Durrance II. 636-673, May 1971

LEONARD CARMICHAEL: An Appreciation. By Melvin M. Payne. 871-874, Dec. 1973
See also Carmichael, Leonard C.

LEONOV, ALEKSEY A.:

Apollo-Soyuz: Handclasp in Space. By Thomas Y. Canby. 183-187, Feb. 1976

LEOPARDS. *See* Snow Leopards

LERICI, CARLO M.: Author:
Periscope on the Etruscan Past. 337-350, Sept. 1959

LERNER, IRA S.: Photographer:
Getting to Know the Wild Burros of Death Valley. By Patricia des Roses Moehlman. Photos by Ira S. Lerner and author. 502-517, Apr. 1972

LERNER MARINE LABORATORY, Bahama Islands:
The Bahamas, Isles of the Blue-green Sea. By Carleton Mitchell. Photos by B. Anthony Stewart. 147-203, Feb. 1958
Man-of-War Fleet Attacks Bimini. By Paul A. Zahl. 185-212, Feb. 1952

LERWICK, Shetland Islands. *See* Up Helly Aa

LESAGE, JEAN: Author:
Alexander Graham Bell Museum: Tribute to Genius. 227-256, Aug. 1956

LESBOS (Island), Greece:
The Isles of Greece: Aegean Birthplace of Western Culture. By Melville Bell Grosvenor. Photos by Edwin Stuart Grosvenor and Winfield Parks. 147-193, Aug. 1972

LESSER SUNDA ISLANDS:
Dragon Lizards of Komodo. By James A. Kern. 872-880, Dec. 1968
East From Bali by Seagoing Jeep to Timor. By Helen and Frank Schreider. 236-279, Aug. 1962
See also Bali

LESSING, ERICH: Photographer:
Firsthand Look at the Soviet Union. By Thomas T. Hammond. 352-407, Sept. 1959
Modern Miracle, Made in Germany. By Robert Leslie Conly. 735-791, June 1959
Poland Opens Her Doors. By Delia and Ferdinand Kuhn. 354-398, Sept. 1958

LESSON and Challenge. By James H. Wakelin, Jr. 759-763, June 1964

LETHBRIDGE, JOHN:
The Treasure of Porto Santo. By Robert Sténuit. Photos by author and William R. Curtsinger. 260-275, Aug. 1975

LETTICK, BIRNEY: Artist:
A New Look at Medieval Europe. By Kenneth M. Setton. Paintings by Andre Durenceau and Birney Lettick. 799-859, Dec. 1962

LEVEES. *See* Dikes and Levees

LEVKAS (Island), Greece:
Homeward With Ulysses (Ionian Islands). By Mel-

LEVKAS (Island), Greece—*Continued*
ville Bell Grosvenor. Photos by Edwin Stuart Grosvenor. 1-39, July 1973

LEWIS, DAVID: Author:
Alone to Antarctica. Drawings by Noel Sickles. 808-821, Dec. 1973
Hokule'a Follows the Stars to Tahiti. Photos by Nicholas deVore III. 512-537, Oct. 1976
Wind, Wave, Star, and Bird. Photos by Nicholas deVore III. 747-781, Dec. 1974
Author-Photographer
Ice Bird Ends Her Lonely Odyssey. 216-233, Aug. 1975

LEWIS, G. EDWARD: Author-Photographer:
El Sangay, Fire-breathing Giant of the Andes. 117-138, Jan. 1950

LEWIS, LEWIS: Author-Photographer:
New Life for the "Loneliest Isle" (Tristan da Cunha). 105-116, Jan. 1950

LEWIS, M. LEE: Author:
To 76,000 Feet by *Strato-Lab* Balloon. By Malcolm D. Ross and M. Lee Lewis. 269-282, Feb. 1957

LEWIS, Isle of, Scotland:
Isles on the Edge of the Sea: Scotland's Outer Hebrides. By Kenneth MacLeish. Photos by Thomas Nebbia. 676-711, May 1970

LEWIS AND CLARK EXPEDITION:
Following the Trail of Lewis and Clark. By Ralph Gray. 707-750, June 1953
In the Footsteps of Lewis and Clark. Special Publication announced. 880-884, June 1970
So Long, St. Louis, We're Heading West. By William C. Everhart. 643-669, Nov. 1965

LEXINGTON, Kentucky:
Heart of the Bluegrass. By Charles McCarry. Photos by J. Bruce Baumann. 634-659, May 1974

LEYDET, FRANÇOIS: Author:
Autumn Flames Along the Allagash. Photos by Farrell Grehan. 177-187, Feb. 1974
Jackson Hole: Good-bye to the Old Days? Photos by Jonathan Wright. 768-789, Dec. 1976
The Mazatzal's Harsh but Lovely Land Between. Photos by Farrell Grehan. 161-167, Feb. 1974
Okefenokee, the Magical Swamp. Photos by Farrell Grehan. 169-175, Feb. 1974
The Olympics: Northwest Majesty. Photos by Farrell Grehan. 188-197, Feb. 1974

LHASA, Tibet:
My Life in Forbidden Lhasa. By Heinrich Harrer. 1-48, July 1955

LIBBY, ERNEST L.: Author-Photographer:
Miracle of the Mermaid's Purse (Skate). 413-420, Sept. 1957

LIBERIA:
Africa: The Winds of Freedom Stir a Continent. By Nathaniel T. Kenney. Photos by W. D. Vaughn. 303-359, Sept. 1960
Rubber-cushioned Liberia. By Henry S. Villard. Photos by Charles W. Allmon. 201-228, Feb. 1948

LINDISFARNE (Island), England:
Pilgrimage to Holy Island and the Farnes. By John E. H. Nolan. 547-570, Oct. 1952

LINE, FRANCIS R.: Author-Photographer:
Arizona Sheep Trek. 457-478, Apr. 1950

LINEHAN, EDWARD J.: Author:
Colorado, the Rockies' Pot of Gold. Photos by James L. Amos. 157-201, Aug. 1969
Cuba's Exiles Bring New Life to Miami. Photos by Nathan Benn. 68-95, July 1973
Czechoslovakia: The Dream and the Reality. Photos by James P. Blair. 151-193, Feb. 1968
Dogs Work for Man. Paintings by Edwin Megargee and R. E. Lougheed. 190-233, Aug. 1958
Norway, Land of the Generous Sea. Photos by George F. Mobley. 1-43, July 1971
Old-new Iran, Next Door to Russia. Photos by Thomas J. Abercrombie. 44-85, Jan. 1961

LINK, EDWIN A.:
Exploring the Drowned City of Port Royal. By Marion Clayton Link. Photos by Luis Marden. 151-183, Feb. 1960
Author
Our Man-in-Sea Project. 713-717, May 1963
Outpost Under the Ocean. Photos by Bates Littlehales. 530-533, Apr. 1965
Tomorrow on the Deep Frontier. 778-801, June 1964

LINK, MARION CLAYTON: Author:
Exploring the Drowned City of Port Royal. Photos by Luis Marden. 151-183, Feb. 1960

LINK IGLOO:
Tomorrow on the Deep Frontier. By Edwin A. Link. 778-801, June 1964

LIONS:
Life with the King of Beasts. By George B. Schaller. 494-519, Apr. 1969
Lion Cubs. Children's book announced. 736-738, Nov. 1972
Spearing Lions with Africa's Masai. By Edgar Monsanto Queeny. 487-517, Oct. 1954

LIPAS (Sailing Craft):
Sea Gypsies of the Philippines. By Anne de Henning Singh. Photos by Raghubir Singh. 659-677, May 1976

LIPIZZANERS:
The White Horses of Vienna. By Beverley M. Bowie. Photos by Volkmar Wentzel. 401-419, Sept. 1958

LISBON, Portugal:
Portugal at the Crossroads. By Howard La Fay. Photos by Volkmar Wentzel. 453-501, Oct. 1965
Portugal Is Different. By Clement E. Conger. 583-622, Nov. 1948

LISTER, JOSEPH, LORD:
The British Way. By Sir Evelyn Wrench. 421-541, Apr. 1949

LITERATURE:
The Britain That Shakespeare Knew. By Louis B. Wright. Photos by Dean Conger. 613-665, May 1964

LITERATURE — *Continued*
The British Way. By Sir Evelyn Wrench. 421-541, Apr. 1949
Included: Geoffrey Chaucer, William Shakespeare, James I and the Translation of the Bible, John Milton, Daniel Defoe, Some British Poets, Charles Dickens
Chelsea, London's Haven of Individualists. By James Cerruti. Photos by Adam Woolfitt. 28-55, Jan. 1972
Included: Thomas Carlyle, George Eliot, George Meredith, R. J. Minney, Sir Thomas More, Tom Pocock, Dante Gabriel Rossetti, Jonathan Swift, Algernon Charles Swinburne, Mark Twain
The England of Charles Dickens. By Richard W. Long. Photos by Adam Woolfitt. 443-483, Apr. 1974
A First American Views His Land. By N. Scott Momaday. 13-19, July 1976
The Fragile Beauty All About Us. By Harry S. C. Yen. 785-795, Dec. 1970
Included: Chinese poetry, 6th century B.C.-A.D. 1269
Lake District, Poets' Corner of England. By H. V. Morton. Photos by David S. Boyer. 511-545, Apr. 1956
Landmarks of Literary England. By Leo A. Borah. Photos by Kathleen Revis. 295-350, Sept. 1955
Literary Landmarks of Massachusetts. By William H. Nicholas. Photos by B. Anthony Stewart and John E. Fletcher. 279-310, Mar. 1950
Contents: Adams family, Alcott family, Nathaniel Bowditch, Anne Bradstreet, William Cullen Bryant, Dana family, Emily Dickinson, Ralph Waldo Emerson, Clyde Fitch, Louise Imogen Guiney, Sarah Josepha Hale, Nathaniel Hawthorne, Julia Ward Howe, Henry Wadsworth Longfellow, James Russell Lowell, Herman Melville, John Boyle O'Reilly, Harriet Beecher Stowe, Henry David Thoreau, Noah Webster, John Greenleaf Whittier
Mark Twain: Mirror of America. By Noel Grove. Photos by James L. Stanfield. 300-337, Sept. 1975
Poets' Voices Linger in Scottish Shrines. By Isobel Wylie Hutchison. Photos by Kathleen Revis. 437-488, Oct. 1957
Contents: Sir James Barrie, James Boswell, John Buchan, Robert Burns, Lord Byron, Thomas Carlyle, Sir Arthur Conan Doyle, James Hogg, Violet Jacob, Samuel Johnson, Allan Ramsay, Sir Walter Scott, William Shakespeare, Adam Smith, Tobias Smollett, Robert Louis Stevenson, William Wordsworth
Robert Frost and New England. By Archibald MacLeish. 438-467, Apr. 1976
Look of a Land Beloved. Photos by Dewitt Jones. 444-467
A Stroll to John o' Groat's. By Isobel Wylie Hutchison. 1-48, July 1956
Included: Sir James Barrie, Michael Bruce, Thomas Carlyle, William Shakespeare, Adam Smith, Robert Louis Stevenson
A Stroll to London. By Isobel Wylie Hutchison. Photos by B. Anthony Stewart. 171-204, Aug. 1950
Included: James Boswell, Brontë sisters, Thomas Carlyle, Charles Dickens, George Eliot, Samuel Johnson, Sir Walter Scott, William Shakespeare, William Wordsworth
See also Elizabethan Age; Gilgamesh, Epic of; *Odyssey; Ramayana*

LITTLE AMERICA, Antarctica:
Admiral of the Ends of the Earth (Richard E. Byrd).

LIZARRIETA, Col de, Pyrenees Mountains:

Pigeon Netting—Sport of Basques. Photos by Irene Burdett-Scougall. 405-416, Sept. 1949

LOBSTERS AND LOBSTERING:

The American Lobster, Delectable Cannibal. By Luis Marden. Photos by David Doubilet. 462-487, Apr. 1973

Maine's Lobster Island, Monhegan. By William P. E. Graves. Photos by Kosti Ruohomaa. 285-298, Feb. 1959

Martha's Vineyard. By William P. E. Graves. Photos by James P. Blair. 778-809, June 1961

See also Spiny Lobsters

LOCKE, JUSTIN: Author-Photographer:

Lost Kingdom in Indian Mexico. 517-546, Oct. 1952

Photographer

Adobe New Mexico. By Mason Sutherland. 783-830, Dec. 1949

Amid the Mighty Walls of Zion. By Lewis F. Clark. 37-70, Jan. 1954

Appalachian Valley Pilgrimage. By Catherine Bell Palmer. 1-32, July 1949

Grand Canyon: Nature's Story of Creation. By Louis Schellbach. 589-629, May 1955

Growing Pains Beset Puerto Rico. By William H. Nicholas. 419-460, Apr. 1951

High Road in the Pyrenees. By H. V. Morton. 299-334, Mar. 1956

Life in the Land of the Basques. By John E. H. Nolan. 147-186, Feb. 1954

Mexico's Booming Capital. By Mason Sutherland. 785-824, Dec. 1951

Miami's Expanding Horizons. By William H. Nicholas. 561-594, Nov. 1950

New Orleans: Jambalaya on the Levee. By Harnett T. Kane. 143-184, Feb. 1953

Paris, Home Town of the World. By Donald William Dresden. 767-804, June 1952

Shooting Rapids in Dinosaur Country. By Jack Breed. Photos by author and Justin Locke. 363-390, Mar. 1954

The Smithsonian Institution. By Thomas R. Henry. 325-348, Sept. 1948

So Much Happens Along the Ohio River. By Frederick Simpich. 177-212, Feb. 1950

Vizcaya: An Italian Palazzo in Miami. By William H. Nicholas. 595-604, Nov. 1950

LOCKLEY, R. M.: Author:

The Solemn, Sociable Puffins. 414-422, Sept. 1954

LOCUSTS:

Locusts: "Teeth of the Wind." By Robert A. M. Conley. Photos by Gianni Tortoli. 202-227, Aug. 1969

Report from the Locust Wars. By Tony and Dickey Chapelle. 545-562, Apr. 1953

LOCUSTS, 17-year:

Rip Van Winkle of the Underground. By Kenneth F. Weaver. 133-142, July 1953

LOFOTEN (Islands), Norway:

Fishing in the Lofotens. Photos by Lennart Nilsson. 377-388, Mar. 1947

LOGGERS:

Idaho Loggers Battle a River. 117-130, July 1951

LOIRE RIVER AND VALLEY, France:

River of Counts and Kings: The Loire. By Kenneth MacLeish. Photos by Dean Conger. 822-869, June 1966

LOLOS (Tribespeople):

Adventures in Lololand. By Rennold L. Lowy. 105-118, Jan. 1947

LOMBARDY'S Lakes, Blue Jewels in Italy's Crown. By Franc Shor. Photos by Joseph J. Scherschel. 58-99, July 1968

LOMPOC VALLEY, California:

The Flower Seed Growers: Gardening's Color Merchants. By Robert de Roos. Photos by Jack Fields. 720-738, May 1968

LONDON, England:

"Around the World in Eighty Days." By Newman Bumstead. 705-750, Dec. 1951

"Be Ye Men of Valour" (Churchill's Life; Funeral). By Howard La Fay. 159-197, Aug. 1965

Benjamin Franklin, Philosopher of Dissent. By Alice J. Hall. Photos by Linda Bartlett. 93-123, July 1975

The Britain That Shakespeare Knew. By Louis B. Wright. Photos by Dean Conger. 613-665, May 1964

The British Way. By Sir Evelyn Wrench. 421-541, Apr. 1949

Chelsea, London's Haven of Individualists. By James Cerruti. Photos by Adam Woolfitt. 28-55, Jan. 1972

"The City"—London's Storied Square Mile. By Allan C. Fisher, Jr. 735-777, June 1961

The England of Charles Dickens. By Richard W. Long. Photos by Adam Woolfitt. 443-483, Apr. 1974

The Final Tribute (Churchill's Funeral). Text by Carolyn Bennett Patterson. 199-225, Aug. 1965

Founders of New England. By Sir Evelyn Wrench. Photos by B. Anthony Stewart. 803-838, June 1953

Founders of Virginia. By Sir Evelyn Wrench. Photos by B. Anthony Stewart. 433-462, Apr. 1948

In the London of the New Queen. By H. V. Morton. 291-342, Sept. 1953

Keeping House in London. By Frances James. 769-792, Dec. 1947

Landmarks of Literary England. By Leo A. Borah. Photos by Kathleen Revis. 295-350, Sept. 1955

London's Zoo of Zoos. By Thomas Garner James. 771-786, June 1953

One Man's London. By Allan C. Fisher, Jr. Photos by James P. Blair. 743-791, June 1966

Queen Elizabeth Opens Parliament. By W. E. Roscher. Photos by Robert B. Goodman. 699-707, Nov. 1961

A Stroll to London. By Isobel Wylie Hutchison. Photos by B. Anthony Stewart. 171-204, Aug. 1950

The Thames Mirrors England's Varied Life. By Willard Price. Photos by Robert F. Sisson. 45-93, July 1958

The World of Elizabeth I. By Louis B. Wright. Photos by Ted Spiegel. 668-709, Nov. 1968

LOS ANGELES, California—*Continued*

Photos by Thomas Nebbia. 451-501, Oct. 1962

New Rush to Golden California. By George W. Long. 723-802, June 1954

See also Los Angeles Basin

LOS ANGELES AQUEDUCT:

California's Parched Oasis, the Owens Valley. By Judith and Neil Morgan. Photos by Jodi Cobb and Galen Rowell. 98-127, Jan. 1976

LOS ANGELES BASIN, California:

Southern California's Trial by Mud and Water. By Nathaniel T. Kenney. Photos by Bruce Dale. 552-573, Oct. 1969

LOST COLONY. *See* Roanoke Island, North Carolina

The LOST Empire of the Incas. By Loren McIntyre. Art by Ned and Rosalie Seidler. 729-787, Dec. 1973

LOST Kingdom in Indian Mexico By Justin Locke. 517-546, Oct. 1952

The LOST SIERRA, California:

Golden Ghosts of the Lost Sierra. By Robert Laxalt. Photos by David Hiser. 332-353, Sept. 1973

LOST World of the Galapagos. By Irving and Electa Johnson. 681-703, May 1959

LOTUKA (Tribespeople):

South in the Sudan. By Harry Hoogstraal. 249-272, Feb. 1953

LOUDER, MAX:

North With the Wheat Cutters. By Noel Grove. Photos by James A. Sugar. 194-217, Aug. 1972

LOUGHEED, R. E.: Artist:

Dogs Work for Man. By Edward J. Linehan. Paintings by Edwin Megargee and R. E. Lougheed. 190-233, Aug. 1958

LOUISBOURG (Fortress), Nova Scotia:

Nova Scotia, the Magnificent Anchorage. By Charles McCarry. Photos by Gordon W. Gahan. 334-363, Mar. 1975

The St. Lawrence, River Key to Canada. By Howard La Fay. Photos by John Launois. 622-667, May 1967

LOUISE, Lake, Canada:

Canadian Rockies, Lords of a Beckoning Land. By Alan Phillips. Photos by James L. Stanfield. 353-393, Sept. 1966

LOUISIADE ARCHIPELAGO, Pacific Ocean:

Adventures with the Survey Navy. By Irving Johnson. 131-148, July 1947

LOUISIANA:

Cajunland, Louisiana's French-speaking Coast. By Bern Keating. Photos by Charles Harbutt and Franke Keating. 353-391, Mar. 1966

Land of Louisiana Sugar Kings. By Harnett T. Kane. Photos by Willard R. Culver. 531-567, Apr. 1958

Louisiana Trades with the World. By Frederick Simpich. Photos by J. Baylor Roberts. 705-738, Dec. 1947

The Lower Mississippi. By Willard Price. Photos by W. D. Vaughn. 681-725, Nov. 1960

Skyway Below the Clouds. By Carl R. Markwith. Photos by Ernest J. Cottrell. 85-108, July 1949

LOUISIANA—*Continued*

Included: Monroe; Shreveport; Shreveport Municipal Airport

See also New Orleans

LOUSMA, JACK R.:

Skylab, Outpost on the Frontier of Space. By Thomas Y. Canby. Photos by the nine mission astronauts. 441-469, Oct. 1974

The LOUVRE, Paris:

The Louvre, France's Palace of the Arts. By Hereward Lester Cooke, Jr. 796-831, June 1971

LOVELL, JAMES A., Jr.:

Hubbard Medal recipient. 861, June 1970

"A Most Fantastic Voyage": The Story of Apollo 8's Rendezvous With the Moon. By Sam C. Phillips. 593-631, May 1969

Space Rendezvous, Milestone on the Way to the Moon. By Kenneth F. Weaver. 539-553, Apr. 1966

LOVELL, TOM: Artist:

In the Footsteps of Alexander the Great. By Helen and Frank Schreider. 1-65, Jan. 1968

LOW COUNTRIES, Europe:

France, Belgium, and the Netherlands, Atlas series supplement. June 1960

See also Belgium; Luxembourg; Netherlands

LOWE, GEORGE: Photographer:

The Crossing of Antarctica. By Sir Vivian Fuchs. 25-47, Jan. 1959

Triumph on Everest. 1-63, July 1954
I. Siege and Assault. By Sir John Hunt. 1-43
II. The Conquest of the Summit. By Sir Edmund Hillary. 45-63

LOWELL, JAMES RUSSELL:

Literary Landmarks of Massachusetts. By William H. Nicholas. Photos by B. Anthony Stewart and John E. Fletcher. 279-310, Mar. 1950

LOWELL, Massachusetts:

The Merrimack: River of Industry and Romance. By Albert W. Atwood. Photos by B. Anthony Stewart. 106-140, Jan. 1951

LOWELL OBSERVATORY: Expedition:

New Light on the Changing Face of Mars. By E. C. Slipher. 427-436, Sept. 1955

LOWER CALIFORNIA. *See* Baja California

The LOWER Keys, Florida's "Out Islands." By John Scofield. Photos by Emory Kristof and Bates Littlehales. 72-93, Jan. 1971

The LOWER Mississippi. By Willard Price. Photos by W. D. Vaughn. 681-725, Nov. 1960

LOWER SLAUGHTER, England:

By Cotswold Lanes to Wold's End. By Melville Bell Grosvenor. 615-654, May 1948

LOWER SOURIS NATIONAL WILDLIFE REFUGE, North Dakota:

Duck Hunting with a Color Camera. By Arthur A. Allen. 514-539, Oct. 1951

LOWMAN, PAUL D., Jr.: Author:

The Earth From Orbit. 645-671, Nov. 1966

M

McCARRY, CHARLES: Author:

Heart of the Bluegrass. Photos by J. Bruce Baumann. 634-659, May 1974

Home to the Enduring Berkshires. Photos by Jonathan S. Blair. 196-221, Aug. 1970

Kyoto and Nara: Keepers of Japan's Past. Photos by George F. Mobley. 836-851, June 1976

New Zealand's North Island: The Contented Land. Photos by Bates Littlehales. 190-213, Aug. 1974

Nova Scotia, the Magnificent Anchorage. Photos by Gordon W. Gahan. 334-363, Mar. 1975

Utah's Shining Oasis. Photos by James L. Amos. 440-473, Apr. 1975

Yesterday Lingers Along the Connecticut. Photos by David L. Arnold. 334-369, Sept. 1972

McCLELLAN-KERR ARKANSAS RIVER NAVIGATION SYSTEM:

Oklahoma, the Adventurous One. By Robert Paul Jordan. Photos by Robert W. Madden. 149-189, Aug. 1971

McCONNELL RIVER REGION, Canada:

Beyond the North Wind With the Snow Goose. By Des and Jen Bartlett. 822-843, Dec. 1973
. . . And Then There Was Fred. . . . 843-847

McCRANE, MARION P.: Author:

Zoo Animals Go to School. Photos by W. E. Garrett. 694-706, Nov. 1956

McCUE, J. J. G.: Author:

How Bats Hunt With Sound. 571-578, Apr. 1961

McCURDY, ARTHUR W.: Photographer:

1898: The Bells on Sable. 408-409, 416-417, Sept. 1965

McDADE, MATT C.: Author:

New York State's New Main Street. 567-618, Nov. 1956

McDIVITT, JAMES A.:

America's 6,000-mile Walk in Space. 440-447, Sept. 1965

McDONALD, EDWIN A.: Author:

Exploring Antarctica's Phantom Coast. Photos by W. D. Vaughn. 251-273, Feb. 1962

McDONALD, EUGENE F., Jr.:

The Society's Hubbard Medal Awarded to Commander MacMillan. 563-564, Apr. 1953
Note: Lieutenant Commander McDonald, present at the ceremony, was a member of the 1925 National Geographic Society—United States Navy MacMillan Arctic Expedition.

McDOWELL, BART: Author:

Avalanche! Photos by John E. Fletcher. 855-880, June 1962

The Changing Face of Old Spain. Photos by Albert Moldvay. 291-339, Mar. 1965

Deerfield Keeps a Truce With Time. Photos by Robert W. Madden. 780-809, June 1969

Earthquake in Guatemala. Photos by W. E. Garrett and Robert W. Madden. 810-829, June 1976

Hungary: Changing Homeland of a Tough, Romantic People. Photos by Albert Moldvay and Joseph J. Scherschel. 443-483, Apr. 1971

Mexico in Motion. Photos by Kip Ross. 490-537, Oct. 1961

McDOWELL, BART: Author—*Continued*

Mexico's Window on the Past. Photos by B. Anthony Stewart. 492-519, Oct. 1968

The Most Mexican City, Guadalajara. Photos by Volkmar Wentzel. 412-441, Mar. 1967

Orissa, Past and Promise in an Indian State. Photos by James P. Blair. 546-577, Oct. 1970

Puerto Rico's Seven-league Bootstraps. Photos by B. Anthony Stewart. 755-793, Dec. 1962

Theodore Roosevelt: a Centennial Tribute. 572-590, Oct. 1958

Those Successful Japanese. Photos by Fred Ward. 323-359, Mar. 1974

MACEDONIA (Republic), Yugoslavia:

Yugoslavia: Six Republics in One. By Robert Paul Jordan. Photos by James P. Blair. 589-633, May 1970

McELROY, WILLIAM D.:

Torchbearers of the Twilight (Fireflies). By Frederick G. Vosburgh. 697-704, May 1951

MacFARLAND, CRAIG: Author-Photographer:

Giant Tortoises: Goliaths of the Galapagos. Photos by author and Jan MacFarland. 632-649, Nov. 1972

MacFARLAND, JAN: Photographer:

Giant Tortoises: Goliaths of the Galapagos. By Craig MacFarland. Photos by author and Jan MacFarland. 632-649, Nov. 1972

McGAHAN, JERRY: Author:

The Condor, Soaring Spirit of the Andes. Photos by Libby McGahan. 684-709, May 1971

McGAHAN, LIBBY: Photographer:

The Condor, Soaring Spirit of the Andes. By Jerry McGahan. 684-709, May 1971

MACHIGUENGA INDIANS:

Amazon—The River Sea. By Loren McIntyre. 456-495, Oct. 1972

By Parachute Into Peru's Lost World. By G. Brooks Baekeland. Photos by author and Peter R. Gimbel. 268-296, Aug. 1964

MACHU PICCHU, Peru:

The Five Worlds of Peru. By Kenneth F. Weaver. Photos by Bates Littlehales. 213-265, Feb. 1964

Peru, Homeland of the Warlike Inca. By Kip Ross. 421-462, Oct. 1950
Contents: National Geographic Society—Yale University expeditions

MacINNIS, JOSEPH B.: Author:

Diving Beneath Arctic Ice. Photos by William R. Curtsinger. 248-267, Aug. 1973

McINTYRE, LOREN:

Editorial on writer-photographers. 295, Mar. 1975
Author-Photographer

Amazon—The River Sea. 456-495, Oct. 1972

Colombia, from Amazon to Spanish Main. 235-273, Aug. 1970

Ecuador—Low and Lofty Land Astride the Equator. 259-298, Feb. 1968

Flamboyant Is the Word for Bolivia. 153-195, Feb. 1966

The Lost Empire of the Incas. Art by Ned and Rosalie Seidler. 729-787, Dec. 1973

McMURDO STATION, Antarctica:

First Flight Across the Bottom of the World. By James R. Reedy. Photos by Otis Imboden. 454-464, Mar. 1964

Flight Into Antarctic Darkness. By J. Lloyd Abbot, Jr. Photos by David S. Boyer. 732-738, Nov. 1967

MacNEIL, NORMAN M.: Photographer:

Square-rigger in a Tempest (Pamir). 703-710, May 1948

McNEIL RIVER STATE GAME SANCTUARY, Alaska:

Among Alaska's Brown Bears. By Allan L. Egbert and Michael H. Luque. 428-442, Sept. 1975

McPHEE, JOHN: Author:

The People of New Jersey's Pine Barrens. Photos by William R. Curtsinger. 52-77, Jan. 1974

MACQUARIE ISLAND, South Pacific Ocean:

Nature's Clown, the Penguin. By David Hellyer and Malcolm Davis. 405-428, Sept. 1952

MacSWAIN, J. W.: Author:

Crossroads of the Insect World. Photos by Edward S. Ross. 844-857, Dec. 1966

MADAGASCAR:

Madagascar: Island at the End of the Earth. By Luis Marden. Photos by Albert Moldvay. 443-487, Oct. 1967

Re-creating Madagascar's Giant Extinct Bird. By Alexander Wetmore. 488-493, Oct. 1967

The World in Your Garden. By W. H. Camp. Paintings by Else Bostelmann. 1-65, July 1947

MA'DAN (Tribespeople):

Marsh Dwellers of Southern Iraq. By Wilfred Thesiger. Photos by Gavin Maxwell. 205-239, Feb. 1958

Water Dwellers in a Desert World. By Gavin Young. Photos by Nik Wheeler. 502-523, Apr. 1976

MADDEN, ROBERT W.: Photographer:

Antarctica: Icy Testing Ground for Space. By Samuel W. Matthews. 569-592, Oct. 1968

China Unveils Her Newest Treasures. 848-857, Dec. 1974

Deerfield Keeps a Truce With Time. By Bart McDowell. 780-809, June 1969

Domesticating the Wild and Woolly Musk Ox. By John J. Teal, Jr. 862-879, June 1970

Earthquake in Guatemala. By Bart McDowell. Photos by W. E. Garrett and Robert W. Madden. 810-829, June 1976

Hawaii, Island of Fire and Flowers. By Gordon Young. 399-425, Mar. 1975

Maryland on the Half Shell. By Stuart E. Jones. 188-229, Feb. 1972

Mobile, Alabama's City in Motion. By William Graves. Photos by Joseph J. Scherschel and Robert W. Madden. 368-397, Mar. 1968

Oklahoma, the Adventurous One. By Robert Paul Jordan. 149-189, Aug. 1971

Old Salem, Morning Star of Moravian Faith. By Rowe Findley. 818-837, Dec. 1970

Quicksilver and Slow Death. By John J. Putman. 507-527, Oct. 1972

Toronto: Canada's Dowager Learns to Swing. By Ethel A. Starbird. 190-215, Aug. 1975

MADDEN, ROBERT W.: Photographer—Continued

Venezuela's Crisis of Wealth. By Noel Grove. 175-209, Aug. 1976

MADDEN, WILLIAM D.: Photographer:

Something's Fishy About That Fin! Photos by Robert J. Shallenberger and William D. Madden. 224-227, Aug. 1974

MADEIRA ISLANDS, Atlantic Ocean:

Madeira, Like Its Wine, Improves With Age. By Veronica Thomas. Photos by Jonathan Blair. 488-513, Apr. 1973

Portugal's Gem of the Ocean: Madeira. By David S. Boyer. 364-394, Mar. 1959

The Treasure of Porto Santo. By Robert Sténuit. Photos by author and William R. Curtsinger. 260-275, Aug. 1975

MADISON, DOLLEY:

Inside the White House. By Lonnelle Aikman. Photos by B. Anthony Stewart and Thomas Nebbia. 3-43, Jan. 1961

The Living White House. By Lonnelle Aikman. 593-643, Nov. 1966

MADISON, JAMES:

Profiles of the Presidents: I. The Presidency and How It Grew. By Frank Freidel. 642-687, Nov. 1964

MADOERA (Island), Java. See Madura

MADRID, Spain:

"Around the World in Eighty Days." By Newman Bumstead. 705-750, Dec. 1951

The Changing Face of Old Spain. By Bart McDowell. Photos by Albert Moldvay. 291-339, Mar. 1965

Speaking of Spain. By Luis Marden. 415-456, Apr. 1950

MADRID CODEX:

The Maya. 729-811, Dec. 1975

MADURA (Island), Indonesia:

Postwar Journey Through Java. By Ronald Stuart Kain. 675-700, May 1948

MAGDALENA (River), Colombia:

Cruising Colombia's "Ol' Man River." By Amos Burg. 615-660, May 1947

MAGELLAN, FERDINAND:

Magellan: First Voyage Around the World. By Alan Villiers. Photos by Bruce Dale. 721-753, June 1976

Included: Strait of Magellan, discovered October 21, 1520

Triton Follows Magellan's Wake. By Edward L. Beach. Photos by J. Baylor Roberts. 585-615, Nov. 1960

The MAGIC Lure of Sea Shells. By Paul A. Zahl. Photos by Victor R. Boswell, Jr. and author. 386-429, Mar. 1969

The MAGIC Road Round Ireland. By H. V. Morton. Photos by Robert F. Sisson. 293-333, Mar. 1961

The MAGIC Worlds of Walt Disney. By Robert de Roos. Photos by Thomas Nebbia. 159-207, Aug. 1963

MALEKULA (Island), New Hebrides:
Taboos and Magic Rule Namba Lives. By Kal Muller. 57-83, Jan. 1972

MALI:
Foxes Foretell the Future in Mali's Dogon Country. By Pamela Johnson Meyer. 431-448, Mar. 1969
Freedom Speaks French in Ouagadougou. By John Scofield. 153-203, Aug. 1966
The Niger: River of Sorrow, River of Hope. By Georg Gerster. 152-189, Aug. 1975

The MALIGNED Coyote. By Hope Ryden. Photos by author and David Hiser. 278-294, Aug. 1974

MALLE, LOUIS: Photographer:
Calypso Explores for Underwater Oil. By Jacques-Yves Cousteau. 155-184, Aug. 1955

MALLORCA (Island), Balearic Islands. *See* Majorca

MALTA:
Democracy's Fortress: Unsinkable Malta. By Ernle Bradford. Photos by Ted H. Funk. 852-879, June 1969

MAMMALS:
African Wildlife: Man's Threatened Legacy. By Allan C. Fisher, Jr. Photos by Thomas Nebbia. 147-187, Feb. 1972
A Continent's Living Treasure. Paintings by Ned Seidler. 164-167
An Artist's Glimpses of Our Roadside Wildlife. Paintings by Walter A. Weber. 16-32, July 1950
Contents: Abert's Squirrel, Badgers, Black Bears, Coyotes, Moose, Pronghorn Antelopes, Skunks, Virginia Deer
Exploring the Mind of Ice Age Man. By Alexander Marshack. 64-89, Jan. 1975
Included: Mammals of the Ice Age as depicted in the art of Cro-Magnon man
"Ice Age Mammals of the Alaskan Tundra," painting supplement. Map of Canada. Mar. 1972
London's Zoo of Zoos. By Thomas Garner James. 771-786, June 1953
Mammals of the Alaskan Tundra. 329-337, Mar. 1972
Orphans of the Wild. By Bruce G. Kinloch. 683-699, Nov. 1962
Portrait of a Fierce and Fragile Land. By Paul A. Zahl. 303-314, Mar. 1972
Roaming Africa's Unfenced Zoos. By W. Robert Moore. 353-380, Mar. 1950
Contents: Antelopes, Buffaloes, Elephants, Gazelles, Giraffes, Gorillas, Hippopotamuses, Leopards, Lions, Okapi, Rhinoceroses, Wart Hogs, Zebras
The Romance of American Furs. By Wanda Burnett. 379-402, Mar. 1948
Contents: Beaver, Chinchillas, Foxes, Minks, Muskrats, Seals
Seeking Mindanao's Strangest Creatures. By Charles Heizer Wharton. 389-408, Sept. 1948
Contents: Cloud Rat, Flying Lemur, Tarsier, Tree Shrew
The Wild Animals in My Life. By William M. Mann. 497-524, Apr. 1957
Contents: Animals of the National Zoological Park
Wild Animals of North America. Book announced. 554-557, Oct. 1960
Wildlife In and Near the Valley of the Moon. By H. H. Arnold. Photos by Paul J. Fair. 401-414, Mar. 1950

MAMMALS—*Continued*
Contents: Deer, Elk, Ground Squirrels, Raccoons
Wildlife of Everglades National Park. By Daniel B. Beard. Paintings by Walter A. Weber. 83-116, Jan. 1949
Contents: Bobcat, Manatee, Marsh Rabbit, Otter, Porpoise, Puma, Raccoon
Wolves Versus Moose on Isle Royale. By Durward L. Allen and L. David Mech. 200-219, Feb. 1963
The Wonder City That Moves by Night. By Francis Beverly Kelley. 289-324, Mar. 1948
Zoo Animals Go to School. By Marion P. McCrane. Photos by W. E. Garrett. 694-706, Nov. 1956
See also names of individual species; *and* Paleontology

MAMMOTH:
Wyoming Muck Tells of Battle: Ice Age Man vs. Mammoth. By Cynthia Irwin, Henry Irwin, and George Agogino. 828-837, June 1962

MAN, Isle of, Irish Sea:
The Manx and Their Isle of Man. By Veronica Thomas. Photos by Ted H. Funk. 426-444, Sept. 1972

MAN, Prehistoric:
Adventures in the Search for Man (*Kenyapithecus wickeri*). By Louis S. B. Leakey. Photos by Hugo van Lawick. 132-152, Jan. 1963
A Bold New Look at Our Past. The Editor. 62-63, Jan. 1975
Ethiopia Yields First "Family" of Early Man. By Donald C. Johanson. Photos by David Brill. 790-811, Dec. 1976
Exploring 1,750,000 Years Into Man's Past. By L. S. B. Leakey. Photos by Robert F. Sisson. 564-589, Oct. 1961
Exploring the Mind of Ice Age Man. By Alexander Marshack. 64-89, Jan. 1975
Finding the World's Earliest Man (*Zinjanthropus boisei*). By L. S. B. Leakey. Photos by Des Bartlett. 420-435, Sept. 1960
Ice Age Man, the First American. By Thomas R. Henry. Paintings by Andre Durenceau. 781-806, Dec. 1955
In Search of Man's Past at Lake Rudolf. By Richard E. Leakey. Photos by Gordon W. Gahan. 712-734, May 1970
The Leakey Tradition Lives On. By Melvin M. Payne. 143-144, Jan. 1973
The Leakeys of Africa: Family in Search of Prehistoric Man. By Melvin M. Payne. 194-231, Feb. 1965
Included: *Homo habilis, Kenyapithecus, Proconsul, Zinjanthropus*
Lifelike Man Preserved 2,000 Years in Peat. By P. V. Glob. 419-430, Mar. 1954
Preserving the Treasures of Olduvai Gorge. By Melvin M. Payne. Photos by Joseph J. Scherschel. 701-709, Nov. 1966
Included: *Homo erectus, Homo habilis, Kenyapithecus, Zinjanthropus*
Skull 1470. By Richard E. Leakey. Photos by Bob Campbell. 819-829, June 1973
Vanished Mystery Men of Hudson Bay. By Henry B. Collins. 669-687, Nov. 1956
Included: Dorset Eskimos, Sadlermiuts
Wyoming Muck Tells of Battle: Ice Age Man vs. Mammoth. By Cynthia Irwin, Henry Irwin, and George Agogino. 828-837, June 1962

National Geographic

MARINE BIOLOGY—*Continued*

To the Depths of the Sea by Bathyscaphe. By Jacques-Yves Cousteau. 67-79, July 1954

Two and a Half Miles Down. By Georges S. Houot. 80-86, July 1954

See also Corals and Coral Reefs

MARINE GARDENS. *See* Ras Muhammad

MARINE RESEARCH. *See* Airborne Undersea Expeditions; Marine Biology; Oceanography

MARINELAND, Florida's Giant Fish Bowl. By Gilbert Grosvenor La Gorce. Photos by Luis Marden. 679-694, Nov. 1952

MARINER MISSIONS:

Journey to Mars (Mariner 9). By Kenneth F. Weaver. Paintings by Ludek Pesek. 231-263, Feb. 1973

Mariner Scans a Lifeless Venus (Mariner 2). By Frank Sartwell. Paintings by Davis Meltzer. 733-742, May 1963

Mariner Unveils Venus and Mercury (Mariner 10). By Kenneth F. Weaver. 858-869, June 1975

Voyage to the Planets. By Kenneth F. Weaver. Paintings by Ludek Pesek. 147-193, Aug. 1970
  Included: Mariner 2, Mariner 4, Mariner 5, Mariner 6, Mariner 7

MARINES, U. S. *See* U. S. Marine Corps

Las MARISMAS (Marshes), Spain:

Rare Birds Flock to Spain's Marismas. By Roger Tory Peterson. 397-425, Mar. 1958

MARITIME ALPS, Europe:

Sheep Trek in the French Alps. By Maurice Moyal. Photos by Marcel Coen. 545-564, Apr. 1952

MARITIME PROVINCES, Canada:

Close-up: Canada, Maine, with the Maritime Provinces of Canada, map supplement. Text on reverse. Mar. 1975

See also New Brunswick; Nova Scotia

MARK TWAIN: Mirror of America. By Noel Grove. Photos by James L. Stanfield. 300-337, Sept. 1975

See also Twain, Mark

MARKETS AND STORES:

Keeping House in London. By Frances James. 769-792, Dec. 1947

Paris Flea Market. By Franc Shor. Photos by Alexander Taylor. 318-326, Mar. 1957

MARKWITH, CARL R.: Author:

Skyway Below the Clouds. Photos by Ernest J. Cottrell. 85-108, July 1949

MAROSTICA, Italy:

Chessmen Come to Life in Marostica. By Alexander Taylor. 658-668, Nov. 1956

MARQUESAS ISLANDS, Pacific Ocean:

Shores and Sails in the South Seas. By Charles Allmon. 73-104, Jan. 1950
  Included: Fatu Hiva; Fatu Huku; Hiva Oa; Nuku Hiva; Tahuata; Ua Huka; Ua Pu

MARQUESAS KEYS, Florida:

Atocha, Tragic Treasure Galleon of the Florida Keys. By Eugene Lyon. 787-809, June 1976

MARS (Planet):

Journey to Mars. By Kenneth F. Weaver. Paintings by Ludek Pesek. 231-263, Feb. 1973

Mars: A New World to Explore. By Carl Sagan. 821-841, Dec. 1967

New Light on the Changing Face of Mars. By E. C. Slipher. 427-436, Sept. 1955

The Red Planet Mars; "The Dusty Face of Mars," map-and-painting supplement. Feb. 1973

The Search for Life on Mars. By Kenneth F. Weaver. 264-265, Feb. 1973

Voyage to the Planets. By Kenneth F. Weaver. Paintings by Ludek Pesek. 147-193, Aug. 1970

MARS RESEARCH EXPEDITION: South Africa:

New Light on the Changing Face of Mars. By E. C. Slipher. 427-436, Sept. 1955

MARSEILLE, France:

French Riviera: Storied Playground on the Azure Coast. By Carleton Mitchell. Photos by Thomas Nebbia. 798-835, June 1967

Provence, Empire of the Sun. By William Davenport. Photos by James A. Sugar. 692-715, May 1975

MARSH, DONALD B.: Author-Photographer:

Canada's Caribou Eskimos. 87-104, Jan. 1947

MARSH ARABS. *See* Ma'dan

MARSH DWELLERS of Southern Iraq. By Wilfred Thesiger. Photos by Gavin Maxwell. 205-239, Feb. 1958

MARSHACK, ALEXANDER:

A Bold New Look at Our Past. The Editor. 62-63, Jan. 1975

Author

Exploring the Mind of Ice Age Man. 64-89, Jan. 1975

MARSHALL, GEORGE C.:

Tribute to General George C. Marshall. 113, Jan. 1960

Author

Giant Effigies of the Southwest. 389, Sept. 1952

Our War Memorials Abroad: A Faith Kept. 731-737, June 1957

MARSHALL, LAURENCE K.: Photographer:

Bushmen of the Kalahari. By Elizabeth Marshall Thomas. 866-888, June 1963

MARSHALL ISLANDS, Pacific Ocean:

Pacific Wards of Uncle Sam. By W. Robert Moore. 73-104, July 1948

See also Bikini; Kwajalein

MARSHALL KALAHARI EXPEDITIONS:

Bushmen of the Kalahari. By Elizabeth Marshall Thomas. Photos by Laurence K. Marshall. 866-888, June 1963

MARSHES. *See* Abbotsbury Swannery; Everglades; Iraq (Marsh Dwellers; Water Dwellers); Las Marismas; Salt Marshes

MARSHFIELD, Massachusetts:

Land of the Pilgrims' Pride. By George W. Long. Photos by Robert F. Sisson. 193-219, Aug. 1947

MATHEMATICIANS. *See* Bowditch, Nathaniel; Newton, Isaac

MATO GROSSO (State), Brazil:
Indians of the Amazon Darkness. By Harald Schultz. 737-758, May 1964
The Jungle Was My Home. By Sasha Siemel. 695-712, Nov. 1952
See also Cinta Larga Indians; Kreen-Akarores; Txukahameis

MATS: America's Long Arm of the Air. By Beverley M. Bowie. Photos by Robert F. Sisson. 283-317, Mar. 1957

MATTERNES, JAY H.: Artist:
"Ice Age Mammals of the Alaskan Tundra," painting supplement. Map of Canada. Mar. 1972
Skull 1470. By Richard E. Leakey. Photos by Bob Campbell. 819-829, June 1973

MATTHEWS, SAMUEL W.: Author:
America Goes to the Fair. 293-333, Sept. 1954
Antarctica: Icy Testing Ground for Space. Photos by Robert W. Madden. 569-592, Oct. 1968
Antarctica's Nearer Side. Photos by William R. Curtsinger. 622-655, Nov. 1971
Bali's Sacred Mountain Blows Its Top. 436-458, Sept. 1963
II. Devastated Land and Homeless People. Photos by Robert F. Sisson. 447-458
Beltsville Brings Science to the Farm. 199-218, Aug. 1953
Hunting the Heartbeat of a Whale. By Paul Dudley White and Samuel W. Matthews. 49-64, July 1956
Nevada Learns to Live With the Atom. 839-850, June 1953
Nevada's Mountain of Invisible Gold. Photos by David F. Cupp. 668-679, May 1968
The Night the Mountains Moved (Montana's 1959 Earthquake). Photos by J. Baylor Roberts. 329-359, Mar. 1960
The Phoenicians, Sea Lords of Antiquity. Photos by Winfield Parks. Paintings by Robert C. Magis. 149-189, Aug. 1974
Science Explores the Monsoon Sea. Photos by Robert F. Sisson. 554-575, Oct. 1967
Scientists Drill at Sea to Pierce Earth's Crust (Project Mohole). Photos by J. Baylor Roberts. 686-697, Nov. 1961
This Changing Earth. 1-37, Jan. 1973
What's Happening to Our Climate? 576-615, Nov. 1976

MATTISON, JAMES A., Jr.: Photographer:
Return of the Sea Otter. By Karl W. Kenyon. 520-539, Oct. 1971

MAUI (Island), Hawaii:
Maui, Where Old Hawaii Still Lives. By Kenneth F. Weaver. Photos by Gordon W. Gahan. 514-543, Apr. 1971

MAURI, CARLO: Photographer:
The Voyage of *Ra II*. By Thor Heyerdahl. Photos by Carlo Mauri and Georges Sourial. 44-71, Jan. 1971

MAURITANIA:
Dry-land Fleet Sails the Sahara. By Jean du

MAURITANIA—*Continued*
Boucher. Photos by Jonathan S. Blair. 696-725, Nov. 1967
Freedom Speaks French in Ouagadougou. By John Scofield. 153-203, Aug. 1966

MAURITIUS, Island of the Dodo. By Quentin Keynes. 77-104, Jan. 1956

MAXWELL, GAVIN: Photographer:
Marsh Dwellers of Southern Iraq. By Wilfred Thesiger. 205-239, Feb. 1958

MAYA (Indians):
Dzibilchaltun. 91-129, Jan. 1959
I. Lost City of the Maya. By E. Wyllys Andrews. 91-109
II. Up From the Well of Time. By Luis Marden. 110-129
Guatemala, Maya and Modern. By Louis de la Haba. Photos by Joseph J. Scherschel. 661-689, Nov. 1974
Into the Well of Sacrifice (Chichén Itzá). 540-561, Oct. 1961
I. Return to the Sacred Cenote. By Eusebio Dávalos Hurtado. 540-549
II. Treasure Hunt in the Deep Past. By Bates Littlehales. 550-561
The Maya. 729-811, Dec. 1975
I. Children of Time. By Howard La Fay. Photos by David Alan Harvey. 729-767
II. Riddle of the Glyphs. By George E. Stuart. Photos by Otis Imboden. 768-791
III. Resurrecting the Grandeur of Tikal. By William R. Coe. 792-798
IV. A Traveler's Tale of Ancient Tikal. Paintings by Peter Spier. Text by Alice J. Hall. 799-811
"Pyramids" of the New World. By Neil Merton Judd. 105-128, Jan. 1948

MAYER, FRED: Photographer:
Little Tibet in Switzerland. By Laura Pilarski. 711-727, Nov. 1968

MAYFLOWER (Ship):
Founders of New England. By Sir Evelyn Wrench. Photos by B. Anthony Stewart. 803-838, June 1953

MAYFLOWER II (Ship):
How We Sailed the New *Mayflower* to America. By Alan Villiers. 627-672, Nov. 1957
"Mayflower II," painting supplement. Nov. 1957
We're Coming Over on the *Mayflower*. By Alan Villiers. 708-728, May 1957

MAYTIME Miracle in Sherwood Gardens. By Nathaniel T. Kenney. 700-709, May 1956

MAZAMA, Mount, Oregon:
Crater Lake Summer. By Walter Meayers Edwards. 134-148, July 1962
When Mt. Mazama Lost Its Top: The Birth of Crater Lake. By Lyman J. Briggs. 128-133, July 1962

MAZATZAL WILDERNESS, Arizona:
The Mazatzal's Harsh but Lovely Land Between. By François Leydet. Photos by Farrell Grehan. 161-167, Feb. 1974

MAZZATENTA, O. LOUIS: Author-Photographer:
New England's "Little Portugal." 90-109, Jan. 1975

MELVILLE, HERMAN:

Literary Landmarks of Massachusetts. By William H. Nicholas. Photos by B. Anthony Stewart and John E. Fletcher. 279-310, Mar. 1950

MELVILLE ISLAND, Australia:

Expedition to the Land of the Tiwi. By Charles P. Mountford. 417-440, Mar. 1956

MEMORIAL DAY CEREMONIES:

'Known but to God' (Unknown Heroes). By Beverley M. Bowie. 593-605, Nov. 1958

MEMORIAL TRIBUTES:

Arnold, H. H.: 1886-1950. 400, Mar. 1950

Bowie, Beverley M.: 1914-1958. 214, Feb. 1959

Carmichael, Leonard: An Appreciation. By Melvin M. Payne. 871-874, Dec. 1973

Chapelle, Dickey: What Was a Woman Doing There? By W. E. Garrett. 270-271, Feb. 1966

Churchill, Winston:
"Be Ye Men of Valour." By Howard La Fay. 159-197, Aug. 1965
The Churchill I Knew. By Dwight D. Eisenhower. 153-157, Aug. 1965
The Final Tribute. Text by Carolyn Bennett Patterson. 199-225, Aug. 1965

Eisenhower, Dwight D.: World's Last Salute to a Great American. By William Graves and other members of the National Geographic staff. 40-51, July 1969

Fleming, Robert V.: 1890-1967. By Melville Bell Grosvenor. 526-529, Apr. 1968

Grosvenor, Elsie May Bell: First Lady of the National Geographic. By Gilbert Hovey Grosvenor. 101-121, July 1965

Grosvenor, Gilbert Hovey. To Gilbert Grosvenor: a Monthly Monument 25 Miles High. By Frederick G. Vosburgh and the staff of the National Geographic Society. 445-487, Oct. 1966

Hildebrand, Jesse Richardson: 1888-1951. 104, Jan. 1952

Kennedy, John F.:
The Last Full Measure. By Melville Bell Grosvenor. 307-355, Mar. 1964
To the Memory of Our Beloved President, Friend to All Mankind. 1A-1B, Jan. 1964

La Gorce, John Oliver: Colleague of the Golden Years. By Gilbert Grosvenor. 440-444, Mar. 1960

Leakey, Louis S. B.: The Leakey Tradition Lives On. By Melvin M. Payne. 143-144, Jan. 1973

Long, George W.: 1913-1958. 215, Feb. 1959

Marshall, George C.: 1880-1959. 113, Jan. 1960

MEMORIALS. *See* Monuments and Memorials; Shrines; War Memorials

MEN, Moose, and Mink of Northwest Angle. By William H. Nicholas. Photos by J. Baylor Roberts. 265-284, Aug. 1947

MEN Against the Hurricane. By Andrew H. Brown. 537-560, Oct. 1950

The **MEN** Who Hid the Dead Sea Scrolls. By A. Douglas Tushingham. Paintings by Peter V. Bianchi. 785-808, Dec. 1958

MEN Who Measure the Earth. By Robert Leslie Conly. Photos by John E. Fletcher. 335-362, Mar. 1956

MENEN, AUBREY: Author:

St. Peter's, Rome's Church of Popes. Photos by Albert Moldvay. 865-879, Dec. 1971

MENÉNDEZ DE AVILÉS, DON PEDRO:

St. Augustine, Nation's Oldest City, Turns 400. By Robert L. Conly. 196-229, Feb. 1966

MENHADEN — Uncle Sam's Top Commercial Fish. By Leonard C. Roy. Photos by Robert F. Sisson. 813-823, June 1949

MENNONITES (People):

Amish Folk: Plainest of Pennsylvania's Plain People. By Richard Gehman. Photos by William Albert Allard. 227-253, Aug. 1965

Artists Look at Pennsylvania. By John Oliver La Gorce. 37-56, July 1948

MENOMINEES (Indians):

Wisconsin's Menominees: Indians on a Seesaw. By Patricia Raymer. Photos by Steve Raymer. 228-251, Aug. 1974

MENZEL, DONALD H.:

Devised Star Charts. 811, Dec. 1957

Author

Exploring Our Neighbor World, the Moon. 277-296, Feb. 1958

Solar Eclipse, Nature's Super Spectacular. By Donald H. Menzel and Jay M. Pasachoff. 222-233, Aug. 1970

MEO (Tribespeople). *See* Hmong

MERCHANT MARINE ACADEMY. *See* U. S. Merchant Marine Academy

MERCHANT MARINE TRAINING SHIPS. *See Dar Pomorza; Georg Stage; Joseph Conrad; and* U. S. Merchant Marine Academy

MERCHANTMAN, Nuclear. *See Savannah,* N.S.

MERCURY (Metallic Element):

Quicksilver and Slow Death. By John J. Putman. Photos by Robert W. Madden. 507-527, Oct. 1972

MERCURY (Planet):

Mariner Unveils Venus and Mercury. By Kenneth F. Weaver. 858-869, June 1975
Included: First geological maps of Mercury

Voyage to the Planets. By Kenneth F. Weaver. Paintings by Ludek Pesek. 147-193, Aug. 1970

MERCURY MISSIONS:

Countdown for Space. By Kenneth F. Weaver. 702-734, May 1961

The Earth From Orbit. By Paul D. Lowman, Jr. 645-671, Nov. 1966

Exploring Tomorrow With the Space Agency. By Allan C. Fisher, Jr. Photos by Dean Conger. 48-89, July 1960

The Flight of *Freedom 7.* By Carmault B. Jackson, Jr. 416-431, Sept. 1961

John Glenn Receives the Society's Hubbard Medal. 827, June 1962

John Glenn's Three Orbits in *Friendship 7:* A Minute-by-Minute Account of America's First Orbital Space Flight. By Robert B. Voas. 792-827, June 1962

The Pilot's Story. By Alan B. Shepard, Jr. Photos by Dean Conger. 432-444, Sept. 1961

MERCURY MISSIONS — *Continued*

Tracking America's Man in Orbit. By Kenneth F. Weaver. Photos by Robert F. Sisson. 184-217, Feb. 1962

MERMAID'S PURSE:

Miracle of the Mermaid's Purse. By Ernest L. Libby. 413-420, Sept. 1959

The MERRIMACK: River of Industry and Romance. By Albert W. Atwood. Photos by B. Anthony Stewart. 106-140, Jan. 1951

MESA DEL NAYAR, Mexico:

Mesa del Nayar's Strange Holy Week. By Guillermo Aldana E. 780-795, June 1971

MESA VERDE NATIONAL PARK, Colorado:

Ancient Cliff Dwellers of Mesa Verde. By Don Watson. Photos by Willard R. Culver. 349-376, Sept. 1948

I See America First. By Lynda Bird Johnson. Photos by William Albert Allard. 874-904, Dec. 1965

Searching for Cliff Dwellers' Secrets. By Carroll A. Burroughs. 619-625, Nov. 1959

Solving the Riddles of Wetherill Mesa. By Douglas Osborne. Paintings by Peter V. Bianchi. 155-195, Feb. 1964

20th-century Indians Preserve Customs of the Cliff Dwellers. Photos by William Belknap, Jr. 196-211, Feb. 1964

Your Society to Seek New Light on the Cliff Dwellers. 154-156, Jan. 1959

MESOPOTAMIA:

Abraham, the Friend of God. By Kenneth MacLeish. Photos by Dean Conger. 739-789, Dec. 1966

Ancient Mesopotamia: A Light That Did Not Fail. By E. A. Speiser. Paintings by H. M. Herget. 41-105, Jan. 1951

See also Euphrates (River)

A MESSAGE From the President of the United States. By Dwight D. Eisenhower. 587, May 1960

MESSINA, Strait of, Italy-Sicily:

Fishing in the Whirlpool of Charybdis. By Paul A. Zahl. 579-618, Nov. 1953

Hydrofoil Ferry "Flies" the Strait of Messina. By Gilbert Grosvenor. 493-496, Apr. 1957

METALS. *See* Minerals and Metals

METALWORK:

Priceless Relics of the Spanish Armada. By Robert Sténuit. Photos by Bates Littlehales. 745-777, June 1969

See also Bronzes; Goldsmithing; Silversmiths; Spanish Treasure

METASEQUOIA (Ancient Tree):

Kew: The Commoners' Royal Garden. By Thomas Garner James. Photos by B. Anthony Stewart. 479-506, Apr. 1950

METEORITES:

Have We Solved the Mysteries of the Moon? By Kenneth F. Weaver. Paintings by William H. Bond. 309-325, Sept. 1973

"Rockhounds" Uncover Earth's Mineral Beauty. By George S. Switzer. 631-660, Nov. 1951

METEORITES — *Continued*

See also Apollo Missions (Apollo 15); Chubb Crater

METEOROLOGY. *See* Climate; Weather; Weather Satellites; Weather Stations and Research

METROPOLIS Made to Order: Brasília. By Hernane Tavares de Sá. Photos by Thomas J. Abercrombie. 704-724, May 1960

METZGER, JOHN: Photographer:

Alaskan Family Robinson. By Nancy Robinson. Photos by John Metzger and Peter Robinson. 55-75, Jan. 1973

MEUSE (River), France-Belgium:

Paris to Antwerp With the Water Gypsies. By David S. Boyer. 530-559, Oct. 1955

MEXCALTITÁN, Mexico:

Mexico's Little Venice. By W. E. Garrett. 876-888, June 1968

MEXICO:

Archeological Map of Middle America, Land of the Feathered Serpent, map supplement. Text on reverse. Oct. 1968

Dzibilchaltun. 91-129, Jan. 1959
I. Lost City of the Maya. By E. Wyllys Andrews. 91-109
II. Up From the Well of Time. By Luis Marden. 110-129

Experiment in International Living. By Hugh M. Hamill, Jr. 323-350, Mar. 1953

From Sun-clad Sea to Shining Mountains. By Ralph Gray. Photos by James P. Blair. 542-589, Apr. 1964

Gifts for the Jaguar God. By Philip Drucker and Robert F. Heizer. 367-375, Sept. 1956

How Fruit Came to America. By J. R. Magness. Paintings by Else Bostelmann. 325-377, Sept. 1951

Hunting the Heartbeat of a Whale. By Paul Dudley White and Samuel W. Matthews. 49-64, July 1956

Into the Well of Sacrifice (Chichén Itzá). 540-561, Oct. 1961
I. Return to the Sacred Cenote. By Eusebio Dávalos Hurtado. 540-549
II. Treasure Hunt in the Deep Past. By Bates Littlehales. 550-561

Lost Kingdom in Indian Mexico. By Justin Locke. 517-546, Oct. 1952

The Maya. 729-811, Dec. 1975
I. Children of Time. By Howard La Fay. Photos by David Alan Harvey. 729-767
Included: Archeological sites: Becan; Bonampak; Chichén Itzá; Dzibilchaltún; Jaina Island; Palenque; Tancah; Tulum; Uxmal; and present-day Maya
II. Riddle of the Glyphs. By George E. Stuart. Photos by Otis Imboden. 768-791
Included: Cobá; Kohunlich; Palenque; Tancah; Yaxchilán

Mexico; Central America, double-sided map supplement. May 1973

Mexico and Central America, Atlas series supplement. Oct. 1961

Mexico and Central America, map supplement. Mar. 1953

Mexico in Motion. By Bart McDowell. Photos by Kip Ross. 490-537, Oct. 1961

Mexico's Little Venice. By W. E. Garrett. 876-888, June 1968

MICHELANGELO—*Continued*

When in Rome. . . . By Stuart E. Jones. Photos by Winfield Parks. 741-789, June 1970
Included: Sistine Chapel, Vatican

MICHIGAN:

Close-up: U.S.A., Wisconsin, Michigan, and the Great Lakes, map supplement. Text on reverse. Aug. 1973

The Great Lakes: Is It Too Late? By Gordon Young. Photos by James L. Amos and Martin Rogers. 147-185, Aug. 1973

Ice Fishing's Frigid Charms. By Thomas J. Abercrombie. 861-872, Dec. 1958

The Past Is Present in Greenfield Village (Henry Ford Museum). By Beverley M. Bowie. Photos by Neal P. Davis and Willard R. Culver. 96-127, July 1958

Work-hard, Play-hard Michigan. By Andrew H. Brown. 279-320, Mar. 1952

See also Isle Royale

MICHIGAN, Lake, U. S.:

Wisconsin's Door Peninsula. By William S. Ellis. Photos by Ted Rozumalski. 347-371, Mar. 1969

Work-hard, Play-hard Michigan. By Andrew H. Brown. 279-320, Mar. 1952

MICHIGAN STATE UNIVERSITY. *See* Summer Institute of Glaciological and Arctic Sciences

MICMAC INDIANS:

Nomads of the Far North. By Matthew W. Stirling. Paintings by W. Langdon Kihn. 471-504, Oct. 1949

MICROBIOLOGY:

The Awesome Worlds Within a Cell. By Rick Gore. Photos by Bruce Dale. Paintings by Davis Meltzer. 355-395, Sept. 1976

MICROELECTRONICS:

Crystals, Magical Servants of the Space Age. By Kenneth F. Weaver. Photos by James P. Blair. 278-296, Aug. 1968

MICRONESIA:

Feast Day in Kapingamarangi. By W. Robert Moore. 523-537, Apr. 1950
Note: The natives of Kapingamarangi and Nukuoro are Polynesian and differ in language and customs from those of the other island groups in Micronesia.

Micronesia: The Americanization of Eden. By David S. Boyer. 702-744, May 1967

Pacific Wards of Uncle Sam. By W. Robert Moore. 73-104, July 1948
Contents: Trust Territory of Pacific Islands

See also Bikini; Ifalik; Kwajalein; Nauru; Truk Lagoon; Ulithi; Yap Islands

MICROSCOPIC STUDIES:

A Bold New Look at Our Past. The Editor. 62-63, Jan. 1975

Exploring the Mind of Ice Age Man. By Alexander Marshack. 64-89, Jan. 1975

Finding Rare Beauty in Common Rocks. By Lorence G. Collins. 121-129, Jan. 1966

Life in a "Dead" Sea—Great Salt Lake. By Paul A. Zahl. 252-263, Aug. 1967

See also Microbiology; Photography, Microscope

MICROWAVE RADIO RELAY:

New Miracles of the Telephone Age. By Robert Leslie Conly. 87-120, July 1954

MID-ATLANTIC RIDGE:

Exploring the Mid-Atlantic Ridge. By Maurice Ewing. 275-294, Sept. 1948

New Discoveries on the Mid-Atlantic Ridge. By Maurice Ewing. Photos by Robert F. Sisson. 611-640, Nov. 1949

MID-ATLANTIC RIFT:

Project FAMOUS. Photos by Emory Kristof. 586-615, May 1975
I. Where the Earth Turns Inside Out. By J. R. Heirtzler. 586-603
II. Dive Into the Great Rift. By Robert D. Ballard. 604-615

MID-ATLANTIC STATES:

Close-up: U.S.A., The Mid-Atlantic States, map supplement. Text on reverse. Oct. 1976

MID-CENTURY Holland Builds Her Future. By Sydney Clark. 747-778, Dec. 1950

MIDDLE AGES. *See* Byzantine Empire; Medieval Europe; *and* Crusades

MIDDLE AMERICA:

Archeological Map of Middle America, Land of the Feathered Serpent, map supplement. Text on reverse. Oct. 1968

See also Central America; Mexico; *and* Aztecs; Maya

MIDDLE EAST AND NEAR EAST:

Europe and the Near East, map supplement. June 1949

Eyewitness to War in the Holy Land. By Charles Harbutt. 782-795, Dec. 1967

Journey Into the Great Rift: the Northern Half. By Helen and Frank Schreider. 254-290, Aug. 1965

Lands of the Eastern Mediterranean, Atlas series supplement. Jan. 1959

Our Vegetable Travelers. By Victor R. Boswell. Paintings by Else Bostelmann. 145-217, Aug. 1949

The Peoples of the Middle East, map supplement. Text on reverse. July 1972

Sailing with Sindbad's Sons. By Alan Villiers. 675-688, Nov. 1948

Troubled Waters East of Suez. By Ernest M. Eller. 483-522, Apr. 1954

Twilight of the Arab Dhow. By Marion Kaplan. 330-351, Sept. 1974

See also Arab Nations; Bible Lands; Crusades; Cyprus; Iran; Israel; Kurdistan; Red Sea; Sinai; Trucial Coast; Turkey

MIDDLE FORK SALMON (River), Idaho:

White-water Adventure on Wild Rivers of Idaho. By Frank Craighead, Jr. and John Craighead. 213-239, Feb. 1970

Wild River (Television film). 239A-239B, Feb. 1970

MIDDLE ISLAND, Quebec, Canada. *See* St. Mary Islands Sanctuary

MIDDLE MISSISSIPPI CULTURE. *See* Russell Cave, Alabama

The **MIDLANDS,** England:

Exploring England's Canals. By Bryan Hodgson. Photos by Linda Bartlett. 76-111, July 1974

MINOAN CIVILIZATION:

Thera, Key to the Riddle of Minos. By Spyridon Marinatos. Photos by Otis Imboden. 702-726, May 1972

MINOT, North Dakota:

North Dakota Comes into Its Own. By Leo A. Borah. Photos by J. Baylor Roberts. 283-322, Sept. 1951

Satellites Gave Warning of Midwest Floods. By Peter T. White. Photos by Thomas A. DeFeo. 574-592, Oct. 1969

MINUTEMEN of the Civil Air Patrol. By Allan C. Fisher, Jr. Photos by John E. Fletcher. 637-665, May 1956

MION, PIERRE: Artist:

Footprints on the Moon. By Hugh L. Dryden. Paintings by Davis Meltzer and Pierre Mion. 357-401, Mar. 1964

The Next Frontier? By Isaac Asimov. 76-89, July 1976

Robots to the Moon. By Frank Sartwell. 557-571, Oct. 1962

"Teammates in Mankind's Greatest Adventure" (Apollo Astronauts), painting supplement. Sept. 1973

Tektite II. 256-296, Aug. 1971
I. Science's Window on the Sea. By John G. Van-Derwalker. Photos by Bates Littlehales. 256-289
II. All-girl Team Tests the Habitat. By Sylvia A. Earle. 291-296

MIQUELON. See St. Pierre and Miquelon

MIRACLE Men of the Telephone. By F. Barrows Colton. 273-316, Mar. 1947

MIRACLE of the Mermaid's Purse. By Ernest L. Libby. 413-420, Sept. 1959

MIRACLE of the Potholes. By Rowe Findley. Photos by Robert F. Sisson. 570-579, Oct. 1975

MISHMI HILLS, Assam, India:

Caught in the Assam-Tibet Earthquake. By F. Kingdon-Ward. 403-416, Mar. 1952

MISSILE RANGE. See Atlantic Missile Range

MISSILES. See Guided Missiles; Rockets

The **MISSION** Called 66: Today in Our National Parks. By Conrad L. Wirth. 7-47, July 1966

MISSIONARIES. See Mary-Rousseliere, Guy

MISSIONS:

Carnival in San Antonio. By Mason Sutherland. Photos by J. Baylor Roberts. 813-844, Dec. 1947
Included: Espada, Mission Concepción, San José, San Juan Capistrano, and the Alamo

Cruise to Stone Age Arnhem Land. By Howell Walker. 417-430, Sept. 1949
Included: Mission stations: Croker Island, Elcho Island, Milingimbi Island, South Goulburn Island, and Yirrkala

Far North with "Captain Mac." By Miriam Mac-Millan. 465-513, Oct. 1951
Included: Catholic, Church of England, and Moravian missions

From Tucson to Tombstone. By Mason Sutherland. 343-384, Sept. 1953

MISSIONS—*Continued*

I Live With the Eskimos (Canadian). By Guy Mary-Rousseliere. 188-217, Feb. 1971

See also California, the Golden Magnet; Mesa del Nayar, Mexico; San Diego (California's Plymouth Rock); Sonora (State), Mexico

MISSISSIPPI:

Dixie Spins the Wheel of Industry. By William H. Nicholas. Photos by J. Baylor Roberts. 281-324, Mar. 1949

The Lower Mississippi. By Willard Price. Photos by W. D. Vaughn. 681-725, Nov. 1960

Skyway Below the Clouds. By Carl R. Markwith. Photos by Ernest J. Cottrell. 85-108, July 1949
Included: East Jackson Airport; Hawkins Field, Jackson; Vicksburg

Today Along the Natchez Trace, Pathway Through History. By Bern Keating. Photos by Charles Harbutt. 641-667, Nov. 1968

See also Natchez; Vicksburg

MISSISSIPPI (River), U. S.:

Down Mark Twain's River on a Raft. By Rex E. Hieronymus. 551-574, Apr. 1948

Gettysburg and Vicksburg: the Battle Towns Today. By Robert Paul Jordan. Map notes by Carolyn Bennett Patterson. 4-57, July 1963

Land of Louisiana Sugar Kings. By Harnett T. Kane. Photos by Willard R. Culver. 531-567, Apr. 1958

The Lower Mississippi. By Willard Price. Photos by W. D. Vaughn. 681-725, Nov. 1960

Mark Twain: Mirror of America. By Noel Grove. Photos by James L. Stanfield. 300-337, Sept. 1975

The Mighty Mississippi. Special Publication announced. 882-886, June 1971

New Orleans: Jambalaya on the Levee. By Harnett T. Kane. Photos by Justin Locke. 143-184, Feb. 1953

New Orleans and Her River. By Joseph Judge. Photos by James L. Stanfield. 151-187, Feb. 1971

St. Louis: New Spirit Soars in Mid-America's Proud Old City. By Robert Paul Jordan. Photos by Bruce Dale. 605-641, Nov. 1965

The Upper Mississippi. By Willard Price. 651-699, Nov. 1958

See also Hannibal, Missouri

MISSISSIPPI VALLEY, U. S.:

"Pyramids" of the New World. By Neil Merton Judd. 105-128, Jan. 1948

MISSISSIPPIAN CULTURE:

Who Were the "Mound Builders"? By George E. Stuart. 783-801, Dec. 1972

See also Russell Cave, Alabama

MISSOURI:

Following the Trail of Lewis and Clark. By Ralph Gray. 707-750, June 1953

Mapping the Nation's Breadbasket. By Frederick Simpich. 831-849, June 1948

Skyway Below the Clouds. By Carl R. Markwith. Photos by Ernest J. Cottrell. 85-108, July 1949
Included: The Ozarks; St. Louis; Springfield

Through Ozark Hills and Hollows. By Mike W. Edwards. Photos by Bruce Dale. 656-689, Nov. 1970

MOHAWKS (Indians) — *Continued*

By Robert L. Conly. Photos by B. Anthony Stewart. 133-142, July 1952

MOHOLE, Project:

Scientists Drill at Sea to Pierce Earth's Crust. By Samuel W. Matthews. Photos by J. Baylor Roberts. 686-697, Nov. 1961

MOHR, CHARLES E.: Author:

Exploring America Underground. 803-837, June 1964

MOIZE, ELIZABETH A.: Author:

Amateur Gardener Creates a New Rose. Photos by Farrell Grehan. 286-294, Aug. 1972

In Touch With Nature. Photos by Steve Raymer. 537-543, Apr. 1974

Turnaround Time in West Virginia. Photos by Jodi Cobb. 755-785, June 1976

MOJAVE DESERT, California:

Californians Escape to the Desert. By Mason Sutherland. Photos by Charles W. Herbert. 675-724, Nov. 1957

The Great Mojave Desert (Television film). 294A-294B, Feb. 1971

The Lure of the Changing Desert. 817-824, June 1954

See also Los Angeles Aqueduct

MOLDVAY, ALBERT: Photographer:

The Changing Face of Old Spain. By Bart McDowell. 291-339, Mar. 1965

Gotland: Sweden's Treasure Island. By James Cerruti. 268-288, Aug. 1973

Hungary: Changing Homeland of a Tough, Romantic People. By Bart McDowell. Photos by Albert Moldvay and Joseph J. Scherschel. 443-483, Apr. 1971

Italian Riviera, Land That Winter Forgot. By Howell Walker. 743-789, June 1963

Madagascar: Island at the End of the Earth. By Luis Marden. 443-487, Oct. 1967

Mexico, the City That Founded a Nation. By Louis de la Haba. 638-669, May 1973

New Era in the Loneliest Continent. By David M. Tyree. 260-296, Feb. 1963

Of Planes and Men. By Kenneth F. Weaver. Photos by Emory Kristof and Albert Moldvay. 298-349, Sept. 1965

Pakistan: Problems of a Two-part Land. By Bern Keating. 1-47, Jan. 1967

The Renaissance Lives On in Tuscany. By Luis Marden. 626-659, Nov. 1974

St. Peter's, Rome's Church of Popes. By Aubrey Menen. 865-879, Dec. 1971

Stockholm, Where "Kvalitet" Is a Way of Life. By James Cerruti. Photos by Albert Moldvay and Jonathan Blair. 43-69, Jan. 1976

Venice Fights for Life. By Joseph Judge. 591-631, Nov. 1972

MOLECULAR BIOLOGY:

The Awesome Worlds Within a Cell. By Rick Gore. Photos by Bruce Dale. Paintings by Davis Meltzer. 355-395, Sept. 1976

MOLENAAR, CORNELIUS and DEE: Photographers:

First American Ascent of Mount St. Elias. By Maynard M. Miller. 229-248, Feb. 1948

MOLLUSKS:

The Magic Lure of Sea Shells. By Paul A. Zahl. Photos by Victor R. Boswell, Jr. and author. 386-429, Mar. 1969

Man-of-war Fleet Attacks Bimini. By Paul A. Zahl. 185-212, Feb. 1952
Included: Sea hares

Shells Take You Over World Horizons. By Rutherford Platt. 33-84, July 1949

X-Rays Reveal the Inner Beauty of Shells. By Hilary B. Moore. 427-434, Mar. 1955

See also Abalone; Chambered Nautilus; Mother-of-Pearl; Nudibranchs; Octopuses; Oyster Fleet; Shipworms; Snails; Squids

MOLUCCAS (Islands), Indonesia:

Magellan: First Voyage Around the World. By Alan Villiers. Photos by Bruce Dale. 721-753, June 1976

Shells Take You Over World Horizons. By Rutherford Platt. 33-84, July 1949

Spices, the Essence of Geography. By Stuart E. Jones. 401-420, Mar. 1949

See also Ternate

MOMADAY, N. SCOTT: Author:

A First American Views His Land. 13-19, July 1976

"MONA LISA" (Leonardo da Vinci):

Escorting Mona Lisa to America. By Edward T. Folliard. 838-847, June 1963

MONACO:

Miniature Monaco. By Gilbert M. and Donna Kerkam Grosvenor. 546-573, Apr. 1963

MONARCH BUTTERFLY:

Found at Last: the Monarch's Winter Home. By Fred A. Urquhart. Photos by Bianca Lavies. 161-173, Aug. 1976

Mystery of the Monarch Butterfly. By Paul A. Zahl. 588-598, Apr. 1963

MONASTERIES:

An Archeologist Looks at Palestine. By Nelson Glueck. 739-752, Dec. 1947
Included: St. Saba, St. George, Mount of Temptation

India's Sculptured Temple Caves. By Volkmar Wentzel. 665-678, May 1953

A Journey to "Little Tibet." By Enakshi Bhavnani. Photos by Volkmar Wentzel. 603-634, May 1951
Included: Himis, Lamayuru, Leh, Phayang, and Pituk monasteries

Searching Out Medieval Churches in Ethiopia's Wilds. By Georg Gerster. 856-884, Dec. 1970

A Woman Paints the Tibetans. By Lafugie. 659-692, May 1949
Included: Alchi, Dongse, Gyangtse, Himis, and Sumur monasteries

See also Great St. Bernard Hospice; Rumtek Monastery; St. Catherine's Monastery

MONGOLIAN PEOPLE'S REPUBLIC:

Journey to Outer Mongolia. By William O. Douglas. Photos by Dean Conger. 289-345, Mar. 1962

MONGOLOIDS, Southern (Malays):

Help for Philippine Tribes in Trouble. By Kenneth MacLeish. Photos by Dean Conger. 220-255, Aug. 1971

Mosaic of Cultures. By Peter T. White. Photos by W. E. Garrett. 296-329, Mar. 1971

MONHEGAN ISLAND, Maine:
Maine's Lobster Island, Monhegan. By William P. E. Graves. Photos by Kosti Ruohomaa. 285-298, Feb. 1959

MONITOR (Civil War Gunboat):
How We Found the *Monitor*. By John G. Newton. 48-61, Jan. 1975

MONITOR LIZARDS. *See* Komodo Dragons

MONKEY-EATING EAGLES:
Seeking Mindanao's Strangest Creatures. By Charles Heizer Wharton. 389-408, Sept. 1948

MONKEYS:
Keeping House for a Biologist in Colombia. By Nancy Bell Fairchild Bates. Photos by Marston Bates. 251-272, Aug. 1948
    Included: Cebus, Douroucouli, Howler, Marmoset, Rhesus, Saimiri, Socay, Spider, Woolly
London's Zoo of Zoos. By Thomas Garner James. 771-786, June 1953
Monkeys, Apes, and Man (Television film). 585A-585B, Oct. 1971
Portraits of My Monkey Friends. By Ernest P. Walker. 105-119, Jan. 1956
School for Space Monkeys. 725-729, May 1961
See also Baboons

MONOLITHS. *See* Easter Island; Stonehenge

MONONGAHELA (River), Pennsylvania:
Pittsburgh, Pattern for Progress. By William J. Gill. Photos by Clyde Hare. 342-371, Mar. 1965
Pittsburgh: Workshop of the Titans. By Albert W. Atwood. 117-144, July 1949

MONROE, JAMES:
Inside the White House. By Lonnelle Aikman. Photos by B. Anthony Stewart and Thomas Nebbia. 3-43, Jan. 1961
The Living White House. By Lonnelle Aikman. 593-643, Nov. 1966
Profiles of the Presidents: I. The Presidency and How It Grew. By Frank Freidel. 642-687, Nov. 1964

MONSOONS:
Science Explores the Monsoon Sea. By Samuel W. Matthews. Photos by Robert F. Sisson. 554-575, Oct. 1967

MONTAGNARDS (Vietnamese Mountain People):
American Special Forces in Action in Viet Nam. By Howard Sochurek. 38-65, Jan. 1965
Viet Nam's Montagnards. By Howard Sochurek. 443-487, Apr. 1968

MONTANA:
Following the Trail of Lewis and Clark. By Ralph Gray. 707-750, June 1953
From Sun-clad Sea to Shining Mountains. By Ralph Gray. Photos by James P. Blair. 542-589, Apr. 1964
Montana, Shining Mountain Treasureland. By Leo A. Borah. 693-736, June 1950
The Night the Mountains Moved (1959 Earthquake). By Samuel W. Matthews. Photos by J. Baylor Roberts. 329-359, Mar. 1960
Sharing the Lives of Wild Golden Eagles. By John Craighead. Photos by Charles and Derek Craighead. 420-439, Sept. 1967

MONTANA—*Continued*
Should They Build a Fence Around Montana? By Mike W. Edwards. Photos by Nicholas deVore III. 614-657, May 1976
    Growing Up in Montana. 650-657
See also Glacier National Park; Padlock Ranch; Pryor Mountain Wild Horse Range; Red Rock Lakes National Wildlife Refuge; Scapegoat Wilderness; Surprise Creek Hutterite Colony

MONTENEGRO (Republic), Yugoslavia:
Yugoslavia: Six Republics in One. By Robert Paul Jordan. Photos by James P. Blair. 589-633, May 1970

MONTEREY PENINSULA, California:
California's Land Apart—the Monterey Peninsula. By Mike W. Edwards. 682-703, Nov. 1972
California's Wonderful One (State Highway No. 1). By Frank Cameron. Photos by B. Anthony Stewart. 571-617, Nov. 1959

MONTEVIDEO, Uruguay:
The Purple Land of Uruguay. By Luis Marden. 623-654, Nov. 1948
'Round the Horn by Submarine. By Paul C. Stimson. 129-144, Jan. 1948

MONTICELLO (Estate), Virginia:
Mr. Jefferson's Charlottesville. By Anne Revis. 553-592, May 1950
Mr. Jefferson's Monticello. By Joseph Judge. Photos by Dean Conger and Richard S. Durrance. 426-444, Sept. 1966
Thomas Jefferson: Architect of Freedom. By Mike W. Edwards. Photos by Linda Bartlett. 231-259, Feb. 1976

MONTREAL, Canada:
Canada, My Country. By Alan Phillips. Photos by David S. Boyer and Walter Meayers Edwards. 769-819, Dec. 1961
Montreal Greets the World (Expo 67). By Jules B. Billard. 600-621, May 1967
Quebec's Forests, Farms, and Frontiers. By Andrew H. Brown. 431-470, Oct. 1949
Sea to Lakes on the St. Lawrence. By George W. Long. Photos by B. Anthony Stewart and John E. Fletcher. 323-366, Sept. 1950

MONUMENT VALLEY, Arizona-Utah:
Better Days for the Navajos. By Jack Breed. Photos by Charles W. Herbert. 809-847, Dec. 1958
I See America First. By Lynda Bird Johnson. Photos by William Albert Allard. 874-904, Dec. 1965

MONUMENTS, National. *See* National Monuments

MONUMENTS AND MEMORIALS:
Gettysburg and Vicksburg: the Battle Towns Today. By Robert Paul Jordan. Map notes by Carolyn Bennett Patterson. 4-57, July 1963
Literary Landmarks of Massachusetts. By William H. Nicholas. Photos by B. Anthony Stewart and John E. Fletcher. 279-310, Mar. 1950
    Included: Memorials to: John Adams, Peter Bulkeley, Mary Baker Eddy, Clyde Fitch, Benjamin Franklin, Louise Imogen Guiney, Henry David Thoreau
The Nation Honors Admiral Richard E. Byrd. 567-578, Apr. 1962
Paris: Vibrant Heart of France. 285-302, Aug. 1958

MOORE, W. ROBERT: Photographer—*Continued*
Three Whales That Flew. By Carleton Ray. 346-359, Mar. 1962

MOOREA (Island), Society Islands:
Tahiti, "Finest Island in the World." By Luis Marden. 1-47, July 1962

MOORS (People):
Portugal at the Crossroads. By Howard La Fay. Photos by Volkmar Wentzel. 453-501, Oct. 1965
Portugal Is Different. By Clement E. Conger. 583-622, Nov. 1948
See also Alhambra

MOOSE:
Men, Moose, and Mink of Northwest Angle (Minnesota). By William H. Nicholas. Photos by J. Baylor Roberts. 265-284, Aug. 1947
Wolves Versus Moose on Isle Royale. By Durward L. Allen and L. David Mech. 200-219, Feb. 1963

MORAN, EDMOND J.: Author:
Stop-and-Go Sail Around South Norway. Photos by Randi Kjekstad Bull and Andrew H. Brown. 153-192, Aug. 1954

MORAVIANS:
Far North with "Captain Mac." By Miriam Mac-Millan. 465-513, Oct. 1951
Old Salem, Morning Star of Moravian Faith. By Rowe Findley. Photos by Robert W. Madden. 818-837, Dec. 1970

MORE of Sea Than of Land: The Bahamas. By Carleton Mitchell. Photos by James L. Stanfield. 218-267, Feb. 1967

The MORE Paris Changes.... By Howell Walker. Photos by Gordon W. Gahan. 64-103, July 1972

MORE Years With Mountain Gorillas. By Dian Fossey. Photos by Robert M. Campbell. 574-585, Oct. 1971

MORGAN, AUDREY and FRANK: Photographers:
Alaska's Russian Frontier: Little Diomede. 551-562, Apr. 1951

MORGAN, JAMES K.: Author-Photographer:
Last Stand for the Bighorn. 383-399, Sept. 1973

MORGAN, JUDITH and NEIL: Authors:
California's Parched Oasis, the Owens Valley. Photos by Jodi Cobb and Galen Rowell. 98-127, Jan. 1976
California's Surprising Inland Delta. Photos by Charles O'Rear. 409-430, Sept. 1976

MORGAN, LAEL: Author-Photographer:
Atka, Rugged Home of My Aleut Friends. 572-583, Oct. 1974
"Ocean Mammals Are to Us What the Buffalo Was to the Plains Indian." 354-355, Mar. 1973

MORGAN CREEK, Idaho:
Last Stand for the Bighorn. By James K. Morgan. 383-399, Sept. 1973

MORMONS:
Amid the Mighty Walls of Zion. By Lewis F. Clark. 37-70, Jan. 1954
First Motor Sortie into Escalante Land. By Jack

MORMONS—*Continued*
Breed. 369-404, Sept. 1949
Roaming the West's Fantastic Four Corners. By Jack Breed. 705-742, June 1952
Utah's Shining Oasis. By Charles McCarry. Photos by James L. Amos. 440-473, Apr. 1975
The Family: A Mormon Shrine. 459-463

MOROCCO:
From Sea to Sahara in French Morocco. By Jean and Franc Shor. 147-188, Feb. 1955
Morocco, Land of the Farthest West. By Thomas J. Abercrombie. 834-865, June 1971
Trek by Mule Among Morocco's Berbers. By Victor Englebert. 850-875, June 1968
When the President Goes Abroad (Eisenhower). By Gilbert M. Grosvenor. 588-649, May 1960

MORRIS, JOE ALEX: Author:
Venice, City of Twilight Splendor. Photos by John Scofield. 543-569, Apr. 1961

MORRISON, HEDDA: Author-Photographer:
Jungle Journeys in Sarawak. 710-736, May 1956

MORRISTOWN, New Jersey:
Shrines of Each Patriot's Devotion. By Frederick G. Vosburgh. 51-82, Jan. 1949

MORTON, H. V.: Author:
High Road in the Pyrenees. Photos by Justin Locke. 299-334, Mar. 1956
In the London of the New Queen. 291-342, Sept. 1953
Lake District, Poets' Corner of England. Photos by David S. Boyer. 511-545, Apr. 1956
The Magic Road Round Ireland. Photos by Robert F. Sisson. 293-333, Mar. 1961

MOSAIC of Cultures (Southeast Asia). By Peter T. White. Photos by W. E. Garrett. 296-329, Mar. 1971

MOSAICS:
Here Rest in Honored Glory.... By Howell Walker. 739-768, June 1957
Mount Sinai's Holy Treasures (St. Catherine's Monastery). By Kurt Weitzmann. Photos by Fred Anderegg. 109-127, Jan. 1964
Roman Life in 1,600-year-old Color Pictures. By Gino Vinicio Gentili. Photos by Duncan Edwards. 211-229, Feb. 1957

MOSCOW, U.S.S.R.:
An American in Russia's Capital. By Thomas T. Hammond. Photos by Dean Conger. 297-351, Mar. 1966

MOSELEY, MICHAEL E.: Author:
Chan Chan, Peru's Ancient City of Kings. By Michael E. Moseley and Carol J. Mackey. Photos by David Brill. 318-345, Mar. 1973

MOSER, DON: Author:
The Azores, Nine Islands in Search of a Future. Photos by O. Louis Mazzatenta. 261-288, Feb. 1976
Big Thicket of Texas. Photos by Blair Pittman. 504-529, Oct. 1974

MOSES:
In Search of Moses. By Harvey Arden. Photos by Nathan Benn. 2-37, Jan. 1976

MOSES, Lake, Washington:

From Sagebrush to Roses on the Columbia. By Leo A. Borah. 571-611, Nov. 1952

MOSIER, ROBERT H.: Author-Photographer:

The GI and the Kids of Korea. 635-664, May 1953

MOSLEMS:

Abraham, the Friend of God. By Kenneth Mac-Leish. Photos by Dean Conger. 739-789, Dec. 1966

Afghanistan: Crossroad of Conquerors. By Thomas J. Abercrombie. 297-345, Sept. 1968

Crusader Lands Revisited. By Harold Lamb. Photos by David S. Boyer. 815-852, Dec. 1954

Delhi, Capital of a New Dominion. By Phillips Talbot. 597-630, Nov. 1947

From America to Mecca on Airborne Pilgrimage. By Abdul Ghafur. 1-60, July 1953

Holy Land, My Country. By His Majesty King Hussein of Jordan. 784-789, Dec. 1964

The Idyllic Vale of Kashmir. By Volkmar Wentzel. 523-550, Apr. 1948

Jerusalem, My Home. By Bertha Spafford Vester. 826-847, Dec. 1964

Jerusalem, the Divided City. By John Scofield. Photos by Brian Brake. 492-531, Apr. 1959

The Other Side of Jordan. By Luis Marden. 790-825, Dec. 1964

Reunited Jerusalem Faces Its Problems. By Kenneth MacLeish. Photos by Ted Spiegel. 835-871, Dec. 1968

Saudi Arabia: Beyond the Sands of Mecca. By Thomas J. Abercrombie. 1-53, Jan. 1966

Station Wagon Odyssey: Baghdad to Istanbul. By William O. Douglas. 48-87, Jan. 1959

The Sword and the Sermon. By Thomas J. Abercrombie. 3-45, July 1972

West From the Khyber Pass. By William O. Douglas. Photos by Mercedes H. Douglas and author. 1-44, July 1958

See also Berbers; Ismaili; Kazakhs; Ma'dan; Moors; Mozabites; Sikhs; Tuareg; Turkomans

MOSQUES:

From America to Mecca on Airborne Pilgrimage. By Abdul Ghafur. 1-60, July 1953
Included: The Kaaba, in the courtyard of the Great Mosque, Mecca; Masjid-al-Nabi (Mosque of the Prophet), in Medina; a mosque in Kuba; and Husain's tomb in Karbala

Journey Into Troubled Iran. By George W. Long. Photos by J. Baylor Roberts. 425-464, Oct. 1951
Included: Masjid-i-Shah (King's Mosque), Masjid Sheik Lutf Ullah, and the mosque at Qum

Turkey Paves the Path of Progress. By Maynard Owen Williams. 141-186, Aug. 1951
Included: Beyazit, Blue Mosque, Eyüp Ansari, Suleiman the Magnificent, Yeni Cami (New Mosque), Yeşil Cami (Green Mosque)

MOSQUITOES:

Exploring Ancient Panama by Helicopter. By Matthew W. Stirling. Photos by Richard H. Stewart. 227-246, Feb. 1950
Included: *Aedes aegypti* and *Haemagogus* mosquitoes

Keeping House for a Biologist in Colombia. By Nancy Bell Fairchild Bates. Photos by Marston Bates. 251-274, Aug. 1948
Included: *Anopheles* and *Haemagogus* mosquitoes

"A MOST Fantastic Voyage": The Story of Apollo 8's Rendezvous With the Moon. By Sam C. Phillips. 593-631, May 1969

The MOST Mexican City, Guadalajara. By Bart McDowell. Photos by Volkmar Wentzel. 412-441, Mar. 1967

MOTAGUA FAULT, Guatemala:

Earthquake in Guatemala. By Bart McDowell. Photos by W. E. Garrett and Robert W. Madden. 810-829, June 1976

MOTHER-OF-PEARL:

Twenty Fathoms Down for Mother-of-Pearl. By Winston Williams. Photos by Bates Littlehales. 512-529, Apr. 1962
See also Abalone

MOTHS:

Moths That Behave Like Hummingbirds. Photos by Treat Davidson. 770-775, June 1965

MOTILONES (Indians):

Venezuela Builds on Oil. By Thomas J. Abercrombie. 344-387, Mar. 1963

MOTORCYCLE RACES:

The Manx and Their Isle of Man. By Veronica Thomas. Photos by Ted H. Funk. 426-444, Sept. 1972
Included: International Tourist Trophy Races ("T.T."); Manx Grand Prix

MOTORCYCLE TRIPS:

Two Wheels Along the Mexican Border. By William Albert Allard. 591-635, May 1971

MOULIN, RAYMOND: Photographer:

Saving Earth's Oldest Living Things. By Andrew H. Brown. Photos by Raymond Moulin and author. 679-695, May 1951

MOUND BUILDERS (Ancient Indians):

"Pyramids" of the New World. By Neil Merton Judd. 105-128, Jan. 1948

Who Were the "Mound Builders"? By George E. Stuart. 783-801, Dec. 1972

MOUNDS. See Jericho, Jordan (The Ghosts of Jericho; Jericho Gives Up Its Secrets); La Venta, Mexico; Panama (Exploring Ancient Panama; Exploring the Past); Tepe Gawra

MOUNIER, BRUCE: Photographer:

Strange March of the Spiny Lobster. By William F. Herrnkind. Photos by Rick Frehsee and Bruce Mounier. 819-831, June 1975

MOUNT KENNEDY YUKON EXPEDITION:

Canada's Mount Kennedy. 1-33, July 1965
I. The Discovery. By Bradford Washburn. 1-3
II. A Peak Worthy of the President. By Robert F. Kennedy. 5-9
III. The First Ascent. By James W. Whittaker. Photos by William Albert Allard. 11-33

MOUNT McKINLEY NATIONAL PARK, Alaska:

Mount McKinley Conquered by New Route. By Bradford Washburn. 219-248, Aug. 1953

Wildlife of Mount McKinley National Park. By Adolph Murie. Paintings by Walter A. Weber. 249-270, Aug. 1953

MOUNT RAINIER NATIONAL PARK, Washington. See Pacific Crest Trail; Rainier, Mount

MOUNT RUSHMORE NATIONAL MEMORIAL. *See* Rushmore, Mount

MOUNT SINAI EXPEDITIONS:

Island of Faith in the Sinai Wilderness (St. Catherine's Monastery). By George H. Forsyth. Photos by Robert F. Sisson. 82-106, Jan. 1964
> Sponsors: University of Michigan, Princeton University, University of Alexandria

Mount Sinai's Holy Treasures (St. Catherine's Monastery). By Kurt Weitzmann. Photos by Fred Anderegg. 109-127, Jan. 1964

Sinai Sheds New Light on the Bible. By Henry Field. Photos by William B. and Gladys Terry. 795-815, Dec. 1948
> Sponsor: University of California African Expedition

MOUNT VERNON, Virginia:

Mount Vernon Lives On. By Lonnelle Aikman. 651-682, Nov. 1953

MOUNTAIN CLIMBING:

American and Geographic Flags Top Everest. By Melvin M. Payne. Photos by Barry C. Bishop. 157-157C, Aug. 1963

Beyond Everest. By Sir Edmund Hillary. 579-610, Nov. 1955

Canada's Mount Kennedy. 1-33, July 1965
I. The Discovery. By Bradford Washburn. 1-3
II. A Peak Worthy of the President. By Robert F. Kennedy. 5-9
III. The First Ascent. By James W. Whittaker. Photos by William Albert Allard. 11-33

Climbing Our Northwest Glaciers. Photos by Bob and Ira Spring. 103-114, July 1953

Cloud Gardens in the Tetons. By Frank and John Craighead. 811-830, June 1948

Colorado by Car and Campfire. By Kathleen Revis. 207-248, Aug. 1954

Colorado's Friendly Topland (Rocky Mountains). By Robert M. Ormes. 187-214, Aug. 1951

El Sangay, Fire-breathing Giant of the Andes. By G. Edward Lewis. 117-138, Jan. 1950

The Fabulous Sierra Nevada. By J. R. Challacombe. 825-843, June 1954

First American Ascent of Mount St. Elias. By Maynard M. Miller. 229-248, Feb. 1948

First Conquest of Antarctica's Highest Peaks. By Nicholas B. Clinch. 836-863, June 1967

The First Traverse (Everest). By Thomas F. Hornbein and William F. Unsoeld. 509-513, Oct. 1963

High Adventure in the Himalayas. By Thomas Weir. 193-234, Aug. 1952

How We Climbed Everest. By Barry C. Bishop. 477-507, Oct. 1963

Mount McKinley Conquered by New Route. By Bradford Washburn. 219-248, Aug. 1953

Mount Rainier: Testing Ground for Everest. By Barry C. Bishop. 688-711, May 1963

New Guinea's Paradise of Birds. By E. Thomas Gilliard. 661-688, Nov. 1951
> Note: The true summit of Mount Wilhelm is reached.

Sierra High Trip. By David R. Brower. 844-868, June 1954

Six to the Summit (Everest). By Norman G. Dyhrenfurth. Photos by Barry C. Bishop. 460-473, Oct. 1963

Skyline Trail from Maine to Georgia. By Andrew H. Brown. Photos by Robert F. Sisson. 219-251, Aug. 1949

MOUNTAIN CLIMBING—*Continued*

Switzerland's Enchanted Val d'Hérens. By Georgia Engelhard Cromwell. 825-848, June 1955

To Torre Egger's Icy Summit. By Jim Donini. 813-823, Dec. 1976

Triumph on Everest. 1-63, July 1954
I. Siege and Assault. By Sir John Hunt. 1-43
II. The Conquest of the Summit. By Sir Edmund Hillary. 45-63

Wintering on the Roof of the World (Himalayas). By Barry C. Bishop. 503-547, Oct. 1962

See also Outward Bound School; Rock Climbing

MOUNTAIN LIONS:

Stalking the Mountain Lion—to Save Him. By Maurice G. Hornocker. 638-655, Nov. 1969

MOUNTAIN PEOPLE, American:

American Mountain People. Special Publication announced. 865-868, June 1973

See also Adirondack Mountains; Blue Ridge; Cades Cove; Cumberland Country; Ozark Plateau; West Virginia

MOUNTAIN VILLAGE, Alaska:

The Curlew's Secret. By Arthur A. Allen. 751-770, Dec. 1948

MOUNTAIN Voices, Mountain Days. By Bryan Hodgson. Photos by Linda Bartlett. 118-146, July 1972

MOUNTAINBURG, Arkansas:

An Ozark Family Carves a Living and a Way of Life. Photos by Bruce Dale. 124-133, July 1975

MOUNTAINS:

Afoot in Roadless Nepal. By Toni Hagen. 361-405, Mar. 1960
> Contents: Himalaya, Mahabharat, and Siwalik Ranges

A Map Maker Looks at the United States. By Newman Bumstead. 705-748, June 1951
> Included: Big Hole, Blue, Cascades, Olympics, Rockies, Sawatch, Sierra Nevada, Tetons, Wasatch, Wenatchee

Mountains Top Off New England. By F. Barrows Colton. Photos by Robert F. Sisson. 563-602, May 1951
> Contents: Berkshires, Green Mountains, White Mountains

New Guinea's Paradise of Birds. By E. Thomas Gilliard. 661-688, Nov. 1951
> Included: Bismarck Mountains (including the climbing of Mount Wilhelm); Hagen Range; Kubor Range

New Zealand, Pocket Wonder World. By Howell Walker. 419-460, Apr. 1952

The Night the Mountains Moved (Montana's 1959 Earthquake). By Samuel W. Matthews. Photos by J. Baylor Roberts. 329-359, Mar. 1960

Our Navy Explores Antarctica. By Richard E. Byrd. U. S. Navy official photos. 429-522, Oct. 1947

Preserving America's Last Great Wilderness (Alaska). Text by David Jeffery. 769-791, June 1975
> Included: Aniakchak Caldera; Brooks Range; Katmai; McKinley; Wrangell

Skyline Trail from Maine to Georgia. By Andrew H. Brown. Photos by Robert F. Sisson. 219-251, Aug. 1949

This Changing Earth. By Samuel W. Matthews. 1-37, Jan. 1973

See also names of specific mountain ranges

MOUNTAINS, Lunar. *See* Apollo Missions (Apollo 15)

MOUNTAINS, Submarine. *See* Ocean Floors

MOUNTAINS of the Moon (Ruwenzori). By Paul A. Zahl. 412-434, Mar. 1962

MOUNTAINTOP War in Remote Ladakh. By W. E. Garrett. 664-687, May 1963

MOUNTFORD, CHARLES P.: Author:
Expedition to the Land of the Tiwi. 417-440, Mar. 1956
Exploring Stone Age Arnhem Land. Photos by Howell Walker. 745-782, Dec. 1949

MOUSE RIVER, Canada-U. S.:
Satellites Gave Warning of Midwest Floods. By Peter T. White. Photos by Thomas A. DeFeo. 574-592, Oct. 1969

MOYAL, MAURICE: Author:
Sheep Trek in the French Alps. Photos by Marcel Coen. 545-564, Apr. 1952

MOYNIHAN, MICHAEL: Author:
The Swans of Abbotsbury. Photos by Barnet Saidman. 563-570, Oct. 1959

MOZABITES:
Oasis-hopping in the Sahara. By Maynard Owen Williams. 209-236, Feb. 1949

MOZAMBIQUE:
Mozambique: Land of the Good People. By Volkmar Wentzel. 197-231, Aug. 1964
Safari Through Changing Africa. By Elsie May Bell Grosvenor. Photos by Gilbert Grosvenor. 145-198, Aug. 1953

MRU TRIBE:
The Peaceful Mrus of Bangladesh. By Claus-Dieter Brauns. 267-286, Feb. 1973

MUDIE, COLIN:
Braving the Atlantic by Balloon *(Small World)*. By Arnold Eiloart. 123-146, July 1959

MUDSKIPPERS:
Who Says Fish Can't Climb Trees? By Ivan Polunin. 85-91, Jan. 1972

MUDSLIDES:
Southern California's Trial by Mud and Water. By Nathaniel T. Kenney. Photos by Bruce Dale. 552-573, Oct. 1969

MUIR, JOHN:
John Muir's Wild America. By Harvey Arden. Photos by Dewitt Jones. 433-461, Apr. 1973
John Muir's Wild America. Special Publication announced. 860-864, June 1976

MUJERES, Isla, Mexico:
Into the Lairs of "Sleeping" Sharks. By Eugenie Clark. Photos by David Doubilet. 570-584, Apr. 1975

MUKDEN, China. *See* Shenyang

MULES:
Trek by Mule Among Morocco's Berbers. By Victor Englebert. 850-875, June 1968

MULLER, KAL: Author-Photographer:
Land Diving With the Pentecost Islanders. 799-817, Dec. 1970
Taboos and Magic Rule Namba Lives. 57-83, Jan. 1972
Tanna Awaits the Coming of John Frum. 706-715, May 1974

MUMMIES:
Ancient Cliff Dwellers of Mesa Verde. By Don Watson. Photos by Willard R. Culver. 349-376, Sept. 1948
    Contents: Mummification by natural dehydration; the famous mummy "Esther"
A Lady From China's Past. Photos from *China Pictorial.* Text by Alice J. Hall. 660-681, May 1974
Lifelike Man Preserved 2,000 Years in Peat. By P. V. Glob. 419-430, Mar. 1954
See also Tutankhamun

MUNICH, Germany:
Bavaria: Mod, Medieval—and Bewitching. By Gary Jennings. Photos by George F. Mobley. 409-431, Mar. 1974

MUÑOZ, JUAN: Author-Photographer:
Cliff Dwellers of the Bering Sea. 129-146, Jan. 1954

MUNROE, JOE: Photographer:
The Bonins and Iwo Jima Go Back to Japan. By Paul Sampson. 128-144, July 1968

MURCHISON MOUNTAINS, New Zealand:
Finding an "Extinct" New Zealand Bird. By R. V. Francis Smith. 393-401, Mar. 1952

MURCIA, Spain:
Spain's Silkworm Gut. By Luis Marden. 100-108, July 1951

MURIA GONDS (Tribespeople):
New Life for India's Villagers. By Anthony and Georgette Dickey Chapelle. 572-588, Apr. 1956

MURIE, ADOLPH: Author:
Wildlife of Mount McKinley National Park. Paintings by Walter A. Weber. 249-270, Aug. 1953

MUROC DRY LAKE, California:
Flying in the "Blowtorch" Era. By Frederick G. Vosburgh. 281-322, Sept. 1950

MURPHY, GRACE E. BARSTOW: Photographer:
Peru Profits from Sea Fowl. By Robert Cushman Murphy. Photos by author and Grace E. Barstow Murphy. 395-413, Mar. 1959

MURPHY, JOHN F., Jr.: Author:
Ambassadors of Good Will: The Peace Corps. By Sargent Shriver and Peace Corps Volunteers. 297-345, Sept. 1964
    Gabon. 325-329

MURPHY, ROBERT CUSHMAN: Author-Photographer:
Peru Profits from Sea Fowl. Photos by author and Grace E. Barstow Murphy. 395-413, Mar. 1959

MURRES:
Sea Bird Cities Off Audubon's Labrador. By Arthur A. Allen. 755-774, June 1948

MURUNG (People):
Bangladesh: Hope Nourishes a New Nation. By William S. Ellis. Photos by Dick Durrance II. 295-333, Sept. 1972

MŪSA, Gebel (Mountain), Egypt. *See* Sinai, Mount

MUSCAT AND OMAN:
Troubled Waters East of Suez. By Ernest M. Eller. 483-522, Apr. 1954
See also Oman

MUSEUM OF SCIENCE, Boston, Massachusetts: Expeditions. *See* Mount Kennedy Yukon Expedition

MUSEUMS:
The DAR Story. By Lonnelle Aikman. Photos by B. Anthony Stewart and John E. Fletcher. 565-598, Nov. 1951
Included: Exhibits of early Americana
Florence Rises From the Flood. By Joseph Judge. 1-43, July 1967
Included: Archeological Museum, Bardini Museum, Bargello Museum, Horne Museum, Institute and Museum of the History of Science, Uffizi
See also American Museum of Natural History; Bell Museum; Corning Museum of Glass; Desert Museum; Eastman, George, for Eastman House; Explorers Hall, NGS; Hearst San Simeon State Historical Monument; Henry E. Huntington Library and Art Gallery; Henry Ford Museum; Hermitage; Kunsthistorisches Museum; Louvre; National Gallery of Art; National Museum of Anthropology, Mexico City; Smithsonian Institution; *and* Mystic Seaport, for Maritime Museum; New York (The World in New York City); Worcester, Massachusetts, for arms and armor

MUSHROOMS:
Bizarre World of the Fungi. By Paul A. Zahl. 502-527, Oct. 1965

MUSIC AND MUSICIANS:
The British Way. By Sir Evelyn Wrench. 421-541, Apr. 1949
Included: Sir William Gilbert and Sir Arthur Sullivan
Carnival in Trinidad. By Howard La Fay. Photos by Winfield Parks. 693-701, Nov. 1971
Hunting Musical Game in West Africa. By Arthur S. Alberts. 262-282, Aug. 1951
Miami's Expanding Horizons. By William H. Nicholas. 561-594, Nov. 1950
Included: Barry College Department of Music, Miami Civic Music Association, Opera Guild of Miami, Philharmonic Society of Greater Miami, University of Miami School of Music
Old Salem, Morning Star of Moravian Faith. By Rowe Findley. Photos by Robert W. Madden. 818-837, Dec. 1970
Included: Music of the Moravians
The President's Music Men (Marine Band). By Stuart E. Jones. Photos by William W. Campbell III. 752-766, Dec. 1959
Utah's Shining Oasis. By Charles McCarry. Photos by James L. Amos. 440-473, Apr. 1976
Included: Ballet West, Mormon Tabernacle Choir, Utah Symphony Orchestra
Vienna, City of Song. By Peter T. White. Photos by John Launois. 739-779, June 1968
See also Recordings, NGS; Songs; *and* Austria (Building a New Austria); Berkshires, for Berkshire Music Festival; China (A Lady From); Hungary; Library of Congress; New Orleans, Louisiana, for jazz; Ozark Plateau, for folk music

MUSK OXEN:
Domesticating the Wild and Woolly Musk Ox. By

MUSK OXEN—*Continued*
John J. Teal, Jr. Photos by Robert W. Madden. 862-879, June 1970

MUSKRATS:
The Romance of American Furs. By Wanda Burnett. 379-402, Mar. 1948

MUSTANG, Remote Realm in Nepal. By Michel Peissel. 579-604, Oct. 1965

MUTATIONS. *See* Albino Animals; Goldfish; Onagadori

MY Backyard, the Adirondacks. By Anne LaBastille. Photos by David Alan Harvey. 616-639, May 1975

MY Life Among Wild Chimpanzees. By Jane Goodall. Photos by Baron Hugo van Lawick and author. 272-308, Aug. 1963

MY Life in Forbidden Lhasa. By Heinrich Harrer. 1-48, July 1955

MY Life in the Valley of the Moon. By H. H. Arnold. Photos by Willard R. Culver. 689-716, Dec. 1948

MY Life With Africa's Little People. By Anne Eisner Putnam. 278-302, Feb. 1960

MY Neighbors Hold to Mountain Ways. By Malcolm Ross. Photos by Flip Schulke. 856-880, June 1958

MYCOLOGY:
Bizarre World of the Fungi. By Paul A. Zahl. 502-527, Oct. 1965

MYOJIN ISLAND (Volcano), Pacific Ocean:
The Explosive Birth of Myojin Island. By Robert S. Dietz. 117-128, Jan. 1954

MYSORE (State), India:
Mysore Celebrates the Death of a Demon. By Luc Bouchage. Photos by Ylla. 706-711, May 1958
Wild Elephant Roundup in India. By Harry Miller. Photos by author and James P. Blair. 372-385, Mar. 1969

MYSTERY of the Ancient Nazca Lines. Photos by Loren McIntyre. 716-728, May 1975

MYSTERY of the Monarch Butterfly. By Paul A. Zahl. 588-598, Apr. 1963

MYSTERY Shrouds the Biggest Planet (Jupiter). By Kenneth F. Weaver. 285-294, Feb. 1975

MYSTIC SEAPORT, Connecticut:
The Age of Sail Lives On at Mystic. By Alan Villiers. Photos by Weston Kemp. 220-239, Aug. 1968

MZABIS (People). *See* Mozabites

MZIMA SPRINGS, Tsavo National Park, Kenya:
Mzima, Kenya's Spring of Life. By Joan and Alan Root. 350-373, Sept. 1971

N

NAGA HILLS, India-Burma:
Roaming India's Naga Hills. By S. Dillon Ripley. 247-264, Feb. 1955

NAHA, Okinawa:
Okinawa, the Island Without a Country. By Jules

NATIONAL AUDUBON SOCIETY: United States—
Continued

The Pink Birds of Texas. By Paul A. Zahl. 641-654, Nov. 1949

Saving Man's Wildlife Heritage. By John H. Baker. Photos by Robert F. Sisson. 581-620, Nov. 1954

NATIONAL BUREAU OF STANDARDS, Washington, D. C.:

Split-second Time Runs Today's World. By F. Barrows Colton and Catherine Bell Palmer. 399-428, Sept. 1947

Uncle Sam's House of 1,000 Wonders. By Lyman J. Briggs and F. Barrows Colton. 755-784, Dec. 1951

NATIONAL CIVIL WAR CENTENNIAL COMMISSION: United States:

The Civil War. By Ulysses S. Grant 3rd. 437-449, Apr. 1961

NATIONAL ELK REFUGE, Wyoming:

Jackson Hole: Good-bye to the Old Days? By François Leydet. Photos by Jonathan Wright. 768-789, Dec. 1976

NATIONAL FORESTS: United States:

Adobe New Mexico. By Mason Sutherland. Photos by Justin Locke. 783-830, Dec. 1949
Included: Carson, Santa Fe

Forest Fire: The Devil's Picnic. By Stuart E. Jones and Jay Johnston. 100-127, July 1968
Included: Deschutes, Kaniksu, Nezperce, Ochoco, Snoqualmie, Wallowa-Whitman, Willamette

Mexico to Canada on the Pacific Crest Trail. By Mike W. Edwards. Photos by David Hiser. 741-779, June 1971
Included: Deschutes, Gifford Pinchot, Inyo, San Bernardino, Shasta Sierra, Trinity, Wenatchee, Willamette

Our Green Treasury, the National Forests. By Nathaniel T. Kenney. Photos by J. Baylor Roberts. 287-324, Sept. 1956
Included: Angeles, Beaverhead, Bitterroot, Carson, Coconino, Coronado, Flathead, Gifford Pinchot, Inyo, Kisatchie, Lolo, Mount Hood, Ocala, Osceola, Ottawa, Payette, Pisgah, Priest River Experimental Forest, Sequoia, Siuslaw, Superior; and the U. S. Forest Service

Timber: How Much Is Enough? By John J. Putman. Photos by Bruce Dale. 485-511, Apr. 1974
Included: Monongahela, Tongass, Willamette, and the U. S. Forest Service

Washington Wilderness, the North Cascades. By Edwards Park. Photos by Kathleen Revis. 335-367, Mar. 1961
Included: Mt. Baker, Okanogan, Wenatchee

White-water Adventure on Wild Rivers of Idaho. By Frank Craighead, Jr. and John Craighead. 213-239, Feb. 1970
Included: Bitterroot, Boise, Challis, Nezperce, Payette, Salmon

See also Florida (Florida's Booming), for Ocala National Forest; Inyo National Forest

NATIONAL FOUNDATION FOR THE INDIAN (FUNAI): Brazil. *See* Cinta Larga Indians; Kreen-Akarores; Txukahameis

NATIONAL GALLERY OF ART, Washington, D. C.:

American Masters in the National Gallery. By John Walker. 295-324, Sept. 1948

In Quest of Beauty. Text by Paul Mellon. French Impressionist paintings from the collections of Mr. and Mrs. Paul Mellon and Mrs. Ailsa Mellon

NATIONAL GALLERY OF ART, Washington, D. C.—
Continued
Bruce. 372-385, Mar. 1967

The Kress Collection: A Gift to the Nation. By Guy Emerson. 823-865, Dec. 1961

The National Gallery After a Quarter Century. By John Walker. 348-371, Mar. 1967

The Nation's Newest Old Masters. By John Walker. Paintings from Kress Collection. 619-657, Nov. 1956

The Vienna Treasures and Their Collectors. By John Walker. 737-776, June 1950

Washington: Home of the Nation's Great. By Albert W. Atwood. 699-738, June 1947

Your National Gallery of Art After 10 Years. By John Walker. Paintings from Kress Collection. 73-103, Jan. 1952

See also Chester Dale Collection; *and* Masterpieces; "Mona Lisa"

NATIONAL GEOGRAPHIC ATLAS OF THE WORLD. See Atlases, NGS: World Atlas

NATIONAL GEOGRAPHIC ATLAS SERIES MAPS. *See* Map Supplements

NATIONAL GEOGRAPHIC MAGAZINE (NGM):

Atlases. *See* Atlases, NGS

Awards Received:

Freedoms Foundation awards received by editor and two staff writers. 190, Feb. 1954

La Belle Award Received by Franklin L. Fisher on behalf of the Society for outstanding contributions to the development of color photography in magazine illustration. 692, Nov. 1953

National Geographic Photographers Win Top Magazine Awards. 830-831, June 1959

Photographers amass national awards. 878, 880-881, Dec. 1961; 898, 901, Dec. 1962

U. S. Camera Achievement Award medal (1951). 481, Oct. 1966

University of Missouri's Honor Award for Distinguished Service in Journalism (1954). 539, Oct. 1963

Editor. Gilbert Hovey Grosvenor (1899-1954); John Oliver La Gorce (1954-1957); Melville Bell Grosvenor (1957-1967); Frederick G. Vosburgh (1967-1970); Gilbert M. Grosvenor (1970-   )

Editor, Associate. *See* Scofield, John; Shor, Franc

Editor-in-Chief. *See* Grosvenor, Melville Bell

Editorial, first regular. 587, Nov. 1974

Editorial Policy. 587, Nov. 1974

History:

First Lady of the National Geographic (Elsie May Bell Grosvenor). By Gilbert Hovey Grosvenor. 101-121, July 1965

The National Geographic Society and Its Magazine: A History. By Gilbert H. Grosvenor. 582a, Oct. 1957; 880, Dec. 1964

National Geographic Society Trustees Elect Key Executives. 576-590, Oct. 1967

The Romance of the Geographic: National Geographic Magazine Observes Its Diamond Anniversary. By Gilbert Hovey Grosvenor. 516-585, Oct. 1963

75 Years Exploring Earth, Sea, and Sky: National Geographic Society Observes Its Diamond Anniversary. By Melvin M. Payne. 1-43, Jan. 1963

To Gilbert Grosvenor: A Monthly Monument 25

The NATION'S Newest Old Masters. By John Walker. Paintings from Kress Collection. 619-657, Nov. 1956

The NATION'S River. By Allan C. Fisher, Jr. Photos by James L. Stanfield. 432-469, Oct. 1976

The NATION'S 200th Birthday. By Gilbert M. Grosvenor. 1, July 1974

NATIVE AMERICANS. See Aleuts; Eskimos; Indians of North America

NATIVE'S Return to Norway. By Arnvid Nygaard. Photos by Andrew H. Brown. 683-691, Nov. 1953

NATRON, Lake, Tanzania:
East Africa's Majestic Flamingos. By M. Philip Kahl. 276-294, Feb. 1970

NATURAL ARCHES AND BRIDGES. See Arches National Monument; Canyonlands National Park; Escalante Canyon, for Grosvenor Arch and La Gorce Arch; Natural Bridges National Monument; Rainbow Bridge National Monument; Zion National Park

NATURAL BRIDGES NATIONAL MONUMENT, Utah:
Roaming the West's Fantastic Four Corners. By Jack Breed. 705-742, June 1952

NATURAL GAS:
Alberta Unearths Her Buried Treasures. By David S. Boyer. 90-119, July 1960
Canada's "Now" Frontier. By Robert Paul Jordan. Photos by Lowell Georgia. 480-511, Oct. 1976
Included: Map showing oil pipeline, proposed gas pipeline, and tar sands
The Eternal Flame. By Albert W. Atwood. 540-564, Oct. 1951
The Pipeline: Alaska's Troubled Colossus. By Bryan Hodgson. Photos by Steve Raymer. 684-717, Nov. 1976
Included: Diagram, Anatomy of the pipeline; map showing potential and producing oil and gas areas
Turnaround Time in West Virginia. By Elizabeth A. Moize. Photos by Jodi Cobb. 755-785, June 1976

NATURAL HISTORY:
In the Wake of Darwin's Beagle. By Alan Villiers. Photos by James L. Stanfield. 449-495, Oct. 1969
Our Continent: A Natural History of North America. Book announced. 572-574, Oct. 1976
See also Nature Study; and Biology; Geology; Marine Biology; Paleontology; Plants

NATURAL RESOURCES:
This Land of Ours — How Are We Using It? By Peter T. White. Photos by Emory Kristof. 20-67, July 1976
See also Energy Sources; Lumber Industry; Minerals and Metals; Water Supply

A NATURALIST in Penguin Land. By Niall Rankin. 93-116, Jan. 1955

NATURE Carves Fantasies in Bryce Canyon (Utah). By William Belknap, Jr. 490-511, Oct. 1958

NATURE STUDY:
Animals that Build their Homes. Children's book announced. 718-720, Nov. 1976
Buck Island — Underwater Jewel. By Jerry and Idaz Greenberg. 677-683, May 1971

NATURE STUDY — Continued
Businessman in the Bush. By Frederick Kent Truslow. 634-675, May 1970
A Day in the Woods. Children's book announced. 724-726, Nov. 1975
The Fragile Beauty All About Us. Photos by Harry S. C. Yen. 785-795, Dec. 1970
Frost, Nature's Icing. By Robert F. Sisson. 398-405, Mar. 1976
In the Gardens of Olympus. By Paul A. Zahl. 85-123, July 1955
In the Wilds of a City Parlor. By Paul A. Zahl. 645-672, Nov. 1954
In Touch With Nature. Text by Elizabeth A. Moize. Photos by Steve Raymer. 537-543, Apr. 1974
Nature's Year in Pleasant Valley. By Paul A. Zahl. 488-525, Apr. 1968
Photographing Northern Wild Flowers. By Virginia L. Wells. 809-823, June 1956
Snowflakes to Keep. By Robert F. Sisson. 104-111, Jan. 1970
Teeming Life of a Pond. By William H. Amos. 274-298, Aug. 1970
Tricks Animals Play. Children's book announced. 724-726, Nov. 1975
The World of My Apple Tree. By Robert F. Sisson. 836-847, June 1972
See also the natural sciences; and listing under Animals

NATURE'S Alert Eyes. By Constance P. Warner. 558-569, Apr. 1959

NATURE'S Aquatic Engineers, Beavers. By Des and Jen Bartlett. 716-732, May 1974

NATURE'S Clown, the Penguin. By David Hellyer and Malcolm Davis. 405-428, Sept. 1952

NATURE'S Gifts to Medicine. By Lonnelle Aikman. Paintings by Lloyd K. Townsend and Don Crowley. 420-440, Sept. 1974

NATURE'S Living, Jumping Jewels. By Paul A. Zahl. 130-146, July 1973

NATURE'S Night Lights: Probing the Secrets of Bioluminescence. By Paul A. Zahl. 45-69, July 1971

NATURE'S Tank, the Turtle. By Doris M. Cochran. Paintings by Walter A. Weber. 665-684, May 1952

NATURE'S Toy Train, the Railroad Worm. By Darwin L. Tiemann. Photos by Robert F. Sisson. 56-67, July 1970

NATURE'S Year in Pleasant Valley. By Paul A. Zahl. 488-525, Apr. 1968

NAURU, the World's Richest Nation. By Mike Holmes. 344-353, Sept. 1976

NAUTICAL Norfolk Turns to Azaleas. By William H. Nicholas. Photos by B. Anthony Stewart. 606-614, May 1947

NAUTILUS (Nuclear-powered Submarine):
The Arctic as a Sea Route of the Future. By William R. Anderson. 21-24, Jan. 1959
Submarine Through the North Pole. By William G. Lalor, Jr. Photos by John J. Krawczyk. 1-20, Jan. 1959

NAUTILUS, Chambered:

The Chambered Nautilus, Exquisite Living Fossil. Photos by Douglas Faulkner. 38-41, Jan. 1976

Shells Take You Over World Horizons. By Rutherford Platt. 33-84, July 1949

NAVAJOS (Indians):

Better Days for the Navajos. By Jack Breed. Photos by Charles W. Herbert. 809-847, Dec. 1958

Desert River (San Juan) Through Navajo Land. By Alfred M. Bailey. Photos by author and Fred G. Brandenburg. 149-172, Aug. 1947

The Navajos. By Ralph Looney. Photos by Bruce Dale. 740-781, Dec. 1972

NAVAL AIR TECHNICAL TRAINING UNIT. *See* Parachute Rigger School

NAVAL BASES:

Four-ocean Navy in the Nuclear Age. By Thomas W. McKnew. 145-187, Feb. 1965

Our Navy in the Far East. By Arthur W. Radford. Photos by J. Baylor Roberts. 537-577, Oct. 1953

See also Guantánamo (Cuba); Honolulu, Hawaii, for Pearl Harbor; Key West, Florida; Portsmouth (England); San Diego, California

NAVIGATION:

Charting Our Sea and Air Lanes. By Stuart E. Jones. Photos by J. Baylor Roberts. 189-209, Feb. 1957

See also Hokule'a; Mayflower II; Radar; Sonar; Submarines, Nuclear-powered; *and* Graham, Robin Lee; Henry, Prince, the Navigator; Lewis, David; Schultz, John E.; Vikings

NAVIGATION, Flight:

Our Air Age Speeds Ahead. By F. Barrows Colton. 249-272, Feb. 1948

Skyway Below the Clouds. By Carl R. Markwith. Photos by Ernest J. Cottrell. 85-108, July 1949

See also Balloons

NAVIGATORS. *See* Explorers, Discoverers, and Navigators

NAVY. *See* U. S. Navy; *and* listing under French Navy

NAVY HURRICANE WEATHER CENTRAL, Miami, Florida:

Men Against the Hurricane. By Andrew H. Brown. 537-560, Oct. 1950

NAWANG GOMBU (Sherpa):

American and Geographic Flags Top Everest. By Melvin M. Payne. Photos by Barry C. Bishop. 157-157C, Aug. 1963

See also American Mount Everest Expedition

NAXOS (Island), Greece:

The Isles of Greece: Aegean Birthplace of Western Culture. By Melville Bell Grosvenor. Photos by Edwin Stuart Grosvenor and Winfield Parks. 147-193, Aug. 1972

NAYARIT (State), Mexico. *See* Mesa del Nayar

NAZARÉ, Portugal:

Portugal Is Different. By Clement E. Conger. 583-622, Nov. 1948

NAZARENOS (Penitents):

Holy Week and the Fair in Sevilla. By Luis Marden. 499-530, Apr. 1951

NAZARETH, Israel:

The Land of Galilee. By Kenneth MacLeish. Photos by B. Anthony Stewart. 832-865, Dec. 1965

Where Jesus Walked. By Howard La Fay. Photos by Charles Harbutt. 739-781, Dec. 1967

NAZCA LINES (Figure Tracings):

Mystery of the Ancient Nazca Lines. By Loren McIntyre. 716-728, May 1975

NEALE, GUY: Artist:

The High World of the Rain Forest. By William Beebe. 838-855, June 1958

NEAR EAST. *See* Middle East and Near East

NEAVE, CHARLES: Author-Photographer:

Helping Holland Rebuild Her Land. By Gilbert M. Grosvenor and Charles Neave. 365-413, Sept. 1954

NEBBIA, THOMAS:

National Geographic Photographers Win Top Magazine Awards. 830-831, June 1959

Photographer

African Wildlife: Man's Threatened Legacy. By Allan C. Fisher, Jr. Paintings by Ned Seidler. 147-187, Feb. 1972

Australia's Pacesetter State, Victoria. By Allan C. Fisher, Jr. 218-253, Feb. 1971

California, the Golden Magnet: I. The South. By William Graves. 595-639, May 1966

Canterbury Cathedral. By Kenneth MacLeish. 364-379, Mar. 1976

Cape Canaveral's 6,000-mile Shooting Gallery. By Allan C. Fisher, Jr. Photos by Luis Marden and Thomas Nebbia. 421-471, Oct. 1959

Crusader Road to Jerusalem. By Franc Shor. 797-855, Dec. 1963

Denmark, Field of the Danes. By William Graves. 245-275, Feb. 1974

The Fabulous State of Texas. By Stanley Walker. Photos by B. Anthony Stewart and Thomas Nebbia. 149-195, Feb. 1961

French Riviera: Storied Playground on the Azure Coast. By Carleton Mitchell. 798-835, June 1967

Greenland's "Place by the Icebergs." By Mogens Bloch Poulsen. 849-869, Dec. 1973

Guantánamo: Keystone in the Caribbean. By Jules B. Billard. Photos by W. E. Garrett and Thomas Nebbia. 420-436, Mar. 1961

Haiti: Beyond Mountains, More Mountains. By Carolyn Bennett Patterson. 70-97, Jan. 1976

Hawaii, U.S.A. By Frederick Simpich, Jr. 1-45, July 1960

In the Crusaders' Footsteps. By Franc Shor. Photos by Thomas Nebbia and James P. Blair. 731-789, June 1962

Inside the White House. By Lonnelle Aikman. Photos by B. Anthony Stewart and Thomas Nebbia. 3-43, Jan. 1961

Isles on the Edge of the Sea: Scotland's Outer Hebrides. By Kenneth MacLeish. 676-711, May 1970

Jamaica Goes It Alone. By James Cerruti. 843-873, Dec. 1967

Life in Walled-off West Berlin. By Nathaniel T. Kenney and Volkmar Wentzel. 735-767, Dec. 1961

Los Angeles, City of the Angels. By Robert de Roos. 451-501, Oct. 1962

NEWPORT, Rhode Island—*Continued*

Long. Photos by Willard R. Culver. 137-170, Aug. 1948

Windjamming Around New England. By Tom Horgan. Photos by Robert F. Sisson. 141-169, Aug. 1950

NEWPORT BEACH, California:

Happy Birthday, Otto Lilienthal! By Russell Hawkes. Photos by James Collison. 286-292, Feb. 1972

NEWTON, ISAAC:

The British Way. By Sir Evelyn Wrench. 421-541, Apr. 1949

NEWTON, JOHN G.: Author:

How We Found the *Monitor*. 48-61, Jan. 1975

The NEXT Frontier? By Isaac Asimov. Paintings by Pierre Mion. 76-89, July 1976

The NEXT 100 Years: A Master Plan for Yellowstone. By George B. Hartzog, Jr. 632-637, May 1972

NEXT Steps in Space. By Thomas O. Paine. 793-797, Dec. 1969

NGORONGORO CRATER, Tanzania:

The Flamingo Eaters of Ngorongoro (Hyenas). By Richard D. Estes. 535-539, Oct. 1973

Hyenas, the Hunters Nobody Knows. By Hans Kruuk. Photos by Baron Hugo van Lawick. 44-57, July 1968

Tool-using Bird: The Egyptian Vulture. By Baroness Jane van Lawick-Goodall. Photos by Baron Hugo van Lawick. 631-641, May 1968

NIAGARA FALLS, Canada-U. S.:

The Great Lakes: Is It Too Late? By Gordon Young. Photos by James L. Amos and Martin Rogers. 147-185, Aug. 1973

Niagara Falls, Servant of Good Neighbors. Photos by Walter Meayers Edwards. 574-587, Apr. 1963

NICHOLAS, WILLIAM H.: Author:

America's "Meat on the Hoof." 33-72, Jan. 1952

Biggest Worm Farm Caters to Platypuses. 269-280, Feb. 1949

Deep in the Heart of "Swisssconsin." Photos by J. Baylor Roberts. 781-800, June 1947

Dixie Spins the Wheel of Industry. Photos by J. Baylor Roberts. 281-324, Mar. 1949

Growing Pains Beset Puerto Rico. Photos by Justin Locke. 419-460, Apr. 1951

History Repeats in Old Natchez. Photos by Willard R. Culver. 181-208, Feb. 1949

Literary Landmarks of Massachusetts. Photos by B. Anthony Stewart and John E. Fletcher. 279-310, Mar. 1950

Men, Moose, and Mink of Northwest Angle. Photos by J. Baylor Roberts. 265-284, Aug. 1947

Miami's Expanding Horizons. 561-594, Nov. 1950

Nautical Norfolk Turns to Azaleas. Photos by B. Anthony Stewart. 606-614, May 1947

Shawneetown Forsakes the Ohio. Photos by J. Baylor Roberts. 273-288, Feb. 1948

Switzerland Guards the Roof of Europe. Photos by Willard R. Culver. 205-246, Aug. 1950

Vizcaya: An Italian Palazzo in Miami. Photos by Justin Locke. 595-604, Nov. 1950

NICHOLDS, ELIZABETH: Author:

The Goats of Thunder Hill. Photos by Robert F. Sisson. 625-640, May 1954

NICHOLS, HERBERT B.: Author:

Water for the World's Growing Needs. By Herbert B. Nichols and F. Barrows Colton. 269-286, Aug. 1952

NICHOLSON, ROBERT W.: Artist:

Saving the Ancient Temples at Abu Simbel. By Georg Gerster. 694-742, May 1966

NICKLIN, CHARLES R., Jr.: Photographer:

New Tools for Undersea Archeology. By George F. Bass. 403-423, Sept. 1968

Swimming With Patagonia's Right Whales. By Roger Payne. Photos by William R. Curtsinger and Charles R. Nicklin, Jr. 576-587, Oct. 1972

NICOSIA, Cyprus:

Cyprus Under Four Flags: A Struggle for Unity. By Kenneth MacLeish. Photos by Jonathan Blair. 356-383, Mar. 1973

NIEDRACH, R. J.: Author-Photographer:

Freezing the Flight of Hummingbirds. By Harold E. Edgerton, R. J. Niedrach, and Walker Van Riper. 245-261, Aug. 1951

NIGER, Republic of:

Drought Threatens the Tuareg World. By Victor Englebert. 544-571, Apr. 1974

Freedom Speaks French in Ouagadougou. By John Scofield. 153-203, Aug. 1966

I Joined a Sahara Salt Caravan. By Victor Englebert. 694-711, Nov. 1965

NIGER RIVER, West Africa:

The Niger: River of Sorrow, River of Hope. By Georg Gerster. 152-189, Aug. 1975

NIGERIA:

Beyond the Bight of Benin. By Jeannette and Maurice Fiévet. 221-253, Aug. 1959

The Niger: River of Sorrow, River of Hope. By Georg Gerster. 152-189, Aug. 1975

Progress and Pageantry in Changing Nigeria. By W. Robert Moore. 325-365, Sept. 1956

Safari Through Changing Africa. By Elsie May Bell Grosvenor. Photos by Gilbert Grosvenor. 145-198, Aug. 1953

NIGHT Life in the Gulf Stream. By Paul A. Zahl. 391-418, Mar. 1954

NIGHT of Terror (Alaska Earthquake). By Tay Pryor Thomas. 142-156, July 1964

The NIGHT the Mountains Moved. By Samuel W. Matthews. Photos by J. Baylor Roberts. 329-359, Mar. 1960

NIGHTINGALE, FLORENCE:

The British Way. By Sir Evelyn Wrench. 421-541, Apr. 1949

The NIGHTMARE of Famine. Photos by Steve Raymer. 33-39, July 1975

NIKE (Guided Missile):

New Miracles of the Telephone Age. By Robert Leslie Conly. 87-120, July 1954

NORFOLK ISLAND, South Pacific:

Bounty Descendants Live on Remote Norfolk Island. By T. C. Roughley. Photos by J. Baylor Roberts. 559-584, Oct. 1960

NORKEY, TENZING. *See* Tenzing Norgay

NORMAN, JAMES: Author:

The Tarahumaras: Mexico's Long Distance Runners. Photos by David Hiser. 702-718, May 1976

NORMAN CONQUEST:

The British Way. By Sir Evelyn Wrench. 421-541, Apr. 1949

900 Years Ago: the Norman Conquest. By Kenneth M. Setton. Photos by George F. Mobley. 206-251, Aug. 1966

NORMANDY, France:

Normandy Blossoms Anew. By Howell Walker. 591-631, May 1959

The Vikings. By Howard La Fay. Photos by Ted Spiegel. 492-541, Apr. 1970

NORSEMEN. *See* Vikings

NORTH, WHEELER J.: Author:

Giant Kelp, Sequoias of the Sea. Photos by Bates Littlehales. 251-269, Aug. 1972

NORTH AFRICA. *See* Algeria; Morocco; Tunisia; *and* Carthage

NORTH AMERICA:

America in the Discovery Age: the Molineaux-Wright Chart. 757, June 1953

Clues to America's Past. Special Publication announced. 860-864, June 1976

How Fruit Came to America. By J. R. Magness. Paintings by Else Bostelmann. 325-377, Sept. 1951

Indians of North America; North America Before Columbus, double-sided map supplement. Dec. 1972

North America, Atlas series supplement. Apr. 1964

North America, map supplement. Mar. 1952

Our Continent: A Natural History of North America. Book announced. 572-574, Oct. 1976

Our Vegetable Travelers. By Victor R. Boswell. Paintings by Else Bostelmann. 145-217, Aug. 1949

The World in Your Garden (Flowers). By W. H. Camp. Paintings by Else Bostelmann. 1-65, July 1947

See also Canada; Central America; Greenland; Mexico; United States

NORTH AMERICAN AIR DEFENSE COMMAND (NORAD). *See* U. S. Air Force (Of Planes and Men)

NORTH BIMINI ISLAND, Bahama Islands. *See* Lerner Marine Laboratory

NORTH BORNEO. *See* Sabah

NORTH CALAVERAS GROVE (Sequoias), California. *See* Calaveras Big Trees State Park

NORTH CAROLINA:

Around the "Great Lakes of the South." By Frederick Simpich. Photos by J. Baylor Roberts. 463-491, Apr. 1948

NORTH CAROLINA — *Continued*

Dixie Spins the Wheel of Industry. By William H. Nicholas. Photos by J. Baylor Roberts. 281-324, Mar. 1949

Exploring America's Great Sand Barrier Reef. By Eugene R. Guild. Photos by John E. Fletcher and author. 325-350, Sept. 1947

Great Smokies National Park: Solitude for Millions. By Gordon Young. Photos by James L. Amos. 522-549, Oct. 1968

Here Come the Marines. By Frederick Simpich. 647-672, Nov. 1950
Included: Cherry Point Air Station and Camp Lejeune

Indian Life Before the Colonists Came. By Stuart E. Jones. Engravings by Theodore de Bry, 1590. 351-368, Sept. 1947

Menhaden — Uncle Sam's Top Commercial Fish. By Leonard C. Roy. Photos by Robert F. Sisson. 813-823, June 1949
Included: Morehead City-Beaufort area on Bogue Sound

My Neighbors Hold to Mountain Ways (Blue Ridge). By Malcolm Ross. Photos by Flip Schulke. 856-880, June 1958

North Carolina, Dixie Dynamo. By Malcolm Ross. Photos by B. Anthony Stewart. 141-183, Feb. 1962

Our Changing Atlantic Coastline. By Nathaniel T. Kenney. Photos by B. Anthony Stewart. 860-887, Dec. 1962
Included: Bodie Island; Hatteras Island; Wash Woods

Pack Trip Through the Smokies. By Val Hart. Photos by Robert F. Sisson. 473-502, Oct. 1952

Skyway Below the Clouds. By Carl R. Markwith. Photos by Ernest J. Cottrell. 85-108, July 1949
Included: Charlotte; High Rock Lake

See also Old Salem; Outer Banks; Roan Mountain

NORTH CASCADES NATIONAL PARK, Washington:

New National Park Proposed: The Spectacular North Cascades. By Nathaniel T. Kenney. Photos by James P. Blair. 642-667, May 1968

NORTH CENTRAL UNITED STATES:

Close-up: U.S.A., The North Central States, map supplement. Text on reverse. Mar. 1974

A Map Maker Looks at the United States. By Newman Bumstead. 705-748, June 1951
Included: Illinois: Chicago and Rock Island; Indiana: South Bend and Gary; Iowa: Davenport and Muscatine; Lake Michigan

Mapping the Nation's Breadbasket. By Frederick Simpich. 831-849, June 1948

North Central United States, Atlas series supplement. Nov. 1958

North Central United States, map supplement. June 1948

See also names of individual states

NORTH DAKOTA:

Duck Hunting with a Color Camera. By Arthur A. Allen. 514-539, Oct. 1951

Following the Trail of Lewis and Clark. By Ralph Gray. 707-750, June 1953

North Dakota Comes into Its Own. By Leo A. Borah. Photos by J. Baylor Roberts. 283-322, Sept. 1951

See also Minot

NORTH for Oil: *Manhattan* Makes the Historic Northwest Passage. By Bern Keating. Photos by Tomas Sennett. 374-391, Mar. 1970

NORTH ISLAND, New Zealand:

New Zealand's North Island: The Contented Land. By Charles McCarry. Photos by Bates Littlehales. 190-213, Aug. 1974

See also Waitomo Caves

NORTH KOREA. *See* Korea, North

NORTH MANKATO, Minnesota:

Satellites Gave Warning of Midwest Floods. By Peter T. White. Photos by Thomas A. DeFeo. 574-592, Oct. 1969

NORTH POLE:

North Toward the Pole on Skis. By Bjørn O. Staib. 254-281, Feb. 1965

The Peary Flag Comes to Rest. By Marie Peary Stafford. 519-532, Oct. 1954

Submarine Through the North Pole *(Nautilus)*. By William G. Lalor, Jr. Photos by John J. Krawczyk. 1-20, Jan. 1959

Up Through the Ice of the North Pole *(Skate)*. By James F. Calvert. 1-41, July 1959

We Followed Peary to the Pole. By Gilbert Grosvenor and Thomas W. McKnew. 469-484, Oct. 1953

NORTH SEA:

Oil, the Dwindling Treasure. By Noel Grove. Photos by Emory Kristof. 792-825, June 1974

Pilgrimage to Holy Island and the Farnes. By John E. H. Nolan. 547-570, Oct. 1952

Thumbs Up Round the North Sea's Rim. By Frances James. Photos by Erica Koch. 685-704, May 1952

NORTH SLOPE, Alaska:

Alaska: Rising Northern Star. By Joseph Judge. Photos by Bruce Dale. 730-767, June 1975

Oil, the Dwindling Treasure. By Noel Grove. Photos by Emory Kristof. 792-825, June 1974

The Pipeline: Alaska's Troubled Colossus. By Bryan Hodgson. Photos by Steve Raymer. 684-717, Nov. 1976

Included: Diagram, Anatomy of the pipeline; map showing potential and producing oil and gas areas

Will Oil and Tundra Mix? Alaska's North Slope Hangs in the Balance. By William S. Ellis. Photos by Emory Kristof. 485-517, Oct. 1971

NORTH STAR Cruises Alaska's Wild West. By Amos Burg. 57-86, July 1952

NORTH Through History Aboard *White Mist*. By Melville Bell Grosvenor. Photos by Edwin Stuart Grosvenor. 1-55, July 1970

NORTH Toward the Pole on Skis. By Bjørn O. Staib. 254-281, Feb. 1965

NORTH UIST (Island), Scotland:

Isles on the Edge of the Sea: Scotland's Outer Hebrides. By Kenneth MacLeish. Photos by Thomas Nebbia. 676-711, May 1970

NORTH VIET NAM:

Air Rescue Behind Enemy Lines. By Howard Sochurek. 346-369, Sept. 1968

NORTH With Finland's Lapps. By Jean and Franc Shor. 249-280, Aug. 1954

NORTH With the Snow Goose. By Des and Jen Bartlett. 822-843, Dec. 1973

NORTH With the Wheat Cutters. By Noel Grove. Photos by James A. Sugar. 194-217, Aug. 1972

NORTHAMPTON, Massachusetts. *See* Clarke School for the Deaf

NORTH-EAST NEW GUINEA:

To the Land of the Head-hunters. By E. Thomas Gilliard. 437-486, Oct. 1955

See also Papua New Guinea

NORTHERN IRELAND. *See* Ireland, Northern

NORTHERN LIGHTS. *See* Aurora Borealis

NORTHERN TERRITORY, Australia:

Eden in the Outback. By Kay and Stanley Breeden. 189-203, Feb. 1973

Rock Paintings of the Aborigines. By Kay and Stanley Breeden. 174-187, Feb. 1973

The Top End of Down Under. By Kenneth MacLeish. Photos by Thomas Nebbia. 145-174, Feb. 1973

NORTHWEST (Region), U. S.:

Climbing Our Northwest Glaciers. Photos by Bob and Ira Spring. 103-114, July 1953

Close-up: U.S.A., The Northwest, map supplement. Text on reverse. Mar. 1973

Forest Fire: The Devil's Picnic. By Stuart E. Jones and Jay Johnston. 100-127, July 1968

Included: Worst blazes of 1967 in Northwest

A Map Maker Looks at the United States. By Newman Bumstead. 705-748, June 1951

Mexico to Canada on the Pacific Crest Trail. By Mike W. Edwards. Photos by David Hiser. 741-779, June 1971

Northwestern United States, Atlas series supplement. Apr. 1960

Northwestern United States, map supplement. June 1950

See also names of individual states

NORTHWEST ANGLE, Minnesota:

Men, Moose, and Mink of Northwest Angle. By William H. Nicholas. Photos by J. Baylor Roberts. 265-284, Aug. 1947

NORTHWEST PASSAGE:

North for Oil: *Manhattan* Makes the Historic Northwest Passage. By Bern Keating. Photos by Tomas Sennett. 374-391, Mar. 1970

Trek Across Arctic America. By Colin Irwin. 295-321, Mar. 1974

NORTHWEST TERRITORIES, Canada:

Across Canada by Mackenzie's Track. By Ralph Gray. 191-239, Aug. 1955

Banks Island: Eskimo Life on the Polar Sea. By William O. Douglas. Photos by Clyde Hare. 703-735, May 1964

Included: Inuvik; Sachs Harbour, Banks Island

Canada's Caribou Eskimos (Padlermiut). By Donald B. Marsh. 87-104, Jan. 1947

Canada's "Now" Frontier. By Robert Paul Jordan. Photos by Lowell Georgia. 480-511, Oct. 1976

The Canadian North: Emerging Giant. By David

OPERATION CROSSROADS (Atomic Bomb Tests). Photos by Joint Task Force I. Paintings by Charles Bittinger. 519-530, Apr. 1947

OPERATION DEEP FREEZE:

Across the Frozen Desert to Byrd Station. By Paul W. Frazier. Photos by Calvin L. Larsen. 383-398, Sept. 1957

All-out Assault on Antarctica. By Richard E. Byrd. 141-180, Aug. 1956

Antarctica: Icy Testing Ground for Space. By Samuel W. Matthews. Photos by Robert W. Madden. 569-592, Oct. 1968

Flight Into Antarctic Darkness. By J. Lloyd Abbot, Jr. Photos by David S. Boyer. 732-738, Nov. 1967

Man's First Winter at the South Pole. By Paul A. Siple. 439-478, Apr. 1958

New Era in the Loneliest Continent. By David M. Tyree. Photos by Albert Moldvay. 260-296, Feb. 1963

We Are Living at the South Pole. By Paul A. Siple. Photos by David S. Boyer. 5-35, July 1957

What We've Accomplished in Antarctica. By George J. Dufek. 527-557, Oct. 1959

Year of Discovery Opens in Antarctica. By David S. Boyer. 339-381, Sept. 1957

OPERATION ECLIPSE: 1948. By William A. Kinney. 325-372, Mar. 1949

OPERATION HIGHJUMP:

Our Navy Explores Antarctica. By Richard E. Byrd. U. S. Navy official photos. 429-522, Oct. 1947

OPERATION SAIL:

By Square-rigger from Baltic to Bicentennial. By Kenneth Garrett. 824-857, Dec. 1976

OPIUM:

The Hmong of Laos: No Place to Run. By W. E. Garrett. 78-111, Jan. 1974

Nature's Gifts to Medicine. By Lonnelle Aikman. Paintings by Lloyd K. Townsend and Don Crowley. 420-440, Sept. 1974

Spirits of Change Capture the Karens. By Peter Kunstadter. 267-285, Feb. 1972

OPOSSUMS:

Br'er Possum, Hermit of the Lowlands. By Agnes Akin Atkinson. Photos by Charles Philip Fox. 405-418, Mar. 1953

See also Possums (Phalangers)

OPTICS. See Lasers; Photography, Microscope; Telescopes; and Newton, Isaac, for his spectrum experiments

ORANGES AND ORANGE GROWING:

Florida Rides a Space-age Boom. By Benedict Thielen. Photos by Winfield Parks and James P. Blair. 858-903, Dec. 1963

How Fruit Came to America. By J. R. Magness. Paintings by Else Bostelmann. 325-377, Sept. 1951

ORANGUTANS:

Orangutans, Indonesia's "People of the Forest." By Biruté Galdikas-Brindamour. Photos by Rod Brindamour. 444-473, Oct. 1975

Search for the Great Apes (Television film). cover, Jan. 1976

ORCHIDS:

The Exquisite Orchids. By Luis Marden. 485-513, Apr. 1971

Hawaii, Island of Fire and Flowers. By Gordon Young. Photos by Robert W. Madden. 399-425, Mar. 1975

O'REAR, CHARLES: Photographer:

The Bittersweet Waters of the Lower Colorado. By Rowe Findley. 540-569, Oct. 1973

California's Surprising Inland Delta. By Judith and Neil Morgan. 409-430, Sept. 1976

A New Riviera: Mexico's West Coast. By Nathaniel T. Kenney. 670-699, Nov. 1973

Nikolaevsk: A Bit of Old Russia Takes Root in Alaska. By Jim Rearden. 401-425, Sept. 1972

OREGON:

Following the Trail of Lewis and Clark. By Ralph Gray. 707-750, June 1953

Forest Fire: The Devil's Picnic. By Stuart E. Jones and Jay Johnston. 100-127, July 1968
Included: Big Lake Airstrip blaze in Willamette National Forest; Ochoco National Forest; Wallowa-Whitman National Forest

From Sagebrush to Roses on the Columbia. By Leo A. Borah. 571-611, Nov. 1952

A Map Maker Looks at the United States. By Newman Bumstead. 705-748, June 1951
Included: Albany, Astoria, Blue Mountains, Corvallis, Crater Lake, Diamond Lake, Eugene, Hells Canyon, Mount Hood, Oregon City, Portland, Rush Creek, Salem, Vanport City, Willamette Valley

Oregon's Many Faces. By Stuart E. Jones. Photos by Bates Littlehales. 74-115, Jan. 1969

Oregon's Sidewalk on the Sea. By Paul A. Zahl. 708-734, Nov. 1961

Powerhouse of the Northwest (Columbia River). By David S. Boyer. 821-847, Dec. 1974

A River Restored: Oregon's Willamette. By Ethel A. Starbird. Photos by Lowell J. Georgia. 816-835, June 1972

Sno-Cats Mechanize Oregon Snow Survey. By Andrew H. Brown. Photos by John E. Fletcher. 691-710, Nov. 1949

Timber: How Much Is Enough? By John J. Putman. Photos by Bruce Dale. 485-511, Apr. 1974

The West Through Boston Eyes. By Stewart Anderson. 733-776, June 1949
Included: Columbia River, Crater Lake, Klamath Falls

See also Crater Lake National Park

OREGON TERRITORY:

The Opening of the American West: Burr's 1840 Map. 762-763, June 1953

O'REILLY, JOHN BOYLE:

Literary Landmarks of Massachusetts. By William H. Nicholas. Photos by B. Anthony Stewart and John E. Fletcher. 279-310, Mar. 1950

ORGAN PIPE CACTUS NATIONAL MONUMENT, Arizona:

Abundant Life in a Desert Land. By Walter Meayers Edwards. 424-436, Sept. 1973

ORGANIZATION OF PETROLEUM EXPORTING COUNTRIES (OPEC):

The Arab World, Inc. By John J. Putman. Photos by Winfield Parks. 494-533, Oct. 1975

ORIENTAL, Cordillera, Andes Mountains:
El Sangay, Fire-breathing Giant of the Andes. By G. Edward Lewis. 117-138, Jan. 1950

The ORIGINAL Boston: St. Botolph's Town. By Veronica Thomas. Photos by James L. Amos. 382-389, Sept. 1974

ORIOLES:
An Exotic New Oriole (Spotted-breasted) Settles in Florida. By Charles M. Brookfield and Oliver Griswold. 261-264, Feb. 1956

ORISSA (State), India:
Orissa, Past and Promise in an Indian State. By Bart McDowell. Photos by James P. Blair. 546-577, Oct. 1970

ORKNEY ISLANDS, Scotland:
Shetland and Orkney, Britain's Far North. By Isobel Wylie Hutchison. 519-536, Oct. 1953

ORLANDO, Florida:
Florida's Booming—and Beleaguered—Heartland. By Joseph Judge. Photos by Jonathan Blair. 585-621, Nov. 1973

ORMES, ROBERT M.: Author:
Colorado's Friendly Topland. 187-214, Aug. 1951

ORNITHOLOGY. See Birds

ORPHANS of the Wild. By Bruce G. Kinloch. 683-699, Nov. 1962

OSAKA, Japan:
Kansai, Japan's Historic Heartland. By Thomas J. Abercrombie. 295-339, Mar. 1970

OSBORNE, DOUGLAS: Author:
Solving the Riddles of Wetherill Mesa. Paintings by Peter V. Bianchi. 155-195, Feb. 1964

OSLO, Norway:
"Around the World in Eighty Days." By Newman Bumstead. 705-750, Dec. 1951
Baltic Cruise of the Caribbee. By Carleton Mitchell. 605-646, Nov. 1950
Norway, Land of the Generous Sea. By Edward J. Linehan. Photos by George F. Mobley. 1-43, July 1971
Norway Cracks Her Mountain Shell. By Sydney Clark. Photos by Gilbert Grosvenor and Ole Friele Backer. 171-211, Aug. 1948
Stop-and-Go Sail Around South Norway. By Edmond J. Moran. Photos by Randi Kjekstad Bull and Andrew H. Brown. 153-192, Aug. 1954
The Vikings. By Howard La Fay. Photos by Ted Spiegel. 492-541, Apr. 1970

OSPREYS:
The Osprey, Endangered World Citizen. By Roger Tory Peterson. Photos by Frederick Kent Truslow. 53-67, July 1969

OSSABAW (Island), Georgia:
Sea Islands: Adventuring Along the South's Surprising Coast. By James Cerruti. Photos by Thomas Nebbia and James L. Amos. 366-393, Mar. 1971

OSTEND, Belgium:
Belgium Comes Back. By Harvey Klemmer. Photos by Maynard Owen Williams. 575-614, May 1948

OSTIONAL BEACH, Costa Rica:
One Strange Night on Turtle Beach. By Paul A. Zahl. 570-581, Oct. 1973

OSTROFF, EUGENE: Photographer:
Vanished Mystery Men of Hudson Bay. By Henry B. Collins. 669-687, Nov. 1956

OTAHEITE. See Tahiti

The OTHER Nevada. By Robert Laxalt. Photos by J. Bruce Baumann. 733-761, June 1974

The OTHER Side of Jordan. By Luis Marden. 790-825, Dec. 1964

The OTHER Yosemite. By Nathaniel T. Kenney. Photos by Dean Conger. 762-781, June 1974

OTSEGO COUNTY, New York. See Thunder Hill Goat Farm

OTTAWA, Ontario, Canada:
Exploring Ottawa. By Bruce Hutchison. 565-596, Nov. 1947
Queen of Canada (Elizabeth II). By Phyllis Wilson. Photos by Kathleen Revis. 825-829, June 1959

OTTERS:
Return of the Sea Otter. By Karl W. Kenyon. Photos by James A. Mattison, Jr. 520-539, Oct. 1971

OUAGADOUGOU, Upper Volta:
Freedom Speaks French in Ouagadougou. By John Scofield. 153-203, Aug. 1966

OUESSANT, Ile d', France:
Atlantic Odyssey: Iceland to Antarctica. By Newman Bumstead. Photos by Volkmar Wentzel. 725-780, Dec. 1955

OUR Air Age Speeds Ahead. By F. Barrows Colton. 249-272, Feb. 1948

OUR Best to You—On the Geographic's 75th Birthday. By Melville Bell Grosvenor. 459, Oct. 1963

OUR Changing Atlantic Coastline. By Nathaniel T. Kenney. Photos by B. Anthony Stewart. 860-887, Dec. 1962

OUR Earth as a Satellite Sees It. By W. G. Stroud. 293-302, Aug. 1960

OUR Ecological Crisis. By Gordon Young. Photos by James P. Blair and Harry S. C. Yen. 737-795, Dec. 1970

OUR Friend From the Sea. By Robert and Nina Horstman. Photos by Robert F. Sisson. 728-736, Nov. 1968

OUR Green Treasury, the National Forests. By Nathaniel T. Kenney. Photos by J. Baylor Roberts. 287-324, Sept. 1956

OUR Growing Interstate Highway System. By Robert Paul Jordan. 195-219, Feb. 1968

OUR Home-town Planet, Earth. By F. Barrows Colton. 117-139, Jan. 1952

OUR Land Through Lincoln's Eyes. By Carolyn Bennett Patterson. Photos by W. D. Vaughn. 243-277, Feb. 1960

OUR Last Great Wilderness. By David Jeffery. 769-791, June 1975

OUR Life-giving Star, the Sun. By Herbert Friedman. 713-743, Nov. 1965

OUR Life on a Border Kibbutz. By Carol and Al Abrams. Photos by Al Abrams. 364-391, Sept. 1970

OUR Magnificent Capital City. Photos by B. Anthony Stewart. 715-738, June 1947

OUR Man-in-Sea Project. By Edwin A. Link. 713-717, May 1963

OUR Navy Explores Antarctica. By Richard E. Byrd. U. S. Navy official photos. 429-522, Oct. 1947

OUR Navy in the Far East. By Arthur W. Radford. Photos by J. Baylor Roberts. 537-577, Oct. 1953

OUR Navy's Long Submarine Arm. By Allan C. Fisher, Jr. 613-636, Nov. 1952

OUR Nuclear Navy. By George W. Anderson, Jr. 449-450, Mar. 1963

OUR Only Native Stork, the Wood Ibis. By Robert Porter Allen. Photos by Frederick Kent Truslow. 294-306, Feb. 1964

OUR Restless Earth. By Maynard M. Miller. 140-141, July 1964

OUR Search for British Paintings. By Franklin L. Fisher. 543-550, Apr. 1949

OUR Snake Friends and Foes. By Doris M. Cochran. Paintings by Walter A. Weber. 334-364, Sept. 1954

OUR Society Welcomes Its 3,000,000th Member. By Melville Bell Grosvenor. 579-582, Apr. 1962

OUR Society's 75 Years Exploring Earth, Sea, and Sky. By Melvin M. Payne. 1-43, Jan. 1963

OUR Universe Unfolds New Wonders. By Albert G. Wilson. 245-260, Feb. 1952

OUR Vegetable Travelers. By Victor R. Boswell. Paintings by Else Bostelmann. 145-217, Aug. 1949

OUR Virgin Islands, 50 Years Under the Flag. By Carleton Mitchell. Photos by James L. Stanfield. 67-103, Jan. 1968

OUR War Memorials Abroad: A Faith Kept. By George C. Marshall. 731-737, June 1957

OURO PRÊTO, Minas Gerais, Brazil:
Brazil's Land of Minerals. By W. Robert Moore. 479-508, Oct. 1948

OUTER BANKS, North Carolina:
Exploring America's Great Sand Barrier Reef. By Eugene R. Guild. Photos by John E. Fletcher and author. 325-350, Sept. 1947
How We Found the *Monitor*. By John G. Newton. 48-61, Jan. 1975
  Note: *Monitor* was lost off the Outer Banks during the Civil War.
Lonely Cape Hatteras, Besieged by the Sea. By William S. Ellis. Photos by Emory Kristof. 393-421, Sept. 1969
October Holiday on the Outer Banks. By Nike Anderson. Photos by J. Baylor Roberts. 501-529, Oct. 1955
Our Changing Atlantic Coastline. By Nathaniel T. Kenney. Photos by B. Anthony Stewart. 860-887, Dec. 1962

OUTER HEBRIDES (Islands), Scotland:
From Barra to Butt in the Hebrides. By Isobel Wylie Hutchison. 559-580, Oct. 1954
Hunting Folk Songs in the Hebrides. By Margaret Shaw Campbell. 249-272, Feb. 1947
Isles on the Edge of the Sea. By Kenneth MacLeish. Photos by Thomas Nebbia. 676-711, May 1970
Scotland From Her Lovely Lochs and Seas. By Alan Villiers. Photos by Robert F. Sisson. 492-541, Apr. 1961

OUTER MONGOLIA. *See* Mongolian People's Republic

OUTLAW TRAIL, U. S. West:
Riding the Outlaw Trail. By Robert Redford. Photos by Jonathan Blair. 622-657, Nov. 1976

OUTPOST Under the Ocean. By Edwin A. Link. Photos by Bates Littlehales. 530-533, Apr. 1965

OUTWARD BOUND SCHOOL:
Journey to the Outer Limits (Television film). 150A-150B, Jan. 1974

OVER and Under Chesapeake Bay. By David S. Boyer. 593-612, Apr. 1964

OVER Plains and Hills of South Dakota. Photos by J. Baylor Roberts. 563-586, May 1947

OVER the Sea to Scotland's Skye. By Robert J. Reynolds. 87-112, July 1952

OWENS VALLEY, California:
California's Parched Oasis, the Owens Valley. By Judith and Neil Morgan. Photos by Jodi Cobb and Galen Rowell. 98-127, Jan. 1976

OYSTER FLEET:
The Sailing Oystermen of Chesapeake Bay. By Luis Marden. 798-819, Dec. 1967

OYSTERS:
"Delmarva," Gift of the Sea. By Catherine Bell Palmer. 367-399, Sept. 1950

OZARK PLATEAU, Arkansas-Missouri:
An Ozark Family Carves a Living and a Way of Life. Photos by Bruce Dale. 124-133, July 1975
Through Ozark Hills and Hollows. By Mike W. Edwards. Photos by Bruce Dale. 656-689, Nov. 1970

P

PA PAE, Thailand:
Living With Thailand's Gentle Lua. By Peter Kunstadter. 122-152, July 1966

PACIFIC COAST, U. S.:
California's Land Apart—the Monterey Peninsula. By Mike W. Edwards. 682-703, Nov. 1972
California's Wonderful One (State Highway No. 1). By Frank Cameron. Photos by B. Anthony Stewart. 571-617, Nov. 1959
Oregon's Sidewalk on the Sea. By Paul A. Zahl. 708-734, Nov. 1961

PACIFIC CREST TRAIL, U. S.:
Mexico to Canada on the Pacific Crest Trail. By Mike W. Edwards. Photos by David Hiser. 741-779, June 1971

PAHLAVI, MOHAMMAD REZA. *See* Mohammad Reza Pahlavi

PAINE, THOMAS:

Firebrands of the Revolution. By Eric F. Goldman. Photos by George F. Mobley. 2-27, July 1974

PAINE, THOMAS O.: Author:

Next Steps in Space. 793-797, Dec. 1969

PAINTERS. *See* Artists

PAINTING SUPPLEMENTS:

"The Adoration of the Magi," a reproduction of the tondo by Fra Angelico and Fra Filippo Lippi. Jan. 1952

"The Dusty Face of Mars." Double-sided supplement. Feb. 1973

"How Man Pollutes His World." Map on reverse. Dec. 1970

"Ice Age Mammals of the Alaskan Tundra." Map of Canada on reverse. Mar. 1972

"Mayflower II." Nov. 1957

"Teammates in Mankind's Greatest Adventure" (Apollo Astronauts). Double-sided supplement. Sept. 1973

"Whales of the World." Map on reverse. Dec. 1976

PAKISTAN:

"Around the World in Eighty Days." By Newman Bumstead. 705-750, Dec. 1951
    Included: Karachi, Khyber Pass, Kohat Pass, Peshawar, Swat (State)

Imperiled Phantom of Asian Peaks: First Photographs of Snow Leopards in the Wild. By George B. Schaller. 702-707, Nov. 1971

In the Footsteps of Alexander the Great. By Helen and Frank Schreider. Paintings by Tom Lovell. 1-65, Jan. 1968

Pakistan, New Nation in an Old Land. By Jean and Franc Shor. 637-678, Nov. 1952

Pakistan: Problems of a Two-part Land. By Bern Keating. Photos by Albert Moldvay. 1-47, Jan. 1967

Sky Road East. By Tay and Lowell Thomas, Jr. 71-112, Jan. 1960

Troubled Waters East of Suez. By Ernest M. Eller. 483-522, Apr. 1954

When the President Goes Abroad (Eisenhower Tour). By Gilbert M. Grosvenor. 588-649, May 1960

See also Hunza

PAKISTAN, East:

East Pakistan Drives Back the Jungle. By Jean and Franc Shor. 399-426, Mar. 1955

See also Bangladesh

PALEN, COLE:

World War I Aircraft Fly Again in Rhinebeck's Rickety Rendezvous. By Harvey Arden. Photos by Howard Sochurek. 578-587, Oct. 1970

PALEONTOLOGY:

Adventures in the Search for Man. By Louis S. B. Leakey. Photos by Hugo van Lawick. 132-152, Jan. 1963
    Included: *Kenyapithecus wickeri; and* fossil remains of a giant rhinoceros, giant baboon, and antelope

Big Game Hunting in the Land of Long Ago (South Dakota). By Joseph P. Connolly and James D. Bump. 589-605, May 1947

PALEONTOLOGY—*Continued*

Ethiopia Yields First "Family" of Early Man. By Donald C. Johanson. Photos by David Brill. 790-811, Dec. 1976
    Contents: *Australopithecus, Homo*

Exploring 1,750,000 Years Into Man's Past. By L. S. B. Leakey. Photos by Robert F. Sisson. 564-589, Oct. 1961
    Included: Dinotherium, giant porcupine, saber-toothed tiger, and swamp antelope

Finding the World's Earliest Man. By L. S. B. Leakey. Photos by Des Bartlett. 420-435, Sept. 1960
    Included: *Afrochoerus* (prehistoric pig), *Pelorovis* (giant sheep), *Proconsul africanus* (primitive ape), *Simopithecus jonathani* (giant baboon), *Sivatherium* (short-necked giraffe), *Zinjanthropus boisei* (early man)

Fossils Lift the Veil of Time. By Harry S. Ladd and Roland W. Brown. 363-386, Mar. 1956

In Search of Man's Past at Lake Rudolf. By Richard E. Leakey. Photos by Gordon W. Gahan. 712-734, May 1970

The Leakey Tradition Lives On. By Melvin M. Payne. 143-144, Jan. 1973

The Leakeys of Africa: Family in Search of Prehistoric Man. By Melvin M. Payne. 194-231, Feb. 1965
    Included: *Kenyapithecus, Proconsul, Zinjanthropus; and* the discovery of *Homo habilis; also,* bantam rhinoceros jaw, rodent and bird bones

Preserving the Treasures of Olduvai Gorge. By Melvin M. Payne. Photos by Joseph J. Scherschel. 701-709, Nov. 1966
    Included: *Homo erectus, Homo habilis, Kenyapithecus,* Maiko Gully "George," *Zinjanthropus; and* the broken molar of a dinotherium; the tooth and bones of an extinct elephant

Re-creating a Vanished World. By Russell D. Guthrie. 294-301, Mar. 1972

Skull 1470. By Richard E. Leakey. Photos by Bob Campbell. 819-829, June 1973

A Visit to the Living Ice Age. By Rutherford Platt. 525-545, Apr. 1957

See also Aepyornis; Brontosaurs; *and* American Museum of Natural History; Dinosaur National Monument; Smithsonian Institution

PALERMO, Sicily:

Sicily, Where All the Songs Are Sad. By Howard La Fay. Photos by Jonathan Blair. 407-436, Mar. 1976

PALESTINE. *See* Bible Lands; Israel; Jordan

PALIO (Horse Race), Siena, Italy:

The Palio of Siena. By Edgar Erskine Hume. 231-244, Aug. 1951

The Renaissance Lives On in Tuscany. By Luis Marden. Photos by Albert Moldvay. 626-659, Nov. 1974

PALISADES, New York-New Jersey:

The Mighty Hudson. By Albert W. Atwood. Photos by B. Anthony Stewart. 1-36, July 1948

PALISADES INTERSTATE PARK, New York-New Jersey:

Skyline Trail from Maine to Georgia. By Andrew H. Brown. Photos by Robert F. Sisson. 219-251, Aug. 1949

PALM SPRINGS, California:

Californians Escape to the Desert. By Mason Suth-

The **PEOPLE** of Cades Cove. By William O. Douglas. Photos by Thomas Nebbia and Otis Imboden. 60-95, July 1962

The **PEOPLE** of Cumberland Gap. By John Fetterman. Photos by Bruce Dale. 591-621, Nov. 1971

The **PEOPLE** of New Jersey's Pine Barrens. By John McPhee. Photos by William R. Curtsinger. 52-77, Jan. 1974

PEOPLE'S REPUBLIC OF CHINA. *See* China (People's Republic of)

PERAZIC, ELIZABETH: Author:

Little Laos, Next Door to Red China. 46-69, Jan. 1960

PERFUME, the Business of Illusion. By Lonnelle Aikman. 531-550, Apr. 1951

PERISCOPE on the Etruscan Past. By Carlo M. Lerici. 337-350, Sept. 1959

PERÓN, JUAN DOMINGO:

Which Way Now for Argentina? By Loren McIntyre. 296-333, Mar. 1975

PERRY, MATTHEW CALBRAITH:

The Yankee Sailor Who Opened Japan. By Ferdinand Kuhn. 85-102, July 1953

PERSEPOLIS (Ruins), Iran:

In the Footsteps of Alexander the Great. By Helen and Frank Schreider. Paintings by Tom Lovell. 1-65, Jan. 1968

Iran: Desert Miracle. By William Graves. Photos by James P. Blair. 2-47, Jan. 1975

Journey Into Troubled Iran. By George W. Long. Photos by J. Baylor Roberts. 425-464, Oct. 1951

PERSIAN EMPIRE:

In the Footsteps of Alexander the Great. By Helen and Frank Schreider. Paintings by Tom Lovell. 1-65, Jan. 1968

The Sword and the Sermon. By Thomas J. Abercrombie. 3-45, July 1972
Included: Conquest of the Persian Empire by Arab Moslems; the adoption of Persian arts and sciences by the conquerors

PERSIAN GULF:

The Arab World, Inc. By John J. Putman. Photos by Winfield Parks. 494-533, Oct. 1975

Beside the Persian Gulf. Photos by Maynard Owen Williams. 341-356, Mar. 1947

Boom Time in Kuwait. By Paul Edward Case. 783-802, Dec. 1952

Calypso Explores for Underwater Oil. By Jacques-Yves Cousteau. 155-184, Aug. 1955

In Search of Arabia's Past. By Peter Bruce Cornwall. 493-522, Apr. 1948
Saudi Arabia, Oil Kingdom. Photos by Maynard Owen Williams. 497-512

Troubled Waters East of Suez. By Ernest M. Eller. 483-522, Apr. 1954

See also Dhows

PERTH, Australia:

Western Australia, the Big Country. By Kenneth MacLeish. Photos by James L. Stanfield. 150-187, Feb. 1975

PERU:

The Amazon. Photos by Loren McIntyre. 445-455,

PERU — *Continued*
Oct. 1972

Amazon — The River Sea. By Loren McIntyre. 456-495, Oct. 1972

At Home in the High Andes. By Harry Tschopik, Jr. 133-146, Jan. 1955

Avalanche! By Bart McDowell. Photos by John E. Fletcher. 855-880, June 1962

Birds That "See" in the Dark With Their Ears. By Edward S. Ross. 282-290, Feb. 1965

By Parachute Into Peru's Lost World. By G. Brooks Baekeland. Photos by author and Peter R. Gimbel. 268-296, Aug. 1964
Included: Apurímac River, Cordillera Vilcabamba, Lake Parodi, Urubamba River

Chan Chan, Peru's Ancient City of Kings. By Michael E. Moseley and Carol J. Mackey. Photos by David Brill. 318-345, Mar. 1973

Finding the Tomb of a Warrior-God. By William Duncan Strong. Photos by Clifford Evans, Jr. 453-482, Apr. 1947

The Five Worlds of Peru. By Kenneth F. Weaver. Photos by Bates Littlehales. 213-265, Feb. 1964

The Lost Empire of the Incas. By Loren McIntyre. Art by Ned and Rosalie Seidler. 729-787, Dec. 1973
A Pictorial Chronicle of the Incas. 747-753

The Marvelous Hummingbird Rediscovered. By Crawford H. Greenewalt. 98-101, July 1966

Parks, Plans, and People: How South America Guards Her Green Legacy. By Mary and Laurance Rockefeller. Photos by George F. Mobley. 74-119, Jan. 1967

Peru, Homeland of the Warlike Inca. By Kip Ross. 421-462, Oct. 1950

Peru Profits from Sea Fowl. By Robert Cushman Murphy. Photos by author and Grace E. Barstow Murphy. 395-413, Mar. 1959

Sea Fever. By John E. Schultz. 237-268, Feb. 1949

Titicaca, Abode of the Sun. By Luis Marden. Photos by Flip Schulke. 272-294, Feb. 1971

See also Condor; Vicuñas; *and* Nazca Lines

PESCADORES (Islands), Taiwan:

Pescadores, Wind-swept Outposts of Formosa. By Horace Bristol, Sr. 265-284, Feb. 1956

See also Formosa Strait

PESEK, LUDEK: Artist:

Journey to Mars. By Kenneth F. Weaver. 231-263, Feb. 1973; Supplement, Feb. 1973

Voyage to the Planets. By Kenneth F. Weaver. 147-193, Aug. 1970

PESH MERGAS. *See* Kurds

PESTALOZZI, Switzerland:

Children's Village in Switzerland, Pestalozzi. Photos by Alfred Lammer. 268-282, Aug. 1959

PESTICIDE POLLUTION:

Can the Cooper's Hawk Survive? By Noel Snyder. Photos by author and Helen Snyder. 433-442, Mar. 1974

The Osprey, Endangered World Citizen. By Roger Tory Peterson. Photos by Frederick Kent Truslow. 53-67, July 1969

Pollution, Threat to Man's Only Home. By Gordon Young. Photos by James P. Blair. 738-781, Dec. 1970

PICTURE-BOOK Portofino. By Carleton Mitchell. Photos by Winfield Parks. 232-253, Feb. 1965

PIED-À-TERRE (Motorboat):

French Riviera: Storied Playground on the Azure Coast. By Carleton Mitchell. Photos by Thomas Nebbia. 798-835, June 1967

PIEDRA PARADA, Chiapas, Mexico:

On the Trail of La Venta Man. By Matthew W. Stirling. Photos by Richard H. Stewart. 137-172, Feb. 1947
    Hunting Mexico's Buried Temples. 145-168

PIEL, GERARD: Author:

Five Noted Thinkers Explore the Future. 70-71, July 1976

PIERCE, FRANKLIN:

Profiles of the Presidents: II. A Restless Nation Moves West. By Frank Freidel. 80-121, Jan. 1965

PIGEON NETTING:

Land of the Ancient Basques. By Robert Laxalt. Photos by William Albert Allard. 240-277, Aug. 1968

Pigeon Netting—Sport of Basques. Photos by Irene Burdett-Scougall. 405-416, Sept. 1949

PIGEONS:

The Flying Telegraph. By Joseph F. Spears. Official U. S. Army Signal Corps photos. 531-554, Apr. 1947

PIGS. See Hogs and Hog Raising

PILARSKI, LAURA: Author:

Little Tibet in Switzerland. Photos by Fred Mayer. 711-727, Nov. 1968

PILGRIMAGES:

Himalayan Pilgrimage. By Christopher Rand. 520-535, Oct. 1956

India's Sculptured Temple Caves. By Volkmar Wentzel. 665-678, May 1953

Kunming Pilgrimage. 213-226, Feb. 1950

Pilgrims Follow the Christmas Star. By Maynard Owen Williams. 831-840, Dec. 1952

See also Hadj; and Canterbury Cathedral; Ethiopia (Searching); Ganges; Holy Island; Jerusalem (Home to; Where Jesus Walked); Vézelay

PILGRIMS:

Founders of New England. By Sir Evelyn Wrench. Photos by B. Anthony Stewart. 803-838, June 1953

The PILOT'S Story. By Alan B. Shepard, Jr. Photos by Dean Conger. 432-444, Sept. 1961

PINE BARRENS (Region), New Jersey:

The People of New Jersey's Pine Barrens. By John McPhee. Photos by William R. Curtsinger. 52-77, Jan. 1974

PINEAPPLES AND PINEAPPLE GROWING:

Because It Rains on Hawaii. By Frederick Simpich, Jr. 571-610, Nov. 1949

Hawaii, U.S.A. By Frederick Simpich, Jr. Photos by Thomas Nebbia. 1-45, July 1960

How Fruit Came to America. By J. R. Magness. Paintings by Else Bostelmann. 325-377, Sept. 1951

See also Puya

The PINK Birds of Texas. By Paul A. Zahl. 641-654, Nov. 1949

PINKIANG, China. See Harbin

PIONEER PROBES:

Mystery Shrouds the Biggest Planet (Jupiter). By Kenneth F. Weaver. 285-294, Feb. 1975
    Included: Pioneer 10, Pioneer 11

Reaching for the Moon. By Allan C. Fisher, Jr. Photos by Luis Marden. 157-171, Feb. 1959
    Included: Pioneer I, Pioneer II, Pioneer III

Voyage to the Planets. By Kenneth F. Weaver. Paintings by Ludek Pesek. 147-193, Aug. 1970
    Included: A Pioneer model; and plans for a future Pioneer F and Pioneer G

PIONEERS Head North to Canada's "Now" Frontier. By Robert Paul Jordan. Photos by Lowell Georgia. 480-511, Oct. 1976

PIONEERS in Man's Search for the Universe. Paintings by Jean-Leon Huens. Text by Thomas Y. Canby. 627-633, May 1974

The PIOUS Ones (Brooklyn's Hasidic Jews). By Harvey Arden. Photos by Nathan Benn. 276-298, Aug. 1975

PIPELINES, Natural Gas. See Natural Gas (Canada's; The Pipeline)

PIPELINES, Oil. See North Slope, Alaska; Trans-Andean Pipeline

PIRACY:

The Vikings. By Howard La Fay. Photos by Ted Spiegel. 492-541, Apr. 1970

PIRANHAS:

Seeking the Truth About the Feared Piranha. By Paul A. Zahl. 715-733, Nov. 1970

PISA, Italy:

The Renaissance Lives On in Tuscany. By Luis Marden. Photos by Albert Moldvay. 626-659, Nov. 1974

PITCAIRN ISLAND, South Pacific Ocean:

I Found the Bones of the Bounty. By Luis Marden. 725-789, Dec. 1957

The Yankee's Wander-world. By Irving and Electa Johnson. 1-50, Jan. 1949

The PITFALLS of Success: Yellowstone at 100. By William S. Ellis. Photos by Jonathan Blair. 616-631, May 1972

PITKIN, JOHN G.: Photographer:

Praying Mantis. 685-692, May 1950

PITTMAN, BLAIR: Photographer:

Big Thicket of Texas. By Don Moser. 504-529, Oct. 1974

PITTSBURGH, Pennsylvania:

Artists Look at Pennsylvania. By John Oliver La Gorce. 37-56, July 1948

Pittsburgh, Pattern for Progress. By William J. Gill. Photos by Clyde Hare. 342-371, Mar. 1965

Pittsburgh: Workshop of the Titans. By Albert W. Atwood. 117-144, July 1949

So Much Happens Along the Ohio River. By Frederick Simpich. Photos by Justin Locke. 177-212, Feb. 1950

"PLAIN PEOPLE." *See* Amish; Hutterites; Mennonites

PLAINEST of Pennsylvania's Plain People: Amish Folk. By Richard Gehman. Photos by William Albert Allard. 227-253, Aug. 1965

PLANETS:

First Photographs of Planets and Moon Taken with Palomar's 200-inch Telescope. By Milton L. Humason. 125-130, Jan. 1953

Voyage to the Planets. By Kenneth F. Weaver. Paintings by Ludek Pesek. 147-193, Aug. 1970

See also Earth; Jupiter; Mars; Mercury; Venus

PLANKTON:

Blue-water Plankton: Ghosts of the Gulf Stream. By William M. Hamner. 530-545, Oct. 1974

How the Sun Gives Life to the Sea (Photosynthesis). By Paul A. Zahl. 199-225, Feb. 1961

Night Life in the Gulf Stream. By Paul A. Zahl. 391-418, Mar. 1954

Sailing a Sea of Fire. By Paul A. Zahl. 120-129, July 1960

Strange Babies of the Sea. By Hilary B. Moore. Paintings by Craig Phillips and Jacqueline Hutton. 41-56, July 1952

Teeming Life of a Pond. By William H. Amos. 274-298, Aug. 1970

PLANT EXPLORERS. *See* Agricultural and Botanical Explorers

PLANTATIONS. *See* Estates and Plantations

PLANTS:

Abundant Life in a Desert Land. By Walter Meayers Edwards. 424-436, Sept. 1973

Florida, Noah's Ark for Exotic Newcomers. By Rick Gore. Photos by David Doubilet. 538-559, Oct. 1976

In the Wilds of a City Parlor. By Paul A. Zahl. 645-672, Nov. 1954

Kew: The Commoners' Royal Garden. By Thomas Garner James. Photos by B. Anthony Stewart. 479-506, Apr. 1950

Malaysia's Giant Flowers and Insect-trapping Plants. By Paul A. Zahl. 680-701, May 1964

Mountains of the Moon (Ruwenzori). By Paul A. Zahl. 412-434, Mar. 1962
    Included: Groundsels, Lichens, Lobelias

Nature's Gifts to Medicine. By Lonnelle Aikman. Paintings by Lloyd K. Townsend and Don Crowley. 420-440, Sept. 1974

Nature's Year in Pleasant Valley. By Paul A. Zahl. 488-525, Apr. 1968

Patent Plants Enrich Our World. By Orville H. Kneen. Photos from U.S. Plant Patents. 357-378, Mar. 1948

Plants of the Alaskan Tundra. 315-321, Mar. 1972

Plants That Eat Insects. By Paul A. Zahl. 643-659, May 1961

Stalking the West's Wild Foods. By Euell Gibbons. Photos by David Hiser. 186-199, Aug. 1973

Stalking Wild Foods on a Desert Isle. By Euell Gibbons. Photos by David Hiser. 47-63, July 1972

A Visit to the Living Ice Age (Far North). By Rutherford Platt. 525-545, Apr. 1957

See also Agriculture; Flowers; Fruit and Fruit Growing; Gardens; Trees; Vegetables

PLAQUEMINES PARISH, Louisiana:

New Orleans and Her River. By Joseph Judge. Photos by James L. Stanfield. 151-187, Feb. 1971

PLATE TECTONICS:

Project FAMOUS. Photos by Emory Kristof. 586-615, May 1975
    I. Where the Earth Turns Inside Out. By J. R. Heirtzler. 586-603
    II. Dive Into the Great Rift. By Robert D. Ballard. 604-615

Science Explores the Monsoon Sea. By Samuel W. Matthews. Photos by Robert F. Sisson. 554-575, Oct. 1967

This Changing Earth. By Samuel W. Matthews. 1-37, Jan. 1973

Window on Earth's Interior. By Robert D. Ballard. Photos by Emory Kristof. 228-249, Aug. 1976

PLATT, RUTHERFORD: Author-Photographer:

Shells Take You Over World Horizons. 33-84, July 1949

A Visit to the Living Ice Age. 525-545, Apr. 1957

PLATYPUSES:

Biggest Worm Farm Caters to Platypuses. By W. H. Nicholas. 269-280, Feb. 1949

Flight of the Platypuses. By David Fleay. 512-525, Oct. 1958

PLAYING 3,000 Golf Courses in Fourteen Lands. By Ralph A. Kennedy. 113-132, July 1952

PLEASANT VALLEY, Maryland:

Nature's Year in Pleasant Valley. By Paul A. Zahl. 488-525, Apr. 1968

PLEISTOCENE EPOCH:

In Search of Man's Past at Lake Rudolf. By Richard E. Leakey. Photos by Gordon W. Gahan. 712-734, May 1970

See also Ice Ages

PLUMMETING Missile of Turquoise, the Shy and Spectacular Kingfisher. Photos by Carl-Johan Junge and Emil Lütken. 413-419, Sept. 1974

PLUTO (Planet):

Voyage to the Planets. By Kenneth F. Weaver. Paintings by Ludek Pesek. 147-193, Aug. 1970

PLYWOOD:

Versatile Wood Waits on Man. By Andrew H. Brown. 109-140, July 1951

POETS:

The British Way. By Sir Evelyn Wrench. 421-541, Apr. 1949

Lake District, Poets' Corner of England. By H. V. Morton. Photos by David S. Boyer. 511-545, Apr. 1956
    Included: Samuel Taylor Coleridge, Ralph Waldo Emerson, Thomas Gray, John Keats, Percy Bysshe Shelley, Robert Southey, Alfred, Lord Tennyson, William Wordsworth

Poets' Voices Linger in Scottish Shrines. By Isobel Wylie Hutchison. Photos by Kathleen Revis. 437-488, Oct. 1957
    Included: William E. Aytoun, John Barbour, Harold Boulton, Robert Burns, Lord Byron, William Douglas, James Hogg, Violet Jacob, Marjory Kennedy-Fraser, Andrew Lang, Allan Ramsay, Sir Walter Scott, William Shakespeare, Alexander Smith, Robert Louis Stevenson

See also Frost, Robert; MacLeish, Archibald; Momaday, N. Scott

POSTERS. *See* Painting Supplements; Photo Supplements

POSTWAR Journey Through Java. By Ronald Stuart Kain. 675-700, May 1948

POSTWAR RECOVERY:

Airlift to Berlin. 595-614, May 1949

Backwoods Japan During American Occupation. By M. A. Huberman. 491-518, Apr. 1947

Belgium Comes Back. By Harvey Klemmer. Photos by Maynard Owen Williams. 575-614, May 1948

Berlin, Island in a Soviet Sea. By Frederick G. Vosburgh. Photos by Volkmar Wentzel. 689-704, Nov. 1951

Italy Smiles Again. By Edgar Erskine Hume. 693-732, June 1949

Japan Tries Freedom's Road. By Frederick G. Vosburgh. Photos by J. Baylor Roberts. 593-632, May 1950

Keeping House in London. By Frances James. 769-792, Dec. 1947

Luxembourg, Survivor of Invasions. By Sydney Clark. Photos by Maynard Owen Williams. 791-810, June 1948

Mid-century Holland Builds Her Future. By Sydney Clark. 747-778, Dec. 1950

Occupied Austria, Outpost of Democracy. By George W. Long. Photos by Volkmar Wentzel. 749-790, June 1951

Okinawa, Pacific Outpost. 538-552, Apr. 1950

Pacific Wards of Uncle Sam. By W. Robert Moore. 73-104, July 1948

Scenes of Postwar Finland. By La Verne Bradley. Photos by Jerry Waller. 233-264, Aug. 1947

Turkey Paves the Path of Progress. By Maynard Owen Williams. 141-186, Aug. 1951

Uncle Sam Bends a Twig in Germany. By Frederick Simpich. Photos by J. Baylor Roberts. 529-550, Oct. 1948

War-torn Greece Looks Ahead. By Maynard Owen Williams. 711-744, Dec. 1949

What I Saw Across the Rhine. By J. Frank Dobie. 57-86, Jan. 1947

With the U. S. Army in Korea. By John R. Hodge. 829-840, June 1947

With Uncle Sam and John Bull in Germany. By Frederick Simpich. 117-140, Jan. 1949

POTALA (Palace), Lhasa, Tibet:

My Life in Forbidden Lhasa. By Heinrich Harrer. 1-48, July 1955

POTASSIUM-ARGON DATING:

A Clock for the Ages: Potassium-Argon. By Garniss H. Curtis. 590-592, Oct. 1961

POTATOES AND POTATO GROWING:

Aroostook County, Maine, Source of Potatoes. By Howell Walker. 459-478, Oct. 1948

Our Vegetable Travelers. By Victor R. Boswell. Paintings by Else Bostelmann. 145-217, Aug. 1949

POTHOLES, Desert:

Miracle of the Potholes. By Rowe Findley. Photos by Robert F. Sisson. 570-579, Oct. 1975

POTOMAC (River), U. S.:

Across the Potomac from Washington. By Albert

POTOMAC (River), U. S. — *Continued*

W. Atwood. 1-33, Jan. 1953

Down the Potomac by Canoe. By Ralph Gray. Photos by Walter Meayers Edwards. 213-242, Aug. 1948

The Nation's River. By Allan C. Fisher, Jr. Photos by James L. Stanfield. 432-479, Oct. 1976

A Good Life on the Potomac. 470-479

New Grandeur for Flowering Washington. By Joseph Judge. Photos by James P. Blair. 500-539, Apr. 1967

Waterway to Washington, the C & O Canal. By Jay Johnston. 419-439, Mar. 1960

See also Harpers Ferry

POUCH COVE, Newfoundland:

Newfoundland, Canada's New Province. By Andrew H. Brown. Photos by author and Robert F. Sisson. 777-812, June 1949

POULSEN, MOGENS BLOCH: Author:

Greenland's "Place by the Icebergs." Photos by Thomas Nebbia. 849-869, Dec. 1973

POULTRY:

"Delmarva," Gift of the Sea. By Catherine Bell Palmer. 367-399, Sept. 1950

Easter Egg Chickens. By Frederick G. Vosburgh. Photos by B. Anthony Stewart. 377-387, Sept. 1948

Long Island Outgrows the Country. By Howell Walker. Photos by B. Anthony Stewart. 279-326, Mar. 1951

Included: Duck raising

POWELL, JOHN WESLEY:

Retracing John Wesley Powell's Historic Voyage Down the Grand Canyon. By Joseph Judge. Photos by Walter Meayers Edwards. 668-713, May 1969

POWELL, Lake, Arizona-Utah:

Lake Powell: Waterway to Desert Wonders. By Walter Meayers Edwards. 44-75, July 1967

POWER. *See* Energy Sources

POWER Comes Back to Peiping. By Nelson T. Johnson and W. Robert Moore. 337-368, Sept. 1949

POWERHOUSE of the Northwest (Columbia River). By David S. Boyer. 821-847, Dec. 1974

PRAGUE, Czechoslovakia:

Czechoslovakia: The Dream and the Reality. By Edward J. Linehan. Photos by James P. Blair. 151-193, Feb. 1968

PRAIRIE PROVINCES, Canada:

Canada's Heartland, the Prairie Provinces. By W. E. Garrett. 443-489, Oct. 1970

Contents: Alberta, Manitoba, Saskatchewan

PRATHER, VICTOR A., Jr.:

We Saw the World From the Edge of Space. By Malcolm D. Ross. Ground photos by Walter Meayers Edwards. 671-685, Nov. 1961

PRAYING MANTIS:

Praying Mantis. Photos by John G. Pitkin. 685-692, May 1950

PRE-COLUMBIAN CIVILIZATION: U. S. Southwest:

The Hohokam: First Masters of the American Desert. By Emil W. Haury. Photos by Helga Teiwes. 670-695, May 1967

Q

QUEEN CHARLOTTE ISLANDS, British Columbia, Canada:

Canada's Window on the Pacific: The British Columbia Coast. By Jules B. Billard. Photos by Ted Spiegel. 338-375, Mar. 1972

QUEEN ELIZABETH Opens Parliament. By W. E. Roscher. Photos by Robert B. Goodman. 699-707, Nov. 1961

QUEEN ELIZABETH'S Favorite Sea Dog: Sir Francis Drake. By Alan Villiers. Photos by Gordon W. Gahan. 216-253, Feb. 1975

QUEEN of Canada. By Phyllis Wilson. Photos by Kathleen Revis. 825-829, June 1959

QUEENSLAND (State), Australia:

Queensland: Young Titan of Australia's Tropic North. By Kenneth MacLeish. Photos by Winfield Parks. 593-639, Nov. 1968

See also Great Barrier Reef

QUEENY, EDGAR MONSANTO: Author:

Spearing Lions with Africa's Masai. 487-517, Oct. 1954

QUEMOY (Islands), China:

Life under Shellfire on Quemoy. By Franc Shor. Photos by Wilbur E. Garrett. 415-438, Mar. 1959

QUESTING for Gems. By George S. Switzer. 835-863, Dec. 1971

The **QUETZAL**, Fabulous Bird of Maya Land. By Anne LaBastille Bowes. Photos by David G. Allen. 141-150, Jan. 1969

QUEZALTENANGO, Guatemala:

Guatemala Revisited. By Luis Marden. 525-564, Oct. 1947

QUICKSILVER and Slow Death. By John J. Putman. Photos by Robert W. Madden. 507-527, Oct. 1972

QUITO, Ecuador:

Ecuador—Low and Lofty Land Astride the Equator. By Loren McIntyre. 259-298, Feb. 1968

QUMRĀN. *See* Khirbat Qumrān, Jordan

R

RNA. *See* Ribonucleic Acid

RA II (Papyrus Ship):

The Voyage of *Ra II*. By Thor Heyerdahl. Photos by Carlo Mauri and Georges Sourial. 44-71, Jan. 1971

RACCOONS:

Raccoon: Amiable Rogue in a Black Mask. By Melvin R. Ellis. 841-854, Dec. 1956

RACES. *See* Automobile Race; Boat Races; Bull Derby; Horse Races; Hot-air Balloons; Land Yachts; Motorcycle Races; Olympic Games; Tall-Ships Race

RADAR:

Miracle Men of the Telephone. By F. Barrows Colton. 273-316, Mar. 1947
Birthplace of Telephone Magic. Photos by Willard R. Culver. 289-312

Our Air Age Speeds Ahead. By F. Barrows Colton.

RADAR—*Continued*
249-272, Feb. 1948

See also DEW Line; Remote Sensing

RADFORD, ARTHUR W.: Author:

Our Navy in the Far East. Photos by J. Baylor Roberts. 537-577, Oct. 1953

RADIATION:

The Incredible Universe. By Kenneth F. Weaver. Photos by James P. Blair. 584-625, May 1974

Remote Sensing: New Eyes to See the World. By Kenneth F. Weaver. 46-73, Jan. 1969
Included: Cosmic Rays, Gamma Rays, Infrared Radiation, Microwaves, Radar and Sonar, Ultraviolet Rays

See also Solar Energy

RADIO:

Miracle Men of the Telephone. By F. Barrows Colton. 273-316, Mar. 1947
Birthplace of Telephone Magic. Photos by Willard R. Culver. 289-312

Our Air Age Speeds Ahead. By F. Barrows Colton. 249-272, Feb. 1948

Uncle Sam's House of 1,000 Wonders (National Bureau of Standards). By Lyman J. Briggs and F. Barrows Colton. 755-784, Dec. 1951

Unlocking Secrets of the Northern Lights. By Carl W. Gartlein. Paintings by William Crowder. 673-704, Nov. 1947

See also Microwave Radio Relay

RADIOACTIVITY:

Man's New Servant, the Friendly Atom. By F. Barrows Colton. Photos by Volkmar Wentzel. 71-90, Jan. 1954

Uncle Sam's House of 1,000 Wonders (National Bureau of Standards). By Lyman J. Briggs and F. Barrows Colton. 755-784, Dec. 1951

You and the Obedient Atom. By Allan C. Fisher, Jr. 303-353, Sept. 1958

See also Potassium-Argon Dating; Radiocarbon Dating

RADIOCARBON (Carbon-14) **DATING:**

How Old Is It? By Lyman J. Briggs and Kenneth F. Weaver. 234-255, Aug. 1958

RADIOTELEMETRY:

Antarctica's Nearer Side. By Samuel W. Matthews. Photos by William R. Curtsinger. 622-655, Nov. 1971
Included: Radio-telemetering of penguins

Studying Wildlife by Satellite. By Frank Craighead, Jr., and John Craighead. 120-123, Jan. 1973

See also Bighorn Sheep; Grizzly Bears; Salmon (the Incredible); Whistling Swan

RAFFLESIA (Flower):

Malaysia's Giant Flowers and Insect-trapping Plants. By Paul A. Zahl. 680-701, May 1964

RAFTS:

Down Mark Twain's River on a Raft. By Rex E. Hieronymus. 551-574, Apr. 1948

Rafting Down the Yukon. By Keith Tryck. Photos by Robert Clark. 830-861, Dec. 1975

Retracing John Wesley Powell's Historic Voyage Down the Grand Canyon. By Joseph Judge. Pho-

REMOTE SENSING: New Eyes to See the World. By Kenneth F. Weaver. 46-73, Jan. 1969

RENAISSANCE:

The Renaissance: Maker of Modern Man. Book announced. 588-592, Oct. 1970

The Renaissance Lives On in Tuscany. By Luis Marden. Photos by Albert Moldvay. 626-659, Nov. 1974

See also Dreyfus Collection (Renaissance Bronzes); Florence, for Renaissance art; Folger (Library), for Renaissance literature; Loire River, for Renaissance architecture

RENNER, F. G.: Author:

Erosion, Trojan Horse of Greece. 793-812, Dec. 1947

REPORT from the Locust Wars. By Tony and Dickey Chapelle. 545-562, Apr. 1953

REPORT on Laos. By Peter T. White. Photos by W. E. Garrett. 241-275, Aug. 1961

REPRINTING Brings Earliest Geographics to Life. By Melvin M. Payne. 688-689, Nov. 1964

REPTILES:

Creepy Crawly Things: Reptiles and Amphibians. Children's book announced. 728-730, Nov. 1974

London's Zoo of Zoos. By Thomas Garner James. 771-786, June 1953

The Lure of the Changing Desert. 817-824, June 1954

Reptiles and Amphibians (Television film). 875A-875B, Dec. 1968

Zoo Animals Go to School. By Marion P. McCrane. Photos by W. E. Garrett. 694-706, Nov. 1956

See also Alligators; Caymans; Crocodilians; Dinosaurs; Iguanas; Komodo Dragons; Lizards; Snakes; Tortoises; Turtles

REPUBLICAN Indonesia Tries Its Wings. By W. Robert Moore. 1-40, Jan. 1951

REQUIEM for a Tribe? Brazil's Kreen-Akarores. By W. Jesco von Puttkamer. 254-269, Feb. 1975

REQUIEM SHARKS:

Into the Lairs of "Sleeping" Sharks. By Eugenie Clark. Photos by David Doubilet. 570-584, Apr. 1975

RESCUE CRAFT:

Tomorrow on the Deep Frontier. By Edwin A. Link. 778-801, June 1964

See also Helicopters

RESCUE WORK. *See* Air Rescue; Civil Air Patrol; Diving Bell; Great St. Bernard Hospice; Guatemala (Earthquake); Military Air Transport Service; School for Survival; U. S. Air Force (Artists Roam); U. S. Coast Guard

RESEARCH REPORTS, NGS:

Research Reports. Compiled and edited by Paul H. Oehser. *1890-1954 Projects.* 442, Sept. 1975; *1955-1960 Projects.* 444, Sept. 1972; *1963 Projects.* 296, Aug. 1968; *1964 Projects.* 300, Aug. 1969; *1965 Projects.* 148, July 1971; *1966 Projects.* 146, July 1973; *1967 Projects.* 148, July 1974; *1968 Projects.* 296, Aug. 1976

RESEARCH VESSELS:

Antarctica's Nearer Side. By Samuel W. Matthews.

RESEARCH VESSELS—*Continued*

Photos by William R. Curtsinger. 622-655, Nov. 1971

Included: *Alpha Helix, Bransfield, Endurance, Hero, Professor Viese*

How We Found the *Monitor.* By John G. Newton. 48-61, Jan. 1975

Included: *Alcoa Seaprobe, Eastward*

Project FAMOUS. Photos by Emory Kristof. 586-615, May 1975

I. Where the Earth Turns Inside Out. By J. R. Heirtzler. 586-603

II. Dive Into the Great Rift. By Robert D. Ballard. 604-615

Included: *Glomar Challenger; Knorr,* R.V.; *Mizar,* U.S.N.S.; *and* submersibles *Alvin; Archimède; Cyana; Lulu*

Science Explores the Monsoon Sea. By Samuel W. Matthews. Photos by Robert F. Sisson. 554-575, Oct. 1967

Thresher: Lesson and Challenge. By James H. Wakelin, Jr. 759-763, June 1964

Included: *Atlantis II, Conrad, Gilliss*

See also Alvin; Asherah; Calypso; Deepstar; Glomar Challenger; John Elliott Pillsbury; Sea Diver

RESOLUTE BAY, Canada:

Diving Beneath Arctic Ice. By Joseph B. MacInnis. Photos by William R. Curtsinger. 248-267, Aug. 1973

RESOLUTION (Sloop):

Captain Cook: The Man Who Mapped the Pacific. By Alan Villiers. Photos by Gordon W. Gahan. 297-349, Sept. 1971

A RESTLESS Nation Moves West. By Frank Freidel. 80-121, Jan. 1965

RESURRECTING the Grandeur of Tikal. By William R. Coe. 792-798, Dec. 1975

RESURRECTING the Oldest Known Greek Ship. By Michael L. Katzev. Photos by Bates Littlehales. 841-857, June 1970

RETRACING John Wesley Powell's Historic Voyage Down the Grand Canyon. By Joseph Judge. Photos by Walter Meayers Edwards. 668-713, May 1969

THE RETURN OF DOVE (Sloop):

Robin Sails Home. By Robin Lee Graham. 504-545, Oct. 1970

RETURN of the Sea Otter. By Karl W. Kenyon. Photos by James A. Mattison, Jr. 520-539, Oct. 1971

RETURN of the Trumpeter. By Frederick Kent Truslow. 134-150, July 1960

RETURN to Changing China. By Audrey Topping. 801-833, Dec. 1971

RETURN to Lonely Tristan da Cunha. By James P. Blair. 60-81, Jan. 1964

REUNITED Jerusalem Faces Its Problems. By Kenneth MacLeish. Photos by Ted Spiegel. 835-871, Dec. 1968

REVIS, ANNE: Author:

Mr. Jefferson's Charlottesville. 553-592, May 1950

REVIS, KATHLEEN: Author-Photographer:

Colorado by Car and Campfire. 207-248, Aug. 1954

Skiing in the United States. 216-254, Feb. 1959

REVIS, KATHLEEN: Author-Photographer—*Continued*

Winter Brings Carnival Time to Quebec. 69-97, Jan. 1958

Photographer

The Friendly Huts of the White Mountains. By William O. Douglas. 205-239, Aug. 1961

Landmarks of Literary England. By Leo A. Borah. 295-350, Sept. 1955

Many-splendored Glacierland. By George W. Long. 589-636, May 1956

Poets' Voices Linger in Scottish Shrines. By Isobel Wylie Hutchison. 437-488, Oct. 1957

Queen of Canada (Elizabeth II). By Phyllis Wilson. 825-829, June 1959

Soaring on Skis in the Swiss Alps. By Carolyn Bennett Patterson. 94-121, Jan. 1961

Washington Wilderness, the North Cascades. By Edwards Park. 335-367, Mar. 1961

Westminster, World Series of Dogdom. By John W. Cross, Jr. 91-116, Jan. 1954

The World in Dolls. By Samuel F. Pryor. 817-831, Dec. 1959

REVOLUTION, American. *See* American Revolution

The **REVOLUTION** in American Agriculture. By Jules B. Billard. Photos by James P. Blair. 147-185, Feb. 1970

REVOLUTIONARY View of the 48 (Contiguous) States. By Barry C. Bishop. 140-147, July 1976

REWATI (White Tiger):

White Tiger in My House. By Elizabeth C. Reed. Photos by Donna K. Grosvenor. 482-491, Apr. 1970

REYNOLDS, ROBERT J.: Author-Photographer:

Over the Sea to Scotland's Skye. 87-112, July 1952

RHINE (River), Europe:

The Rhine: Europe's River of Legend. By William Graves. Photos by Bruce Dale. 449-499, Apr. 1967

RHINEBECK, New York. *See* Old Rhinebeck Aerodrome

RHINOCEROSES:

Stalking the Great Indian Rhino. By Lee Merriam Talbot. 389-398, Mar. 1957

Where Elephants Have Right of Way. By George and Jinx Rodger. 363-389, Sept. 1960
Included: Black Rhinoceros, White Rhinoceros

RHODE, CECIL E.: Author-Photographer:

When Giant Bears Go Fishing. 195-205, Aug. 1954

RHODE ISLAND:

New England's "Little Portugal." By O. Louis Mazzatenta. 90-109, Jan. 1975

New England's "Lively Experiment," Rhode Island. By Robert de Roos. Photos by Fred Ward. 370-401, Sept. 1968

Rhode Island, Modern City-State. By George W. Long. Photos by Willard R. Culver. 137-170, Aug. 1948

See also Newport

RHODE ISLAND (Sidewheeler):

How We Found the *Monitor*. By John G. Newton. 48-61, Jan. 1975

RHODE ISLAND (Sidewheeler)—*Continued*

Note: A search area was established for the *Monitor* based on the log of *Rhode Island,* which had the *Monitor* in tow.

RHODES, CECIL:

The British Way. By Sir Evelyn Wrench. 421-541, Apr. 1949

RHODES (Island), Greece:

The Isles of Greece: Aegean Birthplace of Western Culture. By Melville Bell Grosvenor. Photos by Edwin Stuart Grosvenor and Winfield Parks. 147-193, Aug. 1972

On the Winds of the Dodecanese. By Jean and Franc Shor. 351-390, Mar. 1953

RHODESIA:

Africa: The Winds of Freedom Stir a Continent. By Nathaniel T. Kenney. Photos by W. D. Vaughn. 303-359, Sept. 1960

Freedom's Progress South of the Sahara. By Howard La Fay. Photos by Joseph J. Scherschel. 603-637, Nov. 1962

Rhodesia, a House Divided. By Allan C. Fisher, Jr. Photos by Thomas Nebbia. 641-671, May 1975

Safari Through Changing Africa. By Elsie May Bell Grosvenor. Photos by Gilbert Grosvenor. 145-198, Aug. 1953

RHODODENDRONS:

Pack Trip Through the Smokies. By Val Hart. Photos by Robert F. Sisson. 473-502, Oct. 1952

Rhododendron Glories of Southwest Scotland. By David S. Boyer. Photos by B. Anthony Stewart and author. 641-664, May 1954

Rhododendron Time on Roan Mountain. By Ralph Gray. 819-828, June 1957

See also Azaleas

RHÔNE RIVER DELTA, France. *See* Camargue

RIBONUCLEIC ACID (RNA):

The Awesome Worlds Within a Cell. By Rick Gore. Photos by Bruce Dale. Paintings by Davis Meltzer. 355-395, Sept. 1976
Included: The Language of Life, foldout showing replication of DNA and manufacture of RNA and proteins

RIBOUD, MARC: Photographer:

Cappadocia: Turkey's Country of Cones. 122-146, Jan. 1958

Coronation in Katmandu. By E. Thomas Gilliard. 139-152, July 1957

RICE GROWING:

Backwoods Japan During American Occupation. By M. A. Huberman. 491-518, Apr. 1947

Bangladesh: Hope Nourishes a New Nation. By William S. Ellis. Photos by Dick Durrance II. 295-333, Sept. 1972

Spirits of Change Capture the Karens. By Peter Kunstadter. 267-285, Feb. 1972

RICHARD THE LIONHEART:

The British Way. By Sir Evelyn Wrench. 421-541, Apr. 1949

RICHELIEU (River), Canada:

North Through History Aboard *White Mist.* By Melville Bell Grosvenor. Photos by Edwin Stuart Grosvenor. 1-55, July 1970

RICKER, P. L.: Author-Photographer:
American Wild Flower Odyssey. 603-634, May 1953

RIDDLE of the Glyphs. By George E. Stuart. Photos by Otis Imboden. 768-791, Dec. 1975

RIDING SCHOOL. *See* Spanish Riding School

RIDING the Outlaw Trail. By Robert Redford. Photos by Jonathan Blair. 622-657, Nov. 1976

RIDLEY TURTLES. *See* Pacific Ridley Turtles

RIFLE BIRDS. *See* Birds of Paradise

RIFTS, Ocean. *See* Mid-Atlantic Rift

RIGHT WHALES:
At Home With Right Whales. By Roger Payne. Photos by Des and Jen Bartlett. 322-339, Mar. 1976

Swimming With Patagonia's Right Whales. By Roger Payne. Photos by William R. Curtsinger and Charles R. Nicklin, Jr. 576-587, Oct. 1972

RINGLING BROS. AND BARNUM & BAILEY CIRCUS:
The Wonder City That Moves by Night. By Francis Beverly Kelley. 289-324, Mar. 1948

RIO DE JANEIRO, Brazil:
Brazil, Ôba! By Peter T. White. Photos by Winfield Parks. 299-353, Sept. 1962

Spectacular Rio de Janeiro. By Hernane Tavares de Sá. Photos by Charles Allmon. 289-328, Mar. 1955

RIO GRANDE (River), U. S.-Mexico:
Two Wheels Along the Mexican Border. By William Albert Allard. 591-635, May 1971
See also Big Bend National Park

RÍO INDIO (Town and River), Panama:
Hunting Prehistory in Panama Jungles. By Matthew W. Stirling. Photos by Richard H. Stewart. 271-290, Aug. 1953

RÍO MUNI (Spanish Province), Africa:
In Quest of the World's Largest Frog. By Paul A. Zahl. 146-152, July 1967

"Snowflake," the World's First White Gorilla. By Arthur J. Riopelle. Photos by Paul A. Zahl. 443-448, Mar. 1967

RIOPELLE, ARTHUR J.: Author:
Growing Up With Snowflake. Photos by Michael Kuh. 491-503, Oct. 1970

"Snowflake," the World's First White Gorilla. Photos by Paul A. Zahl. 443-448, Mar. 1967

RIP VAN WINKLE of the Underground. By Kenneth F. Weaver. 133-142, July 1953

RIPLEY, S. DILLON: Author:
Peerless Nepal—A Naturalist's Paradise. Photos by Volkmar Wentzel. 1-40, Jan. 1950

Saving the Nene, World's Rarest Goose. Photos by Jerry Chong. 745-754, Nov. 1965

Strange Courtship of Birds of Paradise. Paintings by Walter A. Weber. 247-278, Feb. 1950
Author-Photographer
Roaming India's Naga Hills. 247-264, Feb. 1955

RIPLEY, California:
Seeking the Secret of the Giants. By Frank M.

RIPLEY, California—*Continued*
Setzler. Photos by Richard H. Stewart. 390-404, Sept. 1952

RIVER GYPSY (Houseboat):
The Jungle Was My Home. By Sasha Siemel. 695-712, Nov. 1952

RIVER PRESERVATION. *See* Wild Rivers: Preservation

RIVERS AND RIVER TRIPS:
The Coast Guard: Small Service With a Big Mission. By William S. Ellis. 113-139, July 1974

Cruising Florida's Western Waterways. By Rube Allyn. Photos by Bates Littlehales. 49-76, Jan. 1955
Contents: Chassahowitzka, Crystal, Homosassa, Suwannee, Weekiwachee, Withlacoochee

Desert River Through Navajo Land. By Alfred M. Bailey. Photos by author and Fred G. Brandenburg. 149-172, Aug. 1947
Contents: A 200-mile journey down the swift San Juan and Colorado Rivers, from Mexican Hat, Utah, to Lees Ferry, Arizona

Following the Trail of Lewis and Clark. By Ralph Gray. 707-750, June 1953

From Sagebrush to Roses on the Columbia. By Leo A. Borah. 571-611, Nov. 1952
Contents: Columbia River and Basin, Willamette River and Valley, Yakima River region

Geographical Twins a World Apart. By David S. Boyer. 848-859, Dec. 1958
Included: A comparison of the Jordan River in the Holy Land with its namesake in Utah

Hunting Prehistory in Panama Jungles. By Matthew W. Stirling. Photos by Richard H. Stewart. 271-290, Aug. 1953
Included: Cascaja, Coclé del Norte, Coclecito, Indio

Inside Europe Aboard *Yankee.* By Irving and Electa Johnson. Photos by Joseph J. Scherschel. 157-195, Aug. 1964

Jungle Jaunt on Amazon Headwaters. By Bernice M. Goetz. 371-388, Sept. 1952
Contents: Aiari, Querari, Vaupés

Jungle Journey to the World's Highest Waterfall. By Ruth Robertson. 655-690, Nov. 1949
Included: Acanán, Carrao, and Churún Rivers

The Jungle Was My Home. By Sasha Siemel. 695-712, Nov. 1952
Included: Cara Cara, Miranda, Paraguay, Paraguay-mirim (Estuary)

Labrador Canoe Adventure. By Andrew Brown and Ralph Gray. 65-99, July 1951
Contents: Ashuanipi, Atikonak, Hamilton, Unknown

A Map Maker Looks at the United States. By Newman Bumstead. 705-748, June 1951
Included: Arkansas, Chicago, Colorado, Columbia, Dosewallips, Duckabush, East (New York), Elwha, Gunnison, McCloud, Mississippi, Niagara, Pit, Potomac, Rock, Sacramento, Snake, Spokane

New St. Lawrence Seaway Opens the Great Lakes to the World. By Andrew H. Brown. 299-339, Mar. 1959

North Through History Aboard *White Mist.* By Melville Bell Grosvenor. Photos by Edwin Stuart Grosvenor. 1-55, July 1970
Included: Hudson, Richelieu, Saguenay, St. Lawrence

Oklahoma, the Adventurous One. By Robert Paul Jordan. Photos by Robert W. Madden. 149-189, Aug. 1971

ROBERTS, J. BAYLOR: Photographer—*Continued*

Hunting the Heartbeat of a Whale. By Paul Dudley White and Samuel W. Matthews. 49-64, July 1956

Indochina Faces the Dragon. By George W. Long. 287-328, Sept. 1952

Iraq—Where Oil and Water Mix. By Jean and Franc Shor. 443-489, Oct. 1958

Japan Tries Freedom's Road. By Frederick G. Vosburgh. 593-632, May 1950

Journey Into Troubled Iran. By George W. Long. 425-464, Oct. 1951

La Jolla, a Gem of the California Coast. By Deena Clark. 755-782, Dec. 1952

Louisiana Trades with the World. By Frederick Simpich. 705-738, Dec. 1947

Macau, a Hole in the Bamboo Curtain. By George W. Long. 679-688, May 1953

Malaya Meets Its Emergency. By George W. Long. 185-228, Feb. 1953

Men, Moose, and Mink of Northwest Angle. By William H. Nicholas. 265-284, Aug. 1947

New Rush to Golden California. By George W. Long. 723-802, June 1954

The Night the Mountains Moved. By Samuel W. Matthews. 329-359, Mar. 1960

North Dakota Comes into Its Own. By Leo A. Borah. 283-322, Sept. 1951

October Holiday on the Outer Banks. By Nike Anderson. 501-529, Oct. 1955

Our Green Treasury, the National Forests. By Nathaniel T. Kenney. 287-324, Sept. 1956

Our Navy in the Far East. By Arthur W. Radford. 537-577, Oct. 1953

Over Plains and Hills of South Dakota. 563-586, May 1947

Pittsburgh: Workshop of the Titans. By Albert W. Atwood. 117-144, July 1949

Saving Man's Wildlife Heritage. By John H. Baker. 581-620, Nov. 1954

Scientists Drill at Sea to Pierce Earth's Crust (Project Mohole). By Samuel W. Matthews. 686-697, Nov. 1961

Seeing the Earth from 80 Miles Up. By Clyde T. Holliday. 511-528, Oct. 1950

Shawneetown Forsakes the Ohio. By William H. Nicholas. 273-288, Feb. 1948

Slow Boat to Florida. By Dorothea and Stuart E. Jones. 1-65, Jan. 1958

This Young Giant, Indonesia. By Beverley M. Bowie. 351-392, Sept. 1955

Triton Follows Magellan's Wake. By Edward L. Beach. 585-615, Nov. 1960

Uncle Sam Bends a Twig in Germany. By Frederick Simpich. 529-550, Oct. 1948

The Wonder City That Moves by Night. By Francis Beverly Kelley. 289-324, Mar. 1948

ROBERTS, WALTER ORR: Author:

We're Doing Something About the Weather! 518-555, Apr. 1972

ROBERTSON, RUTH: Author-Photographer:

Jungle Journey to the World's Highest Waterfall. 655-690, Nov. 1949

ROBIN Sails Home. By Robin Lee Graham. 504-545, Oct. 1970

ROBINSON, ANNE GROSVENOR: Author:

Seattle, City of Two Voices. Photos by B. Anthony Stewart. 494-513, Apr. 1960

ROBINSON, G. D.: Author:

Exploring Aleutian Volcanoes. 509-528, Oct. 1948

ROBINSON, NANCY: Author:

Alaskan Family Robinson. Photos by John Metzger and Peter Robinson. 55-75, Jan. 1973

ROBINSON, PETER: Photographer:

Alaskan Family Robinson. By Nancy Robinson. Photos by John Metzger and Peter Robinson. 55-75, Jan. 1973

ROBOTS to the Moon. By Frank Sartwell. Paintings by Pierre Mion. 557-571, Oct. 1962

ROCHESTER, New York:

Eastman of Rochester: Photographic Pioneer. By Allan C. Fisher, Jr. 423-438, Sept. 1954

ROCK CARVINGS:

The Caves of the Thousand Buddhas. By Franc and Jean Shor. 383-415, Mar. 1951

Darius Carved History on Ageless Rock. By George G. Cameron. 825-844, Dec. 1950

India's Sculptured Temple Caves. By Volkmar Wentzel. 665-678, May 1953

Searching Out Medieval Churches in Ethiopia's Wilds. By Georg Gerster. 856-884, Dec. 1970

See also Cappadocia; Petra

ROCK CLIMBING:

Climbing Half Dome the Hard Way. By Galen Rowell. 782-791, June 1974

We Climbed Utah's Skyscraper Rock. By Huntley Ingalls. Photos by author and Barry C. Bishop. 705-721, Nov. 1962

ROCK PAINTINGS:

Rock Paintings of the Aborigines. By Kay and Stanley Breeden. 174-187, Feb. 1973

Searching Out Medieval Churches in Ethiopia's Wilds. By Georg Gerster. 856-884, Dec. 1970

ROCKEFELLER, LAURANCE S.:

Board of Trustees, member. 647, 655, May 1958; 5, 46, 55, July 1966; 531, 533, Oct. 1966; 80, Jan. 1967; 588, Oct. 1967; 542, Apr. 1971; 227, Aug. 1976

Author

Parks, Plans, and People: How South America Guards Her Green Legacy. By Mary and Laurance Rockefeller. Photos by George F. Mobley. 74-119, Jan. 1967

Problems in Paradise. By Mary and Laurance S. Rockefeller. Photos by Thomas Nebbia. 782-793, Dec. 1974

ROCKEFELLER, MARY FRENCH: Author:

Parks, Plans, and People: How South America Guards Her Green Legacy. By Mary and Laurance Rockefeller. Photos by George F. Mobley. 74-119, Jan. 1967

Problems in Paradise. By Mary and Laurance S. Rockefeller. Photos by Thomas Nebbia. 782-793, Dec. 1974

YWCA: International Success Story. Photos by Otis Imboden. 904-933, Dec. 1963

ROMANCHE TRENCH, Atlantic Ocean:

Calypso Explores an Undersea Canyon. By Jacques-Yves Cousteau. Photos by Bates Littlehales. 373-396, Mar. 1958

ROMANIA:

Americans Afoot in Rumania. By Dan Dimancescu. Photos by Dick Durrance II and Christopher G. Knight. 810-845, June 1969

The Balkans, Atlas series supplement. Feb. 1962

Down the Danube by Canoe. By William Slade Backer. Photos by Richard S. Durrance and Christopher G. Knight. 34-79, July 1965

Romania: Maverick on a Tightrope. By William S. Ellis. Photos by Winfield Parks. 688-713, Nov. 1975

ROMANIES. *See* Gypsies

ROME, Italy:

Italy Smiles Again. By Edgar Erskine Hume. 693-732, June 1949

Jerusalem to Rome in the Path of St. Paul. By David S. Boyer. 707-759, Dec. 1956

Rome: Eternal City with a Modern Air. By Harnett T. Kane. Photos by B. Anthony Stewart. 437-491, Apr. 1957

St. Peter's, Rome's Church of Popes. By Aubrey Menen. Photos by Albert Moldvay. 865-879, Dec. 1971

A Traveler's Map of Italy, map supplement. Text on reverse. June 1970

When in Rome. . . . By Stuart E. Jones. Photos by Winfield Parks. 741-789, June 1970

RONNING, CHESTER:

Return to Changing China. By Audrey Topping. 801-833, Dec. 1971

ROOKERIES. *See* Bird Sanctuaries and Rookeries; Pribilof Islands, for Polovina Seal Rookery

ROOSEVELT, FRANKLIN D.:

Inside the White House. By Lonnelle Aikman. Photos by B. Anthony Stewart and Thomas Nebbia. 3-43, Jan. 1961

The Living White House. By Lonnelle Aikman. 593-643, Nov. 1966

Profiles of the Presidents: V. The Atomic Age: Its Problems and Promises. By Frank Freidel. 66-119, Jan. 1966

ROOSEVELT, THEODORE:

Inside the White House. By Lonnelle Aikman. Photos by B. Anthony Stewart and Thomas Nebbia. 3-43, Jan. 1961

The Living White House. By Lonnelle Aikman. 593-643, Nov. 1966

North Dakota Comes into Its Own. By Leo A. Borah. Photos by J. Baylor Roberts. 283-322, Sept. 1951

Included: Roosevelt's log cabin, now a museum on the State Capitol grounds

Profiles of the Presidents: IV. America Enters the Modern Era. By Frank Freidel. 537-577, Oct. 1965

Theodore Roosevelt: a Centennial Tribute. By Bart McDowell. 572-590, Oct. 1958

ROOT, ALAN: Photographer:

Freeing Flamingos From Anklets of Death. By John G. Williams. 934-944, Dec. 1963

ROOT, ALAN: Photographer—*Continued*

The Galapagos, Eerie Cradle of New Species. By Roger Tory Peterson. Photos by Alan and Joan Root. 541-585, Apr. 1967

Inside a Hornbill's Walled-up Nest. By Joan and Alan Root. 846-855, Dec. 1969

Mzima, Kenya's Spring of Life. By Joan and Alan Root. 350-373, Sept. 1971

ROOT, JOAN: Photographer:

The Galapagos, Eerie Cradle of New Species. By Roger Tory Peterson. Photos by Alan and Joan Root. 541-585, Apr. 1967

Inside a Hornbill's Walled-up Nest. By Joan and Alan Root. 846-855, Dec. 1969

Mzima, Kenya's Spring of Life. By Joan and Alan Root. 350-373, Sept. 1971

ROSCHER, W. E.: Author:

Queen Elizabeth Opens Parliament. Photos by Robert B. Goodman. 699-707, Nov. 1961

ROSE APHIDS. By Treat Davidson. 851-859, June 1961

ROSEATE SPOONBILLS:

The Pink Birds of Texas. By Paul A. Zahl. 641-654, Nov. 1949

Roseate Spoonbills, Radiant Birds of the Gulf Coast. By Robert Porter Allen. Photos by Frederick Kent Truslow. 274-288, Feb. 1962

Saving Man's Wildlife Heritage. By John H. Baker. Photos by Robert F. Sisson. 581-620, Nov. 1954

ROSENSTIEL SCHOOL OF MARINE SCIENCE. *See* University of Miami: Marine Research

ROSES:

Amateur Gardener Creates a New Rose (Portrait). By Elizabeth A. Moize. Photos by Farrell Grehan. 286-294, Aug. 1972

Patent Plants Enrich Our World. By Orville H. Kneen. Photos from U. S. Plant Patents. 357-378, Mar. 1948

See also Tournament of Roses

ROSIER CREEK, Virginia:

A Good Life on the Potomac. By James L. Stanfield. 470-479, Oct. 1976

ROSS, EDWARD S.: Author:

Hunting Africa's Smallest Game. 406-419, Mar. 1961

Author-Photographer

Asian Insects in Disguise. 433-439, Sept. 1965

Birds That "See" in the Dark With Their Ears. 282-290, Feb. 1965

Photographer

Crossroads of the Insect World. By J. W. MacSwain. 844-857, Dec. 1966

ROSS, KIP: Author-Photographer:

Chile, the Long and Narrow Land. 185-235, Feb. 1960

Peru, Homeland of the Warlike Inca. 421-462, Oct. 1950

South Africa Close-up. 641-681, Nov. 1962

We Drove Panama's Darién Gap. 368-389, Mar. 1961

Photographer

Mexico in Motion. By Bart McDowell. 490-537, Oct. 1961

RUSHMORE, Mount, South Dakota—*Continued*

South Dakota Keeps Its West Wild. By Frederick Simpich. 555-588, May 1947

RUSSELL, Kansas:

Hays, Kansas, at the Nation's Heart. By Margaret M. Detwiler. Photos by John E. Fletcher. 461-490, Apr. 1952

RUSSELL CAVE, Alabama:

Life 8,000 Years Ago Uncovered in an Alabama Cave. By Carl F. Miller. 542-558, Oct. 1956

National Geographic Society Presents Russell Cave to the American People. By Melville Bell Grosvenor. 438, Mar. 1958

Russell Cave: New Light on Stone Age Life. By Carl F. Miller. 427-437, Mar. 1958

Russell Cave Dedicated; New Visitor Center Named for Gilbert H. Grosvenor. 440-442, Sept. 1967

RUSSIA. *See* Union of Soviet Socialist Republics

RUSSIANS:

Nikolaevsk: A Bit of Old Russia Takes Root in Alaska. By Jim Rearden. Photos by Charles O'Rear. 401-425, Sept. 1972

RUSSIA'S Mighty River Road, the Volga. By Howard Sochurek. 579-613, May 1973

RUSSIA'S Window on the West: Leningrad. By Howard La Fay. Photos by Dick Durrance II. 636-673, May 1971

RUTHERFORD, ERNEST, LORD:

The British Way. By Sir Evelyn Wrench. 421-541, Apr. 1949

RUWENZORI (Mountains of the Moon), Africa:

Mountains of the Moon. By Paul A. Zahl. 412-434, Mar. 1962

RWANDA. *See* Virunga Mountains

RYDEN, HOPE: Author-Photographer:

The "Lone" Coyote Likes Family Life. Photos by author and David Hiser. 278-294, Aug. 1974

On the Track of the West's Wild Horses. Photos by author and Dick Durrance II. 94-109, Jan. 1971

RYUKYU ISLANDS. *See* Okinawa

S

SÁ, HERNANE TAVARES DE: Author:

Brasília, Metropolis Made to Order. Photos by Thomas J. Abercrombie. 704-724, May 1960

Spectacular Rio de Janeiro. Photos by Charles Allmon. 289-328, Mar. 1955

SAAR:

Coal Makes the Saar a Prize. By Franc Shor. 561-576, Apr. 1954

SAARINEN, EERO:

St. Louis: New Spirit Soars in Mid-America's Proud Old City. By Robert Paul Jordan. Photos by Bruce Dale. 605-641, Nov. 1965
Included: The Gateway Arch, designed by Saarinen

SABA (Island), West Indies:

A Fresh Breeze Stirs the Leewards. By Carleton Mitchell. Photos by Winfield Parks. 488-537, Oct. 1966

SABA (Island), West Indies—*Continued*

The Netherlands Antilles: Holland in the Caribbean. By James Cerruti. Photos by Emory Kristof. 115-146, Jan. 1970

SABAH (North Borneo):

In Storied Lands of Malaysia. By Maurice Shadbolt. Photos by Winfield Parks. 734-783, Nov. 1963

Malaysia's Giant Flowers and Insect-trapping Plants. By Paul A. Zahl. 680-701, May 1964

SABLE ISLAND, Nova Scotia:

Safe Landing on Sable, Isle of 500 Shipwrecks. By Melville Bell Grosvenor. 398-431, Sept. 1965
Included: Maps, 1766 to 1964, indicating eastward shift of the island; map of known shipwreck sites
1898: The Bells on Sable. Photos by Arthur W. McCurdy. 408-409, 416-417

SACRAMENTO, California:

California, Horn of Plenty. By Frederick Simpich. Photos by Willard R. Culver. 553-594, May 1949

California, the Golden Magnet. By William Graves. 595-679, May 1966
II. Nature's North. Photos by James P. Blair and Jonathan S. Blair. 641-679

New Rush to Golden California. By George W. Long. 723-802, June 1954

A **SACRED** Symbol Comes Home: Afo-A-Kom. By William S. Ellis. Photos by James P. Blair. 141-148, July 1974

SADLERMIUTS (Eskimos):

Vanished Mystery Men of Hudson Bay. By Henry B. Collins. 669-687, Nov. 1956

SAFARI from Congo to Cairo. By Elsie May Bell Grosvenor. Photos by Gilbert Grosvenor. 721-771, Dec. 1954

SAFARI Through Changing Africa. By Elsie May Bell Grosvenor. Photos by Gilbert Grosvenor. 145-198, Aug. 1953

SAFE Landing on Sable, Isle of 500 Shipwrecks. By Melville Bell Grosvenor. 398-431, Sept. 1965

SAGA of a Ship, the *Yankee* (Brigantine). By Luis Marden. 263-269, Feb. 1966

SAGAN, CARL: Author:

Mars: a New World to Explore. 821-841, Dec. 1967

SAGUARO (Cactus):

Abundant Life in a Desert Land. By Walter Meayers Edwards. 424-436, Sept. 1973

SAGUENAY RIVER REGION, Canada:

North Through History Aboard *White Mist*. By Melville Bell Grosvenor. Photos by Edwin Stuart Grosvenor. 1-55, July 1970

Quebec's Forests, Farms, and Frontiers. By Andrew H. Brown. 431-470, Oct. 1949

Sea to Lakes on the St. Lawrence. By George W. Long. Photos by B. Anthony Stewart and John E. Fletcher. 323-366, Sept. 1950

SAHARA (Desert), Africa:

Algeria: France's Stepchild, Problem and Promise. By Howard La Fay. Photos by Robert F. Sisson. 768-795, June 1960

Algeria: Learning to Live With Independence. By Thomas J. Abercrombie. 200-233, Aug. 1973

SAPELO (Island), Georgia:
Sea Islands: Adventuring Along the South's Surprising Coast. By James Cerruti. Photos by Thomas Nebbia and James L. Amos. 366-393, Mar. 1971

SAPPORO, Japan:
Snow Festival in Japan's Far North. By Eiji Miyazawa. 824-833, Dec. 1968

SAPSUCKER WOODS, Cornell University's Exciting New Bird Sanctuary. By Arthur A. Allen. 530-551, Apr. 1962

SARA (Tribespeople):
Into the Heart of Africa. By Gertrude S. Weeks. 257-263, Aug. 1956

SARAWAK:
Ambassadors of Good Will: The Peace Corps. By Sargent Shriver and Peace Corps Volunteers. 297-345, Sept. 1964
Sarawak. By Edwin C. Price, Jr. 334-337
In Storied Lands of Malaysia. By Maurice Shadbolt. Photos by Winfield Parks. 734-783, Nov. 1963
Jungle Journeys in Sarawak. By Hedda Morrison. 710-736, May 1956

SARCOPHAGI:
Ancient Shipwreck Yields New Facts—and a Strange Cargo. By Peter Throckmorton. Photos by Kim Hart and Joseph J. Scherschel. 282-300, Feb. 1969
Fresh Treasures from Egypt's Ancient Sands. By Jefferson Caffery. Photos by David S. Boyer. 611-650, Nov. 1955

SARGASSO SEA:
Night Life in the Gulf Stream. By Paul A. Zahl. 391-418, Mar. 1954

SARGASSUM:
Adrift on a Raft of Sargassum. Photos by Robert F. Sisson. 188-199, Feb. 1976

SARGASSUM FISH:
Adrift on a Raft of Sargassum. Photos by Robert F. Sisson. 188-199, Feb. 1976

SARGON II, King (Assyria):
Ancient Mesopotamia: A Light That Did Not Fail. By E. A. Speiser. Paintings by H. M. Herget. 41-105, Jan. 1951

SARK (Island), English Channel:
Britain's "French" Channel Islands. By James Cerruti. Photos by James L. Amos. 710-740, May 1971

SARTWELL, FRANK: Author:
Mariner Scans a Lifeless Venus. Paintings by Davis Meltzer. 733-742, May 1963
Robots to the Moon. Paintings by Pierre Mion. 557-571, Oct. 1962

SASKATCHEWAN (Province), Canada:
Canada's Heartland, the Prairie Provinces. By W. E. Garrett. 443-489, Oct. 1970
The Canadian North: Emerging Giant. By David S. Boyer. 1-43, July 1968
Hunting Uranium Around the World. By Robert D. Nininger. Photos by Volkmar Wentzel. 533-558, Oct. 1954

SASS, HERBERT RAVENEL: Author:
South Carolina Rediscovered. Photos by Robert F. Sisson. 281-321, Mar. 1953

SATELLITE FINDER:
The National Geographic Society Satellite Finder (Map overlay). 808-809, Dec. 1957

SATELLITES:
How Man-made Satellites Can Affect Our Lives. By Joseph Kaplan. 791-810, Dec. 1957
The Next Frontier? By Isaac Asimov. Paintings by Pierre Mion. 76-89, July 1976
Satellites Gave Warning of Midwest Floods. By Peter T. White. Photos by Thomas A. DeFeo. 574-592, Oct. 1969
Space Satellites, Tools of Earth Research. By Heinz Haber. Paintings by William N. Palmstrom. 487-509, Apr. 1956
Telephone a Star: the Story of Communications Satellites. By Rowe Findley. 638-651, May 1962
See also DODGE; Landsat; Mariner Missions; Nimbus

SATMAR HASIDIM. *See* Hasidic Jews

SATURN (Planet):
Voyage to the Planets. By Kenneth F. Weaver. Paintings by Ludek Pesek. 147-193, Aug. 1970

SATURN V (Rocket):
First Explorers on the Moon: The Incredible Story of Apollo 11. 735-797, Dec. 1969
III. The Flight of Apollo 11: "One giant leap for mankind." By Kenneth F. Weaver. 752-787
V. Next Steps in Space. By Thomas O. Paine. 793-797
"A Most Fantastic Voyage": The Story of Apollo 8's Rendezvous With the Moon. By Sam C. Phillips. 593-631, May 1969

SAUDI ARABIA:
Africa and the Arabian Peninsula, map supplement. Mar. 1950
The Arab World. 712-732, Nov. 1958
The Arab World, Inc. By John J. Putman. Photos by Winfield Parks. 494-533, Oct. 1975
From America to Mecca on Airborne Pilgrimage. By Abdul Ghafur. 1-60, July 1953
In Search of Arabia's Past. By Peter Bruce Cornwall. 493-522, Apr. 1948
Saudi Arabia, Oil Kingdom. Photos by Maynard Owen Williams. 497-512
Oil, the Dwindling Treasure. By Noel Grove. Photos by Emory Kristof. 792-825, June 1974
Saudi Arabia: Beyond the Sands of Mecca. By Thomas J. Abercrombie. 1-53, Jan. 1966
The Sword and the Sermon. By Thomas J. Abercrombie. 3-45, July 1972
Included: Mecca; Medina
Troubled Waters East of Suez. By Ernest M. Eller. 483-522, Apr. 1954

SAVANNAH, N.S.:
Aboard the N.S. *Savannah:* World's First Nuclear Merchantman. By Alan Villiers. Photos by John E. Fletcher. 280-298, Aug. 1962

SAVE-THE-REDWOODS League. 682, May 1951; 510, Oct. 1957; 658, Nov. 1963; 15, 28, 44, July 1964; 60, 63, 67, July 1966

SAVING Brazil's Stone Age Tribes From Extinction. By Orlando and Claudio Villas Boas. Photos by W. Jesco von Puttkamer. 424-444, Sept. 1968

SAVING Earth's Oldest Living Things. By Andrew H. Brown. Photos by Raymond Moulin and author. 679-695, May 1951

SAVING Man's Wildlife Heritage. By John H. Baker. Photos by Robert F. Sisson. 581-620, Nov. 1954

SAVING the Ancient Temples at Abu Simbel. By Georg Gerster. Paintings by Robert W. Nicholson. 694-742, May 1966

SAVING the Nene, World's Rarest Goose. By S. Dillon Ripley. Photos by Jerry Chong. 745-754, Nov. 1965

SCALLOPS:

The Magic Lure of Sea Shells. By Paul A. Zahl. Photos by Victor R. Boswell, Jr. and author. 386-429, Mar. 1969

Shells Take You Over World Horizons. By Rutherford Platt. 33-84, July 1949

SCAMMON LAGOON, Baja California, Mexico:

The California Gray Whale Comes Back. By Theodore J. Walker. 394-415, Mar. 1971

Hunting the Heartbeat of a Whale. By Paul Dudley White and Samuel W. Matthews. 49-64, July 1956

SCANDINAVIA:

Friendly Flight to Northern Europe. By Lyndon B. Johnson. Photos by Volkmar Wentzel. 268-293, Feb. 1964

Northern Europe, map supplement. Aug. 1954
Scandinavia, Atlas series supplement. Apr. 1963
See also Denmark; Finland; Iceland; Norway; Sweden

SCAPEGOAT WILDERNESS, Montana:

Studying Grizzly Habitat by Satellite. By John Craighead. 148-158, July 1976

SCARLET IBIS:

New Scarlet Bird in Florida Skies. By Paul A. Zahl. 874-882, Dec. 1967

Search for the Scarlet Ibis in Venezuela. By Paul A. Zahl. 633-661, May 1950

SCENES of Postwar Finland. By La Verne Bradley. Photos by Jerry Waller. 233-264, Aug. 1947

SCHALLER, GEORGE B.: Author-Photographer:

Imperiled Phantom of Asian Peaks: First Photographs of Snow Leopards in the Wild. 702-707, Nov. 1971

Life with the King of Beasts. 494-519, Apr. 1969

SCHEFFER, VICTOR B.: Author:

Exploring the Lives of Whales. 752-767, Dec. 1976
Author-Photographer

The Fur Seal Herd Comes of Age. By Victor B. Scheffer and Karl W. Kenyon. 491-512, Apr. 1952

SCHELLBACH, LOUIS: Author:

Grand Canyon: Nature's Story of Creation. Photos by Justin Locke. 589-629, May 1955

SCHERSCHEL, JOSEPH J.: Photographer:

Ancient Shipwreck Yields New Facts—and a

SCHERSCHEL, JOSEPH J.: Photographer—*Continued*

Strange Cargo. By Peter Throckmorton. Photos by Kim Hart and Joseph J. Scherschel. 282-300, Feb. 1969

Andalusia, the Spirit of Spain. By Howard La Fay. 833-857, June 1975

Freedom's Progress South of the Sahara. By Howard La Fay. 603-637, Nov. 1962

Guatemala, Maya and Modern. By Louis de la Haba. 661-689, Nov. 1974

Hungary: Changing Homeland of a Tough, Romantic People. By Bart McDowell. Photos by Albert Moldvay and Joseph J. Scherschel. 443-483, Apr. 1971

Illinois: The City and the Plain. By Robert Paul Jordan. Photos by James L. Stanfield and Joseph J. Scherschel. 745-797, June 1967

Inside Europe Aboard *Yankee*. By Irving and Electa Johnson. 157-195, Aug. 1964

Lombardy's Lakes, Blue Jewels in Italy's Crown. By Franc Shor. 58-99, July 1968

Macao Clings to the Bamboo Curtain. By Jules B. Billard. 521-539, Apr. 1969

Mobile, Alabama's City in Motion. By William Graves. Photos by Joseph J. Scherschel and Robert W. Madden. 368-397, Mar. 1968

Preserving the Treasures of Olduvai Gorge. By Melvin M. Payne. 701-709, Nov. 1966

South Australia, Gateway to the Great Outback. By Howell Walker. 441-481, Apr. 1970

Sunny Corsica: French Morsel in the Mediterranean. By Robert Cairns. 401-423, Sept. 1973

Yankee Cruises Turkey's History-haunted Coast. By Irving and Electa Johnson. 798-845, Dec. 1969

SCHIRRA, WALTER M., Jr.:

Space Rendezvous, Milestone on the Way to the Moon. By Kenneth F. Weaver. 539-553, Apr. 1966

SCHMIDT, BERNHARD:

Mapping the Unknown Universe. By F. Barrows Colton. 401-420, Sept. 1950
Note: Bernhard Schmidt invented the "Big Schmidt" telescope.

SCHMITT, HARRISON H.: Author-Photographer:

Exploring Taurus-Littrow. 290-307, Sept. 1973
Photographer

"The Earth From Space," photo supplement. Painting on reverse. Sept. 1973

SCHNEEBERGER, JON: Author-Photographer:

Escalante Canyon—Wilderness at the Crossroads. 270-285, Aug. 1972

SCHOOL BULLETIN, NGS:

The *School Bulletin* is retired after 56 years; replaced by *WORLD*. 299, Sept. 1975

SCHOOL for Space Monkeys. 725-729, May 1961

SCHOOL for Survival. By Curtis E. LeMay. 565-602, May 1953

SCHOOLS:

The DAR Story. By Lonnelle Aikman. Photos by B. Anthony Stewart and John E. Fletcher. 565-598, Nov. 1951
Note: DAR partially supports a dozen schools and

SEMINOLES (Indians)—*Continued*

Florida's "Wild" Indians, the Seminole. By Louis Capron. Photos by Willard R. Culver. 819-840, Dec. 1956

Haunting Heart of the Everglades. By Andrew H. Brown. Photos by author and Willard R. Culver. 145-173, Feb. 1948

SENEGAL:

Freedom Speaks French in Ouagadougou. By John Scofield. 153-203, Aug. 1966

SENGSENG (People):

Blowgun Hunters of the South Pacific. By Jane C. Goodale. Photos by Ann Chowning. 793-817, June 1966

SENNETT, TOMAS: Photographer:

North for Oil: *Manhattan* Makes the Historic Northwest Passage. By Bern Keating. 374-391, Mar. 1970

SENTINEL RANGE, Antarctica:

First Conquest of Antarctica's Highest Peaks. By Nicholas B. Clinch. 836-863, June 1967

SENTINELESE (Negrito Tribe):

The Last Andaman Islanders. By Raghubir Singh. 66-91, July 1975

SEOUL, South Korea:

Roaming Korea South of the Iron Curtain. By Enzo de Chetelat. 777-808, June 1950

South Korea: Success Story in Asia. By Howard Sochurek. 301-345, Mar. 1969

South Korea: What Next? By Peter T. White. Photos by H. Edward Kim. 394-427, Sept. 1975

With the U. S. Army in Korea. By John R. Hodge. 829-840, June 1947

SEPIK RIVER, and Region, New Guinea:

Change Ripples New Guinea's Sepik River. By Malcolm S. Kirk. 354-381, Sept. 1973

To the Land of the Head-hunters. By E. Thomas Gilliard. 437-486, Oct. 1955

SEQUOIA GIGANTEA:

The General Sherman: Earth's Biggest Living Thing. 605-608, May 1958

SEQUOIA NATIONAL PARK, California:

Giant Sequoias Draw Millions to California Parks. By John Michael Kauffmann. Photos by B. Anthony Stewart. 147-187, Aug. 1959

Saving Earth's Oldest Living Things. By Andrew H. Brown. Photos by Raymond Moulin and author. 679-695, May 1951

SEQUOIA SEMPERVIRENS. See Redwoods

SEQUOIAS of the Sea: Giant Kelp. By Wheeler J. North. Photos by Bates Littlehales. 251-269, Aug. 1972

SERBIA (Republic), Yugoslavia:

Yugoslavia: Six Republics in One. By Robert Paul Jordan. Photos by James P. Blair. 589-633, May 1970

SERENGETI NATIONAL PARK, Tanzania:

African Wildlife: Man's Threatened Legacy. By Allan C. Fisher, Jr. Photos by Thomas Nebbia. Paintings by Ned Seidler. 147-187, Feb. 1972

Hyenas, the Hunters Nobody Knows. By Hans

SERENGETI NATIONAL PARK, Tanzania—*Continued*

Kruuk. Photos by Baron Hugo van Lawick. 44-57, July 1968

Life With the King of Beasts. By George B. Schaller. 494-519, Apr. 1969

Man of the Serengeti (Television film). 179A-179B, Feb. 1972

Tool-using Bird: The Egyptian Vulture. By Baroness Jane van Lawick-Goodall. Photos by Baron Hugo van Lawick. 631-641, May 1968

SERTÃO (Brazilian Backland):

Drought Bedevils Brazil's Sertão. By John Wilson. Photos by Gordon W. Gahan. 704-723, Nov. 1972

SETO NAIKAI. *See* Inland Sea, Japan

SETTON, KENNETH M.: Author:

A New Look at Medieval Europe. Paintings by Andre Durenceau and Birney Lettick. 799-859, Dec. 1962

900 Years Ago: the Norman Conquest. Photos by George F. Mobley. 206-251, Aug. 1966

SETÚBAL CANYON, Atlantic Ocean:

Four Years of Diving to the Bottom of the Sea. By Georges S. Houot. 715-731, May 1958

SETZLER, FRANK M.: Author:

Seeking the Secret of the Giants (Gravel Figures). Photos by Richard H. Stewart. 390-404, Sept. 1952

SEVEN Giants Who Led the Way. Paintings by Ned Seidler. Text by Rick Gore. 401-407, Sept. 1976

SEVEN Men Who Solved Riddles of the Cosmos. Paintings by Jean-Leon Huens. Text by Thomas Y. Canby. 627-633, May 1974

SEVENTH FLEET, U. S.:

Our Navy in the Far East. By Arthur W. Radford. Photos by J. Baylor Roberts. 537-577, Oct. 1953

Pacific Fleet: Force for Peace. By Franc Shor. Photos by W. E. Garrett. 283-335, Sept. 1959

Patrolling Troubled Formosa Strait. 573-588, Apr. 1955

75 YEARS Exploring Earth, Sea, and Sky: National Geographic Society Observes Its Diamond Anniversary. By Melvin M. Payne. 1-43, Jan. 1963

SEVERY, MERLE: Author:

Northwest Wonderland: Washington State. Photos by B. Anthony Stewart. 445-493, Apr. 1960

SEVILLA, Spain:

Andalusia, the Spirit of Spain. By Howard La Fay. Photos by Joseph J. Scherschel. 833-857, June 1975

Holy Week and the Fair in Sevilla. By Luis Marden. 499-530, Apr. 1951

SEYCHELLES, Tropic Isles of Eden. By Quentin Keynes. 670-695, Nov. 1959

'S GRAVENHAGE (The Hague), Netherlands:

Mid-century Holland Builds Her Future. By Sydney Clark. 747-778, Dec. 1950

The Netherlands: Nation at War With the Sea. By Alan Villiers. Photos by Adam Woolfitt. 530-571, Apr. 1968

SHA'AB RŪMI (Reef), Red Sea:

At Home in the Sea. By Jacques-Yves Cousteau. 465-507, Apr. 1964

SHACKLETON, SIR ERNEST H.:

Our Navy Explores Antarctica. By Richard E. Byrd. U. S. Navy official photos. 429-522, Oct. 1947

SHAD in the Shadow of Skyscrapers. By Dudley B. Martin. Photos by Luis Marden. 359-376, Mar. 1947

SHADBOLT, MAURICE: Author:

In Storied Lands of Malaysia. Photos by Winfield Parks. 734-783, Nov. 1963

New Zealand: Gift of the Sea. Photos by Brian Brake. 465-511, Apr. 1962

New Zealand's Cook Islands: Paradise in Search of a Future. Photos by William Albert Allard. 203-231, Aug. 1967

Western Samoa, the Pacific's Newest Nation. Photos by Robert B. Goodman. 573-602, Oct. 1962

The SHADOWY World of Salamanders. By Paul A. Zahl. 104-117, July 1972

SHAKERS (Religious Sect):

Home to the Enduring Berkshires. By Charles McCarry. Photos by Jonathan S. Blair. 196-221, Aug. 1970

SHAKESPEARE, WILLIAM:

The Britain That Shakespeare Knew. By Louis B. Wright. Photos by Dean Conger. 613-665, May 1964

The British Way. By Sir Evelyn Wrench. 421-541, Apr. 1949

Founders of Virginia. By Sir Evelyn Wrench. Photos by B. Anthony Stewart. 433-462, Apr. 1948
    Included: Stratford on Avon and *The Tempest*

Shakespeare's Britain, map supplement. May 1964

A Stroll to London. By Isobel Wylie Hutchison. Photos by B. Anthony Stewart. 171-204, Aug. 1950

The World of Elizabeth I. By Louis B. Wright. 668-709, Nov. 1968

See also Folger (Library); Henry E. Huntington Library and Art Gallery

SHALLENBERGER, ROBERT J.: Photographer:

Something's Fishy About That Fin! Photos by Robert J. Shallenberger and William D. Madden. 224-227, Aug. 1974

SHAN STATE, Burma. *See* Inle (Lake)

SHANGHAI, China:

Along the Yangtze, Main Street of China. By W. Robert Moore. 325-356, Mar. 1948

Eyes on the China Coast. By George W. Long. 505-512, Apr. 1953

This Is the China I Saw. By Jørgen Bisch. 591-639, Nov. 1964

SHARING the Lives of Wild Golden Eagles. By John Craighead. Photos by Charles and Derek Craighead. 420-439, Sept. 1967

SHARKS:

Calypso Explores for Underwater Oil. By Jacques-Yves Cousteau. 155-184, Aug. 1955
    Included: Aqualung divers' war on sharks in the Indian Ocean

SHARKS — *Continued*

Fish Men Explore a New World Undersea. By Jacques-Yves Cousteau. 431-472, Oct. 1952

Into the Lairs of "Sleeping" Sharks. By Eugenie Clark. Photos by David Doubilet. 570-584, Apr. 1975

Marineland, Florida's Giant Fish Bowl. By Gilbert Grosvenor La Gorce. Photos by Luis Marden. 679-694, Nov. 1952

The Red Sea's Sharkproof Fish. By Eugenie Clark. Photos by David Doubilet. 718-727, Nov. 1974

Sharks: Wolves of the Sea. By Nathaniel T. Kenney. 222-257, Feb. 1968

SHAWNEETOWN Forsakes the Ohio. By William H. Nicholas. Photos by J. Baylor Roberts. 273-288, Feb. 1948

SHEATS, DOROTHEA: Author-Photographer:

I Walked Some Irish Miles. 653-678, May 1951

See also Jones, Dorothea

SHEEP AND SHEEP RAISING:

America's "Meat on the Hoof." By William H. Nicholas. 33-72, Jan. 1952

Better Days for the Navajos. By Jack Breed. Photos by Charles W. Herbert. 809-847, Dec. 1958

Housewife at the End of the World. By Rae Natalie P. Goodall. Photos by James L. Stanfield. 130-150, Jan. 1971

Land of the Ancient Basques. By Robert Laxalt. Photos by William Albert Allard. 240-277, Aug. 1968

Lonely Sentinels of the American West: Basque Sheepherders. By Robert Laxalt. Photos by William Belknap, Jr. 870-888, June 1966

The Navajos. By Ralph Looney. Photos by Bruce Dale. 740-781, Dec. 1972

New South Wales, the State That Cradled Australia. By Howell Walker. Photos by David Moore. 591-635, Nov. 1967

New Zealand: Gift of the Sea. By Maurice Shadbolt. Photos by Brian Brake. 465-511, Apr. 1962

New Zealand's Bountiful South Island. By Peter Benchley. Photos by James L. Amos. 93-123, Jan. 1972

New Zealand's North Island: The Contented Land. By Charles McCarry. Photos by Bates Littlehales. 190-213, Aug. 1974

People and Penguins of the Faraway Falklands. By Olin Sewall Pettingill, Jr. 387-416, Mar. 1956

Scotland's Inner Hebrides: Isles of the Western Sea. By Kenneth MacLeish. Photos by R. Stephen Uzzell III. 690-717, Nov. 1974

Sheep Airlift in New Guinea. Photos by Ned Blood. 831-844, Dec. 1949

Winter Caravan to the Roof of the World. By Sabrina and Roland Michaud. 435-465, Apr. 1972

Yugoslavia: Six Republics in One. By Robert Paul Jordan. Photos by James P. Blair. 589-633, May 1970

See also Bighorn Sheep

SHEEP TREK:

Arizona Sheep Trek. By Francis R. Line. 457-478, Apr. 1950

Sheep Trek in the French Alps. By Maurice Moyal. Photos by Marcel Coen. 545-564, Apr. 1952

SHELLFISH. *See* Crustaceans; Mollusks

SHELLS (Mollusks):

Little Horses of the Sea. By Paul A. Zahl. 131-153, Jan. 1959
> Note: Sanibel Island, Florida, is one of the most famous shelling centers in the world.

The Magic Lure of Sea Shells. By Paul A. Zahl. Photos by Victor R. Boswell, Jr. and author. 386-429, Mar. 1969
> Contents: More than 100 kinds of shells

On Australia's Coral Ramparts. By Paul A. Zahl. 1-48, Jan. 1957

Shells Take You Over World Horizons. By Rutherford Platt. 33-84, July 1949
> Contents: *Conus, Helicostyla, Liguus, Murex, Patella, Pecten, Pelecypoda, Tellina, Terebra, Thais, Tridacna, Trochus, Voluta*

X-Rays Reveal the Inner Beauty of Shells. By Hilary B. Moore. 427-434, Mar. 1955

See also Abalone; Mother-of-Pearl; Nautilus, Chambered

SHENANDOAH NATIONAL PARK, Virginia:

Skyline Trail from Maine to Georgia. By Andrew H. Brown. Photos by Robert F. Sisson. 219-251, Aug. 1949

SHENANDOAH VALLEY, Virginia-West Virginia:

Appalachian Valley Pilgrimage. By Catherine Bell Palmer. Photos by Justin Locke. 1-32, July 1949

Shenandoah, I Long to Hear You. By Mike W. Edwards. Photos by Thomas Anthony DeFeo. 554-588, Apr. 1970

SHENYANG (Mukden), Manchuria:

In Manchuria Now. By W. Robert Moore. 389-414, Mar. 1947

SHEPARD, ALAN B., Jr.:

The Flight of *Freedom 7.* By Carmault B. Jackson, Jr. 416-431, Sept. 1961

Author

The Pilot's Story. Photos by Dean Conger. 432-444, Sept. 1961

Photographer

The Climb Up Cone Crater. By Alice J. Hall. Photos by Edgar D. Mitchell and Alan B. Shepard, Jr. 136-148, July 1971

SHERPAS:

Sherpaland, My Shangri-La. By Desmond Doig. 545-577, Oct. 1966

We Build a School for Sherpa Children. By Sir Edmund Hillary. 548-551, Oct. 1962

See also American Mount Everest Expedition; British Mount Everest Expedition

SHERWOOD GARDENS, Baltimore, Maryland:

Maytime Miracle in Sherwood Gardens. By Nathaniel T. Kenney. 700-709, May 1956

SHETLAND ISLANDS, Scotland:

Shetland and Orkney, Britain's Far North. By Isobel Wylie Hutchison. 519-536, Oct. 1953

Viking Festival in the Shetlands. Photos by Karl W. Gullers. 853-862, Dec. 1954

SHINTOISM:

Cruising Japan's Inland Sea. By Willard Price. 619-650, Nov. 1953

SHINTOISM—*Continued*

Kayak Odyssey: From the Inland Sea to Tokyo. By Dan Dimancescu. Photos by Christopher G. Knight. 295-337, Sept. 1967

See also Kansai; Kyoto

SHIPBUILDING:

Ships Through the Ages: A Saga of the Sea. By Alan Villiers. 494-545, Apr. 1963

See also Kyrenia Ship; *Mayflower II;* Vikings

SHIPLIFT:

Passage to Freedom in Viet Nam. By Gertrude Samuels. 858-874, June 1955

SHIPPING:

The Coming Revolution in Transportation. By Fredric C. Appel. Photos by Dean Conger. 301-341, Sept. 1969
> Included: Containerized cargo, Hovercraft, hydrofoils, supertankers

Here's New York Harbor. By Stuart E. Jones. Photos by Robert F. Sisson and David S. Boyer. 773-813, Dec. 1954

Louisiana Trades with the World. By Frederick Simpich. Photos by J. Baylor Roberts. 705-738, Dec. 1947

New Era on the Great Lakes. By Nathaniel T. Kenney. 439-490, Apr. 1959

New Orleans: Jambalaya on the Levee. By Harnett T. Kane. Photos by Justin Locke. 143-184, Feb. 1953

Norway, Land of the Generous Sea. By Edward J. Linehan. Photos by George F. Mobley. 1-43, July 1971

Portsmouth, Britannia's Sally Port. By Thomas Garner James. Photos by B. Anthony Stewart. 513-544, Apr. 1952

Work-hard, Play-hard Michigan. By Andrew H. Brown. 279-320, Mar. 1952

See also Tankers; U. S. Merchant Marine Academy; *and* Panama Canal; St. Lawrence Seaway; Suez Canal

SHIPS:

The Marvelous Maldive Islands. By Alan Villiers. 829-849, June 1957
> Included: Indian and Maldivian *baggalas*

Men, Ships, and the Sea. Book announced. 552-555, Oct. 1962

Milestones in My Arctic Journeys. By Willie Knutsen. 543-570, Oct. 1949
> Included: *Effie M. Morrissey, Endurance, Northland, Polarbjörn, Quest, Ringsel (En Avant)*

Ships Through the Ages: A Saga of the Sea. By Alan Villiers. 494-545, Apr. 1963

The Yankee Sailor Who Opened Japan. By Ferdinand Kuhn. 85-102, July 1953

See also Dhows; Galleons; Junks; Longships; Mohole, Project; Research Vessels; Sailing Vessels; Shipping; Shipwrecks; Submarines; Tall-Ships Race; U. S. Coast Guard; U. S. Navy; listing under Yachts; *and Af Chapman; Amphitrite; Beagle,* H.M.S.; *Bounty; Endeavour; J. W. Westcott; Mayflower II; Ra II; Savannah,* N.S.

SHIPWORMS, Saboteurs of the Sea. By F. G. Walton Smith. 559-566, Oct. 1956

SHIPWRECKS:

Ancient Shipwreck Yields New Facts—and a

SICILY (Island), Italy—*Continued*

Sicily, Where All the Songs Are Sad. By Howard La Fay. Photos by Jonathan Blair. 407-436, Mar. 1976

Sicily the Three-cornered. By Luis Marden. 1-48, Jan. 1955

SICKLES, NOEL: Artist:

Alone to Antarctica. By David Lewis. 808-821, Dec. 1973

SIDEWHEELER. *See Rhode Island*

SIEMEL, SASHA: Author-Photographer:

The Jungle Was My Home. 695-712, Nov. 1952

SIENA, Italy:

The Palio of Siena. By Edgar Erskine Hume. 231-244, Aug. 1951

The Renaissance Lives On in Tuscany. By Luis Marden. Photos by Albert Moldvay. 626-659, Nov. 1974
Included: The Palio

SIERRA LEONE. *See Freetown*

SIERRA MADRE OCCIDENTAL (Mountain Range), Mexico:

Found at Last: the Monarch's Winter Home. By Fred A. Urquhart. Photos by Bianca Lavies. 161-173, Aug. 1976

The Tarahumaras: Mexico's Long Distance Runners. By James Norman. Photos by David Hiser. 702-718, May 1976

SIERRA NEVADA (Mountains), California:

The Fabulous Sierra Nevada. By J. R. Challacombe. 825-843, June 1954

Golden Ghosts of the Lost Sierra. By Robert Laxalt. Photos by David Hiser. 332-353, Sept. 1973

John Muir's Wild America. By Harvey Arden. Photos by Dewitt Jones. 433-461, Apr. 1973

Mexico to Canada on the Pacific Crest Trail. By Mike W. Edwards. Photos by David Hiser. 741-779, June 1971

School for Survival. By Curtis E. LeMay. 565-602, May 1953

Sierra High Trip. By David R. Brower. 844-868, June 1954

See also Kings Canyon National Park; Yosemite National Park

SIFFRE, MICHEL: Author-Photographer:

Six Months Alone in a Cave (Biorhythm Research). 426-435, Mar. 1975

SIKANG (Former Chinese Province):

Adventures in Lololand. By Rennold L. Lowy. 105-118, Jan. 1947

A SIKH Discovers America. By Joginder Singh Rekhi. 558-590, Oct. 1964

SIKHS:

India's Energetic Sikhs. By John E. Frazer. Photos by James P. Blair. 528-541, Oct. 1972

SIKKIM:

Gangtok, Cloud-wreathed Himalayan Capital. By John Scofield. 698-713, Nov. 1970

Sikkim. By Desmond Doig. 398-429, Mar. 1963

Wedding of Two Worlds. By Lee E. Battaglia. 708-727, Nov. 1963

SILK:

A Lady From China's Past. Photos from *China Pictorial*. Text by Alice J. Hall. 660-681, May 1974

Thailand Bolsters Its Freedom. By W. Robert Moore. 811-849, June 1961

SILKWORMS:

Silkworms in England Spin for the Queen. By John E. H. Nolan. 689-704, May 1953

Spain's Silkworm Gut. By Luis Marden. 100-108, July 1951

This Is the China I Saw. By Jørgen Bisch. 591-639, Nov. 1964

SILVER. *See Slot ter Hooge;* Spanish Treasure

SILVER DART I and II (Airplanes):

Canada's Winged Victory: the *Silver Dart*. By Gilbert M. Grosvenor. 254-267, Aug. 1959

SILVERSMITHS:

Better Days for the Navajos. By Jack Breed. Photos by Charles W. Herbert. 809-847, Dec. 1958

SILVERSTONE, MARILYN: Photographer:

Royal Wedding at Jaisalmer. 66-79, Jan. 1965

SIMLA, Trinidad:

Keeping House for Tropical Butterflies. By Jocelyn Crane. Photos by M. Woodbridge Williams. 193-217, Aug. 1957

SIMONS, VERA: Author:

Laboratory in a Dirty Sky. By Rudolf J. Engelmann and Vera Simons. 616-621, Nov. 1976

SIMPICH, FREDERICK: Author:

Around the "Great Lakes of the South." Photos by J. Baylor Roberts. 463-491, Apr. 1948

California, Horn of Plenty. Photos by Willard R. Culver. 553-594, May 1949

4-H Boys and Girls Grow More Food. 551-582, Nov. 1948

From Indian Canoes to Submarines at Key West. Photos by J. Baylor Roberts. 41-72, Jan. 1950

Here Come the Marines. 647-672, Nov. 1950

Louisiana Trades with the World. Photos by J. Baylor Roberts. 705-738, Dec. 1947

Mapping the Nation's Breadbasket. 831-849, June 1948

So Much Happens Along the Ohio River. Photos by Justin Locke. 177-212, Feb. 1950

South Dakota Keeps Its West Wild. 555-588, May 1947

Uncle Sam Bends a Twig in Germany. Photos by J. Baylor Roberts. 529-550, Oct. 1948

With Uncle Sam and John Bull in Germany. 117-140, Jan. 1949

SIMPICH, FREDERICK, Jr.: Author:

Because It Rains on Hawaii. 571-610, Nov. 1949

Changing Formosa, Green Island of Refuge. Photos by Horace Bristol. 327-364, Mar. 1957

Fountain of Fire in Hawaii. Photos by Robert B. Goodman and Robert Wenkam. 303-327, Mar. 1960

Hawaii, U.S.A. Photos by Thomas Nebbia. 1-45, July 1960

Honolulu, Mid-ocean Capital. Photos by B. Anthony Stewart. 577-624, May 1954

SIMPSON, HUGH: Photographer:

First Woman Across Greenland's Ice. By Myrtle Simpson. 264-279, Aug. 1967

SIMPSON, MYRTLE: Author:

First Woman Across Greenland's Ice. Photos by Hugh Simpson. 264-279, Aug. 1967

SINAI, Mount, and Peninsula, Egypt:

In Search of Moses. By Harvey Arden. Photos by Nathan Benn. 2-37, Jan. 1976

Island of Faith in the Sinai Wilderness (St. Catherine's Monastery). By George H. Forsyth. Photos by Robert F. Sisson. 82-106, Jan. 1964

Mount Sinai's Holy Treasures (St. Catherine's Monastery). By Kurt Weitzmann. Photos by Fred Anderegg. 109-127, Jan. 1964

New Life for the Troubled Suez Canal. By William Graves. Photos by Jonathan Blair. 792-817, June 1975

Sinai Sheds New Light on the Bible. By Henry Field. Photos by William B. and Gladys Terry. 795-815, Dec. 1948

See also Ras Muhammad

SING-SING (Fair):

Australian New Guinea. By John Scofield. 604-637, May 1962

Blowgun Hunters of the South Pacific. By Jane C. Goodale. Photos by Ann Chowning. 793-817, June 1966

New Guinea Festival of Faces. By Malcolm S. Kirk. 148-156, July 1969

New Guinea's Rare Birds and Stone Age Men. By E. Thomas Gilliard. 421-488, Apr. 1953

To the Land of the Head-hunters. By E. Thomas Gilliard. 437-486, Oct. 1955

SINGAPORE:

In Storied Lands of Malaysia. By Maurice Shadbolt. Photos by Winfield Parks. 734-783, Nov. 1963

Malaya Meets Its Emergency. By George W. Long. Photos by J. Baylor Roberts and author. 185-228, Feb. 1953

Singapore, Reluctant Nation. By Kenneth MacLeish. Photos by Winfield Parks. 269-300, Aug. 1966

SINGH, ANNE DE HENNING: Author:

Sea Gypsies of the Philippines. Photos by Raghubir Singh. 659-677, May 1976

SINGH, RAGHUBIR: Author-Photographer:

The Last Andaman Islanders. 66-91, July 1975

Photographer

Calcutta, India's Maligned Metropolis. By Peter T. White. 534-563, Apr. 1973

The Ganges, River of Faith. By John J. Putman. 445-483, Oct. 1971

Sea Gypsies of the Philippines. By Anne de Henning Singh. 659-677, May 1976

SINKIANG:

The Caves of the Thousand Buddhas. By Franc and Jean Shor. 383-415, Mar. 1951
    Included: Urumchi, Turfan, and Qomul (Hami), visited on way to the caves in Kansu Province

How the Kazakhs Fled to Freedom. By Milton J. Clark. 621-644, Nov. 1954

SINT EUSTATIUS (Island), Netherlands Antilles:

A Fresh Breeze Stirs the Leewards. By Carleton Mitchell. Photos by Winfield Parks. 488-537, Oct. 1966

The Netherlands Antilles: Holland in the Caribbean. By James Cerruti. Photos by Emory Kristof. 115-146, Jan. 1970

SINT MAARTEN (Island), Netherlands Antilles:

The Netherlands Antilles: Holland in the Caribbean. By James Cerruti. Photos by Emory Kristof. 115-146, Jan. 1970

SIOUX FALLS, South Dakota:

Satellites Gave Warning of Midwest Floods. By Peter T. White. Photos by Thomas A. DeFeo. 574-592, Oct. 1969

SIOUX INDIANS:

Back to the Historic Black Hills. By Leland D. Case. Photos by Bates Littlehales. 479-509, Oct. 1956

South Dakota Keeps Its West Wild. By Frederick Simpich. 555-588, May 1947

SIPLE, GREG and JUNE:

Bikepacking Across Alaska and Canada. By Dan Burden. 682-695, May 1973

SIPLE, PAUL A.:

All-out Assault on Antarctica. By Richard E. Byrd. 141-180, Aug. 1956

Antarctic Scientist Honored by the Society. 792-793, June 1958

Our Navy Explores Antarctica. By Richard E. Byrd. U. S. Navy official photos. 429-522, Oct. 1947

To the Men at South Pole Station. By Richard E. Byrd. 1-4, July 1957

Author

Man's First Winter at the South Pole. 439-478, Apr. 1958

We Are Living at the South Pole. Photos by David S. Boyer. 5-35, July 1957

SIR FRANCIS DRAKE. By Alan Villiers. Photos by Gordon W. Gahan. 216-253, Feb. 1975

SISSON, ROBERT F.:

Octopus-training experiments. 788-789, 792, 794-795, Dec. 1971

Photographic feats. 880, Dec. 1961; 901, Dec. 1962; 107, Jan. 1970; 692, Nov. 1970; 265, 266, Feb. 1971; 727, 748, June 1973

Author-Photographer

Aha! It Really Works! 143-147, Jan. 1974

At Home With the Bulldog Ant. 62-75, July 1974
    Face-to-Face With a World of Ants. 72-75

Frost, Nature's Icing. 398-405, Mar. 1976

Life Cycle of a Coral. 780-793, June 1973

Snowflakes to Keep. 104-111, Jan. 1970

The Spider That Lives Under Water. 694-701, May 1972

The Wasp That Plays Cupid to a Fig. 690-697, Nov. 1970

The World of My Apple Tree. 836-847, June 1972

Photographer

Adrift on a Raft of Sargassum. 188-199, Feb. 1976

Algeria: France's Stepchild, Problem and Promise. By Howard La Fay. 768-795, June 1960

SOC (Sub-ice Observation Chamber):

Stalking Seals Under Antarctic Ice. By Carleton Ray. 54-65, Jan. 1966

SOCHUREK, HOWARD: Author-Photographer:

Air Rescue Behind Enemy Lines (North Viet Nam). 346-369, Sept. 1968

American Special Forces in Action in Viet Nam. 38-65, Jan. 1965

Berlin, on Both Sides of the Wall. 1-47, Jan. 1970

Slow Train Through Viet Nam's War. 412-444, Sept. 1964

South Korea: Success Story in Asia. 301-345, Mar. 1969

Viet Nam's Montagnards. 443-487, Apr. 1968

The Volga, Russia's Mighty River Road. 579-613, May 1973

Photographer

The Laser's Bright Magic. By Thomas Meloy. 858-881, Dec. 1966

World War I Aircraft Fly Again in Rhinebeck's Rickety Rendezvous. By Harvey Arden. 578-587, Oct. 1970

SOCIETY Honors the Conquerors of Antarctica. 589-590, Apr. 1959

SOCIETY ISLANDS, South Pacific Ocean:

The *Yankee*'s Wander-world. By Irving and Electa Johnson. 1-50, Jan. 1949

See also Tahiti

The SOCIETY Reports to Its Members on Russia Today. The Editor. 351, Sept. 1959

The SOCIETY'S Great 75th Anniversary Issue. Introduction by Melville Bell Grosvenor. 459, Oct. 1963

The SOCIETY'S Hubbard Medal Awarded to Commander MacMillan. 563-564, Apr. 1953

SOCKEYE SALMON:

The Incredible Salmon. By Clarence P. Idyll. Photos by Robert F. Sisson. Paintings by Walter A. Weber. 195-219, Aug. 1968

SOIL EROSION:

Erosion, Trojan Horse of Greece. By F. G. Renner. 793-812, Dec. 1947

This Land of Ours — How Are We Using It? By Peter T. White. Photos by Emory Kristof. 20-67, July 1976

Water for the World's Growing Needs. By Herbert B. Nichols and F. Barrows Colton. 269-286, Aug. 1952

See also Forests and Reforestation; U. S. Soil Conservation Service

SOLAR ECLIPSE, Nature's Super Spectacular. By Donald H. Menzel and Jay M. Pasachoff. 222-233, Aug. 1970

The SOLAR ECLIPSE From a Jet. By Wolfgang B. Klemperer. 785-796, Nov. 1963

SOLAR ENERGY:

The Next Frontier? By Isaac Asimov. Paintings by Pierre Mion. 76-89, July 1976

The Search for Tomorrow's Power. By Kenneth F. Weaver. Photos by Emory Kristof. 650-681, Nov. 1972

Solar Energy, the Ultimate Powerhouse. By John L. Wilhelm. Photos by Emory Kristof. 381-397, Mar. 1976

The Sun. By Herbert Friedman. 713-743, Nov. 1965

What's Happening to Our Climate? By Samuel W. Matthews. 576-615, Nov. 1976

SOLAR SYSTEM. *See* Comets; Moon; Planets; Sun

SOLE:

The Red Sea's Sharkproof Fish. By Eugenie Clark. Photos by David Doubilet. 718-727, Nov. 1974

The SOLEMN, Sociable Puffins. By R. M. Lockley. 414-422, Sept. 1954

SOLHEIM, WILHELM G., II: Author:

New Light on a Forgotten Past. 330-339, Mar. 1971

SOLOMON ISLANDS, South Pacific Ocean:

A Teen-ager Sails the World Alone. By Robin Lee Graham. 445-491, Oct. 1968

Yankee Roams the Orient. By Irving and Electa Johnson. 327-370, Mar. 1951

See also Florida Island

SOLVING Life Secrets of the Sailfish. By Gilbert Voss. Photos by B. Anthony Stewart. Paintings by Craig Phillips. 859-872, June 1956

SOLVING the Mystery of Mexico's Great Stone Spheres. By Matthew W. Stirling. Photos by David F. Cupp. 295-300, Aug. 1969

SOLVING the Riddle of Chubb Crater. By V. Ben Meen. Photos by Richard H. Stewart. 1-32, Jan. 1952

SOLVING the Riddles of Wetherill Mesa. By Douglas Osborne. Paintings by Peter V. Bianchi. 155-195, Feb. 1964

SOMETHING'S Fishy About That Fin! Photos by Robert J. Shallenberger and William D. Madden. 224-227, Aug. 1974

SONAKUL, D.: Author:

Pageantry of the Siamese Stage. Photos by W. Robert Moore. 201-212, Feb. 1947

SONAR (Sound Navigation and Ranging):

Down to *Thresher* by Bathyscaph. By Donald L. Keach. 764-777, June 1964

From Indian Canoes to Submarines at Key West. By Frederick Simpich. Photos by J. Baylor Roberts. 41-72, Jan. 1950

Our Navy's Long Submarine Arm. By Allan C. Fisher, Jr. 613-636, Nov. 1952

SONAR ABILITY. *See* Bats; Killer Whales; Oilbirds; Porpoises; Weddell Seals

SONGHAIS (Tribespeople):

The Niger: River of Sorrow, River of Hope. By Georg Gerster. 152-189, Aug. 1975

SONGS:

Hunting Folk Songs in the Hebrides. By Margaret Shaw Campbell. 249-272, Feb. 1947

Hunting Musical Game in West Africa. By Arthur S. Alberts. 262-282, Aug. 1951

SONOMA VALLEY, California. *See* Valley of the Moon

SOUTH SEA ISLANDS — *Continued*

See also Melanesia; Micronesia; Polynesia

SOUTH SHETLAND ISLANDS, Antarctica. *See* Deception Island

SOUTH to Mexico City. By W. E. Garrett. 145-193, Aug. 1968

SOUTH UIST (Island), Scotland:

Isles on the Edge of the Sea: Scotland's Outer Hebrides. By Kenneth MacLeish. Photos by Thomas Nebbia. 676-711, May 1970

SOUTH VIET NAM. *See* Viet Nam, South

SOUTHAMPTON, THIRD EARL OF (Henry Wriothesley):

Founders of Virginia. By Sir Evelyn Wrench. Photos by B. Anthony Stewart. 433-462, Apr. 1948

SOUTHAMPTON ISLAND, Northwest Territories, Canada:

Twelve National Geographic Society Scientific Projects Under Way. 869-870, June 1954

Vanished Mystery Men of Hudson Bay. By Henry B. Collins. 669-687, Nov. 1956

SOUTHEAST (Region), U. S.:

Close-up: U.S.A., The Southeast, map supplement. Text on reverse. Oct. 1975

Southeastern United States, Atlas series supplement. Jan. 1958

Southeastern United States, map supplement. Feb. 1947

See also names of individual states

SOUTHEAST ASIA:

The Lands and Peoples of Southeast Asia. 295-365, Mar. 1971
 1. Mosaic of Cultures. By Peter T. White. Photos by W. E. Garrett. 296-329
 2. New Light on a Forgotten Past. By Wilhelm G. Solheim II. 330-339
 3. Pagan, on the Road to Mandalay. By W. E. Garrett. 343-365

The Mekong, River of Terror and Hope. By Peter T. White. Photos by W. E. Garrett. 737-787, Dec. 1968

The Peoples of Mainland Southeast Asia, double-sided map supplement. Mar. 1971

Southeast Asia, Atlas series supplement. May 1961

Southeast Asia, map supplement. Sept. 1955

Southeast Asia, map supplement. Dec. 1968

Viet Nam, Cambodia, Laos, and Eastern Thailand, map supplement. Text on reverse. Jan. 1965

Viet Nam, Cambodia, Laos, and Thailand, map supplement. Feb. 1967

See also Burma; Cambodia; Hong Kong; Indochina; Indonesia; Laos; Macao; Malaysia; Philippines; Singapore; Taiwan; Thailand; Viet Nam

SOUTHERN California's Trial by Mud and Water. By Nathaniel T. Kenney. Photos by Bruce Dale. 552-573, Oct. 1969

SOUTHERN RAILWAY SYSTEM:

Dixie Spins the Wheel of Industry. By William H. Nicholas. Photos by J. Baylor Roberts. 281-324, Mar. 1949

SOUTHWEST (Region), U. S.:

Southwestern United States, Atlas series supplement. Nov. 1959

SOUTHWEST (Region), U. S. — *Continued*

Southwestern United States, map supplement. Dec. 1948

Two Wheels Along the Mexican Border. By William Albert Allard. 591-635, May 1971

See also names of individual states; *and* Colorado (River); Four Corners Country; *and* Pre-Columbian Civilization

SOUTHWEST AUSTRALIA'S Wild Gardens: Bizarre and Beautiful. By Paul A. Zahl. 858-868, Dec. 1976

SOYUZ-APOLLO MISSION:

Apollo-Soyuz: Handclasp in Space. By Thomas Y. Canby. 183-187, Feb. 1976

SPACE COLONIES:

The Next Frontier? By Isaac Asimov. Paintings by Pierre Mion. 76-89, July 1976

SPACE FLIGHTS AND RESEARCH:

Awesome Views of the Forbidding Moonscape. 233-239, Feb. 1969

Behold the Computer Revolution. By Peter T. White. Photos by Bruce Dale and Emory Kristof. 593-633, Nov. 1970

The Long, Lonely Leap. By Joseph W. Kittinger, Jr. Photos by Volkmar Wentzel. 854-873, Dec. 1960

Man's Conquest of Space. Special Publication announced. 844-849, June 1968

The Sun. By Herbert Friedman. 713-743, Nov. 1965
 Included: U. S. Naval Research Laboratory studies

We Saw the World From the Edge of Space. By Malcolm D. Ross. Ground photos by Walter Meayers Edwards. 671-685, Nov. 1961

See also Apollo Missions; Gemini Missions; Mariner Missions; Mercury Missions; Pioneer Probes; Ranger Spacecraft; Rockets; Satellites; Skylab Missions; Surveyor Spacecraft; Viking Lander; Voyager; X-15

SPACE MEDICINE:

Aviation Medicine on the Threshold of Space. By Allan C. Fisher, Jr. Photos by Luis Marden. 241-278, Aug. 1955

The Flight of *Freedom 7.* By Carmault B. Jackson, Jr. 416-431, Sept. 1961

The Making of an Astronaut. By Robert R. Gilruth. 122-144, Jan. 1965

School for Space Monkeys. 725-729, May 1961

Skylab, Outpost on the Frontier of Space. By Thomas Y. Canby. Photos by the nine mission astronauts. 441-469, Oct. 1974

We Saw the World From the Edge of Space. By Malcolm D. Ross. Ground photos by Walter Meayers Edwards. 671-685, Nov. 1961

See also Biorhythm Research; Tektite II

SPACE PIONEERS of NASA Journey Into Tomorrow. By Allan C. Fisher, Jr. Photos by Dean Conger. 48-89, July 1960

SPACE RENDEZVOUS, Milestone on the Way to the Moon. By Kenneth F. Weaver. 539-553, Apr. 1966

SPACE SATELLITES. *See* Satellites

SPACE STATIONS:

The Next Frontier? By Isaac Asimov. Paintings by Pierre Mion. 76-89, July 1976

The **SPECTACULAR** North Cascades: New National Park Proposed. By Nathaniel T. Kenney. Photos by James P. Blair. 642-667, May 1968

SPECTACULAR Rio de Janeiro. By Hernane Tavares de Sá. Photos by Charles Allmon. 289-328, Mar. 1955

SPECTACULAR Treasures From a Chinese Tomb. Photos from *China Pictorial*. Text by Alice J. Hall. 660-681, May 1974

SPEISER, E. A.: Author:
Ancient Mesopotamia: A Light That Did Not Fail. Paintings by H. M. Herget. 41-105, Jan. 1951

SPELEOLOGY:
Exploring America Underground. By Charles E. Mohr. 803-837, June 1964
Probing Ice Caves of the Pyrenees. By Norbert Casteret. 391-404, Mar. 1953

SPENCER, DONALD A.: Author-Photographer:
Porcupines, Rambling Pincushions. 247-264, Aug. 1950

SPICE ISLANDS. *See* Moluccas

SPICES:
Clove-scented Zanzibar. By W. Robert Moore. 261-278, Feb. 1952
Spices, the Essence of Geography. By Stuart E. Jones. 401-420, Mar. 1949

SPID (Submersible Portable Inflatable Dwelling):
The Deepest Days. By Robert Sténuit. 534-547, Apr. 1965
Outpost Under the Ocean. By Edwin A. Link. Photos by Bates Littlehales. 530-533, Apr. 1965

SPIDERS:
The Spider That Lives Under Water. By Robert F. Sisson. 694-701, May 1972
Spiders. Children's book announced. 728-730, Nov. 1974
What's So Special About Spiders? By Paul A. Zahl. 190-219, Aug. 1971

SPIEGEL, TED: Photographer:
Canada's Window on the Pacific: The British Columbia Coast. By Jules B. Billard. 338-375, Mar. 1972
George Washington: The Man Behind the Myths. By Howard La Fay. 90-111, July 1976
Kansas City, Heartland U.S.A. By Rowe Findley. 112-139, July 1976
The Loyalists. By Kent Britt. 510-539, Apr. 1975
The Philippines, Freedom's Pacific Frontier. By Robert de Roos. 301-351, Sept. 1966
Reunited Jerusalem Faces Its Problems. By Kenneth MacLeish. 835-871, Dec. 1968
Scientists Ride Ice Islands on Arctic Odysseys. By Lowell Thomas, Jr. 670-691, Nov. 1965
Those Proper and Other Bostonians. By Joseph Judge. 352-381, Sept. 1974
The Vikings. By Howard La Fay. 492-541, Apr. 1970
The World of Elizabeth I. By Louis B. Wright. 668-709, Nov. 1968

SPIER, PETER: Artist:
A Traveler's Tale of Ancient Tikal. Text by Alice J. Hall. 799-811, Dec. 1975

SPINY BABBLER (Bird):
Peerless Nepal—A Naturalist's Paradise. By S. Dillon Ripley. Photos by Volkmar Wentzel. 1-40, Jan. 1950

SPINY LOBSTERS:
New Life for the "Loneliest Isle" (Tristan da Cunha). By Lewis Lewis. 105-116, Jan. 1950
Strange March of the Spiny Lobster. By William F. Herrnkind. Photos by Rick Frehsee and Bruce Mounier. 819-831, June 1975
Tektite II: Science's Window on the Sea. By John G. VanDerwalker. Photos by Bates Littlehales. 256-289, Aug. 1971

SPIRITS of Change Capture the Karens. By Peter Kunstadter. 267-285, Feb. 1972

SPITSBERGEN Mines Coal Again. 113-120, July 1948

SPLIT, Yugoslavia:
Yugoslavia, Between East and West. By George W. Long. Photos by Volkmar Wentzel. 141-172, Feb. 1951
Yugoslavia's Window on the Adriatic. By Gilbert M. Grosvenor. 219-247, Feb. 1962

SPLIT-SECOND Time Runs Today's World. By F. Barrows Colton and Catherine Bell Palmer. 399-428, Sept. 1947

SPLIT Seconds in the Lives of Birds. By Arthur A. Allen. 681-706, May 1954

SPONGE-FISHING INDUSTRY:
On the Winds of the Dodecanese. By Jean and Franc Shor. 351-390, Mar. 1953
Sponge Fishermen of Tarpon Springs. By Jennie E. Harris. 119-136, Jan. 1947

SPOONBILLS. *See* Roseate Spoonbills

SPORTS:
Around the "Great Lakes of the South." By Frederick Simpich. Photos by J. Baylor Roberts. 463-491, Apr. 1948
Included: Boating, Fishing, Horseback riding, Swimming
Long Island Outgrows the Country. By Howell Walker. Photos by B. Anthony Stewart. 279-326, Mar. 1951
Included: Baseball, Fishing, Golf, Lawn bowling, Sailing, Swimming, Tennis
Mexico's Booming Capital. By Mason Sutherland. Photos by Justin Locke. 785-824, Dec. 1951
Included: Baseball, Bowling, Bullfighting, Football, Swimming
See also Olympic Games; *and* names of individual sports

SPORTS-MINDED Melbourne, Host to the Olympics. 688-693, Nov. 1956

The **SPOTLIGHT** Swings to Suez. By W. Robert Moore. 105-115, Jan. 1952

SPRING, BOB and IRA: Photographers:
Climbing Our Northwest Glaciers. 103-114, July 1953

SPRING CREEK HUTTERITE COLONY, Montana:
The Hutterites, Plain People of the West. By William Albert Allard. 98-125, July 1970

SPRINGFIELD, Illinois:
Illinois—Healthy Heart of the Nation. By Leo A.

SPRINGFIELD, Illinois — *Continued*

Borah. Photos by B. Anthony Stewart and Willard R. Culver. 781-820, Dec. 1953

Vacation Tour Through Lincoln Land. By Ralph Gray. 141-184, Feb. 1952

SPRINGTIME Comes to Yellowstone National Park. By Paul A. Zahl. 761-779, Dec. 1956

SPRINGTIME of Hope in Poland. By Peter T. White. Photos by James P. Blair. 467-501, Apr. 1972

SPRUNT, ALEXANDER, Jr.: Author:

Blizzard of Birds: The Tortugas Terns. 213-230, Feb. 1947

SQUARE-RIGGERS:

By Square-rigger from Baltic to Bicentennial. By Kenneth Garrett. 824-857, Dec. 1976

Included: *Amerigo Vespucci, Christian Radich, Danmark, Dar Pomorza, Eagle, Esmeralda, Gazela Primeiro, Gloria, Gorch Fock, Juan Sebastián de Elcano, Kruzenshtern, Libertad, Mircea, Nippon Maru, Sagres II, Tovarishch*

Windjamming Around New England. By Tom Horgan. Photos by Robert F. Sisson. 141-169, Aug. 1950

See also Charles W. Morgan; Eagle; Georg Stage; Joseph Conrad; Pamir; Yankee (Brigantine)

SQUAWS Along the Yukon. By Ginny Hill Wood. 245-265, Aug. 1957

SQUIDS:

Nature's Night Lights: Probing the Secrets of Bioluminescence. By Paul A. Zahl. 45-69, July 1971

Squids: Jet-powered Torpedoes of the Deep. By Gilbert L. Voss. Photos by Robert F. Sisson. 386-411, Mar. 1967

SQUIRRELS, Flying:

"Flying" Squirrels, Nature's Gliders. By Ernest P. Walker. 663-674, May 1947

SRI LANKA. *See* former name, Ceylon

SRINAGAR, Kashmir:

The Idyllic Vale of Kashmir. By Volkmar Wentzel. 523-550, Apr. 1948

STAFFORD, MARIE PEARY:

Gold Medal Awarded to Mrs. Robert E. Peary. 148, Jan. 1956

Note: Mrs. Stafford accepted the Special Gold Medal on behalf of her mother.

Author

The Peary Flag Comes to Rest. 519-532, Oct. 1954

STAFFORD, THOMAS P.:

Apollo-Soyuz: Handclasp in Space. By Thomas Y. Canby. 183-187, Feb. 1976

Space Rendezvous, Milestone on the Way to the Moon. By Kenneth F. Weaver. 539-553, Apr. 1966

STAIB, BJØRN O.: Author:

North Toward the Pole on Skis. 254-281, Feb. 1965

STAINED GLASS:

Chartres: Legacy From the Age of Faith. By Kenneth MacLeish. Photos by Dean Conger. 857-882, Dec. 1969

STALINGRAD, U.S.S.R. *See* Volgograd

STALKING Central Africa's Wildlife. By T. Donald Carter. Paintings by Walter A. Weber. 264-286, Aug. 1956

STALKING Seals Under Antarctic Ice. By Carleton Ray. 54-65, Jan. 1966

STALKING the Great Indian Rhino. By Lee Merriam Talbot. 389-398, Mar. 1957

STALKING the Mountain Lion — to Save Him. By Maurice G. Hornocker. 638-655, Nov. 1969

STALKING the West's Wild Foods. By Euell Gibbons. Photos by David Hiser. 186-199, Aug. 1973

STALKING Wild Foods on a Desert Isle. By Euell Gibbons. Photos by David Hiser. 47-63, July 1972

STAMPS, Postage:

Everyone's Servant, the Post Office. By Allan C. Fisher, Jr. Photos by Volkmar Wentzel. 121-152, July 1954

Liechtenstein Thrives on Stamps. By Ronald W. Clark. 105-112, July 1948

STANDARD OIL COMPANY OF CALIFORNIA:

Barehanded Battle to Cleanse the Bay. By Peter T. White. Photos by Jonathan S. Blair. 866-881, June 1971

STANDARD WEIGHTS AND MEASURES:

Uncle Sam's House of 1,000 Wonders (U. S. Bureau of Standards). By Lyman J. Briggs and F. Barrows Colton. 755-784, Dec. 1951

STANFIELD, JAMES L.: Photographer:

Big Bend: Jewel in the Texas Desert. By Nathaniel T. Kenney. 104-133, Jan. 1968

Canadian Rockies, Lords of a Beckoning Land. By Alan Phillips. 353-393, Sept. 1966

Gold, the Eternal Treasure. By Peter T. White. 1-51, Jan. 1974

Golden Masterpieces. 29-39

Housewife at the End of the World. By Rae Natalie P. Goodall. 130-150, Jan. 1971

Human Treasures of Japan. By William Graves. 370-379, Sept. 1972

Illinois: The City and the Plain. By Robert Paul Jordan. Photos by James L. Stanfield and Joseph J. Scherschel. 745-797, June 1967

In the Wake of Darwin's *Beagle*. By Alan Villiers. 449-495, Oct. 1969

The Investiture of Great Britain's Prince of Wales. By Allan C. Fisher, Jr. Photos by James L. Stanfield and Adam Woolfitt. 698-715, Nov. 1969

Iran's Shah Crowns Himself and His Empress. By Franc Shor. Photos by James L. Stanfield and Winfield Parks. 301-321, Mar. 1968

Life's Tempo on Nantucket. By Peter Benchley. 810-839, June 1970

Living in a Japanese Village. By William Graves. 668-693, May 1972

Mark Twain: Mirror of America. By Noel Grove. 300-337, Sept. 1975

More of Sea Than of Land: The Bahamas. By Carleton Mitchell. 218-267, Feb. 1967

The Nation's River. By Allan C. Fisher, Jr. 432-469, Oct. 1976

A Good Life on the Potomac. 470-479

New Orleans and Her River. By Joseph Judge. 151-187, Feb. 1971

STIRLING, MATTHEW W.: Author—*Continued*
Richard H. Stewart. 271-290, Aug. 1953

Indians of the Far West (United States). Paintings by W. Langdon Kihn. 175-200, Feb. 1948

Nomads of the Far North. Paintings by W. Langdon Kihn. 471-504, Oct. 1949

On the Trail of La Venta Man. Photos by Richard H. Stewart. 137-172, Feb. 1947

Solving the Mystery of Mexico's Great Stone Spheres. Photos by David F. Cupp. 295-300, Aug. 1969

STOCKHOLM, Sweden:
Baltic Cruise of the *Caribbee*. By Carleton Mitchell. 605-646, Nov. 1950

Stockholm, Where "Kvalitet" Is a Way of Life. By James Cerruti. Photos by Albert Moldvay and Jonathan Blair. 43-69, Jan. 1976

Sweden, Quiet Workshop for the World. By Andrew H. Brown. 451-491, Apr. 1963

Thumbs Up Round the North Sea's Rim. By Frances James. Photos by Erica Koch. 685-704, May 1952

See also Vasa

STONE. *See* Marble; Rocks

STONE AGE. *See* Eskimos (Vanished Mystery Men); Ice Age Man; Russell Cave, Alabama

STONE AGE PEOPLES of Today. *See* Arnhem Land; Cinta Larga Indians; Kreen-Akarores; Negritos; New Guinea; Tasaday Tribe; Xingu National Park

STONE SPHERES:
Solving the Mystery of Mexico's Great Stone Spheres. By Matthew W. Stirling. Photos by David F. Cupp. 295-300, Aug. 1969

STONEHENGE—New Light on an Old Riddle. By Harold E. Edgerton. Paintings by Brian Hope-Taylor. 846-866, June 1960

STONES, Precious and Semiprecious. *See* Gems

STONEY INDIANS:
On the Ridgepole of the Rockies. By Walter Meayers Edwards. 745-780, June 1947

STOP-AND-GO Sail Around South Norway. By Edmond J. Moran. Photos by Randi Kjekstad Bull and Andrew H. Brown. 153-192, Aug. 1954

STORES. *See* Markets and Stores; *and* names of cities

STORIED Lands of Malaysia. By Maurice Shadbolt. Photos by Winfield Parks. 734-783, Nov. 1963

STORKS:
Our Only Native Stork, the Wood Ibis. By Robert Porter Allen. Photos by Frederick Kent Truslow. 294-306, Feb. 1964

White Storks, Vanishing Sentinels of the Rooftops. By Roger Tory Peterson. 838-853, June 1962

STORMS:
Our Changing Atlantic Coastline (U. S.). By Nathaniel T. Kenney. Photos by B. Anthony Stewart. 860-887, Dec. 1962

We're Doing Something About the Weather! By Walter Orr Roberts. 518-555, Apr. 1972

See also Hurricanes; Monsoons; *and* Okinawa, for typhoons

STRACHAN, ROBIN: Author:
With the Nuba Hillmen of Kordofan. 249-278, Feb. 1951

STRANGE Animals of Australia. By David Fleay. Photos by Stanley Breeden. 388-411, Sept. 1963

STRANGE Babies of the Sea. By Hilary B. Moore. Paintings by Craig Phillips and Jacqueline Hutton. 41-56, July 1952

STRANGE Courtship of Birds of Paradise. By S. Dillon Ripley. Paintings by Walter A. Weber. 247-278, Feb. 1950

STRANGE Courtship of the Cock-of-the-Rock. By E. Thomas Gilliard. 134-140, Jan. 1962

STRANGE Little World of the Hoatzin. By J. Lear Grimmer. Photos by M. Woodbridge Williams. 391-401, Sept. 1962

STRANGE March of the Spiny Lobster. By William F. Herrnkind. Photos by Rick Frehsee and Bruce Mounier. 819-831, June 1975

The STRANGEST Sea. By Eugenie Clark. Photos by David Doubilet. 338-343, Sept. 1975

STRASBOURG, France:
The Rhine: Europe's River of Legend. By William Graves. Photos by Bruce Dale. 449-499, Apr. 1967

STRATEGIC AIR COMMAND (SAC):
Of Planes and Men (U. S. Air Force). By Kenneth F. Weaver. Photos by Emory Kristof and Albert Moldvay. 298-349, Sept. 1965

School for Survival. By Curtis E. LeMay. 565-602, May 1953

See also DEW Line

STRATFORD-UPON-AVON, England:
The Britain That Shakespeare Knew. By Louis B. Wright. Photos by Dean Conger. 613-665, May 1964

STRATOBOWL, South Dakota. *See Explorer II; Strato-Lab* (To 76,000 Feet)

STRATO-LAB (Balloon):
To 76,000 Feet by *Strato-Lab* Balloon. By Malcolm D. Ross and M. Lee Lewis. 269-282, Feb. 1957

We Saw the World From the Edge of Space. By Malcolm D. Ross. Ground photos by Walter Meayers Edwards. 671-685, Nov. 1961

STRIFE-TORN Indochina. By W. Robert Moore. 499-510, Oct. 1950

STRIP MINING:
Illinois—Healthy Heart of the Nation. By Leo A. Borah. Photos by B. Anthony Stewart and Willard R. Culver. 781-820, Dec. 1953

The People of Cumberland Gap. By John Fetterman. Photos by Bruce Dale. 591-621, Nov. 1971

Should They Build a Fence Around Montana? By Mike W. Edwards. Photos by Nicholas deVore III. 614-649, May 1976

This Land of Ours—How Are We Using It? By Peter T. White. Photos by Emory Kristof. 20-67, July 1976

Will Coal Be Tomorrow's "Black Gold"? By Gordon Young. Photos by James P. Blair. 234-259, Aug. 1975

National Geographic

A **STROLL** to John o' Groat's. By Isobel Wylie Hutchison. 1-48, July 1956

A **STROLL** to London. By Isobel Wylie Hutchison. Photos by B. Anthony Stewart. 171-204, Aug. 1950

A **STROLL** to Venice. By Isobel Wylie Hutchison. 378-410, Sept. 1951
Note: The author trekked from Innsbruck, Austria, through the Tyrol and Dolomites, to Venice, Italy.

STRONG, ARLINE: Author-Photographer:
Seashore Summer. 436-444, Sept. 1960

STRONG, WILLIAM DUNCAN: Author:
Finding the Tomb of a Warrior-God. Photos by Clifford Evans, Jr. 453-482, Apr. 1947

STROUD, W. G.: Author:
Our Earth as a Satellite Sees It. 293-302, Aug. 1960

STRUM, SHIRLEY C.: Author:
Life with the "Pumphouse Gang": New Insights Into Baboon Behavior. Photos by Timothy W. Ransom. 672-691, May 1975

STRUTT, JOHN WILLIAM (Third Baron Rayleigh):
The British Way. By Sir Evelyn Wrench. 421-541, Apr. 1949

STUART, GEORGE E.: Author:
The Maya: Riddle of the Glyphs. Photos by Otis Imboden. 768-791, Dec. 1975
Who Were the "Mound Builders"? 783-801, Dec. 1972

STUBENRAUCH, ROBERT: Photographer:
Okinawa, Pacific Outpost. 538-552, Apr. 1950

STUDENTS:
Helping Holland Rebuild Her Land. By Gilbert M. Grosvenor and Charles Neave. 365-413, Sept. 1954
Norway Cracks Her Mountain Shell. By Sydney Clark. Photos by Gilbert H. Grosvenor and Ole Friele Backer. 171-211, Aug. 1948
See also Experiment in International Living; Schools; Universities and Colleges; YWCA

STUDYING Grizzly Habitat by Satellite. By John Craighead. 148-158, July 1976

STUDYING Wildlife by Satellite. By Frank Craighead, Jr. and John Craighead. 120-123, Jan. 1973

SUB-IGLOO (Underwater Workshop):
Diving Beneath Arctic Ice. By Joseph B. MacInnis. Photos by William R. Curtsinger. 248-267, Aug. 1973

SUBMARINES:
From Indian Canoes to Submarines at Key West. By Frederick Simpich. Photos by J. Baylor Roberts. 41-72, Jan. 1950
Our Navy's Long Submarine Arm. By Allan C. Fisher, Jr. 613-636, Nov. 1952
Pacific Fleet: Force for Peace. By Franc Shor. Photos by W. E. Garrett. 283-335, Sept. 1959
Included: *Grayback, Gudgeon, Sterlet*
See also Sea Robin; and Submersibles

SUBMARINES, Nuclear-powered:
Four-ocean Navy in the Nuclear Age. By Thomas

SUBMARINES, Nuclear-powered—*Continued*
W. McKnew. 145-187, Feb. 1965
Included: *Nautilus, Shark, Skate, Triton*
Man's New Servant, the Friendly Atom. By F. Barrows Colton. Photos by Volkmar Wentzel. 71-90, Jan. 1954
Included: *Nautilus, Seawolf*
Our Nuclear Navy. By George W. Anderson, Jr. 449-450, Mar. 1963
You and the Obedient Atom. By Allan C. Fisher, Jr. 303-353, Sept. 1958
Included: *Nautilus, Seawolf*
See also Nautilus; Skate; Thresher; Triton

SUBMERSIBLES:
Diving Saucer *(Denise)* Takes to the Deep. By Jacques-Yves Cousteau. 571-586, Apr. 1960
Project FAMOUS. 586-615, May 1975
I. Where the Earth Turns Inside Out. By J. R. Heirtzler. Photos by Emory Kristof. 586-603
II. Dive Into the Great Rift. By Robert D. Ballard. Photos by Emory Kristof. 604-615
Included: *Alvin, Archimède, Cyana*
Window on Earth's Interior. By Robert D. Ballard. Photos by Emory Kristof. 228-249, Aug. 1976
See also Asherah; Bathyscaphs; DS-2; Deep Diver; Deepstar; Denise; Submarines

SUDAN:
Africa: Countries of the Nile, Atlas series supplement. Oct. 1963
Journey Into the Great Rift: the Northern Half. By Helen and Frank Schreider. 254-290, Aug. 1965
Kayaks Down the Nile. By John M. Goddard. 697-732, May 1955
Locusts: "Teeth of the Wind." By Robert A. M. Conley. Photos by Gianni Tortoli. 202-227, Aug. 1969
Proud Primitives, the Nuba People. By Oskar Luz. Photos by Horst Luz. 673-699, Nov. 1966
Safari from Congo to Cairo. By Elsie May Bell Grosvenor. Photos by Gilbert Grosvenor. 721-771, Dec. 1954
South in the Sudan. By Harry Hoogstraal. 249-272, Feb. 1953
See also Kordofan; Nubia (Region)

SUEHSDORF, ADOLPH: Author:
The Cats in Our Lives. Photos by Walter Chandoha. 508-541, Apr. 1964

SUEZ CANAL:
An Engineer's View of the Suez Canal. By Glen E. Edgerton. 123-140, Jan. 1957
New Life for the Troubled Suez Canal. By William Graves. Photos by Jonathan Blair. 792-817, June 1975
The Spotlight Swings to Suez. By W. Robert Moore. 105-115, Jan. 1952

SUGAR, JAMES A.: Author-Photographer:
The Family Farm Ain't What It Used to Be. 391-411, Sept. 1974
Starfish Threaten Pacific Reefs. 340-353, Mar. 1970
Trucks Race the Clock From Coast to Coast. 226-243, Feb. 1974
Photographer
Easter Greetings From the Ukrainians. By Robert Paul Jordan. 556-563, Apr. 1972

SURPRISING Switzerland. By Jean and Franc Shor. 427-478, Oct. 1956

SURTSEY (Island), North Atlantic Ocean:
Surtsey: Island Born of Fire. By Sigurdur Thorarinsson. 713-726, May 1965

"SURVEY NAVY":
Adventures with the Survey Navy. By Irving Johnson. 131-148, July 1947

SURVEY SHIP, U. S. See Sumner, U.S.S.

SURVEYOR SPACECRAFT:
Surveyor: Candid Camera on the Moon. By Homer E. Newell. 578-592, Oct. 1966
That Orbèd Maiden . . . the Moon. By Kenneth F. Weaver. 207-230, Feb. 1969

SURVIVAL TRAINING:
Journey to the Outer Limits (Television film). 150A-150B, Jan. 1974
Contents: Outward Bound School
The Making of an Astronaut. By Robert R. Gilruth. 122-144, Jan. 1965
Nevada Learns to Live with the Atom. By Samuel W. Matthews. 839-850, June 1953
Philmont Scout Ranch Helps Boys Grow Up. By Andrew H. Brown. 399-416, Sept. 1956
School for Survival. By Curtis E. LeMay. 565-602, May 1953
We Survive on a Pacific Atoll. By John and Frank Craighead. 73-94, Jan. 1948
Wind River Range: Many-treasured Splendor. By Joseph Judge. 198-205, Feb. 1974
See also Wild Foods

SUSQUEHANNA (River), New York-Pennsylvania-Maryland:
Down the Susquehanna by Canoe. By Ralph Gray. Photos by Walter Meayers Edwards. 73-120, July 1950

SUTHERLAND, MASON: Author:
Adobe New Mexico. Photos by Justin Locke. 783-830, Dec. 1949
Californians Escape to the Desert. Photos by Charles W. Herbert. 675-724, Nov. 1957
Carlsbad Caverns in Color. Photos by E. "Tex" Helm. 433-468, Oct. 1953
Carnival in San Antonio. Photos by J. Baylor Roberts. 813-844, Dec. 1947
From Tucson to Tombstone (Arizona). 343-384, Sept. 1953
Mexico's Booming Capital. Photos by Justin Locke. 785-824, Dec. 1951
Sonora (Mexico) Is Jumping. 215-246, Feb. 1955

SUYÁ INDIANS:
Brazil's Big-lipped Indians. By Harald Schultz. 118-133, Jan. 1962

SVALBARD (Archipelago), Arctic Ocean:
Polar Bear: Lonely Nomad of the North. By Thor Larsen. 574-590, Apr. 1971
Spitsbergen Mines Coal Again. 113-120, July 1948

The SWALLOW-TAILED KITE: Graceful Aerialist of the Everglades. 496-505, Oct. 1972

SWAMPS. See Big Cypress Swamp; Northern Territory, Australia; Okefenokee; Pine Barrens

SWANS:
The Swans of Abbotsbury (England). By Michael Moynihan. Photos by Barnet Saidman. 563-570, Oct. 1959
See also Trumpeter Swans; Whistling Swans

SWAT (State), Pakistan:
Pakistan, New Nation in an Old Land. By Jean and Franc Shor. 637-678, Nov. 1952

SWATEK, PHILLIP M.: Author:
Rugged Is the Word for Bravo. 829-843, Dec. 1955

SWAZILAND Tries Independence. By Volkmar Wentzel. 266-293, Aug. 1969

SWEDEN:
Baltic Cruise of the Caribbee. By Carleton Mitchell. 605-646, Nov. 1950
Friendly Flight to Northern Europe. By Lyndon B. Johnson. Photos by Volkmar Wentzel. 268-293, Feb. 1964
Ghost From the Depths: the Warship Vasa. By Anders Franzén. 42-57, Jan. 1962
Sweden, Quiet Workshop for the World. By Andrew H. Brown. 451-491, Apr. 1963
Thumbs Up Round the North Sea's Rim. By Frances James. Photos by Erica Koch. 685-704, May 1952
The Vikings. By Howard La Fay. Photos by Ted Spiegel. 492-541, Apr. 1970
See also Gotland; Stockholm

SWEET, O. C.: Photographer:
Busy Fairbanks Sets Alaska's Pace. By Bruce A. Wilson. 505-523, Oct. 1949

SWIMMING With Patagonia's Right Whales. By Roger Payne. Photos by William R. Curtsinger and Charles R. Nicklin, Jr. 576-587, Oct. 1972

SWINE. See Hogs and Hog Raising

SWISS COLONISTS: United States:
Deep in the Heart of "Swissconsin." By William H. Nicholas. Photos by J. Baylor Roberts. 781-800, June 1947

SWITZER, GEORGE S.: Author:
The Many-sided Diamond. 568-586, Apr. 1958
Questing for Gems. 835-863, Dec. 1971
"Rockhounds" Uncover Earth's Mineral Beauty. 631-660, Nov. 1951

SWITZERLAND:
Across the Alps in a Wicker Basket (Bernina). By Phil Walker. 117-131, Jan. 1963
The Alps: Man's Own Mountains. By Ralph Gray. Photos by Walter Meayers Edwards and William Eppridge. 350-395, Sept. 1965
"Around the World in Eighty Days." By Newman Bumstead. 705-750, Dec. 1951
Included: Geneva; Jungfraujoch, in the Alps
Children's Village in Switzerland, Pestalozzi. Photos by Alfred Lammer. 268-282, Aug. 1959
Europe Via the Hostel Route. By Joseph Nettis. 124-154, July 1955
The Great St. Bernard Hospice Today. By George Pickow. 49-62, Jan. 1957
Little Tibet in Switzerland. By Laura Pilarski. Photos by Fred Mayer. 711-727, Nov. 1968
The Rhine: Europe's River of Legend. By William

T

TALBOT, PHILLIPS: Author:

Delhi, Capital of a New Dominion. 597-630, Nov. 1947

TALL-SHIPS RACE:

By Square-rigger from Baltic to Bicentennial. By Kenneth Garrett. 824-857, Dec. 1976
Included: Training ships from Argentina, Chile, Colombia, Denmark, England, Italy, Japan, Norway, Poland, Portugal, Romania, Spain, Union of Soviet Socialist Republics, United States, West Germany

TAMPA, Florida:

America Goes to the Fair. By Samuel W. Matthews. 293-333, Sept. 1954
Included: Florida State Fair, Gasparilla Celebration

TAMPA BAY, Gulf of Mexico:

Cruising Florida's Western Waterways. By Rube Allyn. Photos by Bates Littlehales. 49-76, Jan. 1955

TANA TORADJA (Region), Sulawesi:

Life and Death in Tana Toradja. By Pamela and Alfred Meyer. 793-815, June 1972

TANGANYIKA:

Ambassadors of Goodwill: The Peace Corps. By Sargent Shriver and Peace Corps Volunteers. 297-345, Sept. 1964
Tanganyika. By Ruth E. Dygert. 321-323
Britain Tackles the East African Bush. By W. Robert Moore. 311-352, Mar. 1950
The Last Great Animal Kingdom. 390-409, Sept. 1960
Roaming Africa's Unfenced Zoos. By W. Robert Moore. 353-380, Mar. 1950
Spearing Lions with Africa's Masai. By Edgar Monsanto Queeny. 487-517, Oct. 1954
Weighing the Aga Khan in Diamonds. Photos by David J. Carnegie. 317-324, Mar. 1947
See also Tanzania

TANGIER ISLAND, Virginia:

This Is My Island, Tangier. By Harold G. Wheatley. Photos by David Alan Harvey. 700-725, Nov. 1973

TANJUNG PUTING RESERVE, Indonesia:

Orangutans, Indonesia's "People of the Forest." By Biruté Galdikas-Brindamour. Photos by Rod Brindamour. 444-473, Oct. 1975

TANKERS, Oil:

Oil, the Dwindling Treasure. By Noel Grove. Photos by Emory Kristof. 792-825, June 1974
See also Manhattan, S.S.; Oil Spills

TANNA (Island), New Hebrides:

Tanna Awaits the Coming of John Frum. By Kal Muller. 706-715, May 1974

TANZANIA, United Republic of:

Tanzania Marches to Its Own Drum. By Peter T. White. Photos by Emory Kristof. 474-509, Apr. 1975
See also Gombe Stream Game Reserve; Natron, Lake; Ngorongoro Crater; Olduvai Gorge; Serengeti National Park; Tanganyika; Zanzibar

TAOIST SHRINES:

Kunming Pilgrimage. 213-226, Feb. 1950

TAPESTRIES. *See* Bayeux Tapestry

TARAHUMARA INDIANS:

South to Mexico City. By W. E. Garrett. 145-193, Aug. 1968
The Tarahumaras: Mexico's Long Distance Runners. By James Norman. Photos by David Hiser. 702-718, May 1976

TARANTO, Gulf of, Italy:

Ancient Shipwreck Yields New Facts—and a Strange Cargo. By Peter Throckmorton. Photos by Kim Hart and Joseph J. Scherschel. 282-300, Feb. 1969

TARANTULAS:

What's So Special About Spiders? By Paul A. Zahl. 190-219, Aug. 1971

TARASCANS (Indians):

Lost Kingdom in Indian Mexico. By Justin Locke. 517-546, Oct. 1952
South to Mexico City. By W. E. Garrett. 145-193, Aug. 1968

TARAWA (Atoll), Gilbert Islands:

Adventures with the Survey Navy. By Irving Johnson. 131-148, July 1947

TARPON KEY, Florida:

Bad Days for the Brown Pelican. By Ralph W. Schreiber. Photos by William R. Curtsinger and author. 111-123, Jan. 1975

TARPON SPRINGS, Florida:

Sponge Fishermen of Tarpon Springs. By Jennie E. Harris. 119-136, Jan. 1947

TARSIERS:

Seeking Mindanao's Strangest Creatures. By Charles Heizer Wharton. 389-408, Sept. 1948

TASADAY TRIBE:

First Glimpse of a Stone Age Tribe. 881-882, Dec. 1971
The Last Tribes of Mindanao (Television film). 882A-882B, Dec. 1971; 227, Aug. 1972
The Tasadays, Stone Age Cavemen of Mindanao. By Kenneth MacLeish. Photos by John Launois. 219-249, Aug. 1972

TASMANIA, Australia's Island State. By Howell Walker. 791-818, Dec. 1956

TAUFA'AHAU TUPOU IV, King (Tonga):

South Seas' Tonga Hails a King. By Melville Bell Grosvenor. Photos by Edwin Stuart Grosvenor. 322-343, Mar. 1968

TAURUS-LITTROW (Valley), Moon:

Exploring Taurus-Littrow. By Harrison H. Schmitt. 290-307, Sept. 1973

A **TAXI** for the Deep Frontier. By Kenneth MacLeish. Photos by Bates Littlehales. 139-150, Jan. 1968

TAYLOR, ALEXANDER: Author-Photographer:

Chessmen Come to Life in Marostica. 658-668, Nov. 1956

Photographer

By Full-rigged Ship to Denmark's Fairyland. By Alan Villiers. Photos by Alexander Taylor and author. 809-828, Dec. 1955
Paris Flea Market. By Franc Shor. 318-326, Mar. 1957

THOMAS, MARJORY C.: Author:
Copra-ship Voyage to Fiji's Outlying Islands. 121-140, July 1950

THOMAS, TAY: Author:
An Alaskan Family's Night of Terror (Earthquake). 142-156, July 1964
Author-Photographer
Flight to Adventure. By Tay and Lowell Thomas, Jr. 49-112, July 1957
Sky Road East. By Tay and Lowell Thomas, Jr. 71-112, Jan. 1960

THOMAS, VERONICA: Author:
The Arans, Ireland's Invincible Isles. Photos by Winfield Parks. 545-573, Apr. 1971
Madeira, Like Its Wine, Improves With Age. Photos by Jonathan Blair. 488-513, Apr. 1973
The Manx and Their Isle of Man. Photos by Ted H. Funk. 426-444, Sept. 1972
The Original Boston: St. Botolph's Town (England). Photos by James L. Amos. 382-389, Sept. 1974

THOMAS JEFFERSON: Architect of Freedom. By Mike W. Edwards. Photos by Linda Bartlett. 231-259, Feb. 1976
See also Jefferson, Thomas

THOMPSON, J. CHARLES: Photographer:
Trawling the China Seas. 381-395, Mar. 1950

THOMSON, DONALD F.: Author-Photographer:
An Arnhem Land Adventure. 403-430, Mar. 1948

THOMSON, SIR J. J.:
The British Way. By Sir Evelyn Wrench. 421-541, Apr. 1949

THOR HEYERDAHL'S Own Story of Ra II. Photos by Carlo Mauri and Georges Sourial. 44-71, Jan. 1971

THORARINSSON, SIGURDUR: Author:
Surtsey: Island Born of Fire. 713-726, May 1965

THOREAU, HENRY DAVID:
Literary Landmarks of Massachusetts. By William H. Nicholas. Photos by B. Anthony Stewart and John E. Fletcher. 279-310, Mar. 1950

THOROUGHBREDS:
Heart of the Bluegrass (Kentucky). By Charles McCarry. Photos by J. Bruce Baumann. 634-659, May 1974

THOSE Fiery Brazilian Bees. By Rick Gore. Photos by Bianca Lavies. 491-501, Apr. 1976

THOSE Outlandish Goldfish! By Paul A. Zahl. 514-533, Apr. 1973

THOSE Popular Pandas. By Theodore H. Reed. Photos by Donna K. Grosvenor. 803-815, Dec. 1972

THOSE Proper and Other Bostonians. By Joseph Judge. Photos by Ted Spiegel. 352-381, Sept. 1974

THOSE Successful Japanese. By Bart McDowell. Photos by Fred Ward. 323-359, Mar. 1974

THREATENED Glories of Everglades National Park. By Frederick Kent Truslow and Frederick G. Vosburgh. Photos by Frederick Kent Truslow and Otis Imboden. 508-553, Oct. 1967

THREATENED Treasures of the Nile. By Georg Gerster. 587-621, Oct. 1963

THREE Months on an Arctic Ice Island. By Joseph O. Fletcher. 489-504, Apr. 1953

THREE Roads to Rainbow. By Ralph Gray. 547-561, Apr. 1957

THREE Whales That Flew. By Carleton Ray. Photos by W. Robert Moore. 346-359, Mar. 1962

THRESHER, U.S.S. (Submarine):
Thresher Tragedy Spurs Deep-sea Research. 759-777, June 1964
I. Lesson and Challenge. By James H. Wakelin, Jr. 759-763
II. Down to Thresher by Bathyscaph. By Donald L. Keach. 764-777

THROCKMORTON, PETER: Author:
Ancient Shipwreck Yields New Facts—and a Strange Cargo. Photos by Kim Hart and Joseph J. Scherschel. 282-300, Feb. 1969
Oldest Known Shipwreck Yields Bronze Age Cargo. 697-711, May 1962
Thirty-three Centuries Under the Sea. 682-703, May 1960

THRONE Above the Euphrates. By Theresa Goell. 390-405, Mar. 1961

THROUGH Europe by Trailer Caravan. By Norma Miller. Photos by Ardean R. Miller III. 769-816, June 1957

THROUGH Ozark Hills and Hollows. By Mike W. Edwards. Photos by Bruce Dale. 656-689, Nov. 1970

THROUGH the Northwest Passage for Oil. By Bern Keating. Photos by Tomas Sennett. 374-391, Mar. 1970

The THRUSH on the Island of Barra. By Archibald MacLeish. 692-693, May 1970

THULE AIR BASE, Greenland:
We Followed Peary to the Pole. By Gilbert Grosvenor and Thomas W. McKnew. 469-484, Oct. 1953
Weather from the White North. By Andrew H. Brown. Photos by John E. Fletcher. 543-572, Apr. 1955

THUMBS Up Round the North Sea's Rim. By Frances James. Photos by Erica Koch. 685-704, May 1952

THUNDER HILL GOAT FARM, New York:
The Goats of Thunder Hill. By Elizabeth Nicholds. Photos by Robert F. Sisson. 625-640, May 1954

THURBER, MURIEL: Photographer:
Squaws Along the Yukon. By Ginny Hill Wood. 245-265, Aug. 1957

TIBET:
Caught in the Assam-Tibet Earthquake. By F. Kingdon-Ward. 403-416, Mar. 1952
A Woman Paints the Tibetans. By Lafugie. 659-692, May 1949
See also Lhasa

TIBETANS:
A Journey to "Little Tibet" (Ladakh). By Enakshi Bhavnani. Photos by Volkmar Wentzel. 603-634, May 1951

TIVOLI, Copenhagen, Denmark:

Copenhagen, Wedded to the Sea. By Stuart E. Jones. Photos by Gilbert M. Grosvenor. 45-79, Jan. 1963

Denmark, Field of the Danes. By William Graves. Photos by Thomas Nebbia. 245-275, Feb. 1974

TIWI (People):

Expedition to the Land of the Tiwi. By Charles P. Mountford. 417-440, Mar. 1956

TLINGIT INDIANS:

Alaska's Marine Highway: Ferry Route to the North. By W. E. Garrett. 776-819, June 1965

TO Europe with a Racing Start. By Carleton Mitchell. 758-791, June 1958

TO Gilbert Grosvenor: a Monthly Monument 25 Miles High. By Frederick G. Vosburgh and the staff of the National Geographic Society. 445-487, Oct. 1966

TO 76,000 Feet by *Strato-Lab* Balloon. By Malcolm D. Ross and M. Lee Lewis. 269-282, Feb. 1957

TO the Depths of the Sea by Bathyscaphe. By Jacques-Yves Cousteau. 67-79, July 1954

TO the Land of the Head-hunters. By E. Thomas Gilliard. 437-486, Oct. 1955

TO the Memory of Our Beloved President, Friend to All Mankind. 1A-1B, Jan. 1964

TO the Men at South Pole Station. By Richard E. Byrd. 1-4, July 1957

TO the Mountains of the Moon. By Kenneth F. Weaver. Photos from NASA. 233-265, Feb. 1972

TO Torre Egger's Icy Summit. By Jim Donini. 813-823, Dec. 1976

TOADS:

Voices of the Night. By Arthur A. Allen. 507-522, Apr. 1950

Included: Canadian toad, Common toad, Common tree toad, Oak toad, Spadefoot toad, Western toad

TOADSTOOLS:

Bizarre World of the Fungi. By Paul A. Zahl. 502-527, Oct. 1965

TOBACCO GROWING:

Cuba—American Sugar Bowl. By Melville Bell Grosvenor. 1-56, Jan. 1947

Heart of the Bluegrass. By Charles McCarry. Photos by J. Bruce Baumann. 634-659, May 1974

North Carolina, Dixie Dynamo. By Malcolm Ross. Photos by B. Anthony Stewart. 141-183, Feb. 1962

Yesterday Lingers Along the Connecticut. By Charles McCarry. Photos by David L. Arnold. 334-369, Sept. 1972

TOBAGO (Island), West Indies:

Feathered Dancers of Little Tobago. By E. Thomas Gilliard. Photos by Frederick Kent Truslow. 428-440, Sept. 1958

Happy-go-lucky Trinidad and Tobago. By Charles Allmon. 35-75, Jan. 1953

TODAY Along the Natchez Trace, Pathway Through History. By Bern Keating. Photos by Charles Harbutt. 641-667, Nov. 1968

TODAY and Tomorrow in Our National Parks. By Melville Bell Grosvenor. 1-5, July 1966

TODAY on the Delaware, Penn's Glorious River. By Albert W. Atwood. Photos by Robert F. Sisson. 1-40, July 1952

TODD, BURT KERR: Author-Photographer:

Bhutan, Land of the Thunder Dragon. 713-754, Dec. 1952

TOKYO, Japan:

Japan, the Exquisite Enigma. By Franc Shor. 733-777, Dec. 1960

Japan Tries Freedom's Road. By Frederick G. Vosburgh. Photos by J. Baylor Roberts. 593-632, May 1950

Operation Eclipse: 1948. By William A. Kinney. 325-372, Mar. 1949

Note: Tokyo's location error was discovered by expedition scientists.

Those Successful Japanese. By Bart McDowell. Photos by Fred Ward. 323-359, Mar. 1974

Tokyo, the Peaceful Explosion. By William Graves. Photos by Winfield Parks. 445-487, Oct. 1964

TOKYO BAY, Japan:

The Yankee Sailor Who Opened Japan. By Ferdinand Kuhn. 85-102, July 1953

TOLLUND MAN:

Lifelike Man Preserved 2,000 Years in Peat. By P. V. Glob. 419-430, Mar. 1954

TOLTEC CULTURE. *See* Teotihuacán

TOM SAWYER'S Town. By Jerry Allen. 121-140, July 1956

TOMBS:

An Archeologist Looks at Palestine. By Nelson Glueck. 739-752, Dec. 1947

Finding the Tomb of a Warrior-God. By William Duncan Strong. Photos by Clifford Evans, Jr. 453-482, Apr. 1947

Fresh Treasures from Egypt's Ancient Sands. By Jefferson Caffery. Photos by David S. Boyer. 611-650, Nov. 1955

See also Arlington National Cemetery; Etruscans; Han Dynasty Tombs; La Venta; Maya; Petra; Tutankhamun; Ur

TOMBSTONE, Arizona:

From Tucson to Tombstone. By Mason Sutherland. 343-384, Sept. 1953

TOMORROW on the Deep Frontier. By Edwin A. Link. 778-801, June 1964

TONGA:

Coronations a World Apart. By the Editor. 299, Mar. 1968

The Friendly Isles of Tonga. By Luis Marden. 345-367, Mar. 1968

Problems in Paradise. By Mary and Laurance S. Rockefeller. Photos by Thomas Nebbia. 782-793, Dec. 1974

South Seas' Tonga Hails a King. By Melville Bell Grosvenor. Photos by Edwin Stuart Grosvenor. 322-343, Mar. 1968

TONLÉ SAP (Lake and River), Cambodia:

Cambodia: Indochina's "Neutral" Corner. By

TRADE ROUTES. *See* St. Lawrence Seaway; *and* Phoenicians; Vikings

TRADEWINDS (Ketch):

Slow Boat to Florida. By Dorothea and Stuart E. Jones. 1-65, Jan. 1958

TRAFALGAR, Battle of:

The British Way. By Sir Evelyn Wrench. 421-541, Apr. 1949

Portsmouth, Britannia's Sally Port. By Thomas Garner James. Photos by B. Anthony Stewart. 513-544, Apr. 1952

TRAILING Cosmic Rays in Canada's North. By Martin A. Pomerantz. 99-115, Jan. 1953

TRAILING Yellowstone's Grizzlies by Radio. By Frank Craighead, Jr., and John Craighead. 252-267, Aug. 1966

TRAILS. *See* Appalachian Trail; Great Divide Trail; Lewis and Clark Expedition; Natchez Trace; Outlaw Trail; Pacific Crest Trail; Yukon Territory, for Yukon Trail; *and* Sheep Trek

TRAINING SHIPS:

By Full-rigged Ship to Denmark's Fairyland. By Alan Villiers. Photos by Alexander Taylor and author. 809-828, Dec. 1955
Included: *Arken, Danmark, Georg Stage, Lilla Dan, Peder Most*

By Square-rigger from Baltic to Bicentennial. By Kenneth Garrett. 824-857, Dec. 1976
Included: *Amerigo Vespucci, Christian Radich, Danmark, Dar Pomorza, Eagle, Esmeralda, Gazela Primeiro, Gloria, Gorch Fock, Juan Sebastián de Elcano, Kruzenshtern, Libertad, Mircea, Nippon Maru, Sagres II, Tovarishch*
See also Eagle; Midshipmen's Cruise; *and* Portsmouth; *and* listing under Merchant Marine Training Ships

TRAINS:

The Coming Revolution in Transportation. By Fredric C. Appel. Photos by Dean Conger. 301-341, Sept. 1969
Included: Air-cushion trains, High-speed trains, Pneumatic trains, "Unit trains"

Freedom Train Tours America. 529-542, Oct. 1949

The Friendly Train Called Skunk. By Dean Jennings. Photos by B. Anthony Stewart. 720-734, May 1959

Railroads: The Great American Adventure. Special Publication announced. 860-864, June 1976

Slow Train Through Viet Nam's War. By Howard Sochurek. 412-444, Sept. 1964

See also Southern Railway System

TRANS-ANDEAN PIPELINE:

Colombia, from Amazon to Spanish Main. By Loren McIntyre. 235-273, Aug. 1970

TRANS-DARIÉN EXPEDITION:

We Drove Panama's Darién Gap. By Kip Ross. 368-389, Mar. 1961

TRANSPORTATION:

The Coming Revolution in Transportation. By Fredric C. Appel. Photos by Dean Conger. 301-341, Sept. 1969

See also specific modes of transportation

TRANS-SAHARA SAND AND LAND YACHT RALLY:

Dry-land Fleet Sails the Sahara. By Jean du

TRANS-SAHARA SAND AND LAND YACHT RALLY—*Continued*
Boucher. Photos by Jonathan S. Blair. 696-725, Nov. 1967

A TRAVELER'S Tale of Ancient Tikal. Paintings by Peter Spier. Text by Alice J. Hall. 799-811, Dec. 1975

TRAWLERS. *See* Oyster Fleet; Shrimp Fishing

TRAWLING the China Seas. Photos by J. Charles Thompson. 381-395, Mar. 1950

TREASURE, Sunken:

Bermuda—Balmy, British, and Beautiful. By Peter Benchley. Photos by Emory Kristof. 93-121, July 1971

Treasure! (Television film). 575, Nov. 1976; cover announcement, Dec. 1976

The Treasure of Porto Santo. By Robert Sténuit. Photos by author and William R. Curtsinger. 260-275, Aug. 1975

Treasures in the Sea. Children's book announced. 736-738, Nov. 1972

Undersea Treasures. Special Publication announced. 870-874, June 1974

See also Spanish Treasure

TREE FROGS:

Voices of the Night. By Arthur A. Allen. 507-522, Apr. 1950

TREE-RING DATING:

Bristlecone Pine, Oldest Known Living Thing. By Edmund Schulman. Photos by W. Robert Moore. 355-372, Mar. 1958

What's Happening to Our Climate? By Samuel W. Matthews. 576-615, Nov. 1976

TREE SHREWS:

Seeking Mindanao's Strangest Creatures. By Charles Heizer Wharton. 389-408, Sept. 1948

TREE SNAILS, Gems of the Everglades. By Treat Davidson. 372-387, Mar. 1965

TREES:

Beauty and Bounty of Southern State Trees. By William A. Dayton. Paintings by Walter A. Weber. 508-552, Oct. 1957
Contents: Cottonwood, Eastern (Kansas); Dogwood (Missouri, Virginia); Live Oak (Georgia); Magnolia (Mississippi); Palmetto, Cabbage (Florida, South Carolina); Paloverde, Blue (Arizona); Pecan (Texas); Pine, Longleaf (Alabama); Pine, Shortleaf (Arkansas); Piñon (New Mexico); Piñon, Singleleaf (Nevada); Redbud, Eastern (Oklahoma); Redwood, Coast (California); Spruce, Blue (Colorado, Utah); Tulip (Indiana, Kentucky, Tennessee); White Oak (Connecticut, Maryland)

A Tree Is an Amazing Mechanism. 672-673, Nov. 1955

Wealth and Wonder of Northern State Trees. By William A. Dayton. Paintings by Walter A. Weber. 651-691, Nov. 1955
Contents: Birch (New Hampshire); Buckeye (Ohio); Douglas Fir (Oregon); Elm, American (Massachusetts, Nebraska, North Dakota); Hemlock, Eastern (Pennsylvania); Hemlock, Western (Washington); Holly (Delaware); Maple, Red (Rhode Island); Maple, Sugar (New York, Vermont, West Virginia, Wisconsin); Oak, Bur (Illinois); Oak, Northern Red (New Jersey); Pine, Ponderosa (Montana); Pine, Red (Minnesota); Pine, West-

TRUSLOW, FREDERICK KENT:
Author-Photographer
Businessman in the Bush. 634-675, May 1970
The Dauntless Little Stilt. 241-245, Aug. 1960
Eye to Eye With Eagles. 123-148, Jan. 1961
Limpkin, the "Crying Bird" That Haunts Florida Swamps. 114-121, Jan. 1958
Return of the Trumpeter. 134-150, July 1960
Threatened Glories of Everglades National Park. By Frederick Kent Truslow and Frederick G. Vosburgh. Photos by Frederick Kent Truslow and Otis Imboden. 508-553, Oct. 1967
When Disaster Struck a Woodpecker's Home. 882-884, Dec. 1966
Photographer
Feathered Dancers of Little Tobago (Greater Birds of Paradise). By E. Thomas Gilliard. 428-440, Sept. 1958
The Osprey, Endangered World Citizen. By Roger Tory Peterson. 53-67, July 1969
Our Only Native Stork, the Wood Ibis. By Robert Porter Allen. 294-306, Feb. 1964
Roseate Spoonbills, Radiant Birds of the Gulf Coast. By Robert Porter Allen. 274-288, Feb. 1962
Whooping Cranes Fight for Survival. By Robert Porter Allen. 650-669, Nov. 1959

TRUST TERRITORY OF NEW GUINEA. *See* Australian New Guinea; New Britain

TRUST TERRITORY OF THE PACIFIC ISLANDS:
Micronesia: The Americanization of Eden. By David S. Boyer. 702-744, May 1967
Pacific Wards of Uncle Sam. By W. Robert Moore. 73-104, July 1948
See also Ifalik; Kapingamarangi; Kwajalein; Truk Lagoon; Yap Islands

TRYCK, KEITH: Author:
Rafting Down the Yukon. Photos by Robert Clark. 830-861, Dec. 1975

TSAVO NATIONAL PARK, Kenya:
Inside a Hornbill's Walled-up Nest. By Joan and Alan Root. 846-855, Dec. 1969
See also Mzima Springs

TSCHOPIK, HARRY, Jr.: Author-Photographer:
At Home in the High Andes. 133-146, Jan. 1955

TSETSE FLY:
Britain Tackles the East African Bush. By W. Robert Moore. 311-352, Mar. 1950
Safari Through Changing Africa. By Elsie May Bell Grosvenor. Photos by Gilbert H. Grosvenor. 145-198, Aug. 1953

TSUNAMIS:
Earthquake! By William P. E. Graves. 112-139, July 1964
Hawaii, Island of Fire and Flowers. By Gordon Young. Photos by Robert W. Madden. 399-425, Mar. 1975
Thera, Key to the Riddle of Minos. By Spyridon Marinatos. Photos by Otis Imboden. 702-726, May 1972

TUAMOTU ARCHIPELAGO, South Pacific Ocean:
Twenty Fathoms Down for Mother-of-Pearl. By

TUAMOTU ARCHIPELAGO, South Pacific Ocean—
Continued
Winston Williams. Photos by Bates Littlehales. 512-529, Apr. 1962

TUAREG (Tribespeople):
Drought Threatens the Tuareg World. By Victor Englebert. 544-571, Apr. 1974
I Joined a Sahara Salt Caravan. By Victor Englebert. 694-711, Nov. 1965
The Niger: River of Sorrow, River of Hope. By Georg Gerster. 152-189, Aug. 1975
Sand in My Eyes. By Jinx Rodger. 664-705, May 1958

TUCK, JOHN, Jr.:
Man's First Winter at the South Pole. By Paul A. Siple. 439-478, Apr. 1958
We Are Living at the South Pole. By Paul A. Siple. Photos by David S. Boyer. 5-35, July 1957

TUCSON, Arizona:
From Tucson to Tombstone. By Mason Sutherland. 343-384, Sept. 1953
See also Desert Museum

TUKUNA INDIANS:
Tukuna Maidens Come of Age. By Harald Schultz. 629-649, Nov. 1959

TULANE UNIVERSITY:
Delta Regional Primate Research Center. *See* Snowflake (White Gorilla)
Expedition. *See* Dzibilchaltun, Yucatán, Mexico

TULSA, Oklahoma:
Oklahoma, the Adventurous One. By Robert Paul Jordan. Photos by Robert W. Madden. 149-189, Aug. 1971

TUNA:
Golden Beaches of Portugal. By Alan Villiers. 673-696, Nov. 1954
Quicksilver and Slow Death. By John J. Putman. Photos by Robert W. Madden. 507-527, Oct. 1972
Included: Mercury found in tuna
The *Yankee*'s Wander-world. By Irving and Electa Johnson. 1-50, Jan. 1949
Included: Portuguese fishermen, out from San Diego, tuna fishing in Tagus Cove, Galapagos Islands

TUNDRA: North America:
Beyond the North Wind With the Snow Goose. By Des and Jen Bartlett. 822-843, Dec. 1973
. . . And Then There Was Fred. . . . 843-847
Caribou: Hardy Nomads of the North. By Jim Rearden. 858-878, Dec. 1974
North to the Tundra. 293-337, Mar. 1972
I. Re-creating a Vanished World. By Russell D. Guthrie. 294-301
"Ice Age Mammals of the Alaskan Tundra." Painting supplement by Jay H. Matternes
II. Portrait of a Fierce and Fragile Land. By Paul A. Zahl. 303-314
III. Plants of the Alaskan Tundra. 315-321
IV. Birds of the Alaskan Tundra. 322-327
V. Mammals of the Alaskan Tundra. 329-337
The Pipeline: Alaska's Troubled Colossus. By Bryan Hodgson. Photos by Steve Raymer. 684-717, Nov. 1976

TWELVE National Geographic Society Scientific Projects Under Way. 869-870, June 1954

TWENTIETH Anniversary of the Epoch-making Stratosphere Flight by *Explorer II*. 707, Nov. 1955

20TH-CENTURY Indians Preserve Customs of the Cliff Dwellers. Photos by William Belknap, Jr. 196-211, Feb. 1964

TWENTY Fathoms Down for Mother-of-Pearl. By Winston Williams. Photos by Bates Littlehales. 512-529, Apr. 1962

TWILIGHT Hope for Big Cypress. By Rick Gore. Photos by Patricia Caulfield. 251-273, Aug. 1976

TWILIGHT of the Arab Dhow. By Marion Kaplan. 330-351, Sept. 1974

The TWO Acapulcos. By James Cerruti. Photos by Thomas Nebbia. 848-878, Dec. 1964

TWO and a Half Miles Down. By Georges S. Houot. 80-86, July 1954

2,000 Miles Through Europe's Oldest Kingdom. By Isobel Wylie Hutchison. Photos by Maynard Owen Williams. 141-180, Feb. 1949

2,300-YEAR-OLD Greek Ship Reaches Port at Last. By Susan W. and Michael L. Katzev. 618-625, Nov. 1974

TWO Wheels Along the Mexican Border. By William Albert Allard. 591-635, May 1971

TXUKAHAMEIS (Indians):

Amazon—The River Sea. By Loren McIntyre. 456-495, Oct. 1972

Brazil's Txukahameis: Good-bye to the Stone Age. Photos by W. Jesco von Puttkamer. 270-283, Feb. 1975

TYLER, JOHN:

Profiles of the Presidents: II. A Restless Nation Moves West. By Frank Freidel. 80-121, Jan. 1965

TYREE, DAVID M.: Author:

New Era in the Loneliest Continent (Antarctica). Photos by Albert Moldvay. 260-296, Feb. 1963

TYROL (Region), Austria-Italy:

Occupied Austria, Outpost of Democracy. By George W. Long. Photos by Volkmar Wentzel. 749-790, June 1951

A Stroll to Venice. By Isobel Wylie Hutchison. 378-410, Sept. 1951

Tirol, Austria's Province in the Clouds. By Peter T. White. Photos by Volkmar Wentzel. 107-141, July 1961

TYRRHENIAN SEA:

Fishing in the Whirlpool of Charybdis. By Paul A. Zahl. 579-618, Nov. 1953

TYUMEN OBLAST (Region), U.S.S.R.:

Siberia's Empire Road, the River Ob. By Robert Paul Jordan. Photos by Dean Conger. 145-181, Feb. 1976

U

U.S.S.R. *See* Union of Soviet Socialist Republics

UAUPÉS (River), South America. *See* Vaupés

"UBANGI" (Tribespeople). *See* Sara

UBO TRIBE:

Help for Philippine Tribes in Trouble. By Kenneth MacLeish. Photos by Dean Conger. 220-255, Aug. 1971

The Last Tribes of Mindanao (Television film). 882A-882B, Dec. 1971

UDORN ROYAL THAI AIR FORCE BASE, Thailand:

Air Rescue Behind Enemy Lines. By Howard Sochurek. 346-369, Sept. 1968

UGANDA:

Britain Tackles the East African Bush. By W. Robert Moore. 311-352, Mar. 1950

Kayaks Down the Nile. By John M. Goddard. 697-732, May 1955

Orphans of the Wild. By Bruce G. Kinloch. 683-699, Nov. 1962

Roaming Africa's Unfenced Zoos. By W. Robert Moore. 353-380, Mar. 1950

Safari from Congo to Cairo. By Elsie May Bell Grosvenor. Photos by Gilbert Grosvenor. 721-771, Dec. 1954

Uganda, Africa's Uneasy Heartland. By Howard La Fay. Photos by George F. Mobley. 708-735, Nov. 1971

Where Elephants Have Right of Way. By George and Jinx Rodger. Photos by George Rodger. 363-389, Sept. 1960

See also Ruwenzori; Virunga Mountains

UIST, North, and South Uist (Islands), Scotland:

Isles on the Edge of the Sea: Scotland's Outer Hebrides. By Kenneth MacLeish. Photos by Thomas Nebbia. 676-711, May 1970

UKRAINIANS: United States and Canada:

Easter Greetings From the Ukrainians. By Robert Paul Jordan. Photos by James A. Sugar. 556-563, Apr. 1972

ULITHI (Atoll), Caroline Islands:

Adventures with the Survey Navy. By Irving Johnson. 131-148, July 1947

ULSTER. *See* Ireland, Northern

ULYSSES. *See Odyssey*

UNCLE Sam Bends a Twig in Germany. By Frederick Simpich. Photos by J. Baylor Roberts. 529-550, Oct. 1948

UNCLE Sam's House of 1,000 Wonders. By Lyman J. Briggs and F. Barrows Colton. 755-784, Dec. 1951

UNDER Canvas in the Atomic Age. By Alan Villiers. 49-84, July 1955

UNDER the Dome of Freedom: The United States Capitol. By Lonnelle Aikman. Photos by George F. Mobley. 4-59, Jan. 1964

UNDERWATER Archeology: Key to History's Warehouse. By George F. Bass. Photos by Thomas J. Abercrombie and Robert B. Goodman. 138-156, July 1963

See also Archeology, Underwater

U. S. NAVAL ACADEMY, Annapolis, Maryland:

Midshipmen's Cruise. By William J. Aston and Alexander G. B. Grosvenor. 711-754, June 1948

U. S. NAVAL AIR STATION, Lakehurst, New Jersey. *See* Parachute Rigger School

U. S. NAVAL OBSERVATORY, Washington, D. C.:

Split-second Time Runs Today's World. By F. Barrows Colton and Catherine Bell Palmer. 399-428, Sept. 1947

U. S. NAVY:

Adventures with the Survey Navy. By Irving Johnson. 131-148, July 1947

Expeditions and Research. *See* American Antarctic Mountaineering Expedition; Operation Deep Freeze; Operation Highjump

First Flight Across the Bottom of the World. By James R. Reedy. Photos by Otis Imboden. 454-464, Mar. 1964

Flags of the Americas. By Elizabeth W. King. 633-657, May 1949

Flying in the "Blowtorch" Era. By Frederick G. Vosburgh. 281-322, Sept. 1950

Four-ocean Navy in the Nuclear Age. By Thomas W. McKnew. 145-187, Feb. 1965

From Indian Canoes to Submarines at Key West. By Frederick Simpich. Photos by J. Baylor Roberts. 41-72, Jan. 1950
Included: U. S. Naval Station Submarine Base, Air Station, and Fleet Sonar School

The Gooney Birds of Midway. By John W. Aldrich. 839-851, June 1964

Medals awarded the Navy:
Replica of first La Gorce Medal for support of American Antarctic Mountaineering Expedition. 865, 867, June 1967
Society Honors the Conquerors of Antarctica (U. S. Navy Antarctic Expeditions, 1955-1959). 589-590, Apr. 1959

Men Against the Hurricane. By Andrew H. Brown. 537-560, Oct. 1950

Midshipmen's Cruise. By William J. Aston and Alexander G. B. Grosvenor. 711-754, June 1948

Our Navy Explores Antarctica. By Richard E. Byrd. U. S. Navy official photos. 429-522, Oct. 1947

Our Navy in the Far East. By Arthur W. Radford. Photos by J. Baylor Roberts. 537-577, Oct. 1953

Our Navy's Long Submarine Arm. By Allan C. Fisher, Jr. 613-636, Nov. 1952

Our Nuclear Navy. By George W. Anderson, Jr. 449-450, Mar. 1963

Pacific Fleet: Force for Peace. By Franc Shor. Photos by W. E. Garrett. 283-335, Sept. 1959

Patrolling Troubled Formosa Strait. 573-588, Apr. 1955

'Round the Horn by Submarine. By Paul C. Stimson. 129-144, Jan. 1948

Sailors in the Sky: Fifty Years of Naval Aviation. By Patrick N. L. Bellinger. 276-296, Aug. 1961

Troubled Waters East of Suez. By Ernest M. Eller. 483-522, Apr. 1954

We Survive on a Pacific Atoll. By John and Frank Craighead. 73-94, Jan. 1948

The Yankee Sailor Who Opened Japan. By Ferdinand Kuhn. 85-102, July 1953

U. S. NAVY—*Continued*

Yemen Opens the Door to Progress. By Harry Hoogstraal. 213-244, Feb. 1952
Included: A United States Navy team of medical research workers

See also Guantánamo; Honolulu, Hawaii, for Pearl Harbor; San Diego, California; *and* Aviation Medicine; *Enterprise;* MATS; Office of Naval Research; Shiplift; *Strato-Lab;* Submarines; *Trieste;* Unknown Servicemen; War Memorials

U. S. PATENT OFFICE:

Patent Plants Enrich Our World. By Orville H. Kneen. 357-378, Mar. 1948

U. S. POSTAL SERVICE:

Everyone's Servant, the Post Office. By Allan C. Fisher, Jr. Photos by Volkmar Wentzel. 121-152, July 1954

See also J. W. Westcott (Mail Boat); Post Roads

U. S. PUBLIC HEALTH SERVICE:

Immigrants Still Flock to Liberty's Land. By Albert W. Atwood. 708-724, Nov. 1955

U. S. ROUTE 40:

From Sea to Shining Sea. By Ralph Gray. Photos by Dean Conger and author. 1-61, July 1961

U. S. ROUTE 89:

From Sun-clad Sea to Shining Mountains. By Ralph Gray. Photos by James P. Blair. 542-589, Apr. 1964

U. S. SOIL CONSERVATION SERVICE:

Sno-Cats Mechanize Oregon Snow Survey. By Andrew H. Brown. Photos by John E. Fletcher. 691-710, Nov. 1949

U. S. SUBMARINE SCHOOL, New London, Connecticut:

Our Navy's Long Submarine Arm. By Allan C. Fisher, Jr. 613-636, Nov. 1952

U. S. TRUST TERRITORY OF THE PACIFIC ISLANDS. *See* Trust Territory of the Pacific Islands

U. S. VIRGIN ISLANDS. *See* Virgin Islands

U. S. WEATHER BUREAU:

Men Against the Hurricane. By Andrew H. Brown. 537-560, Oct. 1950

Milestones in My Arctic Journeys. By Willie Knutsen. 543-570, Oct. 1949

River Forecasting Center. *See* Midwest Flood

Rugged Is the Word for Bravo. By Phillip M. Swatek. 829-843, Dec. 1955

Weather from the White North. By Andrew H. Brown. Photos by John E. Fletcher. 543-572, Apr. 1955

See also National Weather Service

UNIVERSE:

The Amazing Universe. Special Publication announced. 870-874, June 1975

The Incredible Universe. By Kenneth F. Weaver. Photos by James P. Blair. 589-625, May 1974
Pioneers in Man's Search for the Universe. Paintings by Jean-Leon Huens. Text by Thomas Y. Canby. 627-633

UNIVERSITIES AND COLLEGES:

Atlanta, Pacesetter City of the South. By William S.

UNKNOWN FALLS, Upper and Lower, Labrador:
Labrador Canoe Adventure. By Andrew H. Brown and Ralph Gray. 65-99, July 1951

UNKNOWN SERVICEMEN: World War II and Korea:
'Known But to God.' By Beverley M. Bowie. 593-605, Nov. 1958

UNLOCKING Secrets of the Northern Lights. By Carl W. Gartlein. Paintings by William Crowder. 673-704, Nov. 1947

UNOTO (Masai Ceremony):
Spearing Lions with Africa's Masai. By Edgar Monsanto Queeny. 487-517, Oct. 1954

UNSINKABLE Malta. By Ernle Bradford. Photos by Ted H. Funk. 852-879, June 1969

UNSOELD, WILLIAM F.: Author:
The First Traverse. By Thomas F. Hornbein and William F. Unsoeld. 509-513, Oct. 1963
See also American Mount Everest Expedition

UNSUNG Beauties of Hawaii's Coral Reefs. By Paul A. Zahl. 510-525, Oct. 1959

UP HELLY AA (Festival):
Viking Festival in the Shetlands. Photos by Karl W. Gullers. 853-862, Dec. 1954

UP Through the Ice of the North Pole. By James F. Calvert. 1-41, July 1959

The **UPPER** Mississippi. By Willard Price. 651-699, Nov. 1958

UPPER VOLTA:
Freedom Speaks French in Ouagadougou. By John Scofield. 153-203, Aug. 1966

Al 'UQAYR, Saudi Arabia. *See* Gerrha

UR (Ancient City):
Abraham, the Friend of God. By Kenneth MacLeish. Photos by Dean Conger. 739-789, Dec. 1966

URANIUM:
The Canadian North: Emerging Giant. By David S. Boyer. 1-43, July 1968
Included: Eldorado Mining and Refining Ltd.'s uranium mine in Saskatchewan
Hunting Uranium Around the World. By Robert D. Nininger. Photos by Volkmar Wentzel. 533-558, Oct. 1954
Man's New Servant, the Friendly Atom. By F. Barrows Colton. Photos by Volkmar Wentzel. 71-90, Jan. 1954
White Magic in the Belgian Congo. By W. Robert Moore. 321-362, Mar. 1952
See also Nuclear Energy

URANUS (Planet):
Voyage to the Planets. By Kenneth F. Weaver. Paintings by Ludek Pesek. 147-193, Aug. 1970

URBAN LIFE:
Five Noted Thinkers Explore the Future. 68-75, July 1976
Included: Isaac Asimov, Richard F. Babcock, Edmund N. Bacon, Buckminster Fuller, Gerard Piel

URBAN RENEWAL:
Atlanta, Pacesetter City of the South. By William S.

URBAN RENEWAL — *Continued*
Ellis. Photos by James L. Amos. 246-281, Feb. 1969
Baltimore: The Hidden City. By Fred Kline. Photos by Martin Rogers. 188-215, Feb. 1975
Kansas City, Heartland U.S.A. By Rowe Findley. Photos by Ted Spiegel. 112-139, July 1976
Massachusetts Builds for Tomorrow. By Robert de Roos. Photos by B. Anthony Stewart. 790-843, Dec. 1966
New Grandeur for Flowering Washington. By Joseph Judge. Photos by James P. Blair. 500-539, Apr. 1967
Pittsburgh, Pattern for Progress. By William J. Gill. Photos by Clyde Hare. 342-371, Mar. 1965
St. Louis: New Spirit Soars in Mid-America's Proud Old City. By Robert Paul Jordan. Photos by Bruce Dale. 605-641, Nov. 1965
Stockholm, Where "Kvalitet" Is a Way of Life. By James Cerruti. Photos by Albert Moldvay and Jonathan Blair. 43-69, Jan. 1976
Venice Fights for Life. By Joseph Judge. Photos by Albert Moldvay. 591-631, Nov. 1972
Washington, the City Freedom Built. By William Graves. Photos by Bruce Dale and Thomas Nebbia. 735-781, Dec. 1964

URICK, FRANK, and Family:
Growing Up in Montana. Photos by Nicholas deVore III. 650-657, May 1976

URQUHART, FRED A.: Author:
Found at Last: the Monarch's Winter Home. Photos by Bianca Lavies. 161-173, Aug. 1976

URU INDIANS:
Titicaca, Abode of the Sun. By Luis Marden. Photos by Flip Schulke. 272-294, Feb. 1971

URUGUAY:
Parks, Plans, and People: How South America Guards Her Green Legacy. By Mary and Laurance Rockefeller. Photos by George F. Mobley. 74-119, Jan. 1967
The Purple Land of Uruguay. By Luis Marden. 623-654, Nov. 1948

URUMCHI (Wulumuchi), Sinkiang:
The Caves of the Thousand Buddhas. By Franc and Jean Shor. 383-415, Mar. 1951

UTAH:
From Sun-clad Sea to Shining Mountains. By Ralph Gray. Photos by James P. Blair. 542-589, Apr. 1964
A Map Maker Looks at the United States. By Newman Bumstead. 705-748, June 1951
Included: Arches National Monument; Bryce Canyon; Price; Provo; Roan (Brown) Cliffs; Salt Lake City
Miracle of the Potholes. By Rowe Findley. Photos by Robert F. Sisson. 570-579, Oct. 1975
Riding the Outlaw Trail. By Robert Redford. Photos by Jonathan Blair. 622-657, Nov. 1976
Skiing in the United States. By Kathleen Revis. 216-254, Feb. 1959
Utah's Shining Oasis. By Charles McCarry. Photos by James L. Amos. 440-473, Apr. 1975
See also Arches National Monument; Bear River Migratory Bird Refuge; Bryce Canyon National Park; Canyonlands National Park; Dinosaur National Monument; Escalante Canyon; Fisher

VOURAIKOS RIVER WATERSHED, Greece:
Erosion, Trojan Horse of Greece. By F. G. Renner. 793-812, Dec. 1947

A VOYAGE Into the Unknown Changed Man's Understanding of His World. By Alan Villiers. Photos by Bruce Dale. 721-753, June 1976

The VOYAGE of *Ra II*. By Thor Heyerdahl. Photos by Carlo Mauri and Georges Sourial. 44-71, Jan. 1971

VOYAGE to the Planets. By Kenneth F. Weaver. Paintings by Ludek Pesek. 147-193, Aug. 1970

VOYAGE to Venus: The Story of Mariner II. By Frank Sartwell. Paintings by Davis Meltzer. 733-742, May 1963

VOYAGER (Spacecraft):
Mars: A New World to Explore. By Carl Sagan. 821-841, Dec. 1967

VOYAGERS, Solo. *See* Graham, Robin Lee; *Ice Bird*, for David Lewis; Schultz, John E.

VOYAGES. *See* Cruises and Voyages

The VOYAGES and Historic Discoveries of Capt. Jas. Cook. By Alan Villiers. Photos by Gordon W. Gahan. 297-349, Sept. 1971

VOYAGEURS:
Relics from the Rapids. By Sigurd F. Olson. Photos by David S. Boyer. 413-435, Sept. 1963

VULTURES. *See* Andean Condors; Egyptian Vulture

W

WAGNER, KIP: Author:
Drowned Galleons Yield Spanish Gold. Photos by Otis Imboden. 1-37, Jan. 1965

WAHGI VALLEY, New Guinea:
New Guinea's Paradise of Birds. By E. Thomas Gilliard. 661-688, Nov. 1951
New Guinea's Rare Birds and Stone Age Men. By E. Thomas Gilliard. 421-488, Apr. 1953
Sheep Airlift in New Guinea. Photos by Ned Blood. 831-844, Dec. 1949

WAI WAI INDIANS:
Life Among the Wai Wai Indians. By Clifford Evans and Betty J. Meggers. 329-346, Mar. 1955

WAITOMO CAVES, New Zealand:
Nature's Night Lights: Probing the Secrets of Bioluminescence. By Paul A. Zahl. 45-69, July 1971

WAKELIN, JAMES H., Jr.: Author:
Thresher: Lesson and Challenge. 759-763, June 1964

WAKHAN (Region), Afghanistan:
Afghanistan: Crossroad of Conquerors. By Thomas J. Abercrombie. 297-345, Sept. 1968
We Took the Highroad in Afghanistan. By Jean and Franc Shor. 673-706, Nov. 1950
Winter Caravan to the Roof of the World. By Sabrina and Roland Michaud. 435-465, Apr. 1972

WAKHI (People):
Winter Caravan to the Roof of the World. By Sabrina and Roland Michaud. 435-465, Apr. 1972

WALES:
British Castles, History in Stone. By Norman Wilkinson. 111-129, July 1947
The Investiture of Great Britain's Prince of Wales. By Allan C. Fisher, Jr. Photos by James L. Stanfield and Adam Woolfitt. 698-715, Nov. 1969
Included: Caernarvon Castle
A Traveler's Map of the British Isles, map supplement. Text on reverse. Apr. 1974
Wales, Land of Bards. By Alan Villiers. Photos by Thomas Nebbia. 727-769, June 1965
See also Caldy; Skomer

A WALK Through the Wilderness: Yellowstone at 100. By Karen and Derek Craighead. Photos by Sam Abell. 579-603, May 1972

WALKER, ERNEST P.: Author:
"Flying" Squirrels, Nature's Gliders. 663-674, May 1947

Author-Photographer
Portraits of My Monkey Friends. 105-119, Jan. 1956

Photographer
The Wild Animals in My Life. By William M. Mann. 497-524, Apr. 1957

WALKER, HOWELL: Author:
Italian Riviera, Land That Winter Forgot. 743-789, June 1963
Long Island Outgrows the Country. Photos by B. Anthony Stewart. 279-326, Mar. 1951
The Making of a West Pointer. 597-626, May 1952
The More Paris Changes. . . . Photos by Gordon W. Gahan. 64-103, July 1972
New South Wales, the State That Cradled Australia. Photos by David Moore. 591-635, Nov. 1967
South Australia, Gateway to the Great Outback. Photos by Joseph J. Scherschel. 441-481, Apr. 1970
Washington Lives Again at Valley Forge. 187-202, Feb. 1954

Author-Photographer
Air Age Brings Life to Canton Island. 117-132, Jan. 1955
Aroostook County, Maine, Source of Potatoes. 459-478, Oct. 1948
Belgium Welcomes the World (1958 World's Fair). 795-837, June 1958
Cities Like Worcester Make America. 189-214, Feb. 1955
Cruise to Stone Age Arnhem Land. 417-430, Sept. 1949
France Meets the Sea in Brittany. 470-503, Apr. 1965
From Spear to Hoe on Groote Eylandt. 131-142, Jan. 1953
The Greener Fields of Georgia. Photos by author and B. Anthony Stewart. 287-330, Mar. 1954
Here Rest in Honored Glory . . . (War Memorials). 739-768, June 1957
History Keeps House in Virginia. 441-484, Apr. 1956
Lafayette's Homeland, Auvergne. 419-436, Sept. 1957
The Making of a New Australia. 233-259, Feb. 1956
New Zealand, Pocket Wonder World. 419-460, Apr. 1952

WATT, JAMES:

The British Way. By Sir Evelyn Wrench. 421-541, Apr. 1949

WAURÁ (Indians):

Amazon — The River Sea. By Loren McIntyre. 456-495, Oct. 1972

The Waurá: Brazilian Indians of the Hidden Xingu. By Harald Schultz. 130-152, Jan. 1966

WAVES (Women's Reserve of the U. S. Naval Reserve). *See* Parachute Rigger School

WE're Coming Over on the *Mayflower*. By Alan Villiers. 708-728, May 1957

WE're Doing Something About the Weather! By Walter Orr Roberts. 518-555, Apr. 1972

WE Are Living at the South Pole. By Paul A. Siple. Photos by David S. Boyer. 5-35, July 1957

WE Build a School for Sherpa Children. By Sir Edmund Hillary. 548-551, Oct. 1962

WE Captured a 'Live' Brontosaur. By Roland T. Bird. 707-722, May 1954

WE Climbed Utah's Skyscraper Rock. By Huntley Ingalls. Photos by author and Barry C. Bishop. 705-721, Nov. 1962

WE Drove Panama's Darién Gap. By Kip Ross. 368-389, Mar. 1961

WE Dwelt in Kashgai Tents. By Jean and Franc Shor. 805-832, June 1952

WE Followed Peary to the Pole. By Gilbert Grosvenor and Thomas W. McKnew. 469-484, Oct. 1953

WE Lived in Turbulent Tehran. By Rebecca Shannon Cresson. 707-720, Nov. 1953

WE Saw the World From the Edge of Space. By Malcolm D. Ross. Ground photos by Walter Meayers Edwards. 671-685, Nov. 1961

WE Survive on a Pacific Atoll. By John and Frank Craighead. 73-94, Jan. 1948

WE Took the Highroad in Afghanistan. By Jean and Franc Shor. 673-706, Nov. 1950

"WE Who Face Death." By LeRoy Woodson, Jr. 364-387, Mar. 1975

WEALTH and Wonder of Northern State Trees. By William A. Dayton. Paintings by Walter A. Weber. 651-691, Nov. 1955

WEATHER:

Extraordinary Photograph Shows Earth Pole to Pole. Photos by Nimbus I. 190-193, Feb. 1965

Men Against the Hurricane. By Andrew H. Brown. 537-560, Oct. 1950

Our Changing Atlantic Coastline (March 1962 Storm). By Nathaniel T. Kenney. Photos by B. Anthony Stewart. 860-887, Dec. 1962

We're Doing Something About the Weather! By Walter Orr Roberts. 518-555, Apr. 1972

See also Climate; Drought; Lightning; Storms

WEATHER SATELLITES:

The Earth From Orbit. By Paul D. Lowman, Jr. 645-671, Nov. 1966

Extraordinary Photograph Shows Earth Pole to Pole. Photos by Nimbus I. 190-193, Feb. 1965

How Man-made Satellites Can Affect Our Lives.

WEATHER SATELLITES — *Continued*

By Joseph Kaplan. Paintings by Gilbert Emerson. 791-810, Dec. 1957

Our Earth as a Satellite (*Tiros I*) Sees It. By W. G. Stroud. 293-302, Aug. 1960

Satellites Gave Warning of Midwest Floods. By Peter T. White. Photos by Thomas A. DeFeo. 574-592, Oct. 1969

Space Satellites, Tools of Earth Research. By Heinz Haber. Paintings by William N. Palmstrom. 487-509, Apr. 1956

See also Remote Sensing

WEATHER STATIONS AND RESEARCH:

Man's First Winter at the South Pole. By Paul A. Siple. 439-478, Apr. 1958

Men Against the Hurricane. By Andrew H. Brown. 537-560, Oct. 1950
  Included: Joint Hurricane Warning Center, Miami

Milestones in My Arctic Journeys. By Willie Knutsen. 543-570, Oct. 1949
  Included: Weather stations in Arctic Canada

Our Navy Explores Antarctica. By Richard E. Byrd. U. S. Navy official photos. 429-522, Oct. 1947

Rugged Is the Word for Bravo (Weather Patrol). By Phillip M. Swatek. 829-843, Dec. 1955

Three Months on an Arctic Ice Island. By Joseph O. Fletcher. 489-504, Apr. 1953

We Followed Peary to the Pole. By Gilbert Grosvenor and Thomas W. McKnew. 469-484, Oct. 1953

Weather from the White North. By Andrew H. Brown. Photos by John E. Fletcher. 543-572, Apr. 1955

We're Doing Something About the Weather! By Walter Orr Roberts. 518-555, Apr. 1972

Year of Discovery Opens in Antarctica. By David S. Boyer. 339-381, Sept. 1957

WEAVER, KENNETH F.: Author:

And Now to Touch the Moon's Forbidding Face. 633-635, May 1969

Apollo 15 Explores the Mountains of the Moon. Photos from NASA. 233-265, Feb. 1972

Athens: Her Golden Past Still Lights the World. Photos by Phillip Harrington. 100-137, July 1963

Countdown for Space. 702-734, May 1961

Crystals, Magical Servants of the Space Age. Photos by James P. Blair. 278-296, Aug. 1968

The Five Worlds of Peru. Photos by Bates Littlehales. 213-265, Feb. 1964

The Flight of Apollo 11: "One giant leap for mankind." 752-787, Dec. 1969

Giant Comet Grazes the Sun. 259-261, Feb. 1966

Have We Solved the Mysteries of the Moon? Paintings by William H. Bond. 309-325, Sept. 1973

Historic Color Portrait of Earth From Space. Photos by DODGE Satellite. 726-731, Nov. 1967

How Old Is It? By Lyman J. Briggs and Kenneth F. Weaver. 234-255, Aug. 1958

How to Catch a Passing Comet. 148-150, Jan. 1974

The Incredible Universe. Photos by James P. Blair. 589-625, May 1974

Journey to Mars. Paintings by Ludek Pesek. 231-263, Feb. 1973

Magnetic Clues Help Date the Past. 696-701, May 1967

WEST from the Khyber Pass. By William O. Douglas. Photos by Mercedes H. Douglas and author. 1-44, July 1958

WEST GERMANY. *See* Germany, Federal Republic of

WEST INDIES:

Cape Canaveral's 6,000-mile Shooting Gallery. By Allan C. Fisher, Jr. Photos by Luis Marden and Thomas Nebbia. 421-471, Oct. 1959
Included: Antigua; Bahama Islands; Dominican Republic; Grand Turk; Puerto Rico; St. Lucia

Carib Cruises the West Indies. By Carleton Mitchell. 1-56, Jan. 1948

Christopher Columbus and the New World He Found. By John Scofield. Photos by Adam Woolfitt. 584-625, Nov. 1975

Countries of the Caribbean, including Mexico, Central America, and the West Indies, map supplement. Oct. 1947

Finisterre Sails the Windward Islands. By Carleton Mitchell. Photos by Winfield Parks. 755-801, Dec. 1965

Flags of the Americas. By Elizabeth W. King. 633-657, May 1949
Included: Cuba; Dominican Republic; Haiti

A Fresh Breeze Stirs the Leewards. By Carleton Mitchell. Photos by Winfield Parks. 488-537, Oct. 1966

How Fruit Came to America. By J. R. Magness. Paintings by Else Bostelmann. 325-377, Sept. 1951

Our Vegetable Travelers. By Victor R. Boswell. Paintings by Else Bostelmann. 145-217, Aug. 1949

Robin Sails Home. By Robin Lee Graham. 504-545, Oct. 1970

Sea Fever. By John E. Schultz. 237-268, Feb. 1949

West Indies, Atlas series supplement. Dec. 1962

West Indies, map supplement. Mar. 1954

West Indies and Central America, map supplement. Jan. 1970

See also Bahama Islands; Barbados; Bimini Islands; Cuba; Haiti; Jamaica; Martinique; Netherlands Antilles; Puerto Rico; Trinidad and Tobago; Virgin Islands

WEST IRIAN: People. *See* Asmat

WEST POINT, New York:

The Making of a West Pointer. By Howell Walker. 597-626, May 1952

The Mighty Hudson (River). By Albert W. Atwood. Photos by B. Anthony Stewart. 1-36, July 1948

WEST VIRGINIA:

Appalachian Valley Pilgrimage. By Catherine Bell Palmer. Photos by Justin Locke. 1-32, July 1949

Down the Potomac by Canoe. By Ralph Gray. Photos by Walter Meayers Edwards. 213-242, Aug. 1948

Mountain Voices, Mountain Days. By Bryan Hodgson. Photos by Linda Bartlett. 118-146, July 1972

The Nation's River. By Allan C. Fisher, Jr. Photos by James L. Stanfield. 432-469, Oct. 1976

Shenandoah, I Long to Hear You. By Mike W. Edwards. Photos by Thomas Anthony DeFeo. 554-588, Apr. 1970

So Much Happens Along the Ohio River. By Fred

WEST VIRGINIA—*Continued*

erick Simpich. Photos by Justin Locke. 177-212, Feb. 1950

Turnaround Time in West Virginia. By Elizabeth A. Moize. Photos by Jodi Cobb. 755-785, June 1976

See also Harpers Ferry

WESTCOTT (Mail Boat). *See J. W. Westcott*

WESTERN AUSTRALIA (State), Australia:

Western Australia, the Big Country. By Kenneth MacLeish. Photos by James L. Stanfield. 150-187, Feb. 1975

WESTERN SAMOA, the Pacific's Newest Nation. By Maurice Shadbolt. Photos by Robert B. Goodman. 573-602, Oct. 1962

WESTMANN ISLANDS, Iceland. *See* Heimaey

WESTMINSTER KENNEL CLUB DOG SHOW, New York City:

Westminster, World Series of Dogdom. By John W. Cross, Jr. 91-116, Jan. 1954

WETHERILL MESA, Colorado:

Searching for Cliff Dwellers' Secrets. By Carroll A. Burroughs. 619-625, Nov. 1959

Solving the Riddles of Wetherill Mesa. By Douglas Osborne. Paintings by Peter V. Bianchi. 155-195, Feb. 1964

20th-century Indians Preserve Customs of the Cliff Dwellers. Photos by William Belknap, Jr. 196-211, Feb. 1964
Included: Artifacts of Mesa Verde

Your Society to Seek New Light on the Cliff Dwellers. 154-156, Jan. 1959

WETLANDS:

Florida's Booming—and Beleaguered—Heartland. By Joseph Judge. Photos by Jonathan Blair. 585-621, Nov. 1973

See also listings under Marshes; Swamps

WETMORE, ALEXANDER:

Board of Trustees, member. 595, May 1947; 344, Sept. 1948; 65A-65B, July 1954; 364, Mar. 1956; 835, Dec. 1959; 883, Dec. 1960; 555, Oct. 1964; 485, Oct. 1966; 839, Dec. 1970; 151, Aug. 1975; 227, Aug. 1976

Committee for Research and Exploration, Vice Chairman. 705, June 1947; 175, Feb. 1960; 532, Oct. 1965; 489, Oct. 1967; 881-882, Dec. 1967

Hubbard Medal recipient (1975). 151, Aug. 1975

Author

Re-creating Madagascar's Giant Extinct Bird. 488-493, Oct. 1967

WHALES:

Calypso Explores for Underwater Oil. By Jacques-Yves Cousteau. Photos by Louis Malle. 155-184, Aug. 1955

Hunting the Heartbeat of a Whale. By Paul Dudley White and Samuel W. Matthews. 49-64, July 1956

Namu. Children's book announced. 726-728, Nov. 1973

Whales of the World. 722-767, Dec. 1976
I. The Imperiled Giants. By William Graves. 722-751
II. Exploring the Lives of Whales. By Victor B. Scheffer. 752-767

WILLAMETTE RIVER AND VALLEY, Oregon—*Continued*

A. Starbird. Photos by Lowell J. Georgia. 816-835, June 1972

WILLCOX, ALEX R.: Photographer:

Africa's Bushman Art Treasures. By Alfred Friendly. 848-865, June 1963

WILLEMSTAD, Curaçao, Netherlands Antilles:

The Netherlands Antilles: Holland in the Caribbean. By James Cerruti. Photos by Emory Kristof. 115-146, Jan. 1970

WILLIAM THE CONQUEROR:

The British Way. By Sir Evelyn Wrench. 421-541, Apr. 1949

A New Look at Medieval Europe. By Kenneth M. Setton. Paintings by Andre Durenceau and Birney Lettick. 799-859, Dec. 1962

900 Years Ago: the Norman Conquest. By Kenneth M. Setton. Photos by George F. Mobley. 206-251, Aug. 1966

WILLIAM AND MARY COLLEGE, Williamsburg, Virginia:

Williamsburg: Its College and Its Cinderella City. By Beverley M. Bowie. 439-486, Oct. 1954

WILLIAMS, JOHN G.: Author:

Freeing Flamingos From Anklets of Death. Photos by Alan Root. 934-944, Dec. 1963

WILLIAMS, M. WOODBRIDGE: Author-Photographer:

The Wichitas: Land of the Living Prairie. 661-697, May 1957

Photographer

History and Beauty Blend in a Concord Iris Garden. By Robert T. Cochran, Jr. 705-719, May 1959

Keeping House for Tropical Butterflies. By Jocelyn Crane. 193-217, Aug. 1957

Strange Little World of the Hoatzin. By J. Lear Grimmer. 391-401, Sept. 1962

WILLIAMS, MAYNARD OWEN:

Chief of the NGS Foreign Staff for 20 years; total service, 34 years. 627, Oct. 1963

Author

Pilgrims Follow the Christmas Star. 831-840, Dec. 1952

Portrait of Indochina. By W. Robert Moore and Maynard Owen Williams. Paintings by Jean Despujols. 461-490, Apr. 1951

Turkey Paves the Path of Progress. 141-186, Aug. 1951

War-torn Greece Looks Ahead. 711-744, Dec. 1949

Author-Photographer

Crete, Cradle of Western Civilization. 693-706, Nov. 1953

Dublin's Historic Horse Show. 115-132, July 1953

Home to the Holy Land. 707-746, Dec. 1950

Oasis-hopping in the Sahara. 209-236, Feb. 1949

Pennsylvania Dutch Folk Festival. 503-516, Oct. 1952

Photographer

Belgium Comes Back. By Harvey Klemmer. 575-614, May 1948

Beside the Persian Gulf. 341-356, Mar. 1947

Lascaux Cave, Cradle of World Art. By Norbert

WILLIAMS, MAYNARD OWEN—*Continued*

Casteret. 771-794, Dec. 1948

Luxembourg, Survivor of Invasions. By Sydney Clark. 791-810, June 1948

Operation Eclipse: 1948. By William A. Kinney. 325-372, Mar. 1949

Saudi Arabia, Oil Kingdom. 497-512, Apr. 1948

2,000 Miles Through Europe's Oldest Kingdom (Denmark). By Isobel Wylie Hutchison. 141-180, Feb. 1949

WILLIAMS, WINSTON: Author:

Twenty Fathoms Down for Mother-of-Pearl. Photos by Bates Littlehales. 512-529, Apr. 1962

WILLIAMSBURG, Brooklyn, New York:

The Pious Ones (Hasidic Jews). By Harvey Arden. Photos by Nathan Benn. 276-298, Aug. 1975

WILLIAMSBURG, Virginia:

Firebrands of the Revolution. By Eric F. Goldman. Photos by George F. Mobley. 2-27, July 1974

Williamsburg, City for All Seasons. By Joseph Judge. Photos by James L. Amos. 790-823, Dec. 1968

Williamsburg: Its College and Its Cinderella City. By Beverley M. Bowie. 439-486, Oct. 1954

WILLM, PIERRE HENRI:

Two and a Half Miles Down. By Georges S. Houot. 80-86, July 1954

WILSON, ALBERT G.: Author:

Our Universe Unfolds New Wonders. 245-260, Feb. 1952

WILSON, BRUCE A.: Author:

Busy Fairbanks Sets Alaska's Pace. 505-523, Oct. 1949

WILSON, JAY: Photographer:

To Torre Egger's Icy Summit. By Jim Donini. 813-823, Dec. 1976

WILSON, JOHN: Author:

Drought Bedevils Brazil's Sertão. Photos by Gordon W. Gahan. 704-723, Nov. 1972

WILSON, PHYLLIS: Author:

Queen of Canada (Elizabeth II). Photos by Kathleen Revis. 825-829, June 1959

WILSON, WOODROW:

Inside the White House. By Lonnelle Aikman. Photos by B. Anthony Stewart and Thomas Nebbia. 3-43, Jan. 1961

The Living White House. By Lonnelle Aikman. 593-643, Nov. 1966

Profiles of the Presidents: IV. America Enters the Modern Era. By Frank Freidel. 537-577, Oct. 1965

WIND, Wave, Star, and Bird. By David Lewis. Photos by Nicholas deVore III. 747-781, Dec. 1974

WIND-POWER RESEARCH:

Can We Harness the Wind? By Roger Hamilton. Photos by Emory Kristof. 812-829, Dec. 1975

WIND RIVER RANGE, Wyoming:

Wind River Range: Many-treasured Splendor. By Joseph Judge. 198-205, Feb. 1974

WINDJAMMING Around New England. By Tom Horgan. Photos by Robert F. Sisson. 141-169, Aug. 1950

WOMEN of the Revolution: Patriots in Petticoats. By Lonnelle Aikman. Paintings by Louis S. Glanzman. 475-493, Oct. 1975

WOMEN'S RESERVE OF THE U.S. NAVAL RESERVE (WAVES). *See* Parachute Rigger School

The WONDER City That Moves by Night. By Francis Beverly Kelley. 289-324, Mar. 1948

WONDERLAND in Longwood Gardens. By Edward C. Ferriday, Jr. 45-64, July 1951

WOOD, GINNY HILL: Author:
Squaws Along the Yukon. 245-265, Aug. 1957

WOOD:
Versatile Wood Waits on Man. By Andrew H. Brown. 109-140, July 1951
See also Lumber Industry; Paper and Pulp Industry

WOOD CARVING:
An Ozark Family Carves a Living and a Way of Life. By Bruce Dale. 124-133, July 1975
See also Afo-A-Kom

WOOD IBIS. *See* Wood Storks

WOOD STORKS:
Our Only Native Stork, the Wood Ibis. By Robert Porter Allen. Photos by Frederick Kent Truslow. 294-306, Feb. 1964

WOODLAND PERIOD. *See* Russell Cave, Alabama

WOODPECKERS:
The Bird's Year. By Arthur A. Allen. 791-816, June 1951
Included: Gila, Golden-fronted, Red-bellied woodpeckers
When Disaster Struck a Woodpecker's Home. By Frederick Kent Truslow. 882-884, Dec. 1966

WOODS, Lake of the, Canada-U. S.:
Men, Moose, and Mink of Northwest Angle. By William H. Nicholas. Photos by J. Baylor Roberts. 265-284, Aug. 1947

WOODS HOLE, Massachusetts:
Cape Cod, Where Sea Holds Sway Over Man and Land. By Nathaniel T. Kenney. Photos by Dean Conger. 149-187, Aug. 1962
Windjamming Around New England. By Tom Horgan. Photos by Robert F. Sisson. 141-169, Aug. 1950

WOODS HOLE OCEANOGRAPHIC INSTITUTION:
Expeditions and Research. *See* Mid-Atlantic Ridge; Mid-Atlantic Rift; *and* Weddell Seals

WOODSON, LeROY, Jr.:
Editorial on writer-photographers. 295, Mar. 1975
Author-Photographer
The Kurds of Iraq: "We Who Face Death." 364-387, Mar. 1975

WOOL:
The Cotswolds, "Noicest Parrt o'England." By James Cerruti. Photos by Adam Woolfitt. 846-869, June 1974
High, Wild World of the Vicuña. By William L. Franklin. 77-91, Jan. 1973
See also Qiviut; Tweed

WOOLFITT, ADAM: Photographer:
Amiable Amsterdam. By William Davenport. 683-705, May 1974
Chelsea, London's Haven of Individualists. By James Cerruti. 28-55, Jan. 1972
Christopher Columbus and the New World He Found. By John Scofield. 584-625, Nov. 1975
The Cotswolds, "Noicest Parrt o'England." By James Cerruti. 846-869, June 1974
Edinburgh: Capital in Search of a Country. By James Cerruti. 274-296, Aug. 1976
The England of Charles Dickens. By Richard W. Long. 443-483, Apr. 1974
The Faeroes, Isles of Maybe. By Ernle Bradford. 410-442, Sept. 1970
The Investiture of Great Britain's Prince of Wales. By Allan C. Fisher, Jr. Photos by James L. Stanfield and Adam Woolfitt. 698-715, Nov. 1969
The Netherlands: Nation at War With the Sea. By Alan Villiers. 530-571, Apr. 1968
New Mexico: The Golden Land. By Robert Laxalt. 299-345, Sept. 1970

WORCESTER, Massachusetts:
Cities Like Worcester Make America. By Howell Walker. 189-214, Feb. 1955

WORDEN, ALFRED M.:
Apollo 15 Explores the Mountains of the Moon. By Kenneth F. Weaver. Photos from NASA. 233-265, Feb. 1972

WORDSWORTH, WILLIAM:
The British Way. By Sir Evelyn Wrench. 421-541, Apr. 1949
Lake District, Poets' Corner of England. By H. V. Morton. Photos by David S. Boyer. 511-545, Apr. 1956

WORK-HARD, Play-hard Michigan. By Andrew H. Brown. 279-320, Mar. 1952

WORKING for Weeks on the Sea Floor. By Jacques-Yves Cousteau. Photos by Philippe Cousteau and Bates Littlehales. 498-537, Apr. 1966

WORLD:
The Political World; The Physical World, double-sided map supplement. Nov. 1975
The World, Atlas series supplement. Nov. 1960
The World, map supplement. Mar. 1957; Feb. 1965
The World, map supplement. Painting and text on reverse. Dec. 1970; Dec. 1976
The World Map, supplement. Dec. 1951
See also Earth

WORLD (Magazine for Young Readers):
The *School Bulletin* is retired after 56 years; replaced by *WORLD.* 299, Sept. 1975
Start the World, I Want to Get On! Text announcing National Geographic *WORLD.* 148-150, July 1975

WORLD ATLAS. *See* Atlases, NGS: World

WORLD CRUISES AND VOYAGES:
"Around the World in Eighty Days." By Newman Bumstead. 705-750, Dec. 1951
Captain Cook: The Man Who Mapped the Pacific. By Alan Villiers. Photos by Gordon W. Gahan. 297-349, Sept. 1971